Political Technology and the Erosion of the Rule of Law

ELGAR MONOGRAPHS IN CONSTITUTIONAL AND ADMINISTRATIVE LAW

Series editors: Rosalind Dixon, *University of New South Wales, Australia,* Susan Rose-Ackerman, *Yale University and* Mark Tushnet, *Harvard University, USA*

Constitutions are a country's most important legal document, laying the foundation not just for politics, but for all other areas of law. They allocate power among different levels and branches of government, record and promote a society's shared values, and protect the rights of citizens. Countries around the world are adopting written constitutions, though what defines a constitution is evolving to include a variety of sources beyond canonical texts, such as political conventions, statutes, judicial decisions and administrative law norms.

This cosmopolitan monograph series provides a forum for the best and most original scholarship in constitutional and administrative law, with each book offering an international, comparative, or multi-jurisdictional approach to this complex and fascinating field of research.

Political Technology and the Erosion of the Rule of Law

Normalizing the State of Exception

Günter Frankenberg

Professor of Public Law, Legal Philosophy and Comparative Law, Goethe University, Germany

ELGAR MONOGRAPHS IN CONSTITUTIONAL AND ADMINISTRATIVE LAW

Edward Elgar

Cheltenham, UK • Northampton, MA, USA

Published in German as *Staatstechnik: Perspektiven auf Rechtsstaat und Ausnahmezustand*, Berlin: Suhrkamp Verlag

Translated by Harry Bauer and Günter Frankenberg

Published by
Edward Elgar Publishing Limited
The Lypiatts
15 Lansdown Road
Cheltenham
Glos GL50 2JA
UK

Edward Elgar Publishing, Inc.
William Pratt House
9 Dewey Court
Northampton
Massachusetts 01060
USA

A catalogue record for this book
is available from the British Library

Library of Congress Control Number: 2013949875

This book is available electronically in the ElgarOnline.com Law Subject Collection, E-ISBN 978 1 78347 252 9

FSC www.fsc.org MIX Paper from responsible sources FSC® C013056

ISBN 978 1 78347 250 5 (cased)

Typeset by Columns Design XML Ltd, Reading
Printed and bound in Great Britain by T.J. International Ltd, Padstow

To Emily, Anya, Jenny, Max and Lucas

Contents

Preface

One would expect to find neither angels nor paradise in secular societies; rather one would be prepared to encounter conflicts of all kinds. In pluralist societies dispute and dissent are ubiquitous. Rulers have a tendency to dislike conflict and dissent. Therefore, the rule of law is brought in, not to make the 'powers that be' like controversy, but to prevent them from arbitrarily intervening in disputes and stifling dissent as well as, incidentally, to keep the passions of civil society at bay. Thereby law-rule – in the guise of the rule of law, *Rechtsstaat* or *état de droit* – is widely credited with setting up a regime of distance.

In comparison with democracy, republic or human rights, law-rule musters significantly less enthusiasm. 'Democracy' echoes the desire for participation by promising a government by the people. 'Republic' stands for accountability and transparency and, arguably, government in the public interest and the light of the public. And human rights are generally regarded as the basis of government and are expected to prevent or redress human suffering. In comparison with these rather popular elements of government, law-rule lacks glamour, although it is set up to magically transform personal rule into an impersonal 'government of laws' and, as a theoretical component of self-government, to ensure that rulers rule in the form of law, observe rights and exercise restraint – not exactly a modest agenda.

Law-rule's discrete charm becomes apparent, though, once one turns to political regimes that know no legal constraints and claim extraordinary powers by dint of emergency law under whatever pretext – curbing terrorism and organized crime, defending the stability of the regime against 'extremist elements', punishing traitors (preferably from foreign countries), averting dangers or, more generally, providing security.

This book is about security. More to the point: how it happened that torture turned out to be security's companion and how the state of exception revealed itself as the twin brother of law-rule – not in distant, barbaric regions of the world but in our backyard, in consolidated democracies and rule-of-law countries, like the United States, England and Germany, where power is claimed and widely believed to be civilized; at least: constrained by law. Throughout the last decade state practice – waging the 'war on terror and organized crime' – covered not only extensive surveillance and other secret measures[1] but also torture, the cruel and degrading treatment of prisoners and detainees, illegal renditions, indefinite detention of suspects and more.[2] These measures have undermined the general belief in the effectiveness of law-rule and, by the same token, the liberal imagination of a just world. Lawyers and legal scholars have been and still are deeply divided over whether or not to condemn Guantánamo, justify (rescue) torture in emergency situations, and how to deal with 'enemies' whoever they may be.[3] They disagree, more generally, on whether and how to balance liberty and security and whether the loss of freedom is justified by its trade-offs for security.[4]

It would be overly ambitious to choose 'in defence of the rule of law' as the motto for the following considerations, since the allusion to Foucault's *In Defence of Society* would be all too obvious. Besides, such a motto would be inappropriate for a critique of the concept and practices of *Staatstechnik*, the original title of the book, translated here as 'political technology' to accentuate the exercise of power as a collective singular and 'techniques of government' to stress the various mechanisms and measures of governing. Furthermore, I want to show how, during the series of 'wars on terror, organized crime' and other targets, the state of exception has been normalized, the extraordinary has been reduced to a phenomenon of the everyday, and even the taboo of torture has been touched upon – also under cover of law-rule.

The analysis of political technology is confronted with a twofold challenge: on the one hand, it has to throw light on the ambivalences of law-rule, while, on the other hand, it has to defend democratic legality against fantasies of extraordinary threats and extraordinary practices of power. Because things could be different in the world of law, security regimes and counter-terrorism, it seems in order to begin with a critique.

---

1 Cole et al., *Secrecy, National Security and the Vindication of Constitutional Law*.

2 From the burgeoning literature see only Cole and Dempsey, *Terrorism and the Constitution*; and the impressive, empirically informed normative critique submitted by Waldron, *Torture, Terror, and Trade-Offs*.

3 See e.g. Greenberg, *The Torture Debate in America*; Waldron, *Torture, Terror, and Trade-Offs*.

4 For a critique of balancing and justificatory trade-offs: Waldron, *Torture, Terror and Trade-Offs*, ch. 2. For an apology and the complementary thesis that the executive branch should make the trade-offs between liberty and security: Posner and Vermeule, *Terror in the Balance*.

The first chapter introduces the mindset of engineers and experts as well as the typical methods characterizing political technology. I introduce the proposition that political technology as security technique is developed in the legal regime of the prevention of danger. Guiding the subsequent argument, in this section I argue that the security state exceeds the constraints of law-rule and works to normalize emergency powers (Chapter 1). Then a *tour d'horizon* through the conceptual repository of modernity follows. Using the example of a number of influential pre-modern and modern notions of the state, this part of the book illustrates and conceptualizes the change and trajectory of political technology from Hobbes to Foucault and draws attention to the relationships between conception and images of power (Chapter 2).

Reconstructing the emergence and development of law-rule, the next section of the book aims to highlight the ambivalences entailed in the liberal paradigm of law-rule and its corresponding political technology. These ambivalences become apparent in the different pathways of the rule of law and *Rechtsstaat* as well as in constellations of law-rule and the state of exception. They also surface in a number of legal controversies over the contents and scope of the rule of law in England and the German *Rechtsstaat* (Chapter 3).

Thereupon, the liberal imagination and mantra of law-rule, which have always already been threatened by the unruly prerogative, is contrasted with fantasies of the extraordinary. These fantasies are based on the very political and legal-doctrinal thinking that – inspired by and following on from Carl Schmitt – currently indulges in apocalyptic scenarios meant to force open the gates to emergency legislation in the name of security (like the Prevention of Terrorism Acts in England and the Patriot Act in the United States).[5] This chapter addresses Carl Schmitt's and the latter-day Schmittians' romance with the exception and traces its impact on Schmitt's legal theory and on the recent jurisprudence of 'rescue torture', the 'rescue downing' of aircraft and an 'enemy criminal law' (Chapter 4).

How the state of exception is normalized, and how the instruments of emergency law and their corresponding juridical justifications infiltrate the doctrines of 'normal' law will be illustrated by examining two post-World War II crises of law-rule, the first focusing on the German *Rechtsstaat*, once it was challenged by 'political extremism' and attacked by a national terrorist group (Chapter 5). The second crisis was triggered by terrorist networks operating transnationally; it requires a more global

[5] See Ferejohn and Pasquino, 'The Law of Exception', at 215.

(though hardly comprehensive) discussion (Chapter 6). These two phases of counter-terrorism and crises of law-rule are particularly instructive as they not only highlight the different strategies and mechanisms employed to integrate the state of exception into ordinary law-rule but also demonstrate that things had already changed, at least in some European countries, before 9/11.[6] One of the basic changes appears to be the shift from the direct regulation of individual behaviour to the monitoring of social processes and the screening of communication by the police, security and intelligence agencies. The phenomena of crisis, however 'modern', like the 'roving surveillance' of the internet, bring to the fore that law-rule has always been uneasily connected with the prerogative of the ruler to cope with whatever emergency might occur or be perceived as such.

The concluding chapter focuses on the normalization of torture as a technique of governing (Chapter 7). The comparative remarks on torture practices and torture doctrines neither exhaust the matter nor will they end the normalizing juridical discourse. An end of political technology, informed by one or the other security agenda, is not in sight. Therefore I only offer some comparisons on the return of torture and today's attempts to legally justify its practice. The focus will be on United States and German jurisprudence as well as the practitioners of state-organized and -executed brutality.

[6] Jeremy Waldron argues 'Things changed on September 9, 2001.' (id., *Torture, Terror and Trade-Offs* (supra note 2), 1).

Acknowledgements

This book developed out of timely, often spontaneous reactions to events and tendencies I interpret retrospectively as an underlying trend towards the normalization of the state of emergency. In particular the justificatory discourse on torture and juridical apologies for an ever-expanding security imperative, dictated by the varieties of counter-terrorism, made me write this book. Many colleagues, friends and collaborators supported me with ideas and criticism. They contributed to both the original *Staatstechnik – Perspektiven auf Rechtsstaat und Ausnahmezustand* (Berlin: Suhrkamp, 2010) and later to this considerably revised and updated version. I have to thank Erhard Denninger, Rainer Forst, Klaus Günther, Michael Stolleis, Thomas Vesting and Hans Vorländer for their comments on essays included in this book and on the new chapters. Martin Loughlin offered valuable comments on Chapter 1. As always, I profited greatly from discussion with my Critical Legal Studies friends and the co-editors of *Kritische Justiz*. Without the support of Petra Czoik, Asmaa El Idrissi, Yasmina Aznei, Lisa Tuchscherer and especially Helena Lindemann and Cara Röhner I would never have completed the manuscript in such a short time. Nina Malaviya deserves credit for the arduous task of revising the notes and bibliography of the original text. I am indebted to Tara Gorvine for paving the way for the English publication and to Virginia Williams for her superb editing of the manuscript. I am very grateful to Harry Bauer who translated Chapters 1–6; for revisions of the translation I assume responsibility. The translation was sponsored by the Cluster of Excellence 'Formation of Normative Orders' at the Goethe University, Frankfurt. For the English publication, the text and notes of the original were considerably revised, abridged and supplemented. The book is dedicated to my children.

Günter Frankenberg
Frankfurt,
June 2009–June 2013

1. A critique of political technology

1.1 POLITICAL TECHNOLOGY, GOOD GOVERNANCE AND STATECRAFT

Political technology refers to the exercise of political power. 'Technology' includes the entirety of practices, norms and principles, forms of knowledge and skills, calculations, strategies and tactics that state actors and institutions use in their operations. 'Political' and 'legal' characterize modalities of how power is exercised. They address an important component of Michel Foucault's multifaceted concept of governmentality.[1] However, in contrast, political technology stresses statehood as a sphere of activity and intervention for intersecting goals and operative strategies; and it also highlights the importance of law as a form of intervention and basis of authority in the exercise of power. The more common but narrower concept of governmental technology encompasses in its conventional use only the executive and administrative aspects of political technology and emphasizes practice, namely governing itself, whereas political technology also encompasses legislative practices of power as well as private agencies acting in the service of the state.

The technology of governing is not always clearly distinguished from the art of government or *statecraft* with its rather mixed fortunes. From antiquity to the Enlightenment, political philosophy conceived the art of government mainly as the virtuosity or *prudentia* required by a ruler. The art had to show in forward-looking and prudent politics and policy.[2] In

[1] Michel Foucault highlights the specific governmental rationale for raising a problem in a certain manner as well as highlighting the governmental practices and technologies that are applied to solve these problems according to this rationale. As with the concept of power, Michel Foucault's concept of 'governmentality' is complex yet underdetermined. Foucault, *The Birth of Biopolitics*. See also Lemke, 'The Birth of Bio-Politics'.

[2] Accordingly, the title of Machiavelli's *The Prince* was initially translated as *On the Statecraft of a Prince*. Cf. Foucault, 'Governmentality'. For statecraft as virtuosity, see Müller, 'Erste Vorlesung über König Friedrich II', at 189. For statecraft as *prudentia*, see Walter Euchner, 'Demokratietheoretische Aspekte der politischen Ideengeschichte'.

his *Social Contract*, Rousseau painted a rather positive, idyllic picture of statecraft in a monarchy:

> Thus the will of the people, the will of the prince, the public force of the State, and the particular force of the government, all answer to a single motive power; all the springs of the machine are in the same hands, the whole moves towards the same end; there are no conflicting movements to cancel one another, and no kind of constitution can be imagined in which a lesser amount of effort produces a more considerable amount of action. Archimedes, seated quietly on the bank and easily drawing a great vessel afloat, stands to my mind for a skilful monarch, governing vast states from his study, and moving everything while he seems himself unmoved.[3]

Whoever refers to statecraft today may want to stress the difficulty of governing or rather assume a critical or ironic position, but is not likely to have political virtuosity or prudence in mind.[4] Usually presidents, federal chancellors, cabinet members and so forth are seen as neither artists nor magicians, though they may see themselves that way.[5] In the political arena, they rather appear as pragmatic jugglers of things possible. Still, the concept of the art of government is experiencing a modest renaissance at present. In this vein, a bold essay recently vindicated 'craftsmanship in questions of government and administration' as a foundation for reconstructing and renewing the welfare state, with the aim of updating the inner relationship of the state, the art of government and the good life.[6] And the US Department of State went online with its programme of '21st Century Statecraft' 'complementing traditional foreign policy tools with newly innovated and adapted instruments that fully leverage networks, technologies, and demographics of our interconnected world'.[7]

---

[3] Rousseau, 'The Social Contract', Book III, ch. 6.

[4] Hillary Clinton was quite serious when she referred to '21st Century Statecraft'. However, the reference to 'Mugabe's art of government' in Zimbabwe has to be taken as bitter irony; while the characterization of German environmental policy as a 'Dadaist art of government' comes with a much lower degree of bitterness.

[5] As former British Prime Minister Margaret Thatcher reveals in her self-congratulatory political autobiography: *Statecraft: Strategies for a Changing World*.

[6] Vogel, *Die Staatsbedürftigkeit der Gesellschaft*, 97 and 99 ff. (with references to Sternberger, 'Das Menschenrecht nach Glück zu streben' and Mulgan, 'Vom Staat und vom Glück').

[7] http://www.state.gov/statecraft (23 March 2013), see also *The Economic Times*, 17 April 2013.

Moreover, the art of government has for some time now – albeit with a different meaning and lower normative charge – (re)turned to classical semantics and pre-democratic ideas of a good order in the fashionable guise of the concept of *good governance*.[8] However, nowadays it often refers to governmental practice in the developmental context.[9] A brief glance at the respective theoretical and conceptual controversies[10] indicates that, informed by economics, governance describes the practices and techniques of governing in complex regulatory systems. In contrast to government, governance is meant to encompass non-hierarchical structures of order as well as non-imperative, collaborative and informal state actions in order to better capture the effects such disparate phenomena as globalization, supranational multi-level systems or models of new public management have on domestic administration.

So why introduce the concept of political technology executed by state agencies and agents, given that the state as a form of rule seems to cause more problems than it solves, and since the concept of governance, although still somewhat controversial, is readily available? A number of reasons can be marshalled here: first, the state is familiar as a concept and idea and still around, despite theoretical obituaries. Second, there are indications that 'society is in need of the state'.[11] Even in a socio-economic environment driven by technological progress and centred around the economy, there is sufficient theoretical reason and empirical evidence to assume that markets, the financial system, the societal division of labour and the distribution of wealth still reckon with and rely on state intervention. Third, I want to demonstrate that the focus on political technology employed by state agencies and agents captures more accurately than the concept of governance the specific constellations between law-rule and the state of exception in pursuing security

[8] Explicitly in Meinert, 'Städtische Regierungskunst'; implicitly in UNESCAP, 'What is Good Governance?', which lists eight criteria of good governance, and IMF, *Good Governance: The IMF's Role*. See also Theobald, *Zur Ökonomik des Staates*.

[9] See e.g. Smith, *Good Governance and Development*; Noman et al., *Good Growth and Governance in Africa*.

[10] I return to the debate about governance below (Chapter 2). For the different key facets and issues discussed, see the seminal volume by Rosenau and Czempiel (eds.), *Governance without Government*. A critical overview of governance projects at the global level, which is beyond the scope of this book, is provided by Kennedy, 'The Mystery of Global Governance'; see also id., *Global Governance?*

[11] Vogel, *Die Staatsbedürftigkeit der Gesellschaft* (supra note 6).

agendas, like counter-terrorism, fighting 'organized crime' or the self-preservation of the state. Fourth, the following reflections on the technical aspects of statecraft are meant to help demystify the state and, especially, a view of the state as the epitome of the neutral mechanics of the sovereign art of governing. The concept has therefore a critical function. Fifth, this critique has to prove itself vis-à-vis the concept of security, which has worked and still works as the main rationale for and objective of political technology. With regard to this very objective, my analysis addresses threat scenarios, instruments and rules, as well as methods and strategies of threat prevention together with their particular risks and side effects. In the following, the operative methods and techniques that can be attributed to the state are, hence, narrowly understood as security technology, whose rules and measures, forms of knowledge and practices react to situations of risk that range from the specific to the highly general, in both normal but also emergency situations.[12]

Regimes[13] under ordinary law-rule or extraordinary emergency law equip the rationale of political technology with its respective meaning and direction in two areas of conflict: the legal prevention of abuse (directed against the arbitrary use of state power) and the prevention of dangers under emergency law (covering siege, war, insurrection, civil war, disaster, political uprising, etc.). In an ideal-typical contrast, regular law and emergency law mark and structure the areas, in which the security dispositive requires or engenders its specific political technology – depending on whether the task is to regulate, steer, control, inform or discipline under regular law or to monitor, subjugate, put down, pacify, detain or coerce under emergency law.

Law-rule – covering the varieties of the rule of law, *Rechtsstaat* and *état de droit* – and the state of exception, not only as its dark side and nemesis but also its twin brother, are at the heart of the following considerations. They are introduced here as contrasting perspectives for the analysis of fuzzy and topical phenomena, such as the 'preventive state' or 'surveillance state', counter-terrorism and civil sacrifice. They

---

[12] My considerations of political technology refer to the sphere, institutions and agents of domestic and external security but not to the field of social security or other political areas, like financial or fiscal security.

[13] In the following, I use the term regime either to mark the specific and fundamental characteristics of a form of political rule (e.g. authoritarian or democratic regimes) or the ensembles of norms, principles, procedures of decision-making and practices that constitute institutions in particular policy areas (e.g. the human rights regime).

play a crucial role in the discourse on security for both the justification and critique of extreme measures, such as violence and the treatment of 'dangerous persons' as enemies under criminal law.

1.2 POLITICAL TECHNOLOGY AS MINDSET

The Mentality of Engineers

Political technology is defined by an attitude or mindset and a method. The mindset of political technicians is meant to capture the way engineers think and act in political contexts. The engineers of political technology show, therefore, primarily a technical interest in, and a utilitarian and instrumentalist understanding of, the exercise of power, both of which in general allow for a merely tactical relationship to law.[14] Such instrumentalism is reflected in current notions of statecraft as the efficient and up-to-date use of power.[15]

Based on the claim of neutrality and on the legitimacy of expertise, their actions are pragmatically geared towards what is technically feasible. According to their ideology, success is measured by the effective functioning of institutions and the efficient implementation of policies; it can be assessed via the discrepancy between defined and achieved goals as well as the ratio of costs and benefits of, for instance, sweeping surveillance measures, brutal interrogation methods or the military intervention in Iraq.[16] Of course, practice shows that the engineers of and technical experts in governmental and administrative techniques often try to avoid the legal evaluation and monitoring of their actions, despite their focus on functionality and success.[17] They try to be as little bothered as possible by institutional or legal constraints, like civil rights or the test of

---

[14] Jürgen Habermas refers to the construction of social order and not to political technology, when he states in *Theory and Practice*, 43: 'The engineers of the correct order can disregard the categories of ethical social intercourse and confine themselves to the construction of conditions under which human beings, just like objects within nature, will necessarily behave in a calculable manner.' For dictatorship as the approach to the state of exception in political technology, which corresponds to the 'technical interest of an engineer in producing a thing', see Schmitt, *Die Diktatur*, 8 ff.

[15] E.g. the US Department of State's '21st Century Statecraft' programme and Margaret Thatcher's revelations (id., *Statecraft*).

[16] This frame of mind is illustrated by Posner, *The Perils of Global Legalism*.

[17] For the numerous EU-financed legislative projects in the post-socialist states, appropriate investigative research into effectiveness is still lacking.

proportionality, which might impinge on their freedom to decide and act. Unlike public officials who base their mission on a legal or political mandate, if they have not already chosen to mandate themselves, the public official as engineer tends to derive his or her mandate from a superior good, their supposedly superior knowledge and technical expertise.

Charismatic or authoritarian self-mandating and openly elitist mandates on the basis of a higher good or goal (like a revolution or the preservation of national unity) or superior knowledge (like the privileged insight into the historical 'laws' of socialist development) necessarily fade into the background in functioning democracies. In the national and, even more so, the international context, the mentality of political technicians has invaded politics and has come to dominate the various fields of policy.[18] Unlike experts, the protagonists of political technology are neither outsiders nor limited to generally advisory, subaltern roles and functions.[19]

In critical situations, politicians, no matter in what kind of role they appear, tend to shift to an engineering mindset and basically privilege technical rules and standards that apply to the problem or policy they have to cope with, over the principles and standards of law-rule and democracy. In these circumstances, legal concerns and constraints become a secondary priority at best: they are heeded, if they establish weak or no checks on political-technological considerations or can be utilized for legitimizing purposes. To the extent that law is meant to protect individual liberties against state interventions and to question inherent 'necessities', experts usually have a rather ambivalent, tactical take on law. And the ideology and operative implications of a 'lawful government', as is demonstrated by the 'war on terror' or the recent management of the Euro crisis, mutate on the quiet to a style of governing that deviates from democratic law-rule to political technology

---

Security policy-makers show a similar lack of interest in proving the effectiveness of their measures, when they routinely demand the extension of their competences, especially when it comes to the fight against 'organized crime' or terrorism (Hoffmann-Riem, 'Das Bundesverfassungsgericht als Garant von Rechtsstaatlichkeit', at 560).

[18] The problematic nature of a politics of expertise in the international context is discussed by Kennedy, 'Challenging Expert Rule'.

[19] For the distinction between the various types of political-social engineers – the expert, the technocrat and the political technician – see Frankenberg, 'Die europäische Union der Staatstechniker und Experten'.

carried out by state technicians who tend to treat the legislator and the law as hindrances in the way of Pareto-optimal problem solutions.

1.3 POLITICAL TECHNOLOGY AS METHOD

The mindset of political engineering translates into methods of political technology. In general, the term 'method of political technology' encompasses knowledge, practices, tactics, strategies and objectives. These operative aspects are shaped by the acting authorities, their competences, the regime of rules and procedures they have to operate in, their calculations and forms of knowledge as well as their overall characteristic – primarily legislative or executive – style. These methods I distinguish, if only for analytical reasons and ideal-typically, from legal techniques before I introduce four paradigms of political technology.

In the Shadow of Hierarchy

While standard legal techniques of governing operate, as a rule, within hierarchical structures, methods of political technology do not or, at best, remain in the shadow of hierarchy. As regards their general features, methods of political technology differ from legally formed, framed and legitimized techniques, first, in their informality, second, in their indirect impact, and third, and most importantly, in the imperatives of the underlying political (security) project they pursue.

First, conventionally, the predicates 'imperative' and 'formal' refer to the particular characteristics of the legal technique illustrated by parliamentary statutes, ordinances, decrees, administrative acts, etc. In regimes of self-government such decisions place decision-makers in a framework of separated powers and parliamentary, judicial or administrative controls. Dressed in the standard practices of law, the actors – legislators, presidents, administrators, courts, etc. – operate in a (more or less) hierarchically structured and horizontally interconnected system of competences and try to resolve conflicts through imperative, legally framed steering.

In recent times, the set of governmental techniques and practices has also included cooperative and more flexible methods.

With the advent of governance techniques, the world of formal-imperative legal commands and exercise of power has receded or rather shifted visibly to political technology. Power is exercised flexibly and informally not only by public/state authorities but also by private agencies (not always) specially empowered by law. The various new and not so new forms of cooperation are illustrated by public-private partnerships, administrative agreements, 'deals' under criminal law and court settlements. However, all these cooperative forms remain in the 'shadow of hierarchy',[20] because it is always possible to fall back on the imperative arsenal of steering instruments in case informal cooperation fails.

The coordinates of knowledge informing and guiding political decisions shift from power/law to power/expertise.[21] While government had always relied on knowledge, through expertise it receives a special mandate and mostly informal, political legitimation. This shift has become dramatic since the advent and rapid deployment of information technology. All by itself the informal style of governing, based on expertise rather than officially generated and, according to the ideal of parliamentarism, publicly debated knowledge, reveals an affinity between governance and political technology, which is discussed below as one of the ambivalences of the liberal paradigm.

Second, no matter whether it regulates, steers, prohibits, permits, informs, coerces or subjugates, legal technology – as method – is generally and ideal-typically geared towards *directly* intervening in the social sphere and economy or regulating individual behaviour. For this purpose, binding legislative or administrative decisions and court judgments coordinate actions and events and their consequences, if necessary with the help of force. These authoritative decisions concern the interaction between authorities and actors, which either exercise authority or, as societal actors, are involved in or affected by them. Also, conventional methods have basically and ideal-typically relied on *regulation* based on 'conditional programmes', i.e. the legal elements of rules authorizing governmental or police action or court sanctions for specific incidences and, respectively, individual cases.

Legal technology has never exclusively been constituted by strictly formalized, directly targeted regulations. It has always comprised provisions leaning towards political technology by granting discretion to administrative agencies and even courts due to indeterminate concepts and blanket clauses which have made the structure of conditional programmes porous, opening them up to consideration of political purposes.

---

20 This metaphor I borrow from Scharpf, *Games Real Actors Play*, 197.

21 See Kennedy, 'Challenging Expert Rule' and Frankenberg, 'Die europäische Union der Staatstechniker und Experten'.

In recent years, however, the standard modalities of legal technology have shifted considerably from the direct regulation of behaviour to the indirect disciplining of social processes. Information technology permits the monitoring of the movement of individuals and groups, the screening of social communication and economic transactions, and surveillance not only of public spaces. 'Dummy' clauses authorize the sweeping collection and processing of data; and statutes authorizing operative police action contain a variety of not only preventive but pre-emptive screening and surveillance measures.[22] They testify, if not to a paradigmatic shift, to the rapid advance of relatively new forms of indirect steering mechanisms to generate knowledge from military, secret service, police and also private sources. This new knowledge production is not only run by experts in information technology, it is also only very loosely connected with legal forms and legal constraints, thus opening up spaces for tactical manoeuvres, such as cooperation and data exchange between the police and secret services as well as the symbiosis of the military and commercial rationality in the collection, aggregation, exchange and use of data. Therefore, this ensemble of post-1984 measures qualifies as political technology.

The semantic and theoretical shift from government to governance captures some aspects of the general features of and the transition to a technology with a political DNA. With this shift the overall perspective changes from formal to informal rules, from direct to indirect modes of operation involving both state institutions and agents as well as private actors – companies, networks and civil society associations – as in principle equal partners in the decision-making process.[23] The governance perspective includes the whole variety of collective actors, their connections and relationships and the diversity of new instruments of (self-)steering within the activating nation-state and in complex multilevel systems, like the European Union,[24] and may help elucidate the concept and methods of political technology.

---

[22] The shift from prevention to pre-emptive measure or 'hyper-prevention' will be discussed in the context of the two crises of law-rule triggered by national and transnational terrorism (Chapters 5 and 6).

[23] From the plethora of literature on governance, see Mayntz, 'Governance Theory als fortentwickelte Steuerungstheorie'; Arthur Benz, 'Nationalstaat'; and OECD, *Online-Verwaltungslexikon*, http://olev.de; *Report on European Governance (2003–04)*, SEC (2004) 1153, 22 September 2004.

[24] In contrast to government, governance seems to be conceptually geared towards the combination of hierarchy and competition, of command and negotiation structures, of bureaucracy and networks, of formal and informal actions.

Third, from the variety of political projects that can be and are being pursued with the means and methods of political technology, I choose and focus on security because it has pervaded and come to dominate the arenas and discourses of politics, economics and law. More than any other policy topic, the varieties of security – or: the shifts and rifts of the security *dispositif*[25] – testify to the transformation of the methods of governmental techniques and the tension between the normal and exceptional situation. In different security regimes, operative techniques applied by the state change their shape and *modus operandi* significantly. Threats to the safety of the public or the political regime – or at least the official political, military or police perception of them – raise issues that are meant to be addressed by the use of new technologies, especially information technology, and the appropriate expertise. Furthermore, also in the area of security policy questions arise of how, with what methods and instruments, to resolve the conflicts and problems of interdependence that emerge at the territorial, social and functional boundaries of the state as institution. This becomes even more pertinent, since they are accompanied by a loss of certainty[26] and entail, seen from the perspective of the actors, a significant need for uncontrolled, unofficial and informal coordination.[27]

By contrasting law-rule and extraordinary rule beyond the law, i.e. the state of exception, different paradigms of political-technological methods can be teased out. The key criteria for the following distinction and attempt at model building are: first, whether given governmental techniques operate within the context of a predetermined difference between a normal and exceptional situation; second, and relatedly, whether and to what extent they are hemmed in by external legal rules, or whether they follow the rules of their own logic and technical code; and third, which strategic objectives the technicians are required to pursue by the changing *topos* of security.

The modelling that follows does not aim at writing a history of the state or governmental techniques and their inventors. Following Max

---

[25] Following Foucault, '*dispositif*' denotes primarily the heterogeneous ensemble of discourses, institutions, regulatory decisions, law, administrative measures, scientific statements, normative (moral, ethical, etc.) positions. See Foucault, 'The Confessions of the Flesh'.

[26] Baumann, *Modernity and Ambivalence*.

[27] Cf., although not limited to the field of public security, Mayntz, 'Verwaltungsreform und gesellschaftlicher Wandel', and Benz, 'Nationalstaat', 343.

Weber's ideal-types,[28] my aim is rather to emphasize and bundle diffuse and discrete phenomena for heuristic purposes. And I pursue a twofold objective: first, to highlight the different, specific, ideal-typical rationale of the techniques applied; and, second, to emphasize the effect of this rationale on the relationship between the holders and users of state power and their addressees.

The 'Method Machiavelli'

Political technology as a bundle of specific techniques for executing power is here introduced as *method Machiavelli* – not because it was invented or exclusively designed by the author of *The Prince*[29] but since it can arguably be related to what Michel Foucault called an 'abominable text'.[30] Under the guiding principle of the person of the ruler as the linchpin of 'reason of state', it functions as a technology for the acquisition and defence of sovereign power unhampered by moral and legal constraints. Neither concerned with the distinction between normalcy and emergency and the corresponding separation of competences nor hindered by legal rules, ethical principles or duties of virtue, such a political technology is tailored to the prince and therefore focuses on the acquisition and conservation of his power, as in the teachings of the Sophists. According to Machiavelli, political power in the conventional sense, as the control over territory and its resident population, might not be acquired casually by birth but through negotiation or force and is exercised at the will of its owner free of formal or normative constraints: 'There is no fundamental, essential, natural and juridical connection between the prince and his principality.'[31]

The difference between princely authority in a legally normal and an exceptional situation cannot reveal itself in the context of Machiavelli's empirical political sociology and psychology. Only by contrasting the Republic and (Roman) dictatorship is Machiavelli able to draw the

---

[28] Weber, *Economy and Society*, especially 19–22. Here, method does not mean scientific method in the modern sense; the methods outlined in the following are therefore really presented as ideal-types and should not be misconstrued as a scientific product of their respective namesake.

[29] Machiavelli, *The Prince*. See also id., *The Discourses*, ed. Bernard Crick (London: Penguin, 1984). Cf. for this and the following, Skinner, *Machiavelli*; Kersting, *Niccolò Machiavelli* and Münkler, 'Machiavelli, Niccolò'.

[30] Foucault, 'Security, Territory, Population', 73–9.

[31] Michel Foucault, *Security, Territory, Population: Lectures at the Collège de France, 1977–78*, 93.

contours of a 'useful', because temporary, state of exception meant to resolve a crisis quickly.[32]

Shaped by the situation and political climate in the Italian Republics, *The Prince* reads like a sober, sometimes cynical instruction manual for establishing and stabilizing princely families and state structures. Its author advises the ruler to always do what is required to consolidate his power position and to protect his principality. Neither charisma nor ethical leadership is required when dealing with internal and external enemies, but depending on the circumstances the prince has to act like a lion or a fox (Lysander)[33] – cruelty, deceit, fraud, corruption, treason, but also care or incentives, such as rewards or a prospective office, need to be applied. Machiavelli advises the prince to utilize his strategic and tactical skills, which does not equate to the use of statecraft in the sense of a virtuous, wise and economic steering of individuals, goods and wealth.

The Machiavellian scheme, dominated by *technicity*, subverts the clear distinction between regular order and exception and allows for a variety of authoritarian and even dictatorial techniques, which foreshadow the informality of current techniques of governing.[34] Therefore the Machiavellian technology of politics has not died with the demise of its namesake or the Italian republics. Rather, its method and mentality of self-mandating, which refers to sovereignty for use by the sovereign, transcends their original context. Due to its strict focus on the ruler, its formlessness and normative abstinence, the *method Machiavelli* meets the needs of the leadership in authoritarian regimes of all kinds, mainly concerned with maintaining their power, like the regimes of Vladimir Putin and Alexander Lukashenka, both marked by a scheme of power preservation without even a hint of occasional virtue. Not only can the *method Machiavelli* still be observed in its traditional field of application – politics: imperial presidents use it regularly,[35] while less imperial democratic leaders may fall back on it in times of crisis, such as the crisis of the Euro, or at authoritarian moments when preservation of power calls for the suspension or circumvention of democratic law-rule.

However, in constitutional states, the Machiavellian style meets with constraints by the constitution. This is why Machiavellian shifts from law to an 'occasional virtue' or the dictates of raw power require a pseudo-democratic or pseudo-legalist masquerade. Such camouflage tends to

---

[32] Machiavelli, *The Discourses*, chs. XXXIV–XXXV. Cf. Rossiter, *Constitutional Dictatorship*, 301 and Schmitt, *Die Diktatur*, 7 ff.

[33] Cf. Stolleis, 'Löwe und Fuchs'.

[34] See McCormick, 'Addressing the Political Exception'.

[35] Prempeh, 'Presidential Power in Comparative Perspective'.

borrow from the semantics or the arsenal of the state of exception.[36] No masquerade is warranted if the general public relishes rather than objects to the chief executive officer's repeated abuses and breaches of law for the preservation of his power.[37]

More commonly, the Machiavellian method shies away from the democratic and legal life-world and retreats to areas with no or less pronounced legal rules and democratic structures. To (at least semi-political) areas, that is, where the exercise of power means 'to do whatever it takes'[38] with hardly any (legal) restraint and outside control. Private corporations and the European Central Bank qualify as zones for Machiavellian moments and methods; furthermore political parties and, in particular, the World Soccer Association (FIFA), whose presidents have gone out of their way to gain the reputation that they will do 'whatever it takes', including using Mafia methods, to gain and stay in power.[39]

The 'Method Hobbes'

The *method Hobbes* is aligned with more complexity, normatively speaking. Its foundations and various facets can in the main be traced back to the *Elements of Law* and the *Leviathan*.[40] In these politico-philosophical studies, Thomas Hobbes designs a 'physics' of power against a backdrop of the chaotic context of England torn by religious wars and power struggles. Based on the discrepancy between the state of nature and the social condition, he comes up with a concept of abstract sovereignty and constructs the state as a peace machine. Against the tradition of absolutism, which by then dominated political philosophy, he bases the power of the sovereign on a network of reciprocal contracts in

---

[36] The freehand suspension of the German Nuclear Power Act in 2011, which was at the time only a couple of months old, by the government of Chancellor Angela Merkel can be characterized as a Machiavellian emergency measure dictated by the logic of power preservation after the disaster of Fukujima.

[37] As happened, for example, in Italy during the extended populist sultanate of Silvio Berlusconi; see Sartori, *Il Sultanato*.

[38] 'Within our mandate, the ECB (European Central Bank) is ready to do whatever it takes to preserve the euro.' Mario Draghi, Speech at the Global Investment Conference, London, 26 July 2012.

[39] E.g. Jennings, *Foul! The Secret World of FIFA*; Kistner, *FIFA-Mafia*.

[40] Hobbes, *Elements of Law Natural and Politic*; id., *Leviathan*; and id., *De Cive*.

favour of an independent third party.[41] In his *Leviathan*, Hobbes binds this third party, the holder of sovereign authority, to a central political goal: the protection of life to ensure peaceful coexistence. In this way, he attributes for the first time the essential aspects of a security calculation to a political technology, which is concentrated in the hands of the sovereign, oriented towards the executive and imperative; while the security calculation itself is linked to the justification of absolute power. At the same time, Hobbes shifts the rationale for the state from the Machiavellian interest of the prince 'in himself' to the robust interests of the estates and the utility maximizers in the bourgeois competitive society, which emerged before his very eyes.

In the *Elements of Law*, Hobbes specifies the way sovereign power is exercised over the subjects regarding any conflict of life in society. He explicitly regards state technology as the 'art of government'.[42] While the theory of sovereignty is the basis for the supreme duty of the ruler to preserve state and society, to protect them from relapsing into the anarchic state of nature, to enact general laws for this purpose and to enforce them universally, the art of government manifests itself in the 'good government of the people' for the mutual benefit of sovereign and subjects:

> And as the art and duty of the sovereigns consists in the same acts, so also doth their profit. For the end of art is profit; and governing to the profit of the subjects, is governing to the profit of the sovereign. (...) *Salus populi suprema lex*; by which must be understood, not the mere preservation of their lives, but generally their benefit and good.[43]

Thus, Hobbes bases his method of state technology on a double strategy, namely to ensure both the preservation of the state and the safety of the people, which coincides with '*salus populi*' in his *Leviathan* as well as to promote, without obligation, the common good (in the *Elements of Law*).[44]

In light of the Hobbesian theory of sovereignty, the outlines of a bisected rule of law begin to emerge. With the focus on the prevention of

---

41 For a detailed account of this often overlooked innovation in Hobbes' work, see Hampton, *Hobbes and the Social Contract Tradition*, 97–113 and 114–29; Skinner, *Freiheit und Pflicht*.

42 For the following, cf. also Bohlender, 'Metamorphosen des Gemeinwohls', 249 ff.

43 Hobbes, *Elements of Law*, part II, ch. 9.

44 Hobbes, *Leviathan*, ch. 30. Ferejohn and Pasquino ('The Law of the Exception') focus on safety of the people (p. 224).

threats from within and from the outside, the techniques employed by the state turn out to be security technology. Although sovereign rule, unless legitimized by conquest, has its origins in contractual law, the political order guaranteed by the Leviathan entails neither a re-connection to the contracting parties nor a separation of powers. Hobbes rejects both expressly. Due to his fear of possible dangers that threaten the political order and the resulting organization of safety, he consequently arrives at a conception of state power as indivisible: legislation, taxation and jurisdiction, the supreme command of the armed forces and the decision on war and peace – the 'sword of war' and the 'sword of justice'[45] – are to remain in the hands of the sovereign. After all, the ruler has obligations imposed on him by natural and divine rights. However, in the absence of a higher authority, these obligations are not enforceable. In today's terminology, they have rather the character of 'soft law' in the sense of a non-binding voluntary commitment. Derived from the theory of sovereignty, the rationale of obedience ('the purpose of obedience is protection')[46] contradicts the substantive rationale of the art of government (*salus populi*) only at first glance. For on the basis of the asymmetrical relationship between rulers and ruled, the logic of care does not bind the methods and instruments of political technology; rather it remains itself tied 'to the preservation and enhancement of state power'.[47]

Hobbes designs the relationship between the sovereign and its subjects as a general relationship of subordination constituted by reciprocal, third-party beneficiary contracts. The right to sovereignty and the fear 'that disposeth to rebellion is pretence of right'[48] block his way to an even moderately substantial concept of the constitutional state. Only with their agreement that institutes the sovereign, do the individual members of a society as subjects gain membership of the state and its protection. In return, they give up a significant portion of their freedom and their right to everything, including the right to resist, in exchange for their safety, as long as the Leviathan is able to fulfil its protective function. They cannot complain about 'legal violations' committed by or attributed to the sovereign, since they have authorized him by contract to be the source of law: *volenti non fit iniuria*.[49] In the shadow of this absolute

[45] Hobbes, *Elements of Law*, part II, ch. 1 (7–12) and ch. 8, where Hobbes refers to Bodin's *Six Books of the Commonwealth*, Book II, ch. 1.
[46] For the purpose of obedience, see Hobbes, *Leviathan*, ch. 21.
[47] Bohlender, 'Metamorphosen des Gemeinwohls', 251.
[48] Hobbes, *Elements of Law*, part II, ch. 8.
[49] Ibid., ch. 2 (3) and ch. 5 (2), id., *Leviathan*, ch. 21.

power over life and death, they are left with the residual freedom to do what has not been regulated by the ruler and to refuse obedience, if necessary. In the area of what is regulated, civil laws inevitably link the ears of the subjects to the lips of sovereign authority.[50]

If one leaves aside the exceptional situation of the state of nature, the Hobbesian fear-driven theory of sovereignty and conflict lacks the conceptual space for a worldly state of exception and to conceptualize the latter as an alternative to the norm. Nevertheless, the superior purpose of security suggests that Hobbes differentiates in his concept of political technology between 'the greatest inconvenience that can happen to a commonwealth', which is war and civil war, i.e. the ever-looming relapse into a state of nature as exceptional situation, on the one hand, and everyday conflicts triggered by the 'right of self-help' on the other hand.[51] The final chapter of the *Elements of Law* in particular can be read as a manual for the sovereign to prevent revolt:

> For maintaining of peace at home, there be so many things necessarily to be considered, and taken order in, as there be several causes concurring to sedition.[52]

Among other things, Hobbes considers it necessary in order to secure domestic peace 'to set out to every subject his propriety, and distinct lands and goods', 'to divide the burthens, and charge of the commonwealth proportionately' and to exercise 'due … justice' through 'the right performance of their duties, on the parts of those, who are the magistrates'. He also recommends taking measures in order to impose penalties so that 'there ought to be some means for the keeping under of those that are disposed to rebellion by ambition'.

The characteristics of the imperative and executive political technology outlined in the *Elements of Law* and the *Leviathan* have survived its author, work and original context even more successfully than in the case of Machiavelli. For Hobbes, the father of security technology, it was clear that one's neighbour could not be trusted: he might be a supporter of Cromwell or a royalist, a Catholic or Puritan, an aristocrat or a Leveller.

---

50 Hobbes, *Leviathan*, ch. 21. Hobbes mentions as examples of this freedom: 'the liberty to buy, and sell, and otherwise contract with one another; to choose their own abode, their own diet, their own trade of life, and institute their children as they themselves think fit; and the like'.

51 Hobbes, *Elements of Law*, part 2, chs. 5, 8 and 10.

52 Ibid., part 2, ch. 9.

Even in consolidated constitutional democracies, most conservative political philosophers and security policy-makers are prone to such mistrust. They constantly update the Hobbesian question of how political rule can be protected from dangerous individuals (*Gefährder*), harmful elements and exuberant, untamed initiatives of the citizenry. In this way, Hobbes is still regarded as the godfather of the preventive security state – a reading that somewhat unfairly reduces his work to the concept of the security state.

In the subsequent chapters, I will show that even critical situations for internal and external security, which rank below the threshold of a 'major crisis' or the state of emergency, offer the opportunity to apply measures of the *method Hobbes* and to connect it with other methods of political technology.

The 'Method Locke'

The *method Locke* as legal technology introduces elements of the liberal paradigm which at first glance could not be more different from the Hobbesian security state with its emphasis on the protection of natural rights. Nevertheless, the protection of property, liberty and security of the individual as well as the somewhat hidden protection of the 'body politic' is down to the purpose of security:

> But because no *political society* can be, nor subsist, without having in itself the power to preserve the property, and in order thereunto punish the offences of all those of that society, there, and there only, is *political society* where every one of the members hath quitted this natural power, resigned it up into the hands of the community in all cases that exclude him not from appealing for protection to the law established by it.[53]

Security does not vanish as *topos*; rather, its elements are only re-organized. Against the backdrop of the Glorious Revolution of 1688–9, John Locke maintained after his liberal turn that political rule is constituted by social contract. His position was not based on the reciprocal waiver of rights by the subjects in order to secure internal and external peace. Rather, from Locke onwards, the mutual social contract establishes a legislature as supreme authority and thereby institutionalizes majority rule. Absolutist sovereignty is replaced by parliamentary sovereignty, which programmes the actions of the executive with the help of

[53] Locke, *Two Treatises of Government*, 'Second Treatise', ch. 7, § 87 (emphasis added).

laws and finds its limits in the fundamental, natural rights to property and personal freedom. In the field of operative techniques used by the agencies and agents of the state, this legislative method pushes executive thinking into the background and sets out to establish legal restraints on the security-driven power engineer in the form of basic rights and constitutional principles (proportionality; determinacy). While both are rather loose and indeterminate concepts, they can still be reviewed by the courts.

In contrast to the tradition founded by Hobbes, the philosophical protagonists[54] of liberal techniques of governing shift their attention, when it comes to the prevention of dangers, from the potentially rebellious citizenry to potentially arbitrary and despotic state power and its incursion into the sphere of property and liberty. In the name of the security interests of a property-owning, bourgeois, male society,[55] they vie for the institutional design of law-rule that places, on the one hand, limits on the exercise of freedom and ensures, on the other hand, a 'limited and lawful government' basing every exercise of power on a relationship of trust (Locke) or binding it to a contract that establishes rule and authorizes it (Rousseau, Sieyès, Kant) within a system of the separation of powers or checks and balances:[56]

> [T]hat both the people may know their duty, and be safe and secure within the limits of the law, and the rulers, too, kept within their due bounds [...].[57]

In Locke's and other authors' work, varieties of the liberal paradigm replace the central authority with law in the guise of general law that

---

54 Apart from Locke, *Two Treatises on Government*, 'Second Treatise', one should also mention the following classics: Montesquieu, *The Spirit of the Laws*; Kant, *The Metaphysics of Morals*; Sieyès, *Qu'est-ce que le tiers-état?*; von Humboldt, *Ideen zu einem Versuch, die Grenzen der Wirksamkeit des Staates zu bestimmen* and Mill, *On Liberty*. Cf. Boucher and Kelly, *The Social Contract from Hobbes to Rawls* and Kersting, *Die politische Philosophie des Gesellschaftsvertrages*.

55 For a detailed and critical analysis see Neumann, *The Rule of Law*. Cf. Holdsworth, *History of English Law II*, 647 ff.; Macpherson, *The Political Theory of Possessive Individualism: Hobbes to Locke*. For the argument against reducing Locke to such an account of possessive individualism, see Tully, *A Discourse on Property*. Also in this vein, see Pateman, *The Sexual Contract*.

56 Locke's notion of the separation of powers remains vague, while Montesquieu, Kant and Sieyès provide more concrete notions. Today, one can find complex systems of the horizontal and vertical separation of state powers and the checks and balances between them in numerous constitutional orders.

57 Locke, *Two Treatises of Government*, 'Second Treatise', ch. 11, § 137.

provides, if necessary, for direct interventions in social processes and direct regulation of individual behaviour. In the contractualist context, law-rule is meant to guarantee the normalcy of lawful government (Locke). For the first time, the liberal paradigm highlights the contrast between an ordinary, *legally* regulated state of freedom and an exceptional state of unconstrained, sovereign arbitrary use of power (relegated to the prerogative). In this way, the power of the ruler fades into the background, while it was still visible in Hobbes' account. As legal order, the system of general laws is given the task of generating normative normalcy. In the later stages of the liberal paradigm, the problematic relationship between norms and validity vis-à-vis facts and effectiveness is addressed in formulas like the 'normative force of the factual' (Georg Jellinek) or 'the very real force of the counterfactual' (Jürgen Habermas).[58]

With this construction of a state of normal law or later democratic law-rule, the legislative style assumes a guiding role. In the liberal imagination and ideology, law-rule safeguards the transition from the personal to the impersonal exercise of power by untying the bond of personal loyalty to the monarch and turning it into obedience to law. Thus, laws are imagined to control, if not eliminate, the subjective factor of political rule – authoritarian arbitrariness. This very imagination is expressed by the catchy and brilliant formula 'government of laws and not of men' in the Anglo-American constitutional tradition.[59] As foil for the depiction of abuses of state power, the rule of law, constitutional state, *Rechtsstaat* and *état de droit* refer to both the legal form manifest in law and a corresponding, legally bound and normal exercise of political power.[60] At the same time, the underlying security agenda focuses political technology on the direct control of behaviour and direct interventions in the socio-economic sphere in the standard form of legal statutes, administrative acts and so forth.

There is a dark side to this paradigm, though: the prerogative of the monarch. On the quiet it transforms the legal techniques of governing into *political* technology, which is still claimed to be legal. For Locke, the prerogative – the untamed legacy of monarchical despotism – remains

---

[58] Heller, *Staatslehre*, 251; Jellinek, *Allgemeine Staatslehre*, 329–30 and Habermas, *The Philosophical Discourse of Modernity*, 206.

[59] The formula has its origins in Aristotle's work and in Harrington's *The Commonwealth of Oceana*. Cf. Michelman, 'Law's Republic', at 1502.

[60] For a detailed and differentiated account of the respective conceptual history, cf. Heuschling, *État de droit Rechtsstaat Rule of Law*.

in place, albeit not as the centrepiece of the liberal narrative.[61] In his design of the liberal paradigm he also recognizes martial law and executive powers as explicit emergency powers. They appear as deviations from regular law – or more precisely, as exceptions to the law – and indicate the illiberalism woven into the fabric of the liberal paradigm and its political rationale. In the course of historical development, variants of the *method Locke* emerged and included additional exceptional situations that lie outside of the legal framework or transgress its borders.[62] In the constitutional discourse of the 19th century, war was replaced by the prototypical state of siege[63] and, informed by the trauma of the Jacobins, political uprisings took centre stage in the imagination of the extraordinary. Finally, in the 20th century the state of exception (and later: emergency) operates as an overarching term for different forms of extraordinary situations of crisis brought about by war, siege, turmoil and disaster. The varieties of the extraordinary raise the question, addressed below, of whether these extreme situations of crisis can be typified, legalized and dealt with according to the ordinary legal pattern of liberal standardization, even though they lie outside of the legal framework.

The 'Method Foucault'

The *method Foucault* offers a lateral account of the previously introduced, historicized and ideal-typical methods of political technology. It opens a new and critical perspective on both the *method Hobbes* and the *method Locke* as well as on the Machiavellian and non-Machiavellian techniques of exercising power and their underlying threat perceptions and security conceptions. This perspective breaks with the tradition of narratives that justify power and legitimize authority by limiting its scope and exercise. Instead, the strategies and mechanisms of power are analysed without any obvious (or at least: a priori) normative intention. Michel Foucault is not interested in legitimizing but in examining and criticizing the modalities and strategies for the exercise and operation of

---

[61] See Locke, *Two Treatises of Government*, 'Second Treatise', § 159; for a concise analysis see Loughlin, *Foundations of Public Law*, 383–7; Dunn, *The Political Thought of John Locke*, 150 and Pasquino, 'Locke on King's Prerogative', 201.

[62] Chapters 3 and 4 will deal in detail with these exemptions from the normativity of the normal state.

[63] For a detailed and broad account, see Boldt, *Rechtsstaat und Ausnahmezustand*.

power.[64] He brings to the fore the modern version of the Hobbesian paradigm which he detects in the liberal paradigm of governmental technology – the illiberal security paternalism – designed with quite practical-legitimizing intent by liberal political philosophy.

Foucault concedes that the Hobbesian theory of the sovereign state and its corresponding political technology appropriately portrays the everyday experience of political domination in feudal societies and roughly also in the post-feudal society the author of the *Leviathan* was confronted with. The manner in which power was exercised in absolutist times could rightly be captured in the dualism sovereign/subject with regard to its expressions and functions. In contrast to the Hobbesian security dispositive,[65] a new power mechanism emerges in the 17th and 18th centuries; according to Foucault, it seeks to extract time and labour out of bodies rather than out of goods and wealth:

> [T]he body is also directly involved in a political field; power relations have an immediate hold upon it; they invest it, mark it, train it, torture it, force it to carry out tasks, to perform ceremonies, to emit signs.[66]

And these power relations force it, in particular, to emit signs of obedient functioning. Typically, for the *method Foucault*, this new mechanism is exercised through continued monitoring, control and registration as well as discontinuously via the tax system and recurring obligations to pay charges and provide services.[67] Whereas Hobbes legitimizes the position of the sovereign and the techniques of the ruler/Leviathan to preserve peace, after having become free of legal interference following the completion of the contract, and whereas the Lockean focus is directed towards taming the monarch and limiting civil society's exercise of liberty, the *method Foucault* outlines the ensemble of discursive and non-discursive disciplinary techniques and practices of power. Thus, the unitary conception of sovereignty dissolves into various manifestations of 'disciplinary power'.[68]

---

[64] For the following, see Foucault, *Discipline and Punish* and id., *The Birth of the Clinic*.

[65] Following Foucault, I understand 'dispositive' as the heterogeneous ensemble of discourses and institutions, legislative rules and administrative measures, (legal) scientific statements and philosophical considerations. Foucault, *Dispositive der Macht*; Deleuze, 'Was ist ein Dispositiv?'

[66] Foucault, *Discipline and Punish*, 25.

[67] Foucault, *Society must be Defended*, 36.

[68] For this and the following, see especially the Lecture of 14 January 1976 (Foucault, *Society must be Defended*, 36 ff.).

From Foucault's perspective, the Hobbesian concept of ultimate authority emerges with the 'self-exemption of the sovereign',[69] who does not act as a contractual partner but emerges as a unifying effect triggered by the mutual authorization of 'frightened subjects'.[70] With this introduction, Foucault distances himself from both the Hobbesian and post-Hobbesian concepts of legal and political philosophy in Western societies, which revolve at the beginning around royal power, later around its functional equivalent, the sovereign state, and finally around the rule of law.

With his view of the techniques of disciplinary power and later of biopolitics, Foucault rejects not only the absolutist monarch as the central person and living body of sovereignty, but also the liberal obsession with legitimacy, typical of the *method Locke,* and the resulting theoretical focus on how to justify and limit power – and authorize its exercise. This focus displaces actual rule and its consequences by its occupation with the juridical and, we might add here, dressing political technology up as a set of legal techniques.

Rather than looking at the head of state (Hobbes) or the natural rights of the propertied class (Locke), Foucault assumes the perspective of the subjugated in order to reveal the 'fact of domination' in their secret and brutal aspects. He intends to expose the law, which *generates* relations of domination and does not only serve them as a tool, as is suggested in the *method Locke.* This perspective highlights how the life of those under domination and control is standardized and made subject to authoritative regulations following the security rationale of disciplinary power.

In his analysis of power, Foucault takes five 'methodological precautions', which manoeuvre him into strict opposition to a political theory fixated on the sovereign or Leviathan and the legitimate order as well as on formal and direct, executive or legislative techniques of governing. His studies first follow power up to its furthest ramifications, even up to its capillaries, where it becomes paper-thin and less and less determined by law. The legal edifice of sovereignty and the system of individual rights fade thereby into the background.

Second, instead of the formal aspects of legal technology, Foucault examines the practices and techniques of power in order to grasp 'the material operations, forms of subjugation, and the connections among

---

[69] Luhmann, 'Metamorphosen des Staates', 101, 108.

[70] Foucault, *Society must be Defended*, 119, and Opitz, 'Zwischen Sicherheitsdispositiven und Securitization', 201, 208.

and the uses made of the local systems of subjugation'.[71] In this way, he dismisses one of the key problems that has preoccupied political theory and science, namely how, based on the diversity of individuals and efforts of will, a unitary will of the state or a single body politic can form and be given life by the 'soul of the sovereign' or constituted by the constitution, as was argued later. With this focus Foucault teases the illiberal governmentality out of the liberal paradigm and anticipates the shift of techniques of governing from direct regulations of behaviour to the screening of communication and the monitoring of movements and social processes by security and, as we learn these days, also by intelligence agencies.

Third, Foucault does not understand power as a monolithic, homogeneous phenomenon of rule, exercised in a linear fashion by command, but as something that circulates, works as a chain and is passed on to individuals and practised by them via networks.[72] Thereby, he leaves behind the juridical conception of power as property and agency, which is the foundation for the *methods Hobbes* and *Locke,* and introduces the concept of *relational power* – a power which is expressed and valid in the relationships it is constituted by and whose exercise follows the laws of economics.[73]

Fourth, he does not derive power from a central authority but investigates it in an 'ascending analysis of power',[74] starting from the micromechanisms that reveal to him the connections and uses of the local systems of subjugation.[75] Finally and fifth, Foucault refrains from analysing the big power ideologies and, at least initially, also postpones an investigation of law. Instead, he focuses on dispositives and apparatuses of knowledge that emerge at the tapering ends of power networks and become effective as instruments for the accumulation of knowledge, methods of observation, techniques of recording and other more or less subtle mechanisms and practices. In the end he reveals the normative goal of his scientific method: in his lectures on governmentality and of *Society Must Be Defended* it becomes apparent that he wants to liberate

---

71 Foucault, *Society Must Be Defended*, 34.

72 The issues entailed in such a broad concept of power are discussed elsewhere in some detail. Cf. Honneth, *The Critique of Power* and Habermas, *The Philosophical Discourse of Modernity*, chs. IX and X.

73 Foucault, *Society Must Be Defended* and id., *The Birth of Biopolitics*, 144.

74 Foucault, *Dispositive der Macht*, 81 and id., *Society Must Be Defended*, 30.

75 Cf. Foucault, *Madness and Civilization*; id., *Der Wille zum Wissen*.

'subjugated knowledge', whose historical substance was trapped and perished under the pressure of functional contexts and formal systematization.

The characteristics of the *method Foucault* as an established and practised political technology emerge (from Foucault's critical analyses and narratives) when emphasis is given to the strategies of indirect behavioural monitoring executed by the surveillance of events and spaces as well as the screening of communication. These strategies are embedded in the networks of disciplinary power and systems of control in regimes of illiberal governmentality.

Instead of a contractual Hobbesian arrangement covering the security of the territory and its borders or a liberal social contract geared towards the security of property and liberty, in Foucault's studies, at least in his later work, the state is empowered to intervene by a security contract of a different kind. Here we catch a puzzling glimpse of the state of exception defined neither in the traditional nor, as will be shown later, in a Schmittian manner:

> [W]hen the normal course of everyday life is interrupted by an exceptional unique event, then the law is not sufficient. Then interventions are needed, which despite their extraordinary, extra-legal character ought not to appear arbitrary or an abuse of power, but as an expression of caring … This ubiquitous care is the face that the state exposes to its citizens.[76]

The security paternalism diagnosed by Foucault curiously accommodates the aspect of care outlined in Locke's *Elements of Law*, modifies it and turns critically against it, in order to return to an analysis of law, whose concept is anchored in the liberal paradigm.

As is shown in the following chapters, the hyper-Orwellian security paternalism that characterizes the political technology of the *method Foucault* is enhanced by the erosion of structures and categories of law-rule aligned with a drastic reduction of judicial review. Dummy provisions, especially in police law and data protection law, signal the legislature's surrender to the new techniques of governing geared towards the accumulation and processing of data by intercepting communication, registering transactions, screening the internet, monitoring social events and processes, etc., which treat society as a production site for information and turn the state into an 'information-market state'.

---

[76] Foucault, 'Die Sicherheit und der Staat', 140. See also Fitzpatrick and Golder, *Foucault's Law*.

1.4 POLITICAL TECHNOLOGY OF THE SECURITY STATE

Between the Negation and the Juridification of the State of Exception

The function of the liberal-constitutional link between norm and legality is to exclude the arbitrary use of state power and to banish brute force from societal conflicts. Thus, the *method Locke* is accompanied by the – naïve, or at least overly optimistic – idea that it erects a conceptual barrier that separates us from the places and times of savage violence. Unless the defence against unlawful state interference or civil rights violations has to be addressed, the liberal paradigm has considerable difficulty grasping and coping with exceptional situations even conceptually and including them in the framework of legislative political technology.

The theory and practice of Lockean governmental technology oscillate like a will-o'-the-wisp between two extremes.[77] The optimistic version of the rule-of-law project is allowed by its rule rationalism to believe that normal law settles essential matters and any kind of arbitrary use of state power and any recourse to civil feud and law of the jungle are under control. In this way, political uprisings, coup attempts, wars or disasters are negated explicitly or implicitly.[78] The state of exception does not occur; or rather it *must not* take place because its mere standardization would undermine the very normalcy the legal system refers to and relies on. Law-rule may focus on the management of normal situations. An emergency law does not exist; there remains only the prerogative as the power of promoting the public good, where law is silent, and discretion, where the law has no clear answer.

In contrast to the negation of the exceptional case, 'realistic' doctrines of law-rule interpret the rationalist project as the task of regulating all imaginable societal situations and conflicts and, therefore, also the unthinkable case of emergencies. They strive for the delicate 'registration

---

[77] See, in particular, Chapters III and IV below.

[78] Accordingly, Art. 13 of the French Constitution of 14 August 1830 prohibited the monarch from ever suspending the laws or preventing their implementation. Art. 130 of the 1831 Belgian Constitution states similarly: 'The Constitution can neither partly nor totally be suspended.' A comparable validity command can be found in Art. 108 Belgian Constitution.

of the state of exception into the constitutional world'.[79] Under the influence of legal positivism,[80] many legal systems have tried, therefore, to juridify or legalize war, siege, civil war and disasters as exceptional cases, especially since the mid-19th century. In order to prevent extra-legal measures, the manipulators of the method of political technology are given special powers for situations of extraordinary danger. The paradox of standardizing the extraordinary is meant to be overcome by tying the state of exception under emergency law or the rules on a constitutional dictatorship to a formal declaration, to rules of responsibility, deadlines, procedures and substantive objectives – largely according to the pattern of dealing with conflicts in normal situations. Of course, given the fact that these norms are geared towards their own elimination after the end of the state of exception, the paradoxical nature of this project becomes apparent.

Normalizing the State of Exception

The liberal dilemma in the face of extraordinary threats or extreme cases becomes apparent in its unsteady past. Various, early approaches to 'register' the state of exception 'into law-rule' were followed in totalitarian regimes, especially in National Socialism, by the practice of legal masking and perverting the exceptional case with the help of emergency decree law and the Nazis' infamous Enabling Act. After the Second World War, a first phase of resistance followed until emergency provisions – generally no longer related to a state of exception – were included in constitutions around the world. In many countries, the crises of law-rule[81] that began in the 1980s under the banner of counter-terrorism and were continued in the 1990s with the 'war on terror and organized crime', revealed the risks and side effects of the positivist strategy of integrating emergency powers into the law of the normal state. The dynamics of 'registering' the state of exception as part of the norm,

---

[79] Boldt, *Rechtsstaat und Ausnahmezustand*, 162. Typical in this context is the Act on the State of Exception of 4 June 1851, in *Preußische Gesetzes-Sammlung 1851*, 451 ff.

[80] In legal positivism, the state of exception 'formally lives the life of a general norm' as the epitome of the relevant rules under emergency law, which a legal order provides (Boldt, *Rechtsstaat und Ausnahmezustand*, 86 and 166 ff.).

[81] I deal with the crises of the rule of law triggered by political terrorism in later chapters (Chapters 5, 6 and 7).

which is to say the empirical and normative regularity in legal orders,[82] I characterize as a process of its gradual *normalization*.[83] Normalization means that the instruments and ideology of emergency law are step by step wrapped in a cloak of regular normativity, are perpetuated and become part of everyday life through their juridification, their emergence as *topoi* under emergency law as well as their inclusion in the doctrines of regular law. In short: the exception is integrated into the norm.

The normalization of the extraordinary manifests itself at three levels of political technology. First, it becomes visible in a *semantics* camouflaging or trivializing deviance from democratic law-rule. Current examples are the demands of security policy-makers to allow the military to use 'military means' – in plain language, weapons – when they assist domestic authorities or use the armed forces domestically. In the same direction points the trivialization of torture, as 'life-saving forced statement', 'self-inflicted rescue questioning' or 'rescue torture'. This normalizing rhetoric and reasoning uses in each case a vocabulary that strips the respective phenomena of their exceptional nature in order to include them discreetly in the normalcy of the legal everyday. Incidentally, this vocabulary also opens the door for the systematic legal rehabilitation of the concept of the enemy.

Second, normalization also becomes apparent in a new legal *topography*. Boundaries and thresholds for intervention meant to safeguard freedom as well as categorical distinctions relevant for the authoritative 'invention' of citizens' duties are covered up by the new design of a security state. A clear indication of the normalization process are the structural distortions and 'materializations' of danger prevention law (police law) in the framework of a 'new security architecture',[84] which will later be shown to shift from cognitive to (pseudo-)existential security. Within the framework of this architecture, the categorical differences between peacebreaker and peaceful citizen, between danger and risk are eliminated, and danger prevention law is transformed into a 'danger invention law'. Similarly, 'probable cause' loses more of its already endangered protective function in criminal law enforcement. Within the overall new topography of the security state, the protection of persons by guaranteeing the certainty of law falls prey to an illusory

---

[82] For a slightly different definition, see Ferejohn and Pasquino, 'The Law of the Exception', 221.

[83] Regarding the argument that the state of exception becomes normalized and an everyday phenomenon, see Frankenberg, 'Kritik des Bekämpfungsrechts' and Dyzenhaus, 'The Permanence of the Temporary'.

[84] See Burwell et al., *Transatlantic Transformation*.

certainty with regard to the objects protected by law (*Rechtsgüter*). In turn certain 'dangerous elements', types of perpetrators and even suspects are excluded from legal protection and thus are relegated, if so required by necessity, to the status of enemies.

Third, this normalization process becomes functionally manifest in norms which inscribe new tasks and competences into the topography of law, in particular into danger prevention law and criminal codes. In functional terms the characteristics of this 'new security architecture' are (a) the extension of the agenda of counter-terrorism; its areas of threat comprise international terrorist networks, the proliferation of weapons of mass destruction, and human trafficking;[85] (b) data sharing and cooperation between police, security agencies and intelligence services as the inner structure of the surveillance state; (c) efforts to extend the domestic use of the armed forces; (d) the screening of online and offline communication, video-surveillance of public areas, wiretapping, and the registration of economic transactions; and last but not least, (e) the dramatic advance and institutional increase of cyber-espionage.[86] While the 'new security architecture' comprises strategies to control cyberspace, this does not mean that it abandons physically coercive measures. Attempts to normalize torture will be analysed in detail below; along with doctrines designed to legitimize the downing of so-called renegade aircraft.[87]

Political Technology as Security Technology

Normalizing the state of exception begins within law-rule whenever discretionary power is set free from legal restraints and therefore the application of a norm in single cases can scarcely be anticipated. The normalization becomes more general with the integration of extra-ordinary measures into the standard texture of law-rule.[88] Ultimately, the normalizing dynamics submit the rationality of law-rule to the imperatives of the security state. This process and dynamics follow a specific security script: the conventional law-rule prevention of danger gives way to the logic of hyper-prevention. Governmental (police) operations encompass not only concrete threats but also potential, abstract risks and therefore extend spatially far beyond zones of danger and temporally into the future. Hyper-prevention requires that the police are at the scene of

---

85 *Frankfurter Allgemeine Sonntagszeitung*, 16 June 2013, p. 7.

86 Schirrmacher, 'Der verwettete Mensch'; Bobbitt, *Terror and Consent*.

87 See Chapters 4 and 6 (downing of renegade aircraft) and 7 (torture).

88 See Chapters 5 and 6.

the crime before the offender, that the engineers of security know what we will do tomorrow, and that they are largely exempt from legal molestations in order to allow them to operate smoothly in whatever 'war on … ' they are fighting.

The security state has become a global phenomenon[89] and manifests, as was argued and will be shown, a new logic of political technology. Driven by dramatic, anxiety-inducing threat scenarios, like the image of the 'ticking bomb' or the pervasive metaphor of war, the Hobbesian question has directed attention to how a citizenry can be monitored and their energies curbed by government in order to effectively prevent as early as possible excess activities of civil society and, in particular, the criminal activity of 'dangerous elements' – 'organized crime' and terrorists. The Hobbesian scenario has been modernized though: political technicians' operations follow the logic of the undeclared state of exception and the assumption that threats emerge primarily out of the middle of society, emanating not only from 'sleepers', 'dangerous elements' and other incarnations of 'evil' but also from those who do not deviate from what is considered normal behaviour. Therefore, society has to be kept under constant monitoring, screening and surveillance. 'Securitization' in a regime of illiberal governmentality is called for. In this regime the normalized state of exception turns out to be the twin brother of law-rule, which may explain the 'striking fact that, even in those advanced democracies whose constitutions contain provisions for emergency powers, these powers are not used'.[90] Why openly use them when they can be discreetly integrated into the texture of law-rule?

---

[89] For the vast literature on the security state, see e.g. Balkin, 'The Constitution in the National Surveillance State'; Darnstädt, *Der globale Polizeistaat*; Klinsman et al., *Whose National Security?*; Kirshner, *Globalization and National Security*; Lewis, *Globalization and National Security*.

[90] Ferejohn and Pasquino, 'The Law of the Exception'.

2. Visions of political technology

Legal and political techniques of governing are translated into spoken words and written texts. We usually represent, execute, justify or criticize these techniques by dint of language and script. It is rarely observed that throughout history they have also found pictorial expression. To introduce the more elaborate conceptual discussion that will follow, in this chapter I want to present some of the visions and images that illustrate the imagining of rule-law and *Rechtsstaat* and elucidate their conceptual dimension.

2.1 HOBBES AND THE BEGINNING OF MODERN POLITICAL TECHNOLOGY

At the beginning of modern theories of the state, there was Thomas Hobbes and, more precisely, what is undisputedly his most influential work – the *Leviathan* (1651). Some historians and political philosophers would argue for a different starting point, if this were considered important. In fact, when it comes to the origin of unbound state technology, one would need to think of Machiavelli's manual of power (*The Prince*, written in 1513 and published in 1552) or Jean Bodin's *Six Livres de la République* (1576), which identify him as the initiator of the modern doctrine of sovereignty. The mystery posed by every beginning,[1] namely the time before that it deconstructs, is not meant to be pursued further here. Because hardly anyone will dispute that the *Leviathan*, followed by the *Elements of Law Natural and Politic* (1640), belongs to the paramount line of powerful historical myths dealing with state formation and the notions of political technology.

Probably written in 1650 and first published in the following year, Hobbes unleashes with the peace machine, which he names after the Biblical sea monster 'Leviathan', a new political imagination showing distinct features of a fascination with political technology. He portrays a

[1] Vorländer, 'Gründung und Geltung', 243: 'Not only magic dwells in the beginning, but also a mystery'.

number of people, sometimes called society or *civitas*, who leave the apocalypse of the state of nature behind and enter into a civilized, albeit permanently conflictual, social state, which is dominated by the rules of a political mechanics. Released from any hopes for salvation by transcendent powers, society is forced to remember its own strengths. In Hobbes' account, it is still hesitant, half-hearted and yet courageous, but also scared, always gazing at the post-apocalyptic head of the 'mortal god'. Once installed, the latter presents itself as powerful, overlooking people and landscape, and virtually embodies the purpose of security to which the Leviathan is bound. The ruler may also care for the well-being of his subjects, as was shown before, but first and foremost it is his duty to meet the responsibility to protect, as one would say these days.[2]

What other ideas of political technology can be derived from theories of the modern state? First in political philosophy, then in legal philosophy and later under the heading of 'General Theory of the State' (*Allgemeine Staatslehre*), the Hobbesian line of argument was maintained and his executivist view and focus on sovereignty dominated the debate for a long time. Political philosophy and theories of the state follow the guiding concept of Hobbes' governmental techniques – security – and remain fixated upon the executive power: the sovereign monarch, the head of state, the monopolist of legitimate force (Max Weber), and only sometimes upon the rule of law, regularly upon the sovereign state. At its top, the ultimate decision-making power for the issue of security is located. Sovereign is he who is authorized or deemed to be authorized to suspend the law in a state of war or siege and later in a state of emergency. The doctrines of sovereignty ensure that the exercise of power remains largely unconstrained. Where legal bonds are derived from an august tradition, natural law or a social contract, the monarchical or post-monarchical prerogative corrects the limited sovereignty and leaves the door wide open for executive techniques of governing required in exceptional situations.

The picture changes after the revolutions in the United States and in France. Different concepts and imaginations of the sovereign – 'we the people' in the United States, the sovereign *Nation*[3] in France or, latterly, a German *Volk* (people) finally 'united in its tribes'[4] – eclipse the

2 Orford, *International Authority and the Responsibility to Protect*.

3 'Le principe des toute souveraineté réside essentiellement dans la Nation', Art. 3 Déclaration des Droits de l'Homme et du Citoyen (1789). See also Art. 3 of the French 1958 Constitution.

4 The Preamble of the Weimar Constitution of 1919 begins with 'The German people, united in its tribes'.

Leviathan and suspend its mechanics. In this way, monarchical or authoritarian access is no longer permitted among the techniques of the state of exception. At first, the prerogative must negotiate the hopes of salvation held by revolutionaries in the early, still uncertain and self-reassuring modernity; then, it has to accommodate the bourgeois hopes of security, which are directed at the rule of law and the legislator and the *Rechtsstaat*.

In the founding and consolidation phase of bourgeois-capitalist society, the bourgeois imagination is much less troubled by evil that comes in the shape of war, disaster and counter-revolution. The dominant idea is that the technology of power rests in law. It survives numerous wars and revolutions, theoretical challenges and polemical farewells, but not always in good shape. The socialization of the state of bourgeois society, as predicted by Marx and Engels and others, does not take place. They introduce a new and powerful picture of the state's withering away.[5] This happened neither in the 19th century nor in 'real socialism', which did not go beyond the nationalization of the means of production and the authoritarian administration of the public in the name of state security. Even in what is, somewhat rashly, called 'late capitalism', the state does not die or wither away. Recently, the privatization of state functions and globalization affected statehood, changed and weakened it, but did not abolish it. Repeated fears that the constitutional state and its techniques dissolve into the materializations of the social and technical state[6] seem nowadays helplessly outdated.

A similar picture emerges in the sciences of the state, politics and law: in many of his works, such as *Discipline and Punish*, Michel Foucault criticized the political and legal sciences' fixation upon sovereignty and law as a command of the sovereign.[7] In his lectures *Society must be Defended*,[8] he significantly modified this criticism. However, notions of sovereignty as the 'soul of the state' still remain in the background of his

---

[5] Typical are Engels, 'Herrn Eugen Dührings Umwälzung der Wissenschaft (Anti-Dühring)', 261 ff., and Lenin, *Staat und Revolution*, 18 ff., who, however, saw this process as the violent 'abolition' of the bourgeois state by the proletarian revolution after the 'proletarian state or semi-state' 'withers away'.

[6] Forsthoff, *Der Staat der Industriegesellschaft*; against it, Vogel, *Die Staatsbedürftigkeit der Gesellschaft*, 13–30, who counters 'state melancholy' with the 'presence' and functional necessity of the welfare state.

[7] I basically agree with Fitzpatrick and Golder (*Foucault's Law*) that in his early writings Foucault did not 'expel' the law from the analysis of disciplinary mechanisms.

[8] Foucault, *Discipline and Punish* and id., *Society Must be Defended*.

thinking; meanwhile, for a couple of years now, political science has talked more soberly and technically only about sovereign control performances. The latter have come under pressure through arguments stating the failure of politics and law. But even the claims or demands that are sometimes made regarding the retirement of the steering state – or rather of steering theories – seem to have no effect on the idea of the sovereign state and the instruments of political technology; the fragmentation of national sovereignty in supranational multi-level systems or its impotence to control cross-border problems, such as organized crime, terrorism and climate change, has also had little effect.

Recently, it seems, there had been a crisis over the conceptual link between the state and sovereignty; a link which is ritually stressed by political science, state theory and political technology. This can be concluded from the *fin-de-siècle* attitude of rather too rash and nostalgic descriptions and obituaries of the state,[9] from over-critical reflections on the theory of the state and its objectives[10] as well as from the shift in scientific interest to the trans- and international level.[11] Although the supposedly sovereign nation-state barely resembles the biblical sea monster Leviathan today, still, these circumstances do not prevent actors in the economy – a functionally differentiated system organized according to the technical views of systems theory that works best state-free according to the neoliberal vision – from calling for state support and accepting a supranational financial rescue umbrella, whenever there is an obvious market failure or in cases of states approaching insolvency. But once the financial crisis is over, the farewell to the state will be popular again and the functional differentiation between politics and economics will again be insisted upon, as previously.

The situation is confusing. Nevertheless, we can conclude that Hobbes' 'mortal god' and its political technology have suffered from consumption

---

[9] Reinhard, *Geschichte der Staatsgewalt*; van Creveld, *The Rise and Decline of the State*. By the way, both authors invoke, and perhaps not for the last time, the classical founding myth by showing the frontispiece of the *Leviathan* on their front cover. For obituaries, see Albrow, *Abschied vom Nationalstaat*; Losano ('Der nationale Staat zwischen Regionalisierung und Globalisierung') talks about the 'withering away of the state'; Denninger, 'Vom Ende nationalstaatlicher Souveränität in Europa'. Schmitt had already argued: 'The era of the State is now coming to an end. This needs no discussion.' (*The Concept of the Political*, 10).

[10] Vesting, 'Die Staatsrechtslehre und die Veränderung ihres Gegenstandes'.

[11] Instructive here are the publications of the research project 'Transformations of the State': Hurrelmann et al., *Zerfasert der Nationalstaat?*; Mau, *Transnationale Vergesellschaftung*; Zangl, *Die Internationalisierung der Rechtsstaatlichkeit*.

for some time now. If a grand analogy is allowed, they remind us of Freud's 'god with artificial limbs'.[12] Still, this fact has scarcely affected the mentality of the political engineers. The crisis phenomena rather indicate that governments in dire straits opt if in doubt for the legally unbound exercise of power. The monarchical prerogative has changed its appearance; it returns as the executive state's provision to intervene.

2.2 CONSTRUCTION: IMAGES OF THE LEVIATHAN

'Non est potestas Super Terram quae Comparetur ei' and 'When it rises up, the mighty are terrified; they retreat before its thrashing.'[13] Hobbes, who distrusted language,[14] tried to depict the incomparable power of the state graphically. Horst Bredekamp,[15] a historian of culture, reconstructed with almost criminalist meticulousness not only the Hobbesian perspective but also the success story of the visually powerful *Leviathan* in modern state theory. Attributed to Wenzeslaus Hollar and Abraham Bosse according to his prudent research, the Leviathan frontispiece[16] puts into the spotlight the no longer traditional but still not yet modern ruler as sovereign and political technician. On the one hand, the frontispiece, approved by Hobbes, represents the Leviathan's origin and supreme power with regard to 'matter, forme, and power of a commonwealth ecclesiastical and civil'. On the other hand, Hobbes introduces this power in contractual terms.

Stretching to the upper edge of the image, which is probably meant to indicate the firmament, the upper body of a giant towers like a star above a European or perhaps just an English 17th century landscape in this 'tactical portrait': the head crowned, with, following tradition, a sword in his right hand as the epitome of the executive technique of government and, since the religious schism, the crozier provocatively in his left. The contours of the monarch's arms and torso encompass a huge number of people; they represent the estate-based society, disembodied but wrapped

---

[12] Freud, 'Civilization and Its Discontents', 29.

[13] Job 41:24.

[14] Hobbes, *Leviathan*, ch. 26: 'The written laws, if laws, if they be short, are easily misinterpreted, for the diverse significations of a word or two; if long, they be more obscure by the diverse significations of many words …' and later 'for the significations of almost all are either in themselves, or in the metaphorical use of them, ambiguous.'

[15] Bredekamp, *Thomas Hobbes Visuelle Strategien: Der Leviathan – Das Urbild des modernen Staates.*

[16] Bredekamp, *Thomas Hobbes Visuelle Strategien*, ch. 2.

Figure 2.1 *Abraham Bosse,* Leviathan, *Frontispiece of Thomas Hobbes,* Leviathan, *1651 (detail)*

in the mantle of the ruler. Densely packed, the subjects gaze from their respective position to the head of the guarantor of peace; just like the subsequent generation of legal and political philosophers.

With the cooperation of Hobbes and Hollar/Bosse, a unique moment in political iconography occurred: the presentation of the 'body politic' remains unsurpassed. It is the product of the same people, who – in today's parlance, virtually – renounce their 'right to everything' and entrust themselves to political technology:

> I authorise and give up my right of governing myself to this man, or to this assembly of men, on this condition; that thou give up, thy right to him, and authorise all his actions in like manner.[17]

What is more, the image of the Leviathan also remains unsurpassed. It emerges out of that ensemble of agreements as peace machine and a kind

17 Hobbes, *Leviathan*, ch. 17 a. E.

of a state under a semi-rule of law: established through the renunciation of law, but then unbound by law. The powers necessary for collectively preventing danger and safeguarding peace are transferred to the Leviathan. The fixation of the subjects upon the head corresponds to the construct of an agreement entailing a waiver of rights and authorization *uno actu*[18] that allows no other line of vision: the people attach chains – that is civil laws – by mutual agreement, on the one hand, to the lips of the sovereign or the sovereign assembly and, on the other hand, to their own ears.[19] The sovereign speaks; the subjects, bereft of rights, listen.

Consisting of the mortal king and the kingdom that exists in his image, reminiscent of the doctrine of 'the king's two bodies',[20] the paradox of the artefact state is also inscribed upon the political iconography with precision. Although created by people with the help of a contract and, hence, constituted secularly, the image of a 'mortal God' in the legal contract refers back to the theological level of Genesis, as is indicated by how close the head is to the sky and by the term 'mortal god'. At the same time, the mechanics of political technology is transported beyond this world.

Bearing human features, the head[21] towers over a body that sinks into a landscape, represented in what seems to be quite a peaceful manner given the chaotic 17th century. Constituted by contract, the comprehensive claim to power (later criticized by Hobbes' critics as totalitarian) is illustrated by the Leviathan towering over hills, rivers, the sea on the horizon, castles, isolated farms, an urban settlement in the foreground, with a military complex and a civil-urban area as well, of course, as a church. All of this is dominated by the body and decisively by the head as well as overshadowed by the arms. The mantle eventually symbolizes the relationship of sovereignty, which in a feudal society envelopes the social body completely; hence, it again incorporates it symbolically and at the same time hides the mechanics of the peace machine from the viewer's gaze.

In later images and designs, the visual strategy changes slightly but still significantly. The frontispiece of the second volume of Hobbes' (1652) *Elements of Law* maintains the sword and, hence, the idea of an executive political technology, but it replaces the bishop's crozier with a scale, arguably to appease the Church, and softens the torpor of the

---

[18] Cf. Fetscher, 'Einleitung', XXIV ff.

[19] Hobbes, *Leviathan*, ch. 21.

[20] Cf. Kantorowicz, *The King's Two Bodies.*

[21] Interpreters of the image recognize, depending on interpretation, Charles I or his opponent Cromwell, but also Thomas Hobbes himself.

Figure 2.2 Abraham Bosse, Frontispiece of Thomas Hobbes, Le Corps Politique, *1652*

people. Now, their faces turn towards the reader, who can recognize themselves among the men, women and children and in the implied relationships between them. The elements of the 'body politic' appear as agents ('subjects'), but without the capacity to deny the power of the Leviathan.

Bredekamp believes that the abandoning of the bishop's crozier is a tactical move in order to rescind the provocation of the church. This might have been Hobbes' motive, since he wanted to return to England from his French exile. But this point can also be interpreted differently, namely as a change of topic due to the subject of the *Elements of Law*: a shift towards the worldly problems of political technology as an ensemble of security techniques that no longer require justification or pictorial representation of the 'power ecclesiastical'. Unlike the construction of sovereignty in the *Leviathan*, Hobbes' justification of law as a disciplinary regime suggests the use of secular symbols when it comes to his vision of social conflicts. The same applies to his theory of how disputes in the civil state can be settled by law. The frontispiece of the *Elements of Law* does not depict the fear-inspiring, respect or fear-commanding representation of the peace machine to control human greed, pursuit of glory and lust to kill, but the practice of living together in society under law-rule. This interpretation is supported by the fact that subsequent editions of the *Leviathan* maintain the bishop's crozier and depict some countable, yet anonymous members of the body politic, who renounce their 'right to everything' and submit to this semi-immanent and semi-transcendent sovereign power. What remains is the notion of the state as the epitome of a neutral mechanics of sovereign governmental technology.

2.3 SUBVERSION: THE PANOPTICON AND THE CAPILLARIES OF POWER

For four centuries, the Hobbesian visual programme reigns virtually unchallenged and shapes the top-down imagery of the state and political technology with its focus on the head (*caput*) as well as its dichotomy of state and society. Then Michel Foucault enters the picture. Political iconography is certainly not his business. Since he does not share Hobbes' distrust of unreliable language, he does not use an image that supports the written word with the power of a visual representation. He does not devote himself to any of Hobbes' frontispieces or to a visual programme comparable to Hobbes' imaginary fabrication of the social body.

Nevertheless, the gaze, the look and the visual play a significant role in Foucault's studies and concepts of the techniques of disciplinary and bio-power. It is characteristic of the structure and functioning of the secret or anonymous practices and techniques of power and also of the knowledge apparatus examined by him that they want to evade representation, visual representation and imagining – perhaps in the form of an anthropomorphic compound; this is what he attempts to make visible. Geared rather towards the disciplining technology of politics and less towards sovereign statehood, Foucault's grammar of power and society follows an entirely different post-Leviathan logic. Power affects bodies in its capillary networks; it becomes more anonymous and more functional and resists any incarnation. Consequently, in his analyses Foucault cannot even try to inscribe the capillaries and techniques of power upon the collective memory with the help of a frontispiece à la *Leviathan*.

His visual strategy, if one can speak of it at all, unfolds in the medium of language and the scientific method. At a critical distance from Hobbes, the early Foucault illustrates the new power mechanism of permanent surveillance and disciplining of bodies within prison in the example of the institutions of Bentham's Panopticon (Figure 2.3) in *Discipline and Punish*.[22] This mechanism of power installs a central view of bodies enclosed in cells and separated from each other 'to induce in the inmate a state of consciousness and permanent visibility (Figure 2.4) that assures the automatic functioning of power'.[23]

In Foucault's study *The Birth of the Clinic*, this illustrative method falls back on an 'archaeology of gaze'.[24] It is characteristic of the entire work of Foucault that it tracks down the subjects in their respective historical locations and in the discursive networks of disciplinary power, and that it addresses these circumstances. Whereas Hobbes' theory of absolutism and state theories close to his position are concerned with the legal power of crowned heads or of non-monarchically legitimized heads of state, Foucault enters prisons, mental asylums, poorhouses and later the camps of the 20th century, in order to pursue the subversion of crowned knowledge.

One can hardly turn one's back more radically on the Hobbesian theory tradition and its accompanying images than Foucault did. Throughout his life, the French historian-philosopher, contested among

---

22 Foucault, *Discipline and Punish*, especially 195 ff. and (for Figure 2.3) 200 ff.

23 Foucault, *Discipline and Punish*, quoted by Fitzpatrick and Golder, *Foucault's Law*, 20.

24 Foucault, *The Birth of the Clinic*.

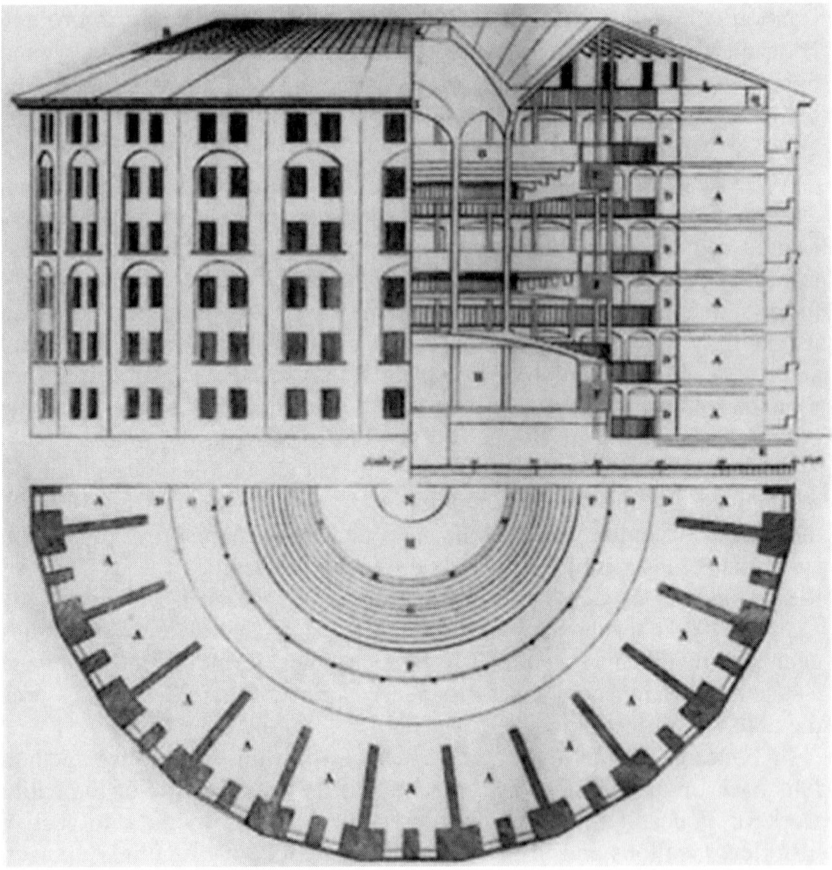

Figure 2.3 Jeremy Bentham, The Works of Jeremy Bentham (1838–1843) *IV, 172: Panopticon Blueprint*

fellow historians, fought against the fixation upon the head of the state and upon sovereignty as its 'soul' with the help of his methodological and theoretical work: through negation in *Discipline and Punish*, through relativization in later works, especially in the lectures in *Society Must be Defended*. The latter's title is meant programmatically, namely as an analysis of rule, which seeks to defend society against the unbridled strategies and tactics of all kinds of technicians of state and not-state power.

Foucault explicitly rejects the notion of the Leviathan as an artificially fabricated human being, whose head symbolizes sovereignty:

Figure 2.4 The former prison Presidio Modelo in Nueva Gerona (Cuba)

> In short, we have to abandon the model of Leviathan, that model of an artificial man who is at once an automaton, a fabricated man, but also a unitary man who contains all real individuals, whose body is made up of citizens but whose soul is sovereignty.[25]

Foucault does not deny that the theory of sovereignty was the instrument that shaped the political and theoretical struggles and imaginations within the power systems of the 16th, 17th and also 18th centuries; when, for instance, Rousseau countered monarchical absolutism – in a revolutionary counter-move – with the model of a republican democracy, and when, mainly in England, the Parliament as the political embodiment of the people stepped out of *The King's Shadow*.[26]

With the emergence and spread of disciplinary power, the subjects' real experience of rule changes and requires a different visual representation: centralized legal sovereignty and its corresponding power techniques lose the importance ascribed to them by classical theories. Disciplinary regimes use different techniques and follow a new 'economy of power'.[27] Their calculation is based on the combination of a minimum of power

25 Foucault, *Society Must be Defended*, 34.
26 Cf. the instructive study by Manow, *In the King's Shadow*.
27 Foucault, *The Birth of Biopolitics*, 166.

use and a maximum of power efficiency. With this turn towards method as political technology, referred to as biopolitics and executed by engineers and experts, the 'economy of power' is different from the lavish sovereign power of a Sun King. Against the juridico-political monism of classical doctrines of sovereignty and their construction of a good order from an engineer's perspective, Foucault always argues for the heterogeneity of power in today's 'normalizing society'. This consists of a dualism: 'an organization of public right articulated around the principle of the sovereignty of the social body … and … a tight grid of disciplinary coercions'.[28] The legal edifice of sovereignty is therefore not nothing, as *Discipline and Punish* may be read to suggest. Of course, sovereignty, for instance as constitutional state, precedes 'disciplinary power' neither in reality nor analytically.

2.4 DECONSTRUCTION: FROM SOVEREIGN TO DEMOCRATIC AESTHETICS

With the impressive reconstruction of the origins and historical impact of the *Leviathan* and its composite structure, Horst Bredekamp guides his audience through an imaginary museum 'in which all images appear in a common room: the memory'.[29] The image of the *Leviathan* and its later variations support language with the power of the visual. They are introduced as a 'higher authority' that dominated the collective memory, which until the 20th century was fascinated by giants with Leviathanian features and the political struggle for the head.

With the later transition to the democratic era, the stately visual programme of absolutism and its corresponding ideas of political technology could have come to an end or could have been replaced by the pictorial translation of the democratic law-rule as a liberal imagination.

However, numerous authors and works state that democracy cannot be embodied *per definitionem*; that it does not know an image of itself because people-authority does not lend itself to visual translation; and that it is precisely characteristic of the pluralism of democratic societies that they cannot agree on a visual programme.[30] Accordingly, one could say that in the case of democracy it may be outdated to assume a conception and a visual idea of an external political technology, bundled in and executed by the state. In plain light, the theory proves wrong that

---

28 Foucault, *Society must be Defended*, 37.

29 Bredekamp, 'Ikonographie des Staates'.

30 References in Manow, 'Der demokratische Leviathan'.

the visual agnosticism of democracy and its technology of rule have to do without a 'coherent aesthetical representation'[31] due to its 'remarkable shortcomings' and its 'embarrassing weakness'. This position is taken in by the ideology of democratic law-rule and ignores the need for symbols of political rule also in the post-monarchical era:

> Thrones may be out of fashion and pageantry, too; but political authority still requires a cultural frame in which to define itself and advance its claims, and so does opposition to it. [...] The extraordinary has not gone out of modern politics, however much the banal may have entered; power not only still intoxicates, it still exalts.[32]

In other words, every political rule relies on being recognized by its subjects[33] – in modern parlance, by its addressees – and for this purpose it regularly uses, in addition to the personnel of political technology – police, military and intelligence agencies – and in addition to more or less good reasons, also the 'beautiful appearance' of images and narratives, myths and representations.

Furthermore, it can be argued against this agnosticism that every society has to represent itself visually as a unit – as a community, people, nation[34] – and has to put itself in the limelight in one or the other way in order to be able to refer operationally to itself by means of its public officials and institutions. Part of the self-design, self-description and imagination of a society (as a national or ethnic or legal community[35]) is always a self-attributed, imaginary foundation. Its 'instituting' (Claude Lefort) requires a common space for the political, within which social differentiation can take place.[36] Modernity emerges with and in this symbolic space of the political. Within this space, the political economy of productive imagination is hardly any longer informed by the pre-modern logic of the embodiment of society in the form of the state or the

---

[31] Cf. Grasskamp, *Die unästhetische Demokratie*, 7 and 9.

[32] Geertz, 'Centers, Kings, and Charisma', 30.

[33] Cf. the clear and substantive studies by Koschorke et al., *Der fiktive Staat* and Manow, *In the King's Shadow*.

[34] In detail Anderson, *Imagined Communities*.

[35] Art. 1(2) Basic Law for the Federal Republic of Germany: 'The German people therefore acknowledge inviolable and inalienable human rights as the basis of every community.'

[36] Cf. Koschorke et al., *Der fiktive Staat*, 60 ff., and Lefort, *Fortdauer des Theologisch-Politischen?*, 38, as well as Rödel et al., *Die demokratische Frage*, especially chs. III and IV.

monarch.[37] On the contrary, it is assumed that political rule rather uses rhetoric, images and performances that differ from the traditional visual programme or re-interprets the latter creatively to banish crude Machiavellianism and crude Hobbesianism of political technology. In the following, three examples are meant to illustrate the political symbolism of modernity.

Symbols of Societal Unity

The first example dates back to the time of the 'Great Revolution' in France. It continued the ongoing departure of the divine right, set off by Hobbes and his disenchantment with the monarchy. In 1793, the execution of the king – under his civil name Louis Capet – made drastically apparent the link between the withdrawal of royal dignity and the symbolic disembodiment of society.[38] The unified corporality of the social dissolves into the '*société des individus*'.[39] The monarch loses the quasi-private, hereditary right to rule and the obligation to loyalty is no longer bound to his person. The place of the personal sovereign remains symbolically empty. Henceforth, political struggles aim to occupy the place of power, at least temporarily. Similarly, the legal relationship of a contract of domination between monarch and subject is broken. Obedience to impersonal laws or constitutional loyalty replace the personal loyalty to the monarch.

In the founding act, society is constituted as a people or nation, and transfers to it collective sovereignty and constituent power.

> At the same place, at which the state previously became manifest personally and bodily in the figure of the monarch, now the abstraction of the modern state idea presents itself as pure text [in the constitutional document – G.F.].[40]

In this way, three things succeed in France almost magically: the subjectification of the collective 'nation', while power is depersonalized and its technical aspect concealed in the Constitution. In England, the single constitutional document is missing, and yet the monarchy and the

---

[37] On the need for a symbolic-ritual embodiment of every institutional order, see the impressive study by Stollberg-Rilinger, *Des Kaisers alte Kleider*.

[38] Cf. Koschorke et al., *Der fiktive Staat*, 229.

[39] It cannot be ruled out that the logic of embodiment continues to have an impact in the democratic republic and the parliamentary democracy, as demonstrated by Manow, *In the King's Shadow*.

[40] Koschorke et al., *Der fiktive Staat*, 248.

people can be tamed in the medium of representation according to the formula 'King/Queen-in-Parliament'.

For all states that declare themselves constitutional democracies the following applies: where the law is to reign, the logic of embodiment fades. Political power becomes unimaginative. The mechanics and strategies of politics are no longer a visible-tangible power technology of the sovereign; their imagery rather follows the *method Locke* and its suggestion and normative claim that it only becomes apparent in rules, procedures and reasons. Law-rule à la Locke lacks plasticity – a lack that is in France compensated by the emblems and staging of the Nation as 'grande nation', 'nation armée', etc. as well as by the cult of the figure of the legislator in the 18th and 19th centuries.[41] In the United States, the lack is overcompensated for by the currently still vivid cult of the 'Founding Fathers' as founders of the democratic constitution. In Germany, which has to do without both a founding myth as well as a national cult, the emphasis (maybe not yet a cult) has shifted towards the Federal Constitutional Court as 'the guardian of the constitution' since the middle of the 20th century.

The Interior Design of Democracy

A second example of the symbolic imagination and images of modernism is the possibility of bringing a republic and democracy to life through its 'interior design', such as the parliamentary seating plan, and at the same time covering up the rough edges of political technology, which fade in importance compared with the creation of social unity (by elections) and parliamentary decision-making, i.e. the legislative style characterizing the *method Locke*.

Both the British House of Commons, with its rows of benches facing each other and the Speaker at the front, as well as the amphitheatre, imitated all over the world and dating back to the Palais Bourbon, also function as new symbolic stages for the new order. Their construction is not accidental nor does it obey functionalist imperatives, such as acoustics. Rather they are tailored to the different forms of the legitimation of rule. According to Philip Manow, the parliamentary seating plan in the House of Commons follows, for instance, the logic of the embodiment of the 'King-in-Parliament':

41 This cult goes back to Rousseau (*The Social Contract*, Book 2, ch. 7). Cf. Wisner, *The Cult of the Legislator in France 1750–1830*.

In the case of England (and later of all the Commonwealth countries), the monarch himself or herself remained this symbol. Although present only as a picture, as a royal head on the wall of the Houses of Commons or as a signature beneath all the Acts of parliament, the monarch bestows on parliament a fiction of unity that does not have to be symbolized in its physical architecture, and particularly not in a seating plan.[42]

Figure 2.5 House of Commons (original chamber), Westminster Parliament, London (England)

By recourse to the doctrine of the king's two bodies,[43] Manow concludes that the Westminster Parliament has successfully filled the idea of the political body of the king (King) without the king's natural body (king) losing its unifying function. Consequently, there is no need to demonstrate distance from the *ancien régime* through a new symbolic form of representing political unity.

In contrast, Manow interprets the shape of the semicircle as an attempt to symbolically heal the irreparable damage done to the body of the French king. Furthermore, the amphitheatre overcomes feudal structures and does not relate to obvious social or political fragmentations. Symbolizing a new social unit, it therefore devotes itself to serving the undivided

42 Cf. in detail Manow, *In the King's Shadow*, ch. 2, who very plausibly rejects the interpretation that the semicircle of the seating order highlighted the left-right scheme or the party system or was functionalist or just arbitrary.

43 Kantorowicz, *The King's Two Bodies*.

Figure 2.6 European Parliament in Strasbourg (France)

nation.[44] With the French Revolution, a new self-image of society as a unit connects with a new political imagination:

> It is not a question of representing parts of society or particulate needs vis-à-vis a supreme authority (king), rather the sovereign will of the nation is meant to find expression by dint of representation. [...] This is, hence, about *the representation of political unity*.[45]

The exercise of power, with its techniques, risks and side effects, is made to disappear in the various forms of representation. Their technicians appear, if at all, only as authorized enforcers of the sovereign will of the nation.

---

[44] According to Mopin, the semicircle is more suited than the circle to represent the 'incarnation of the people' from the point of view of a speaker addressing the stands – Mopin et al., *L'Assemblée nationale*, 33–4; similarly, Manow, 'Der demokratische Leviathan', 15 (emphasis in original).

[45] Duso, 'Repräsentative Demokratie', 11 and 16.

The Architecture of the Republic

The third example leads out of the shadows cast by the body of the king and illustrates not the destruction but the deconstruction of the head, which Hobbes introduced as an icon of state sovereignty; it also stands for the construction of a new image and imagination of political technology.

The dome of the Reichstag in Berlin, which houses the Federal Diet of Germany, opposes the mysteries of the absolutist state[46] as well as its traditional sovereignty and power techniques. On the one hand, the transparent vault fits quasi-seamlessly into the symbolism of republican publicity. Instead of the *arcana imperii*, the glass shell of rule conveys a new transparency of parliamentary decisions and practices. On the other hand, the symbolic head, upon which the author of the *Leviathan* and his contemporaries in 1651, the French revolutionaries and the state theories of the 19th and 20th centuries gazed, is re-imagined and becomes accessible to the citizens of a democratic republic via a spiral ramp.

The architect Norman Foster turned a constructive dilemma, namely the need to integrate an originally unplanned dome into his design, into a brilliant, sovereignty-critical twist, which Foucault might have relished: the glass head of the state is populated. 'The dome of the Reichstag constitutes a kind of upper house', which brings together randomly 'ever new sovereigns'.[47]

Symbolically recalled in the head, the formerly monolithic and closed sovereignty liquefies. In this way, the dome embodies newer theories according to which sovereignty comes into its own only in legally institutionalized procedures.[48] It now flows through the windings of the dome, which is quasi-democratically and casually seized not only by citizens climbing up and down, while simultaneously a 'gestural dis-empowerment of the parliament' takes place, since those represented gaze *down* on their representatives on their 'visites de tous les jours' – perhaps bored, perhaps interested.[49]

In a casual postmodern fashion, the republican and post-national constellation of a new randomness in this transparent and populated

---

[46] Cf. Kantorowicz, 'Mysteries of State'.

[47] Bredekamp, 'Ikonographie des Staates', 407.

[48] Especially, Habermas, *Between Facts and Norms*.

[49] In order to avoid misconceptions, it should be mentioned that no document, not even a passport, permits these citizen-sovereigns access and, hence, participation in the accidental-entertaining permanent party of parliamentary observation.

Source: © 2005 Heiko Burkhardt, Lilano.com

Figure 2.7 Dome of the Reichstag, Berlin (Germany)

dome bids farewell to the image of the sovereign head and the related concept of political technology. The dome of the Reichstag keeps its distance from the Hobbesian strategy of submission in architectural terms as well. Instead of a contractualist big bang, we have to prepare ourselves for the civil-societal practice of permanent justification and re-establishing of politically constituted societies – in short, for contingency – and this not only since the Berlin Republic[50] and its parliamentary dome. The performative democracy, with its procedures, deliberations and restless movements of civil society, replaces the permanently revised social contract. Accordingly, constitutions are not received from the hereafter like the Ten Commandments and set in stone; they are discussed and decided upon in order to become established and changed again.

One might say the dome of the Reichstag symbolically completes the destruction of the absolutist regime and its techniques of governing – a project Hobbes began with the *Leviathan* reluctantly and not without considerable personal risk, and Locke and liberal political philosophers

[50] For German civil society catching up on the founding of the Bonn Republic, see Rödel et al., *Die demokratische Frage*, especially chs. III and IV.

tried to tone down in order to protect private property and liberty. The glass dome translates into a widely visible piece of architecture. It represents the transparent republican promise of modernity and its rejection of arcane politics. By the same token, the capillaries of the dome structure refer to the networks of biopolitics, which Foucault analysed with subversive intent.

In terms of political technology too, the dome of the Reichstag sends an ambivalent signal. During the day, in daylight, it seems to democratize the panoptic gaze. Surveillance, or so it seems, is recoded from a matter of political technology into a civil society project. In darkness, however, the glass dome with its capillaries is rather reminiscent of the eye of the surveillance state, which arches over society, registers citizens' movements and relationships, their travel, cars and bank accounts, and records their conversations. The following chapters pursue this ambivalent impression at the level of legal-political analysis; the chapters turn from the high level of symbolism into the lowlands of tangible concepts and rules of political technology, its history, doctrine and practices.

3. Constellations of law-rule and the state of exception

The methods that constitute the technology of governing and the mindset they presuppose are mainly characterized by their more or less ambivalent relationship to law and their security agenda. How the exercise of political power deals with legal constraints will be discussed with regard to the most prominent variations of law-rule[1] – the Anglo-American rule of law and the German *Rechtsstaat*. In particular, it will be shown how these methods oscillate between legality and the extra-legal exception and thereby privilege specific paradigms of political technology.

3.1 FROM VISUAL MAGIC TO POLYSEMY

Both the rule of law and the *Rechtsstaat* have come of age, but they still do not enjoy a corresponding universal and unanimous appreciation. Despite – or because of – their operative versatility and semantic indeterminacy, they remain controversial. As thoroughly sober rhetorical figures, their 'pathos of distance' from popular passion and political scheming withstands all present-day translations into catchy metaphors. Although the 'eye of the law' follows the logic of organicist embodiment, this metaphor captures only one, albeit important aspect of law-rule: the desacralizing and depersonalizing reification of rule-guided government on its way 'from god to the earthly god of the prince, from there to the mortal god of the *Leviathan* and from there to deified law, which in turn finds its culmination in the constitution'.[2] This partial embodiment remains intact even if one adds the 'arm of the law' as executive extension of the 'eye of the law'. On the other hand, the classic image of a 'government of laws and not of men', laid down in the Constitution of

[1] Frank Michelman, 'Law's Republic', 97 *Yale Law Journal* 1493–1537/1499 (1988). In the following I use 'law-rule' as a shorthand for lawful and limited government that encompasses its most prominent varieties: rule of law, *Rechtsstaat*, and *état de droit*.

[2] Stolleis, *The Eye of the Law*.

Massachusetts in 1780, approximates the heart of law-rule as one of the central aspects of the liberal self-imagination. In striking contrast to the visual magic of the *Leviathan*, this formula emphasizes how the 'eye of the law', as the objectification of power, is meant to exclude the personal arbitrary use of power, as a special feature, but without remedying the lack of intelligibility.

Due to their polysemy[3] and ambiguity,[4] their 'ideological abuse and general over-use'[5] – perhaps also because of their resistance to visualization – both the rule of law and the *Rechtsstaat* are sometimes relegated to the realm of 'empty phrases and concepts'. Proponents as well as critics often respond to their cool rationality with doubt, discomfort or indifference. While the rule of law has been labelled 'just another one of the self-congratulatory rhetorical devices',[6] the *Rechtsstaat* has been presumed to approach its 'dawn' as if it were breathing its last.[7] Both have at times been reduced to emanations of liberal ideology. Proposals to 'deflate the beautiful bubble of the *Rechtsstaat*' or to abandon the term 'rule of law' altogether, though certainly not representative, are nevertheless symptomatic.[8]

As a constitutional principle and normative foundation of governing, the rule of law, *Rechtsstaat* and also the *état de droit* share the semantic indeterminacy of principles and a close affinity to ideology. Nevertheless, they may survive suggestions that they abandon their only vaguely outlined content as general principles in favour of a varying number of individual elements or sub-principles.[9] Does the general (constitutional) principle grounded in august tradition or precise definition still generate the necessary certainty? Given the manifold, sometimes unintentionally deconstructive moves of constitutional theory, scepticism seems justified, although the courts, especially the German Federal Constitutional Court,

---

[3] Jowell, 'The Rule of Law Today', 57; Kelsen, *Reine Rechtslehre*, 314, refers to a pleonasm.

[4] Loughlin, *The Foundations of Public Law*, 312–14.

[5] Shklar, 'Political Theory and the Rule of Law', 1.

[6] Shklar, 'Political Theory and the Rule of Law', 1.

[7] E.g. Merten, 'Rechtsstaatsdämmerung'; Hawel, 'Dämmerung des demokratischen Rechtsstaates?'

[8] For references, see Kunig, *Das Rechtsstaatsprinzip*, 3 ff., 481 ff.

[9] Sobota, *Das Prinzip Rechtsstaat*, lists a staggering 142 sub-principles of the *Rechtsstaat*.

tend to uphold the principle of the rule of law, though not with exuberant enthusiasm.[10]

The jurisdiction and powers of nationally organized public authority have become precarious due to the ongoing trends towards privatization, on the one hand, and the consequences of denationalization – particularly in the context of Europeanization and the transnationalization of political responsibility – on the other hand. Therefore, it is prudent to remain realistic about the order and orientation provided by concepts and their history. Nevertheless, an exegetical retreat, like the elimination of the term *Rechtsstaat* or labelling it an empty formula, is as inappropriate a reaction to the amalgamation of different meanings in the concept and the idea and ideology of the rule of law[11] as the occasional over-emphatic intervention.[12] After all, they only tell the tale of historical conflicts and projects that, under the originally polemical terms rule of law, *Rechtsstaat* or *état de droit*, tried to tame claims to power under absolutist regimes by putting the state and the exercise of power under law and by legitimizing both through law, given that emergency legislation and the fear of the arbitrary use of state power were ubiquitous in absolutism.[13]

Today, however, the varieties of law-rule come in less polemical terms. Rather they are widely accepted as blueprints for the design of institutions and offer criteria, not always clear ones, for their functioning. More importantly in the context of this study, they refer to different constellations of power/sovereignty between state and society, to different functional separations and attributions of political powers as well as to the legal status of individuals under the umbrella of human or fundamental rights. Since the 'entry into a civil condition' (Kant), this formula indicates a normative concept: as the formal principle of a legally framed community, law-rule provides a possible and historically very influential

---

[10] The Federal Constitutional Court was asked a number of times to concretize the *Rechtsstaat* principle; this concerned especially cases regarding expropriation by the Soviet occupation force, East German border guards who shot refugees and often data protection. Cf. *BVerfGE* 92, 277/325 ff.; 95, 96/140 ff.

[11] Hutchinson and Monahan, *The Rule of Law: Ideal or Ideology?*

[12] Baratta ('Zur Entwicklung des modernen Rechtsstaatsbegriffs') calls the *Rechtsstaat* 'one of the most successful formulas of contemporary law', 1. Leisner, 'Rechtsstaat – ein Widerspruch in sich?' calls it a 'true and rare taboo'. Ryffel, *Grundprobleme der Rechts- und Staatsphilosophie* sees it as an 'anthropological necessity', 416, which Behrendt, *Rechtsverzicht als Rechtsgewinn*, even celebrates as the 'perhaps most impressive intellectual achievement for human existence' (5).

[13] Leibholz, *Strukturprobleme der modernen Demokratie*.

answer to the dual task of secular societies, namely to constitute political authority and to socially integrate their members.[14]

With the implementation of the *method Locke* as law enforcement and by suppressing its illiberal valences, the initially liberal, later democratic and social *Rechtsstaat* introduces a fundamental distinction with far-reaching consequences: normal legality emerges out of the universe of the generalized state of exception. At the same time, violence sanctioned by law begins to play a more important role than trust as a resource for political rule.[15] Legal certainty takes centre stage: the subjects are meant to know what they are up against on the part of government and usually may expect that what is supposed to happen will happen.[16] And deviations from normative normalcy are seen as exceptions that require justification.

In the following, rather than dismissing law-rule or delivering another apology, I want to explore its ambivalence, beginning by showing that in practice we are always confronted with a vague and 'essentially contested concept'[17] of democratic law-rule – whether it comes under the heading of rule of law, *Rechtsstaat* or *état de droit*. The constitutive elements of law-rule can be described in various ways and vary considerably and unpredictably against the backdrop of changing political and economic, social and cultural circumstances. The contours of this antonym to the unruly, extra-legal state of exception cannot be defined in a way which removes the varieties of law-rule from past and present conflicts – even if this is what a plethora of interpretations claim – rather they become clear if one reconstructs the historical constellations and crises as well as their accompanying theoretical and doctrinal controversies.

3.2 ORIGINS, AFFINITIES AND DIFFERENCES

The history of law-rule as normal legality and the state of exception must have been written, one might think. However, this assumption turns out to be plausible only by translating it into the plural. For the development

[14] See, in detail, Frankenberg, *Die Verfassung der Republik*, ch. III.

[15] Particularly apparent in John Locke's philosophy, especially in the *Two Treatises of Government*, 'Second Treatise'.

[16] Reemtsma, *Vertrauen und Gewalt*, 87.

[17] Gallie, 'Essentially Contested Concepts', 169 ff.; Heuschling, *État de droit, Rechtsstaat, Rule of Law*, 5 ff. and 31 ff.

of the rule of law and the *Rechtsstaat*[18] was reconstructed in many and diverse ways, while the state of exception[19] was portrayed less extensively. I do not intend to complement or even complete the pluralism of these narratives with a further – and necessarily cursory – account. From the vantage point of law-rule and the state of exception, I reconstruct in the following the gradual emergence and spread of the rule of law and the *Rechtsstaat* as modes for justifying legitimate government and limiting its powers and purposes. I also focus on the development of political technology within regimes of law-rule as the epitome of normal normativity in the state-citizen relationship.

The development of lawful government (and legal techniques of governing) was accompanied by the emergence of rules and theories of the state of exception in times of war, civil war and catastrophe. Whereas I first address the development of the *Rechtsstaat* and its corresponding political technologies from the perspective of normal legality, the following chapter will focus on theories, fantasies and techniques relating to the state of exception, more commonly referred to as the state of emergency.

'Inventing' the *Rechtsstaat*

The interpretative openness of the *Rechtsstaat* as a concept, idea and ideology already begins with the question of its origin. Although the search for origins rarely leads to certainties but rather to myths, as far as the concept of the *Rechtsstaat* is concerned it turns out to be particularly misleading. It is certainly no coincidence that the term *Rechtsstaat* emerged when the individual as citizen was 'invented' in several places in the German-speaking world. Without actually using the literal term, Kant's *Rechtslehre* systematically developed law-rule – as 'the only lasting constitution of the state in which the law is self-governing'.[20] German political theory and administrative science after Kant adopted the concept rather reluctantly and half-heartedly in the first half of the 19th century.[21]

---

18 For the development of the *Rechtsstaat* and the rule of law, see Tamanaha, *On the Rule of Law*; Böckenförde, 'Entstehung und Wandel des Rechtsstaatsbegriffs'; Maus, 'Entwicklung und Funktionswandel der Theorie des bürgerlichen Rechtsstaats'; Neumann, *The Rule of Law*, 179 ff.

19 For the history of the state of emergency, see Reinach, *De l'état de siège*; Boldt, *Rechtsstaat und Ausnahmezustand*; Rossiter, *Constitutional Dictatorship*.

20 Kant, 'On the Old Saw' and *The Metaphysics of Morals*, § 45 seq.

21 Especially Welcker, *Die letzten Gründe von Recht, Staat und Strafe*; von Aretin, *Staatsrecht der konstitutionellen Monarchie I*, 163 and von Mohl,

A birth certificate for the *Rechtsstaat*[22] that would ease any doubt is hard to come by. Law-rule was very much in the air during the revolutionary transition period. We can therefore refrain from reconstructing any genealogy and paternity tests, since many potential fathers had already come across the *problématique*, programmes and principles of legally justifying and moderating political domination. Moreover, for a proper understanding, state practice may be rather more illuminating than a genealogy of the term itself.

The prehistory of just and/or legally constrained government can be traced back to the political thought of antiquity, like other fundamental principles of modern state organization – especially the republic and democracy – and the English tradition of the rule of law. In Greek and Roman antiquity, the legitimation and moderation of government were more important than limiting state purposes. Plato and Aristotle based the viability of a well-ordered political community on justice as the substantive concretization of the common good and stressed the notion of political domination mediated by law. Suggested by them as well as by Polybius and Cicero, a combination of monarchical, aristocratic and democratic elements in a mixed form of government aims at a twofold goal: first, to ensure the rule of the most capable – under the more or less active, but always controlled participation of citizens, which excluded women, children, resident foreigners and slaves. Second, to serve as restrictions of sovereign powers and as a barrier against any despotic change of those supposedly 'good' constitutions.

If one keeps one's distance from the idyllic images of people living a peaceful, philosophical-virtuous life, like Plato's elitist 'worldly city of god' as well as Cicero's obvious idealization of the Roman Republic, then a genuine issue of law-rule becomes apparent, despite the different contexts and programmes of these classical theories of the state. How can government be organized so that it provides effective command of the

---

who uses the term in a book title for the first time in 1832; see *Die Polizei-Wissenschaft nach den Grundsätzen des Rechtsstaates*; cf. also Bähr, *Der Rechtsstaat*.

[22] In 1798, Placidus speaks of a 'Rechts-Staats-Lehre' (*Rechtsstaat* theory) (in his *Litteratur der Staatslehre*, 73); in 1806 Leisler speaks of a 'rechtlicher Staat' (legal state) (cit. in Stolleis, 'Rechtsstaat und Staatsunrecht im 20. Jahrhundert', col. 369). Finally, the little known Harscher von Almendingen refers in *Grundzüge zu einer neuen Theorie über Verletzungen des guten Namens und der Ehre* to the 'Rechtsstaat' (66). It was Marc Bors who directed me to Harscher von Almendingen. Müller is therefore perhaps wrongly credited with the 'invention' of the term (*Elemente der Staatskunst*). Cf. Weinacht, '"Staatsbürger" – Zur Geschichte und Kritik eines politischen Begriffs'.

state but without running the risk of unconstrained action that could ruin the political community through ignorance, incompetence and the arbitrary use of power?

The Rule of Law as a Developmental 'Path'

In comparison with the classical theories of the state, a closer affinity[23] exists between the idea, ideals and ideology of the rule of law, *Rechtsstaat* and the *état de droit.*[24] Despite significant – national, cultural and institutional – differences, they are constituted by a similar set of ambiguous basic principles[25] and share the ambivalence of being both political as well as legal concepts. On the one hand, they are designed programmatically to confine absolutist regimes, but also to legitimize rule and to lend rulers authority. On the other hand, they also limit their functions and powers and avert arbitrary, later called unlawful, interventions in the estates-based or bourgeois society. The common denominator is hence to legally establish an 'authoritative and limited government' as the normal state of being, which in the modern era is accompanied like a shadow by extra-legal states of exception – such as war, state of siege or other emergency situations.

Compared to the ideal and real utopias of the classical theories of the polis and the republic, the rule of law indicates, due to its long genealogy,[26] a developmental path leading up to the liberal paradigm of legal technology. In a first developmental step, trust in the beneficial work of philosophically educated and virtuous elites is replaced by trust in the lawful rights of the (initially still estates-based) parliament and the courts. Parliament is still constituted by an elite, but one of ideology and with a claim to represent the people. There is also a further aspect: the rule of law as a political principle is meant to accomplish the transition from personal to impersonal, namely the law-mediated exercise of power. In a first step, it therefore leaves behind the *method Machiavelli* and, by

---

23 In the affirmative, see MacCormick, 'Der Rechtsstaat und die rule of law', 65; for a contrary position, see Böckenförde, 'Entstehung und Wandel des Rechtsstaatsbegriffs', 144 n. 4. For the differences, overlaps and links between these concepts, see Heuschling, *État de droit, Rechtsstaat, Rule of Law*.

24 Tamanaha, *On the Rule of Law*; Hutchinson and Monahan, *The Rule of Law: Ideal or Ideology?*

25 MacCormick, 'Der Rechtsstaat und die rule of law', 67.

26 For a classical, albeit not very precise, account, see Dicey, *Introduction to the Study of the Law of the Constitution*; Heuschling, *État de droit, Rechtsstaat, Rule of Law*, 165 ff.

virtue of the social contract and the abstract conception of sovereignty, it generates or inaugurates the *method Hobbes*. The second step leads to the *method Locke*. As a legal or constitutional principle, the rule of law is to tame the ruler's prerogatives and any arbitrary use of power by virtue of the legislative style complemented by judicial review.

From then on, abuses of governmental power could be depicted and scandalized against the backdrop of the rule of law, as would later be the case on the continent with the *Rechtsstaat* or the *état de droit*. At the same time, the burden increased for justifying the use of martial law, the royal prerogative or any executive privilege in exceptional situations. In Locke's classical conception, this became manifest in the theory of the prerogative he could not domesticate completely but did restrict in scope and move at least closer to the rule of law.[27] Accordingly, the executive had the right to violate the law by using its discretion in the event of a state of exception, for which no rules existed; but afterwards it had to justify unlawful measures before the public and might even be called to account. The question of who deserved primacy – the king, the parliament or the courts – was at the heart of the key constitutional conflicts and the scientific disputes they entailed from the 16th to the 18th centuries.

A further correspondence exists between the rule of law and the *Rechtsstaat* regarding the aspect of order. Both offer an answer to the question of how social order is possible. However, one can discern different reference points, with significant consequences for the English and German pathways to a project in which society is ordered by law and legislative techniques of governing. The rule of law implies, first and foremost, obedience to the laws passed by parliament, whereas the *Rechtsstaat* accentuates the state or an executive power as primary point of reference. Via the legitimating bridge of parliamentary sovereignty, obedience to the laws can easily be linked with representative democracy. The development of the rule of law can therefore be read as the history of social and political struggles over the justification and development of government controlled by parliament, both constituted by democracy (the people) and restrained by law.[28] Since the separation and juxtaposition of state and (civil) society in continental theory is alien to the English

[27] Locke, *Two Treatises of Government,* 'Second Treatise', ch. 14. Cf. Loughlin, *Public Law and Political Theory*, 376–86.

[28] Dicey, *Introduction to the Study of the Law of the Constitution*, 183 ff.; MacCormick, 'Der Rechtsstaat und die rule of law', 66 and Gough, *Fundamental Law in English Constitutional History*, 137; as well as the philosophical forerunner of 'lawful government', Locke, *Two Treatises of Government*, 'Second Treatise', especially §§ 134–9.

conception of law, the dispute about limiting the purposes of the state becomes therefore less important than theories and doctrines limiting its authority in order to safeguard liberty and property.

In the Tudor period, the Crown's lawyers introduced the doctrine of the 'two bodies of the king', distinguishing the body natural and the king as fallible private person (king) from the body politic and the king as infallible King ('King can do no wrong'). From this distinction the political notion of and legal justification for a depersonalized, permanent political rule could be derived, which immunized its sacred dignity (*dignitas*) against any criticism of its legitimacy.[29] In contrast to the modern continental doctrine of double majesty – the *maiestas realis* of the estates of the empire representing the people vis-à-vis the emperor as *maiestas personalis* – English political theory located sovereignty first with the monarch, after the constitutional conflicts of the 17th century briefly with the people and then with Parliament, before finally the political compromise and ideology of mixed government, the King-in-Parliament, prevailed. The concept of a king responsible to parliament blocked the way for the personal rule of a sovereign with the help of a supreme law and thereby left behind the unruly normalcy of the *ancien régime* characterized by the particular position of the ruler and the personal relationship (loyalty) between the subjects and their ruler.

Designed by Thomas Hobbes in his *Leviathan* and also in his *Elements of Law*, the image of a peace machine and 'mortal god' matched this semi-modern political imagination. On the one hand, it did not have to be an individual who would hold sovereign power, although Hobbes may have seen his theory of the state as a project to save the monarchy. On the other hand, Hobbes did not bolster absolutism with the legitimizing power of the divine right; he rather stressed the interest calculation of the individual members of society. This became manifest in a mutual social contract of the people in favour of a third party, the *Leviathan*.

Before this background, John Locke firmly maintained the contractualist constitution of political rule, although not necessarily so as to justify the Glorious Revolution of 1688/89. Unlike Hobbes' work, his argument was not based on a reciprocal waiver of rights by the subjects in order to secure internal and external peace. Rather, Locke's mutual agreement led to the introduction of a legislature as supreme authority and institutionalized in this way the rule of the minority (the political elite) that

---

[29] Kantorowicz, *The King's Two Bodies* and Gauchet, 'Des deux corps du roi au pouvoir sans corps'. For a critique of this interpretation, see Agamben, *Homo sacer.*

participated in elections as the majority. The exercise of power found its limits at the barrier of fundamental, natural rights to property and personal freedom.[30] With many of the essential elements of the liberal paradigm in place and the complementary doctrine of the prerogative, Locke's theory marked the contrast between a legal state of freedom (legality) and a state of executive emergency powers, which remained, however, bound to the welfare of the people and could be revoked by the people in case of abuse.[31]

Hobbes' political doctrine of enlightened despotism as well as Locke's ultimately liberal political philosophy reflect, each in its own way, the struggles of the English barons, the landed gentry, against the prerogative of the Crown, and later the struggles and political agenda of the property-owning bourgeoisie, aimed at establishing a system of the separation of powers under the rule of law (still rejected by Hobbes).[32] The theoretical and practical enthronement of Parliament as sovereign and the emphasis on the role of the courts as a bulwark against the unlawful meddling with liberty and property constituted the regulatory and institutional conditions for the transition from a feudal society to a simple market society and eventually to the developed, competitive market and society.[33]

To determine the social location of the rule of law and its genesis primarily as the protection of property and traditional rights does not, however, reduce it to a system of class rule and possessive individualism. After all, since the triumph of parliamentary sovereignty in the 19th century, this legal regime fosters the consolidation of parliamentary democracy through the judicial review of the executive and administrative sections of government. In the course of fundamental political and social rights being successfully recognized,[34] the theory and practice of the rule of law becomes more and more detached from its initial and lasting fixation on the protection of property.

---

[30] Locke, *Two Treatises of Government*, 'Second Treatise'.

[31] Ibid., 'Second Treatise', ch. 14. For Locke's problem of the prerogative of the monarch, see Loughlin, *The Foundations of Public Law*, ch. 13; Pasquino, 'Locke on King's Prerogative' and Casson, 'Emergency Judgment'.

[32] As stated in Locke's Second Treatise, 137.

[33] Cf. in more detail Neumann, *The Rule of Law*; Holdsworth, *History of English Law II*, 647 ff.; Macpherson, *The Political Theory of Possessive Individualism.* For a critical perspective, see Tully, *A Discourse on Property*.

[34] MacCormick, 'Der Rechtsstaat und die rule of law', 68 ff.; Marshall, *Citizenship and Social Class*; MacCrudden and Chambers, *Individual Rights and the Law in Britain*.

With the development of citizenship rights, the gradually extended rights to vote and, at long last, the transfer of the European Convention on Human Rights (ECHR) fundamental rights via the 1998 Human Rights Act, British-style law-rule no longer easily equates to a regime of possessive individualism. In the course of its eventful history, this amalgam of principles, rules, standards, conventions and expectations generated a novel fabric of parliamentary acts and judicial rights as well as an unstable climate of legality. Within the latter, the expectation can grow that the use of emergency powers is kept in check by the rule of law or even rejected by the judiciary.

However, until the present, persistent theoretical as well as doctrinal debates reveal the considerable discrepancy between the actually established and practised rule of law and its often invoked and coherent ideal.[35] Controversy is still triggered by conflicting principles entailed in the regime: the judicially developed common law and law enacted by Parliament; law-rule and the doctrine of sovereignty; positivist interpretations of the law and doctrines of natural law; theories of formal legality and substantive justice; freedom and equality; general and situational rules; moral neutrality and the favouring of the common good.[36] These differences and the underlying conflicts over the prerogatives of the king versus parliamentary sovereignty, the separation of powers and fundamental rights signal that the boundaries between the law-regulated normal state and emergency powers in extraordinary situations, which have emerged in almost endless constitutional disputes, are even today, if not contested, still permeable. They shape the exercise of power in the traditional rule-of-law context as well as the context of the *Rechtsstaat*.

3.3 THE *RECHTSSTAAT* – A GERMAN '*SONDERWEG*'

With the combination of law and state, the concept of *Rechtsstaat* illustrates the particular German theoretical and ideological trajectory from enlightened absolutism to a self-governed society under law. The initial and long-term privileged focus on the state constitutes a totally different perspective from the one just presented in the concept of the rule of law: it concentrates on the executive top of the state, its

---

35 For an instructive analysis from the angle of conceptual and theoretical history, see Heuschling, *Etat de droit, Rechtsstaat, Rule of Law*, 165 ff., with detailed references. Cf. also MacCormick, *Rhetoric and the Rule of Law*.

36 Cf. Goldsworthy, 'Legislative Sovereignty and the Rule of Law'; Allan, *Law, Liberty and Justice*; Loughlin, *Public Law and Political Theory*, 151.

bureaucracy and methods and leaves aside parliamentary democracy. Its linchpin is the monosyllabic state as unit, control centre and repository of sovereignty, which is subjected to a review of legality.

To speak of a German *Sonderweg*, which began long before the bourgeois revolution, seems not unreasonable. After all, the theory of the state in the Enlightenment as well as the revolutionary programmes and events since the end of the 18th century – however blurred they were – stress the correspondence between the rule of the laws (*Gesetzesherrschaft*), parliamentary representation and popular sovereignty, while the German theory of the early *Rechtsstaat* in the 19th century is still primarily inspired by an anti-parliamentarian, if not anti-democratic, impetus, despite the identification of justice and law and the invocation of the sovereignty of the legislator. German authors appear to be reluctant to depart from the German reading of Hobbes' political technology, favouring an enlightened despotism with hardly any legal constraints.

Towards the Paternalism of the Authoritarian State

In England, civil society succeeded in securing its acquired rights and enforcing its parliamentary representation in bitter constitutional conflicts, especially in the disputes between the King and Parliament in the 17th century. Above all, the Petition of Right of 1628 and the 1689 Declaration of Rights as fundamental laws with quasi-constitutional status became milestones on the way to a constitutional, not just absolutist, monarchy and a limited government no longer bearing the characteristics of a paternalistic authoritarian state. In contrast, early modern German political theory was guided by the questions of how secular politics could be given direction 'without the compass of religion and morality'; how people with competing religious beliefs could live together peacefully; and how government could be established and consolidated.[37] Its stated goals were (a) to replace the medieval association of persons with a modern territorial state as a secular functional association, (b) to form out of the diversity of sovereign rights the absolute sovereignty of the prince, and (c) to level all feudal differences among the estates and special privileges in the status of the subject.

The key concepts of *raison d'état*, welfare, happiness and necessity removed the limitations of state purposes (*Staatszwecke*) and legitimated governmental paternalism – only hinted at and non-binding in the

---

[37] Cf. for this and the following Stolleis, *Geschichte des öffentlichen Rechts in Deutschland I* and id., *Staat und Staatsräson in der frühen Neuzeit*.

conception of the *method Hobbes*. In the name of *necessitas*, the prince was in charge of legislation and, through the imperative instructions for interpreting the law, collecting taxes and levies, held the power to deprive towns, estates and the nobility of their rights and privileges, and to expropriate church property without compensation. Moreover, the prince was entitled to dispose of any other privileges. A legally trained civil service worked on the concretization of state purposes. Just as the *raison d'état* could serve almost any state purpose as a legitimizing formula, sovereignty as the structural feature of an absolutist state stood in the way of an institutional conjunction of *Rechtsstaat* and parliamentarianism.

The absolute power to issue law for everyone and everything domestically without the consent of third parties and to be independent of all secular and ecclesiastical powers contradicted in the early modern context a subsequently common understanding of law-rule and excluded – in theory and state practice – the contrast between law-rule and a state of exception. With the conception of absolute and unbound sovereignty, Jean Bodin had developed in 1576 the highly influential model of a 'well-ordered commonwealth'.[38] The latter he characterized by the fact that its inner nature allowed all sorts of new rights to be generated for the sovereign prince as holder of the legislative, executive and judicial power. Of course the personalization of sovereignty permitted Bodin to restrict the *potestas legibus soluta* inherently. As the earthly image of God, the sovereign prince was bound by the eternal principles of divine law, natural law and the *leges fundamentales*. It also seems compatible with this concept of sovereignty that his own laws bound the prince and his exercise of power. Neo-Aristotelians introduced 'sovereignty external' constraints of princely power, which came in the form of the common good as state purpose and doctrines of political virtue; with the ruler's duty of loyalty and justice as well as divided sovereignty, they prepared the basis for a 'good government' as the precursor of good governance with imperative features, which can at best be described retrospectively as a regime of generalized emergency law.

Based on natural law, only the social contract theories of the early Enlightenment formulated the transition from absolutist state practice grounded in the *raison d'état* and sovereignty to the theory and practice of the *Rechtsstaat* in the 19th century. Grotius, Pufendorf, Thomasius and Christian Wolff accommodated the absolutist claim to power within a framework of international and domestic rule somewhat restrained by

---

38 Bodin, *Six Books of the Commonwealth*, Book I, chs.1 and 8.

contractualism.[39] With the Janus-faced construction of a social contract mutually protecting the members of a *societas civilis* and a contract of subordination, Pufendorf, in marked contrast to Hobbes, turned the sovereign into an equal contractual party. And in contrast to Locke's philosophy, these social contract theories were primarily dedicated to the 'promotion of general welfare' and 'good order' (*Polizey*). In the tradition of the *leges fundamentales*, they accentuated the fundamental duties of rulers, but gave less emphasis to the rights of citizens compared to their duties – especially obedience, loyalty and the subordination of self-interest. However, in the theories of the state's purpose, the freedom of the citizen as subject remained uncertain. The asymmetric twin character of the virtuous ruler and virtuous citizens indicated a priority for justifying a moderately absolutist rule and its corresponding state purposes. In the absence of an economically and structurally developed, politically conscious and organized bourgeoisie, a social catalyst was missing that could connect the emancipatory idea of natural rights with the principle of equality. Therefore, the *Rechtsstaat* and the legislative style of governing were only outlined vaguely. The danger of power abuse was primarily meant to be combated by state ethics and the right to resistance as a quasi-emergency law from below.

Entering the Bourgeois Era

Compared with developments in Britain, the bourgeois era in Germany began after some delay. It was only in the last decades of the 18th century that treatises of state theory signalled an emerging change.[40] They first split the overall state purpose of happiness into specific individual purposes and replaced them in the end with (the stability and certainty of the) law and civic freedom. Gradually, the perspective shifted from the citizen as subject to the citizen as member of the body of the state, yet still without participation rights.

As a consequence, trust in the state as guarantor of civil liberties was gradually replaced by mistrust of the state as their potential enemy.

---

[39] Hofmann, 'Von den Ursprüngen deutschen Rechtsstaatsdenkens in der nachchristlichen Sozialphilosophie', with further references and Mohnhaupt and Grimm, *Verfassung*.

[40] For this transition, see Scheidemantel, *Das Staatsrecht nach der Vernunft und den Sitten der vornehmsten Völker betrachtet*; von Justi, *Die Natur und das Wesen der Staaten als Grundwissenschaft der Staatskunst, der Policey und aller Regierungswissenschaften*; von Humboldt, *Ideen zu einem Versuch, die Grenzen der Wirksamkeit des Staates zu bestimmen*.

Wariness of the powers of the absolute sovereign and the paternalism of a caring state bureaucracy, up until then almost universally justified with eudaemonist theories of state purposes, became manifest in the 1794 General Civil Code for the Prussian States (*Preussisches Allgemeines Landrecht* (ALR)). This 'monument to the Prussian Enlightenment' reduced, albeit moderately, the government's responsibilities and made provisions for an independent judiciary (ALR II, sec. 13 and 17). The social model of the ALR represented a compromise between an estates-based order and a bourgeois-capitalist society, combining norms of the 'basic law of freedom' with the principle of authority grounded on estates. However, in accordance with the prevailing theory of the state, the ALR maintained the notion that the state grants citizens their rights and therefore may rescind them at will.

The transition to a (rational) legal justification of the state and to the liberal paradigm of governing, already present in the works of Rousseau and Locke, was significantly advanced by Immanuel Kant. He based the liberal paradigm on the rights to political autonomy of the male, property-owning citizenry. Thus, the Kantian *Rechtslehre* developed the conception of the individual as both subject of the law and citizen/author of law. In a freer and more 'modern' way than the contemporary theory of the state, he defined the state as a 'multitude of human beings under laws of right',[41] whose purpose was to realize the well-being of the state.

> By the wellbeing of a state is understood, instead, that condition in which its constitution conforms most fully to principles of right; it is that condition which reason, *by a categorical imperative*, makes it obligatory for us to strive after.[42]

Against Hobbes, Kant stated as a priori conditions for the legal-civil condition: the freedom of each member of society as a human being, his equality as subject and autonomy as citizen.[43] Thus, he based his rational state on the self-fulfilment of individual subjectivity in freedom and equality rather than on transpersonal goods, like happiness; in doing so, he radically departs from both the eudaemonist doctrine of state purposes and the paternalistic authoritarian state.

---

41 Kant, *Metaphysics of Morals*, § 49, Akad. VI, 313.

42 Kant, *Metaphysics of Morals*, § 49, Akad. VI, 318.

43 Kant, 'On the Old Saw', and id., *The Metaphysics of Morals*. Apart from the freedom of the individual and the quality of citizens, in his work *'Perpetual Peace': A Philosophical Essay*, 121, Kant also introduces the concept that all persons are dependent on a single common legislation. Cf. also id., *Metaphysics of Morals*, §§ 46 ff.

However, in accordance with the maturity requirements of Prussian common law, Kant denied women and employees the right to vote. In this way, he was able to avoid the radical implications of Rousseau's conception,[44] according to which the contradiction between freedom and legal coercion can only be reconciled by the fact that all subjects of law are at the same time authors of (coercive) laws through their participation in forming the common will. Kant's restrictive concept of the franchise and his reserve towards a democratic republic suggest that one should not exaggerate the implications and intentions of his approach for democratic theory.[45]

It is not disputed, however, that Kant shifted the justification of state authority from the absolute sovereignty of the prince to a depersonalized sovereignty with a separation of powers: in the realm of ideas, he elevated the 'united will of the people' to the status of sovereign invested with legislative power. The 'ruler' (*Regent*) of the state was defined as its real legislator under the proviso that its laws must be able to find consent, unlike in Bodin's or Hobbes' conception. Consequently, the right of the citizens to contradict replaced their right to resist abuses of power and despotism. Thus, Kant introduced key elements of an emerging democratic *Rechtsstaat* and made it possible to qualify any despotic exercise of power as justifiable only under the extra-legal rules of a state of exception.

Despite its originality and moderation, the Kantian *Rechtsstaat* and its further development of the *method Locke* met with a cool reception in the traditionally conservative and anti-revolutionary German political theory, infected by a widespread fear of Jacobinism, and privileging the state and a stable order over democratic participation and parliamentary representation.

The Rectifying Liberalization of the State

How can the state be constituted as guarantor of civil liberty and security and, at the same time, be controlled as the source of their danger? Linking a Hobbesian approach to political technology with a Lockean legal-technological perspective, this seems to be the key question in the discourses of political theory and administrative science that emerge in the specific 'national constellations' of the 19th century. A special feature

---

[44] Rousseau, 'The Social Contract', especially Book 1, chs. 6–8.

[45] For a different account, see the impressive 'democratic' Kant interpretation by Maus, *Zur Aufklärung der Demokratietheorie*, who derives a strong concept of democracy from Kant's work.

of these political and semantic controversies was the rather narrow perspective, typical of the German *Sonderweg*: law-rule was disconnected from programmes of societal self-government within the confines of a given territory and narrowed down to the guarantee of legal certainty and the effective operation of a functionally and institutionally differentiated administrative state as well as its internal sovereignty and constitutional legitimacy.

Only early constitutionalism[46] adopted the emancipatory approaches of the Enlightenment and the Kantian philosophy of reason and linked them to a formal-substantive concept of the *Rechtsstaat.*[47] At the heart of this primarily formal understanding of the constitution under law-rule and directed against despotic rule were the reinterpretation of the state as a legal person and the formal concept of law. While the state as a legal person offered an escape route from the explosive conflict between the sovereignty of the prince and the people, law – generated with the participation of representatives of the people – from now on steered the activity of the administration and guaranteed citizens 'the certainty of lawful freedom'.[48] The argumentative figure of law-rule secularized the justification of the state and restricted the traditional freedom of the monarch, namely to exercise his power arbitrarily, with the help of a constitutional system that separates and balances the state powers. Despite this rectifying liberalization of the state, the political technology of early constitutionalism was almost exclusively based on the unbroken supremacy of the monarch and beyond legal constraints.

The substantive component of early constitutionalism's concept of the state became manifest at the level of state purposes. Here, welfare and justice subsidiarily established by the '*gute Polizey*' joined the genuine constitutional duties of the liberal minimal state: legal protection and security.[49] With its rejection of the state as seen from the perspective of a master of the house, early constitutionalism in Germany began to follow

---

46 See, especially, Welcker, *Die letzten Gründe von Recht, Staat und Strafe*; Aretin, *Staatsrecht der konstitutionellen Monarchie I*; von Mohl, *Das Staatsrecht des Königreichs Württemberg* and id., *Die Polizei-Wissenschaft nach den Grundsätzen des Rechtsstaates*.

47 Cf. the controversial and differentiated analysis in Maus, 'Theorie des bürgerlichen Rechtsstaats' and Böckenförde, 'Entstehung und Wandel des Rechtsstaatsbegriffs', 149.

48 Von Humboldt, *The Sphere and Duties of Government.*

49 Von Humboldt's narrow definition of state purposes did not succeed in early-constitutional political theory. Cf. Stolleis, *Geschichte des öffentlichen Rechts in Deutschland II*, 156 ff. and 258 ff.

the idea of limited government and a state organization under the principles of rational law (*Vernunftrecht*), featuring the recognition of the rights of the members of the state – although still restricted to male and property-owning citizens – responsible judges, popular representation and a government responsible to representative bodies. Born out of the plight of the early theory of the *Rechtsstaat*, namely 'to claim the sovereignty of law without possession of the sovereignty of parliament',[50] its rational state (under the rule of law) was based on the 'the principle of the free, equal, property generating person' (Böckenförde) and perverted in the end into the virtue of the authoritarian defence against an alleged parliamentary absolutism.

In the first half of the 19th century, the supremacy of the monarch's executive power also found expression in an uncontested extra-legal emergency concept protecting the order of the state. In almost all German territories, this emergency norm is complemented by laws and regulations that gave state authorities the power to use the military domestically in the case of riots and disturbances and to proclaim a state of war or siege as well as to take measures that seemed appropriate in these cases. Altogether these special powers constituted the 'state of exception of the bourgeois *Rechtsstaat*',[51] the declaration, execution and termination of which were left to the discretion of the executive – following the model of the *état de siège* in the French monarchy of the Restoration period.

The Return to the Monarchical Principle

In the aftermath of the revolutionary turmoil in 1848/9, conflicting demands by the politically insecure German bourgeoisie characterized the tension between the formal and substantive[52] *Rechtsstaat*. The bourgeois interest in a state-free, mainly economic sphere was compromised by a desire for state intervention to secure peace and order elsewhere. The interlude of liberal-democratic aspirations was a short one; the aim was to constitutionalize both the monarch's position and his powers under emergency law. After a short while, the property-owning

---

[50] Maus, 'Theorie des bürgerlichen Rechtsstaats', 19; also for the following quote.

[51] Boldt, *Rechtsstaat und Ausnahmezustand*, 60 ff.

[52] Introduced only by Weimar political theory, the 'substantive *Rechtsstaat*' does not confine itself to formal safeguards but includes substantive requirements for state activity, such as justice, protection of those on the breadline and the guarantee of human dignity, which authorizes the state to intervene in social affairs. Cf. Böckenförde, 'Entstehung und Wandel des Rechtsstaatsbegriffs'.

bourgeoisie once again sought its salvation and security in the monarchy. Barely articulated suggestions to restrict the intervention powers of the monarch were overshadowed by the old discretionary state of siege in state theories defending the monarchical principle. The King of Prussia was able to proclaim uncontested: 'In times of high risk, the King takes dictatorship.'[53]

After the failed revolution of 1848/9, Friedrich Julius Stahl, one of the intellectual leaders of the restoration, engaged in rehabilitating the monarchical principle and the representation of the estates 'on the basis of the Christian belief'. Still, he reduced the participation of the estates to a right of veto. In his oft-quoted definition of *Rechtsstaat*, the substantive aspects, i.e. the God-given substance of the 'moral realm', fade initially into the background:

> In the manner of law the *Rechtsstaat* shall determine precisely and secure absolutely the trajectories and limits of its action as well as the free sphere of its citizens and shall realize (enforce) the ethical ideas by command of the state, which is to say: directly, only as far as it belongs to the legal sphere … This is the concept of the *Rechtsstaat*, not by any chance, that the state handles merely the legal order without administrative purposes, or altogether merely protects the rights of the individuals, [the *Rechtsstaat*] denotes not at all the aim and content of the state, but only the way and character to realize them.[54]

In Stahl's conception of the state and, by implication, governmental techniques, the securing of the 'absolute legal order' entered into a highly ambivalent association with the 'constant increase of the ethical and religious content of the state institution'. He committed any exercise of power and application of law to the 'unchangeable rule of the law' and ranked legal certainty among the human rights. However, in exchange, he introduced the 'omnipotence of parliament', i.e. of the prince and the participating estates, which in the end turned out to be the omnipotence of the executive.[55] In his vision of a 'moral empire', Stahl accommodated his double opposition to the 'objectionable teachings of the revolution' and the patrimonial theory of the state, which led him to the '*Staatskönigtum*' of the constitutional monarchy. Despite his affirmation of the

---

53 Cit. in Frahm, 'Entstehungs- und Entwicklungsgeschichte der Preußischen Verfassung', 282.

54 Stahl, *Die Philosophie des Rechts*, II/2, II. Abschnitt, 1. Kap., § 36.

55 Ibid., I. Abschnitt, 2. Kap. and II. Abschnitt, 1. Kap., § 41.

Rechtsstaat, grounded on Christian ethics, he propagated not a legal but an executive political technology, severed from significant legal constraints.

Positivism: Formal *Rechtsstaat* and the Depoliticized State of Exception

In a departure from both the early-constitutionalist affinity to the philosophy of the Enlightenment and the restorative construction of a moral realm, theories of the state in late constitutionalism[56] eradicated all philosophical connotations from the concept of the *Rechtsstaat*. Following the dictates of legal positivism, in a first step theory was separated from the purposes to be pursued by the state. In a second step, the areas of state influence were confined to the prevention of danger[57] and the *Rechtsstaat* was, in formalist fashion, reduced to an 'order of the relationship between law, administration and individual'.[58] The focus shifted to theories of the state as the association of wills (*Willensverband*) and of law as an order given by sovereign legislation unrestrained by substantial confines – both linked under the label *Staatswillenspositivismus* (state-will positivism).

After these conceptual moves, the constitutional-doctrinal concept of the *Rechtsstaat* lost its affinity to economic interests and the political demands of factions within bourgeois society, at least on the surface. With the liberation from substantive constraints, especially from vested rights or state purposes, the voluntaristic concept of law in legal positivism finally allowed the legislature to intervene creatively in the social structure of the state as its natural basis: 'The law can do everything; all civil rights [...] can be curtailed by dint of law.'[59] The 'state of well-ordered administrative law'[60] established in this way a kind of rule of law and primacy of parliament, but touched upon neither the anti-parliamentarian independence of the executive in the German Empire nor the 'special power relationship' of civil servants and soldiers

---

56 Especially, von Gerber, *Grundzüge eines Systems des deutschen Staatsrechts*; Laband, *Das Staatsrecht des Deutschen Reiches II*; Mayer, *Deutsches Verwaltungsrecht I*, 53 ff.

57 Instructive also is the 1882 Kreuzberg ruling by the Prussian Higher Administrative Court (*PrOVG* 9, 353). Cf. also Jellinek, *Allgemeine Staatslehre*, 353 (and 359 ff.): The theory of the *Rechtsstaat* has 'the ultimate purpose to confine the innate un-abolishable power of the supreme bodies of the state'.

58 Meyer and Anschütz, *Lehrbuch des deutschen Staatsrechts*, 29 n. b; Oertzen, *Die soziale Funktion des staatsrechtlichen Positivismus*, 163 ff.

59 Mayer, *Deutsches Verwaltungsrecht I*, 70.

60 Ibid., 58.

in particular – still maintaining the spirit of the traditional fixation on the state. Hence, the dominant discourse pursued the German *Sonderweg* of the *Rechtsstaat*, still characterized by its distance from the liberal paradigm of law-rule and the *method Locke*.

Legal positivism distanced itself from the liberal paradigm in another respect also. While war and other emergency situations point towards the executive prerogative as the 'wholly other' of the normalcy of law-rule, legal positivism took the provisions for exceptional situations – above all special courts, summary executions and rules for suspending civil rights – as an unproblematic given. The programme of legal positivism aimed at juridifying the state of exception. Two legal-positivist operations helped obscure the original political function of the state of siege, namely to defend the order of the bourgeois *Rechtsstaat* against subversion from the left. First, the positivist approach led to a de-politicization by removing the state of exception from political controversy and by integrating it into police law. Second, positivism extended the concept of order by separating the exception from its political implications and by categorizing it as a military 'secondary administrative law meant to generate peace and order'.[61]

3.4 THE CONSTITUTIONALIZATION OF THE *RECHTSSTAAT* AND THE STATE OF EMERGENCY

The two German republics, of Weimar in 1919 and Bonn in 1949, adopted the liberal paradigm; yet, they approached the relationship between the normal situation under constitutional law and the exceptional situation rather differently.

Mutations of Political Technology

The Constitution of the Weimar Republic (CWR) links back to the 1848 *Paulskirchenverfassung* (St Paul's Church Constitution) that never entered into force and, for the first time in German history, took a decisive step away from constitutional monarchy to the democratic republic.[62] The Weimar conception of the *Rechtsstaat*, although not explicitly mentioned as a general principle, became manifest in a scheme of separated powers, especially an independent judiciary, and in a

---

[61] Boldt, *Rechtsstaat und Ausnahmezustand*, 107 ff., especially 170 ff.

[62] Anschütz, *Die Verfassung des Deutschen Reiches vom 11. August 1919* and Gusy, 'Vom Deutschen Reich zur Weimarer Republik', 758 ff.

catalogue of basic rights, even though they had only the normative force of programmatic provisions and were also coupled with fundamental obligations. At the same time, its infamous Article 48, providing for quasi-dictatorial arrangements in states of emergency, was to inspire the burgeoning literature on constitutional dictatorship.[63] The Weimar Constitution institutionalized trust in both the Parliament and the President of the Republic. It attempted therefore to achieve a delicate combination of the legislative and executive styles of political technology.

The *Reichspräsident*, elected directly for a seven-year term, had the power to dissolve the *Reichstag* – a competency foreshadowing his emergency powers. Article 48 CWR significantly exceeded, therefore, the corresponding Article 68 of Bismarck's 1871 Constitution of the German *Reich*. Article 68 provided for a law that would give the Emperor 'the power, if demanded by the public security of the Empire, to declare martial law in any part thereof', whereas the Weimar Constitution untied the traditional link between exception and war by assigning special powers to the President. For the purpose of stability, discipline and risk aversion, he was empowered to use the armed forces domestically against the *Länder* (German states), issue emergency decrees and suspend certain fundamental rights (Article 48(1) and (2) CWR). For the first time, the twin character of the *Rechtsstaat* and the state of exception as an arrangement for crisis situations was manifested in constitutional form:

> In the event of a State not fulfilling the duties imposed upon it by the Reich constitution or by the laws of the Reich, the President of the Reich may make use of the armed forces to compel it to do so.
>
> If public security and order are seriously disturbed or endangered, the President of the Reich may take measures necessary for their restoration intervening if need be with the assistance of the armed forces. For this purpose he may suspend for a while, in whole or in part, the fundamental rights provided in Articles 114, 115, 117, 118, 123 and 153.[64]

During the Weimar Republic, the infamous presidential emergency decrees turned out to be both explosive as well as ultimately destructive. The legal clarification of presidential emergency powers, intended in Article 48 CWR, never materialized. Thus, the general clause led to a

---

[63] Cf. Rossiter, *Constitutional Dictatorship*; Agamben, *State of Exception*.

[64] Accordingly, the following rights could be suspended: freedom of the individual, sanctity of the home, privacy of correspondence, the ban on censorship, freedom of assembly and the guarantee of ownership.

singular extension of the security paradigm as normal political technology[65] in the First German Republic as well as to a transformation of the state of exception from preventing political dangers to also combating economic crises.

> [The governments of the Republic] made continual use of Article 48, proclaiming a state of exception and issuing emergency decrees on more than two hundred and fifty occasions; among other things, they employed it to imprison thousands of communist militants and to set up special tribunals authorized to pronounce capital sentences. On several occasions [...] the government had recourse to Article 48 to cope with the fall of the mark [...].[66]

In its last crisis years, the Weimar Republic mutated beyond all constitutional barriers into a borderless regime of a 'provisional dictatorship' under emergency law.[67]

The *Method Hobbes* or the *Method Locke*?

The explosive nature of presidential emergency powers remained unrecognized in the early years of the Weimar Republic. Consequently, the interpretative struggles and open political confrontations between positivist and anti-positivist theories of the state were rather focused on the status of the notion of a bourgeois *Rechtsstaat* and Parliament as sole legislator.[68]

In accordance with positivist loyalty to the text of the constitution, Hans Kelsen followed Gerber and Laband but took a decisive decision: in his critique of Laband's *Staatswillenspositivismus* (state-will positivism), Kelsen deconstructed the concept of state rule, central in this context, and reduced it to pure normativity. In his strictly anti-metaphysical, sociologically informed theory of the state, the fatal connection between the parliamentary principle and the monarchy came to its belated end, because Kelsen shifted the emphasis from the state to law. He maintained the centrality of (constitutional) law, but relativized the juxtaposition of legislation and jurisdiction under the functional aspect of the generation of law. According to his conception, the *Rechtsstaat* is defined not as a state with specific legal institutions, but as a state all of whose acts are

65 Cf. Agamben, *State of Exception*, 14.

66 Ibid., 15.

67 Schmitt introduces the distinction between acting and sovereign dictatorship in *Die Diktatur*.

68 See Dyzenhaus, *Legality and Legitimacy*; Jacobson and Schlink, *Weimar*.

based upon the legal order.[69] By keeping parliament out of the conflict between the executive and bureaucratic state and the apolitical society of subjects, he prepared the transition from the *method Hobbes* to the *method Locke*.

Richard Thoma adopted to some extent Kelsen's approach of a formal concept of the *Rechtsstaat*. He nevertheless argued in favour of an interventionist state that required 'clear and general rules and comprehensive guarantees of legality'. Thoma also emphasized the legal omnipotence of the legislature bestowed with 'an unlimited power of legislation, which may create, in the interest of the common weal and disregarding all freedoms, rights, privileges and established conditions, new orders of social co-existence'. However, Thoma compromised his conception of the *Rechtsstaat*, since he ultimately defended the state:

> The idea of the *Rechtsstaat* is sacrificed [...], as far as it is meant to bend the state as a whole under some absolute law ridiculing human legislative power.[70]

Hermann Heller in principle shared this perspective of the interventionist state. The outspoken critic of the 'soulless and empty' concept of the *Rechtsstaat* introduced the notion of a 'social *Rechtsstaat*' and extended it to the provisions regarding the economic order covered by the Weimar Constitution (Article 151 et seq. CWR).[71] However, he did not play off a theory of state purposes derived from the Constitution against the positivist conception of law and the legislator's creative (interventionist) freedom. On the contrary, he criticized the authoritarian tendencies of the traditional concept of law and adjusted sovereignty in a quasi-republican move to democratic law-making powers. From a different vantage point than Kelsen, Heller, thus, switched from the *method Hobbes*, which dominated German theories of the state throughout the 19th century and at the beginning of the 20th century, to the *method Locke* by acknowledging the central role of the parliamentary legislator.

In stark contrast, conservative anti-positivists were especially annoyed by and politically suspicious of the Weimar legislature. For the first time since the introduction of universal suffrage, it deserved to be called

[69] Kelsen, *General Theory of Law and State*, 181.

[70] Thoma, 'Rechtsstaatsidee und Verwaltungsrechtswissenschaft', 204, 214; cf. id., 'Der Vorbehalt der Legislative und das Prinzip der Gesetzmäßigkeit von Verwaltung und Rechtsprechung'.

[71] Heller, *Staatslehre*; id., *Rechtsstaat oder Diktatur?*; id., 'Der Begriff des Gesetzes in der Reichsverfassung'.

'democratic' and was seen as threatening the security of the middle class from below in the shape of the parliamentary factions of the various workers' parties. Against the transition to Lockean political technology, arguably introduced by the Weimar Constitution and then theoretically completed by Kelsen and Heller, conservative theory once more brought the *method Hobbes* into play. In polemical attacks on the formal theories of the *Rechtsstaat* and Heller's 'social democracy in the form of a *Rechtsstaat*' and in uncompromising political opposition to the legislative state of Weimar, anti-positivists referred to either neo-natural law foundations or radical anti-parliamentarianism[72] in order to attack parliament with recourse to a higher ranking, substantively charged concept of legitimacy.

In the works of Erich Kaufmann, the undermining of the *Rechtsstaat* remained fairly inconspicuous. He focused on the defence of natural law against neo-Kantianism. He adopted the basic features of conservative anti-parliamentarianism but took an institutional turn. He obliged the democratic legislator to submit to the principles of justice elaborated by the judicature, thus introducing the judiciary as a norm-reviewing institution ranking higher than the parliamentary legislator.

As distinct from Kaufmann's pursuit of justice in the realm of natural law, Carl Schmitt and also Otto Koellreutter turned to the executive power in their anti-parliamentary pursuit of order and stability and accorded it primacy over the legislature. According to a somewhat mysterious general decision and the 'substantial order' they imputed to the Weimar Constitution, they held this primacy to be ensured by a 'political concept of law' to the disadvantage of the democratic parliament. Both political – rather than legal – theorists, they shared the programme of maintaining the socio-economic status quo under property law and therefore aimed to preserve the political domination of the (upper) middle class.

Aimed against law-rule as a state of laws (*Gesetzesstaat)* and the legal techniques of governing, the anti-positivist's unbridled anti-parliamentarianism inscribed into the context of the Weimar Republic, yet again, the German *Sonderweg* of the *Rechtsstaat* as the rule of the

---

[72] For neo-natural law, see Kaufmann, 'Die Gleichheit vor dem Gesetz im Sinne des Art. 109 der Reichsverfassung'. For anti-parliamentarianism, see Schmitt, *Verfassungslehre*, 23 ff., 35 ff. and 138 ff.; id., *Der Hüter der Verfassung*; id., *Unabhängigkeit der Richter, Gleichheit vor dem Gesetz und Gewährleistung des Privateigentums nach der Weimarer Verfassung*. For a critical perspective, see Maus, 'Theorie des bürgerlichen Rechtsstaats', 40 ff. and Dyzenhaus, *Law as Politics – Carl Schmitt's Critique of Liberalism*.

judiciary or the executive respectively. With regard to the state of exception,[73] the openly anti-liberal romantic Carl Schmitt overshadowed the 'merely' conservative Kaufmann. With his 'substantive' (or material) theory of the *Rechtsstaat*, Schmitt designed an emergency law that, charged with substantive values, ranked higher than the legislator and ordinary legislation and thus transgressed the confines of the liberal paradigm of governmental technology. The conception of a two-stage normativity consisting of legality and a higher (political) legitimacy reintroduced the executive prerogative and opened the door for the provisional dictatorship of the President, based on his emergency powers. Deliberately introduced by Schmitt to destroy the parliamentary legislative state,[74] the difference between higher legitimacy and lower-ranking legality fitted seamlessly into his agenda of separating democracy from parliamentarianism, liberating politics from legal constraints and 'removing the death mask from liberalism'.[75]

In the crises of the Weimar Republic, the structural incompatibility of parliamentary rule and dictatorship by emergency decree became obvious. The oscillation of German 19th century theories of the *Rechtsstaat* between utopia and apology, between the idealization of the *Rechtsstaat* and the defence of the status quo, came to an alarming halt. From 1933 on, apologetic and subservient comments on Hitler's tyranny came thick and fast. After conservative theories of the state in Weimar, united in the fight against 'the ideas of 1789', had previously removed the normative core of the concept of the *Rechtsstaat*, they – not all but most of them – now lost all argumentative scruples. In a bid to surpass others in discourse, the dictatorial structure and barbaric practice of the Nazi regime were accommodated under the umbrella of a 'national *Rechtsstaat*' (Otto Koellreutter) or a 'National Socialist German *Rechtsstaat*' (Carl Schmitt).[76] The latter, as a regime of an undeclared state of exception, devoted all powers to the *Führer* and destroyed in the

---

[73] See Chapter 4 for more details.

[74] Schmitt, *Legality and Legitimacy*, 299, 308 ff.; see also Dyzenhaus, *Legality and Legitimacy.* For a critical perspective, Maus, 'Theorie des bürgerlichen Rechtsstaats', 42 ff.; Preuß, *Legalität und Pluralismus.*

[75] Schmitt in a letter to R. Smend on 17 October 1927, cit. in Mehring, *Carl Schmitt*, 217.

[76] Typically, Koellreutter, *Der nationale Rechtsstaat*; Forsthoff, *Der totale Staat*; Binder, 'Autoritärer Staat und Rechtsstaat'; Schmitt, 'Der Rechtsstaat'; id., 'Der Führer schützt das Recht'; Koellreutter, 'Leviathan und totaler Staat'. For a critical account, see Stolleis, *Geschichte des öffentlichen Rechts in Deutschland III*, 330 ff., and Hilger, *Rechtsstaatsbegriffe im Dritten Reich.*

name of a supposedly higher justice all – not only political – opponents and 'alien elements' with murderous consequences and unparalleled brutality.[77]

Always already operating on the defensive in the German 'epistemic community' and state practice, the *method Locke* – and its components: certainty of law, predictability of state action, separation of powers and legal protection – were then mocked as ethnically alien (*volksfremde*), liberalist symptoms of weakness and decay. The liberal constitutional state, 'one of the most effective means of liberal suggestion', was replaced by cynical reinterpretations, like the '*deutsche Rechtsstaat Adolf Hitlers*', in which

> [a]ll law [stems from] the vital right of the people. Every law of the state, every judicial judgment contains only so much law, as flows from this source. The rest is not law, but a 'positive network of coercive norms (*Zwangsnormengeflecht*)', ridiculed by any clever criminal.[78]

Carl Schmitt, who according to his own words wanted to 'lend sense' to National Socialism, aimed openly at the 'polemical victory over the liberalist state of laws (*Gesetzesstaat*)' by the 'ethnic total state' that would find its unity in 'the orientation against the enemy'. In a new state or '*Weltanschauungsstaat*', the *Rechtsstaat* and its corresponding political technology, the *method Locke*, became 'obsolete':

> Then one will hopefully consider the term only as a trophy of the … victory over the bourgeois individualism and its deformations of the concept of law.[79]

Instead of a precarious coexistence between the *Rechtsstaat* and the state of exception, Carl Schmitt, as will be shown in the following chapter, had already opted for the theoretical primacy of the exception in the early years of the Weimar Republic and was prepared to politicize the claims that the exercise of power should follow the legal form and be legally constrained.[80] After celebrating the dictatorial president as 'guardian of the constitution', he finally enthroned the sovereign, dictatorial *Führer* as

---

77 For more details, cf. Peter Schneider, *Ausnahmezustand und Norm*, 211 ff.

78 Schmitt, 'Der Führer schützt das Recht'.

79 Schmitt, 'Was bedeutet der Streit um den Rechtsstaat?', 201.

80 See below Schmitt, *Political Theology. Four Chapters on the Theory of Sovereignty*.

'guardian of the law'[81] – a law, however, that was not even ambivalent as it destroyed all those of 'alien species' (*Artfremde*) and even offered no protection to those who were non-alien: 'Those who remain rooted in the same species as the Führer do not need any guarantees against his avenging hand.'[82] In this way, Schmitt's law fell far behind the Hobbesian *Elements of Law* and the *method Hobbes.*

3.5 THE POST-NAZI CONSTELLATION: LOCKE UNPLUGGED, NATURAL LAW UPDATED

After the Fascist 'rapture in civilization' and the liberation from Nazi dictatorship, the alternative between continuity and change characterized the constellation in Germany. Faced with the terrible legacy of the terror regime, the beginnings of the new West German constitutionalism were shaped less by 'embarrassment about the phenomenon of political domination' (Ernst-Wolfgang Böckenförde) than by an unreflective juxtaposition of *Rechtsstaat* and democracy, updating the *Sonderweg* for the 'Zero Hour' after World War II.[83] This juxtaposition was based on the missing distinction between laws generated under the Nazi regime and laws with a democratic pedigree. In this 'Zero Hour', lack of a grasp of democratic deficits, if not the openly anti-democratic thrust of traditional theories of the *Rechtsstaat*, led many scholars to follow an established statist mode of crisis management and to seek refuge in the *Rechtsstaat* as 'one of the greatest goods of mankind', as had many of the theories of the state during the Weimar period. Under the circumstances, democracy did not seem to be an attractive option.

Unlike the 19th century doctrines of the *Rechtsstaat* and Schmitt's decisionism, the law was emphasized vis-à-vis the state. However, this position unplugged the *method Locke* and legal positivism: 'Mindful of the physical devastation which the survivors of the 2nd World War were led into by a godless state and social order lacking in all conscience or respect for human dignity', as formulated in the Preamble of the 1946

81 Schmitt, *Der Hüter der Verfassung*; id., 'Der Führer schützt das Recht'. Cf. Mehring, *Carl Schmitt*, 165 ff. (for the dictatorship of the *Reichspräsident*), 281 ff. and 319 ff. (for the dictatorship of the *Führer*).

82 Schneider, *Ausnahmezustand und Norm*, 214.

83 Stolleis, 'Besatzungsherrschaft und Wiederaufbau deutscher Staatlichkeit 1945–1949'.

Bavarian Constitution, the 'Zero Hour' became a heyday for the domination of substantive concepts of the *Rechtsstaat*, inspired by neo-Platonism or the renaissance of natural law.[84] These doctrines of law-rule followed the German *Sonderweg* to the extent that they were prepared to tame the emerging rule of the people by inaugurating a rule of laws and a 'supreme court' as a counterweight to popular or parliamentary sovereignty.[85] As a lesson from the recent past, reiterated in the formula 'Bonn is not Weimar', the protagonists of natural law wove into the fabric of the new republic the legend that cast legal positivism as the midwife of the Nazi regime. In implementing this position, they preferred natural law and other extra-positive legal principles and again entrusted legal elites with their implementation, despite their glaring failures in the past. From the fact that National Socialism had left behind 'law [...] as an expanse of ruins', Gustav Radbruch, author of the term 'legal injustice (*gesetzliches Unrecht*)', derived that the task of lawyers was 'to recall again a higher law [...], a natural law [...], in short: a supra-legal law'.[86] In this way, he juxtaposed emergency law, which borrows its questionable philosophic dignity from its extra-positive nature, as against the positive law of the democratic constitutional state.

Although not unimpressed by the renaissance of natural law and partly inspired by Catholic social theory, the authors of the early *Länder* Constitutions followed a slightly different path. They attempted to give the *Rechtsstaat* substantive content by turning to positive constitutional law: the guiding principle of human dignity,[87] socio-ethical principles, like the 'commands of morals and humanity',[88] or state goals, such as the promotion of social justice, welfare and social peace. As a substantive principle, law-rule was meant to legitimize the interventionist politics and freedom of action of the welfare state.

---

84 Already in Weimar political theory, the 'substantive' *Rechtsstaat* had been juxtaposed with the merely formal one. It was characterized by substantive requirements regarding state activities and legislation, in which notions of a material justice can also become manifest.

85 Cf. Kägi, *Die Verfassung als rechtliche Grundordnung des Staates* (for a critical perspective, see Bäumlin and Ridder, 'Art. 20 Abs. 1-3 III Rn. 30 ff.').

86 Radbruch, 'Die Erneuerung des Rechts'.

87 Art. 100 Constitution of Bavaria (1946); Art. 5(1) Constitution of Bremen (1947); Art. 3 Constitution of Hesse (1946).

88 Art. 1 Constitution of Bremen ('commands of ethics and humanity'); Art. 1(3) 1947 Constitution of Rhineland-Palatinate ('requirements of the common weal as determined by natural law'); cf. also Art. 1 Constitution of Baden-Württemberg of 1953 ('fulfilment of the Christian moral law').

Initially only provisional, with an eye to the division of Germany, the 'Basic Law' – the Constitutional Court and the commentators – followed again the German *Sonderweg* of the *Rechtsstaat*. Resuming the theories of the *Rechtsstaat* at the 'Zero Hour', the emphasis shifted again from the state to law. According to the *method Locke*, mistrust of the state correlated with confidence in the law and its ability to tame the government. From this angle, stark controversies arose about the structure and substance of law-rule. They reveal the persistence of considerable uncertainty and unfamiliarity in dealing with the *Rechtsstaat* as a normative principle, institutional structure and an ensemble of legal techniques of governing.

3.6 REINVENTING THE STATE OF EXCEPTION AS 'PROTECTED DEMOCRACY'

Especially with regard to the state of exception, now returning as state of emergency, the Basic Law (BL) still reveals the aftershocks of the failure of the *Rechtsstaat* in the Weimar Republic. Conceptualized as a provisional constitution, the Basic Law, unlike its 19th and 20th century ancestry, originally did not deal with the state of exception and only marginally with emergency situations. Prompted by its 'liberal fundamentalism', noted by observers in comparison with the 1947 Japanese Constitution, also by its concept of governmental technology, the authors, recognizing the limited sovereignty of the Federal Republic, intended to keep aloof from Article 48 CWR. Under the supervision of the Allied Powers, the Parliamentary Council (*Parlamentarischer Rat*) did not make use of the emergency provisions included in the draft Constitution of Herrenchiemsee (Article 111) and some of the *Länder* Constitutions that in part followed the Weimar pathway.

The Marginalization of the State of Emergency in the 'Militant Democracy'

In this way, excursions into emergency territory remained sparse and tentative: the provision for a legislative state of emergency (Article 81 BL) caused by obstructive majorities was meant to come to terms with the Weimar trauma of a powerless parliament without resorting to a presidential dictatorship and to strengthen the federal government temporarily in cases of a dysfunctional Federal Diet (*Bundestag*).[89] Strictly speaking, the legislative emergency clause does not constitute emergency law but provides for temporary crisis management, when the legislative process is blocked due to a failed vote of confidence (Article 68 BL) and a bill marked as urgent or linked to the vote of confidence has to be passed.

Marginal emergency provisions can be found in Article 91 BL, dealing with domestic emergencies. Suspended in its original version by the military governors in accordance with the Occupation Statute until express permission was given,[90] it provided for a transfer of powers in favour of the federal government within the framework of the latter's task to 'safeguard the overall constitution'.[91] Since the 1968 'Emergency Laws', which ended Allied rights under Article 5(2) *Deutschland Vertrag*, the revised Article 91 allows in cases of imminent danger for the existence of the free democratic order of the Federal Republic or of one of its *Länder* that the affected *Land* may request police forces from other *Länder* or that the federal government may intervene, if the *Land* is unwilling or unable to prevent the danger. In such emergency situations, powers are therefore meant to be shifted, but there was and is no intention to suspend the instruments for the prevention of dangers, in particular regular powers and the rules of armament.

Article 91 BL is said to contain another lesson from Weimar, namely the need to strengthen democracy against its 'enemies'.[92] This lesson finds its institutional expression in the concept of a 'militant democracy',[93] which after World War II proliferated and became a global item of constitutionalism.[94] With the ban on parties and associations (Articles 21(2) and 9(2) BL) and the never applied forfeiture of basic rights

---

[89] In constitutional practice, the 'legality provision' of Art. 81 Basic Law has remained insignificant. Brenner, in von Mangoldt et al., *GG*, Art. 81 Rn. 8 ff.; Bryde, in von Münch and Kunig, *GG III*, Art. 81, Rn. 3 ff.

[90] Genehmigungsschreiben der Militärgouverneure zum Grundgesetz vom 12.05.1949, VOBIBZ, 416. Cf. Böckenförde, 'Ausnahmerecht und demokratischer Rechtsstaat'.

[91] Cf. Bryde, in von Münch and Kunig, *GG III*, Art. 81 Rn. 1 ff.; see also *BVerfGE* 13, 54/79.

[92] These 'theories' usually neglect the fact that Weimar lacked not the legal instruments for protecting the republic but the respective personnel in the judiciary and administration. For a detailed and differentiated account, see Gusy, *Weimar, Die wehrlose Republik?*

[93] Loewenstein, 'Militant Democracy and Fundamental Rights'.

[94] Loewenstein is seen as its conceptual father. Cf. also Frankenberg, 'The Learning Sovereign'.

(Article 18 BL), these provisions utilize the arsenal of emergency law. However, these instruments for defending the 'free democratic basic order' keep a low profile as constitutional protection of democracy and constitution.[95] With their constitutionalization, however, they nevertheless indicate a problematic step towards the internalizing and normalizing of the state of exception and its corresponding normalized political technology.[96]

Constitutionalizing the Exception?

At the end of the 1960s, the Bonn Republic, though desperately claiming to have learned from Weimar, resembled its predecessor on one central point: after a series of long and bitter controversies,[97] in which the Federal Government pursued and defended its strategy to constitutionalize the emergency situation, the Basic Law was finally amended with the so-called 'emergency constitution' (*Notstandsverfassung*). After many failed initiatives to control internal and external emergency situations, which began with the lifting of the Occupation Statute,[98] the 1968 emergency constitution determined provisions for a 'state of tension' (*Spannungsfall*) (Arts. 80a and 87a(3)) and a 'state of defence' against armed attacks (Art. 115 ff.), for domestic unrest (Art. 87a(4)) – satirized by Forsthoff as a relic of the 'venerable 19th century'[99] – as well as for disasters and grave accidents (Art. 35(2) and (3)). These provisions offer a fairly broad, albeit systematically flawed, concept of exceptional circumstances and respective powers.

---

[95] Denninger, *Freiheitliche demokratische Grundordnung*.

[96] In my analysis of the regressive *Rechtsstaat* ('Angst im Rechtsstaat') and the normalized state of emergency (Chapters 5 and 6), I come back to the crises triggered by the practice of the political prevention of danger, which aims at protecting the 'free democratic fundamental constitutional order' against political extremism and terrorism.

[97] For the debates about the emergency laws, see Sterzel, *Kritik der Notstandsgesetze*; Seifert, *Der Notstandsausschuß* and id., *Kampf um Verfassungspositionen*. See also Schweitzer, 'Emergency Powers in the Federal Republic of Germany'.

[98] With its abolition the Federal Republic of Germany gains sovereignty but only under the provision that the issues of Germany, Berlin, peace and a state of emergency are settled – Arts. 2 and 5(2) Convention on Relations between the Three Powers and the FRG signed on 26 May 1952 and 23 October 1954 (BGBl. 1955 II, 305). Cf. West German Emergency Laws, HL Deb., 11 July 1968, vol. 294 cc. 1084–5.

[99] Forsthoff, *Der Staat der Industriegesellschaft*.

In contrast to its historical precursors, marked by the technique of the general clause,[100] the regulatory strategy behind the provisions of the Basic Law was owed to the attempt to quasi-anticipate and typify possible exceptional situations as examples for regulation and to integrate them into the overall framework of the Basic Law with as much consideration for fundamental rights as possible: the state of emergency comes as an external or internal one. Its determination and execution aim at protecting the territory and existence of the Federal Republic and its *Länder*, its 'free democratic order', civilian objects and population.[101] For this purpose, the emergency provisions shift powers to the benefit of the Federal Government and allow the domestic use of armed forces. The regulatory framework for the legislative process in the state of defence (Art. 115c–e) and the guarantee of the integrity and functioning of the Federal Constitutional Court (Art. 115g) indicate, however, that not even an armed attack should completely unhinge the constitutionalized political technology, its legislative style and its respect for fundamental rights.[102]

The 'emergency constitution' and the instruments of a 'militant democracy' have not ended attempts to accommodate the state of exception constitutionally. Under the label of 'protected democracy' and after the experience of two world wars and the Weimar emergency decree dictatorship, such attempts have become common in the Federal Republic, as also incidentally in a number of other European countries[103] and the United States.[104]

3.7 THE FORM OF LAW-RULE VERSUS THE SUBSTANCE OF THE WELFARE STATE

In the development of the *Rechtsstaat*, the controversy between 'formalization and materialization' indicates a stark conflict characteristic of the discourse in the Federal Republic; still, it is hardly as significant as the

[100] See, for instance, § 54 Paulskirchenverfassung von 1849, Arts. 66 and 68 Reichverfassung, Art. 66 Weimarer Reichsverfassung and Art. 15 der Europäischen Menschenrechtskonvention (Abweichung von Menschenrechten im Notstandsfall).

[101] Arts. 80a(1), 87a, 91 and 115a GG.

[102] Exceptions: Arts. 9(3)(3), 10(2) and 17a(1) GG.

[103] See Sájo, *Militant Democracy.*

[104] See Rankin and Dallymayr, *Freedom and Emergency Powers in the Cold War*.

fateful controversies between positivists and anti-positivists in Weimar or the *problématique* of the state of exception. The controversial relationship between the form and substance of the *Rechtsstaat* seems, at first glance, to be far removed from the risk horizon of an emergency constitution (and was never a focal point for public protest). At second glance, however, relationships emerge that indicate at least an affinity to extraordinary emergency powers, although they are not meant to prevent a *coup d'état* or an economic crisis.

In Nostalgic Defence of the Formal *Rechtsstaat*

In its Article 28(1), the Basic Law refers *en passant* to Hermann Heller's formula of the 'social *Rechtsstaat*'. In the early phase of the Federal Republic, this ironically provoked some of those political and legal theorists to figure as constitutional architects of the second German Republic, whose licence one would have liked to have seen revoked after their intellectual involvement in building the Hitler-state. This refers to protagonists of the first round in the constitutional debate – of particular prominence were Carl Schmitt, who then reappeared to fight against the 'tyranny of values', and Ernst Forsthoff, the erstwhile supporter of Hitler's 'total state', who now argued against the 'merger of the *Rechtsstaat* and welfare state' in an almost ironic self-disposal of his past.

In the spirit of the 'eternal value' of the *Rechtsstaat*, Ernst Forsthoff argued that there is a structural antinomy between the *Rechtsstaat* and the welfare state.[105] While it is undisputed that the legal form of the *Rechtsstaat* and the demands of the welfare state (= political substance) can come into conflict as legal versus political technology, Forsthoff intended to convey more with his antinomy: the unacknowledged antinomy between the capitalist free market economy and the social market economy served as the backdrop of his argument. He credited the 'rational-normative *Rechtsstaat*' with accepting the social-economic status quo and with keeping a distance from a state-run system of goods distribution. Against the import of questions of justice and democracy,[106] in accordance with his traditional understanding of the state he stylized

---

[105] Forsthoff, 'Begriff und Wesen des sozialen Rechtsstaates'; id., *Der Staat der Industriegesellschaft*, especially 147 ff. Cf. also Huber, 'Niedergang des Rechts und Krise des Rechtsstaates', 77.

[106] Especially, Abendroth, 'Zum Begriff des demokratischen und sozialen Rechtsstaats im Grundgesetz der Bundesrepublik Deutschland'. Cf. Perels, 'Der soziale Rechtsstaat im Widerstreit'.

law-rule into a non-political principle of form. Thus he meant to keep in check powers over distributive policies dictated by the welfare state or at least to keep them at the level of administrative law and thus out of the constitution.

However, circumstances (and accompanying theories of the *Rechtsstaat*) moved on from Forsthoff's nostalgic-ideological and politico-economic interest in a formalist concept, operating with legal-conditional programmes; they also left behind his restriction on indirect social intervention through administrative bodies and tax regimes as the ideal form of a *Rechtsstaat*.[107] With the astounding career of the welfare state and its doctrinal affirmation, the social *Rechtsstaat* became a generally accepted element and principle of constitutional law and increasingly showed the traits of a welfare guaranteeing state, providing especially marketability, redistribution, security and education as well as structures for the private resolution of problems.[108] The welfare state of today has shaped theories and doctrines of basic rights; they almost routinely add claims to social benefits to the traditional defence against state interventions and have extended the objective-legal dimension of fundamental rights into wide-ranging responsibilities to protect. As a matter of consequence, these responsibilities reactivate, strengthen and extend the weak strand of Hobbes' and Locke's conception of techniques of governing – the duty to pursue the *salus populi* – and give the executive and also the judiciary, as far as it controls their implementation, special and wide-ranging powers.

In Defence of Democratic Legality

Attempts to reduce the *Rechtsstaat* to an apolitical formal principle and tendencies to 'materialize' it were repeatedly opposed by formal theories of a different kind. Declared opponents of Forsthoff ignited a second debate about reformalization in the late 1970s and early 1980s.[109] While

---

[107] Cf. the contributions by Bachof, Abendroth and Hesse in Forsthoff, *Rechtsstaatlichkeit und Sozialstaatlichkeit*, as well as Degenhart, 'Rechtsstaat – Sozialstaat, Anmerkungen zum aktuellen Problemstand'; Ridder, 'Die soziale Ordnung des Grundgesetzes'; Zacher, 'Das soziale Staatsziel', with further references, and Perels, 'Der soziale Rechtsstaat im Widerstreit'.

[108] Vogel, *Die Staatsbedürftigkeit der Gesellschaft*, and Hoffmann-Riem, *Modernisierung von Recht und Justiz*.

[109] The controversy between Grimm, 'Reformalisierung des Rechtstaats als Demokratiepostulat?' and Hase/Ladeur/Ridder, 'Nochmals: Reformalisierung des Rechtsstaats als Demokratiepostulat?' is instructive. Cf. also Maus, 'Theorie des

they pursued different aims, they shared the objective of protecting legal form – praised by Rudolf von Jhering as the 'twin sister of freedom' – against its erosion. Their main targets were the doctrine of the 'horizontal effect' of fundamental rights among private individuals, the Federal Constitutional Court's construction of an 'objective value-order' behind and above basic rights, the hypertrophic role of the judiciary and, finally, the burgeoning case law regarding the duty to protect.

Not unaffected by Carl Schmitt's philippics against the 'tyranny of values', protagonists of reformalizing law-rule were committed to a democratic legal positivism incorporating the constitutional principle of the welfare state. Their criticism rested on two pillars: first, some of them criticized the jurisprudence of the Federal Constitutional Court (FCC) and especially its doctrine of an 'objective value-order'[110] arching over the fundamental rights catalogue of the Basic Law as a perversion of the *Rechtsstaat*, and also compromising the basically legislative style of the *method Locke*. The legislative powers of Parliament, they claimed, were preceded by a substantially and institutionally higher-ranking level of legitimacy – rather comparable to Carl Schmitt's double-step concept of legality. They therefore advocated a return to formality and legislation to keep the political process open to social alternatives and to defend the powers of the legislature against the FCC. They based their intervention to correct the 'misery of the legislator' (not atypical for the history of German theories of the *Rechtsstaat*), inter alia, on a passage in the FCC's 1973 *Abortion Decision*. Assuming that 'the law (*Recht*) is not identical with the totality of written statutes (*Gesetze*)', the Court perceived as its task 'to bring to the light values that are immanent in the constitutional order, however, not or only imperfectly expressed in the texts of the written laws' and characterized its hermeneutic operation with subtle

bürgerlichen Rechtsstaats', 46 ff.; Preuß, *Legalität und Pluralismus*; Frankenberg, 'Angst im Rechtsstaat'; Bäumlin and Ridder, in: *AK-GG*², Art. 20 Abs. 1-3 III Rn. 38 ff.; Ridder, 'Vom Wendekreis der Grundrechte'.

110 A classic example is the following passage of the *Lüth* decision, which is heralded as a milestone of democracy: 'There is no doubt that the main purpose of basic rights is to protect the individual's sphere of freedom against encroachment by public power: they are the citizen's bulwark against the state. [...] But far from being a value-free system [references] the Constitution erects an objective system of values in its section on basic rights, and thus expresses and reinforces the validity of the basic rights. [...] This system of values, centring on the freedom of the human being to develop in society, must apply as a constitutional axiom throughout the whole legal system: it must direct and inform legislation, administration, and judicial decision' (*BVerfGE* 7, 198/204 ff.).

irony as 'an act of appraising cognition, not lacking also volitional elements'.[111]

Second, the advocates of reformalization opposed the FCC's interpretation of fundamental rights as a 'value system'. They emphasized instead the process character of rights as establishing the self-definition as well as protecting the capacity of individuals to act and organize. Consequently, they argued against basic rights being monopolized in a functionalist – juridico-objective – fashion and being gradually turned into substantive 'value decisions' that may generate, on the part of the state, a broad responsibility to protect[112] and thus legitimize a more executive style of governing complemented by the supervision of the FCC.

Reformalization was intended to (re-)produce the democratic *Rechtsstaat* as a regime of distance – distance, on the one hand, from daily passions and particular social interests and on the other hand from an all too powerful constitutional court and its jurisprudence of balancing.

To a certain extent the FCC at least semantically accommodated this criticism of its quasi-emergency law jurisdiction. In its recent case law, the justices have refrained from invoking an 'objective value-order'. And fundamental rights no longer function as pillar or 'elements' of this value order but mostly as norms containing basic principles.[113] The vague, juridical-objective dimension of fundamental rights is increasingly concretized through a functional diversification of organizational and procedural safeguards that suggests a return to a Lockean conception.[114]

The debate about reformalizing the *Rechtsstaat* led to controversy about the relationship between the *Rechtsstaat* and democracy. In Forsthoff's attack on the social component of the *Rechtsstaat*, the democratic

---

111 *BVerfGE* 34, 269/287.

112 The prohibition of insufficient means obliges the legislator to sufficiently safeguard objects protected by law, i.e. to carefully assess the actual situation, to weigh conflicting interests against each other and implement effective measures (*BVerfGE* 88, 203/254). For the prohibition of insufficient means, see Canaris, 'Grundrechte und Privatrecht', 228, and Isensee, 'Das Grundrecht als Abwehrrecht und staatliche Schutzpflicht'. For a critical perspective, see Denninger, 'Vom Elend des Gesetzgebers zwischen Übermaßverbot und Untermaßverbot'.

113 For references, see Böckenförde, 'Grundrechte als Grundsatznormen'.

114 Typically, *BVerfGE* 73, 280/296; 77, 170/229. Denninger, 'Staatliche Hilfe zur Grundrechtsausübung durch Verfahren, Organisation und Finanzierung'. As arrangements required by basic rights, organization and procedures still show their origins in the realm of 'objective law', but at the same time, they can be assigned more easily to the juridical-subjective functions of rights.

implications remained unexplored. However, they became apparent in the defensive semantics he used against the legislator who engaged in changing social conditions – rejecting all efforts to 'project changing social and political conditions into the constitution' – and in his, albeit dark, Hegelianizing message of the state as the abstract 'keeper of humanity'.[115]

While Forsthoff derived the tension between *Rechtsstaat* and democracy from the 'de-formalization of constitutional law',[116] the Swiss constitutional lawyer Werner Kägi based his antinomy of the *Rechtsstaat* and democracy, in contrast, on a supposed tendency towards formalization which 'the principle of the *Rechtsstaat* falls victim to'.[117] In the anti-positivist tradition, although not with the Weimar militancy, Kägi took issue with Hermann Heller's worry about the 'de-animation of the idea of the *Rechtsstaat*' and called for a 'community of destiny between *Rechtsstaat* and democracy' – with a vague thrust and a hardly lucid reasoning. As the cause for the crisis of legality, he identified the 'ideology of a massive, anti-representational democraticism', for which he held Rousseau, the positivists and decisionists collectively responsible. Though somehow capturing the post-war resuscitation of natural law, Kägi's attempt to escape the 'core values' of law-rule remained without consequences for the further development, due to its lack of differentiation between constitution-making and constitutional legislation as well as his implausible description of constitutional reality.

The political scientist Fritz Scharpf picked up the theme of law-rule versus political costs, as a 'negative correlation' 'between the perfecting of *Rechtsstaat* structures of the German type and the chances of an effective democratic-political steering and control of the administrative system'.[118] Scharpf addressed a set of problems validated empirically by the extensive literature on juridification and implementation[119] but without claiming that the constitutional state might be solely or even

---

[115] Forsthoff, 'Begriff und Wesen des sozialen Rechtsstaates', 175, and id., *Der Staat der Industriegesellschaft*, 168 ff.

[116] Forsthoff, 'Die Umbildung des Verfassungsgesetzes', 200.

[117] Cf. Kägi, *Die Verfassung als rechtliche Grundordnung des Staates* and id., 'Rechtsstaat und Demokratie'.

[118] Scharpf, *Die politischen Kosten des Rechtsstaats*. For the tension between the *Rechtsstaat* and democracy, see Bettermann, *Der totale Rechtsstaat*, 8 ff., and Püttner, 'Der informale Rechtsstaat', 69.

[119] Cf. only Voigt, *Verrechtlichung*; Zacher et al., *Verrechtlichung von Wirtschaft, Arbeit und sozialer Solidarität*; Vogel, 'Zur Diskussion um die Normenflut' and Starck, 'Übermaß an Rechtsstaat?'

primarily responsible. In its essential features, the criticism of juridification follows the argument of Max Weber, who had opposed substantive law as dissolving law's formal rationality,[120] and compromises, one might add here, the *method Locke*. The democratic implications of these lines of reasoning only become apparent at the level of meta-critique: substantive law is said to destroy the separation of powers by giving the judiciary a central role in the application of 'legal dummies' – an ensemble of general clauses, highly indeterminate legal concepts, vague objectives and experimental statutes. According to the post-Weberian view, the transformation of the *Rechtsstaat* establishes a rule by virtue of judicially sanctioned legitimacy.[121] In other words, the predictable democratic-legislative style of governing technology falls victim to a regime of executive ad hoc measures hardly controlled by, what Max Weber would have called, kadi-casuistry.

In stark contrast to such approaches and maybe also in response to their criticism, the FCC has for some time now attempted to amalgamate *Rechtsstaat* and democracy into a doctrine by interweaving the two complementary principles of legitimation in the institution of democratic law, understood as an expression of state order and popular will. One might say the Court attempted to help to get the *method Locke* accepted. However, the Court has not yet been able to precisely determine the law-rule/democracy issue beyond the separation of powers and has not put to rest the antinomy-dichotomy-tension debate. The Court presented two crucial arguments though: first, law-rule requires, entirely in the *spirit* of the liberal paradigm of legal technology, public power in all its expressions to be legally bound through a clear order of competences and separation of functions so that power abuse can be prevented and the freedom of the individual can be ensured. Second, democracy requires the organization of every crucial area of life by statutes to be based on a decision of the legislative bodies derived from the will of the people.[122] For a long time a hallmark of German theorizing about *law-rule*, the conflict of form and substance has thus been accommodated in the complementarity of the formal and substantive binding quality of law, which incidentally seems to establish the triumph of the *method Locke* at

[120] Max Weber, *Economy and Society*, especially vol. I, 225–6; vol. II, 656–7. For de-formalization, cf. Wiethölter, 'Materialisierungen und Prozeduralisierungen von Recht' and the contributions in Zacher et al., *Verrechtlichung von Wirtschaft, Arbeit und sozialer Solidarität*.

[121] Maus, 'Verrechtlichung, Entrechtlichung und der Funktionswandel von Institutionen' and Denninger, 'Verfassungsrechtliche Schlüsselbegriffe'.

[122] *BVerfGE* 33, 125/158.

the constitutional level. The analysis of the crises of the *Rechtsstaat* (Chapters 5, 6 and 7) will demonstrate that statutory law has a different story to tell.

The Systematic Relationship between *Rechtsstaat* and Democracy

Free from doctrinal constraints, the philosopher Jürgen Habermas draws a line under the traditional opposition of the *Rechtsstaat* and democracy. Continuing the Kantian tradition in his *Discourse Theory of Law and Democracy*,[123] he overcomes the dichotomy between the formal and substantive rationality of law by providing a discourse-theoretical justification for the ethical minimum of the *Rechtsstaat*, which can be read as a normative barrier against the meddling with powers under emergency law. The linchpin of his considerations is the discourse principle according to which all those affected as addressees of legal norms must be able to agree with them as participants in a rational discourse. Following the concepts of Rousseau and Kant, all members of a society play a dual role, both as addressees and authors of law.[124] In this way, Habermas leaves behind those liberal notions of democracy which modelled the latter after the pattern of a contract under private law between market participants. Instead, he introduces democracy as a practice of deliberation between the participants of public discourse. Here the communicative actor moves to the centre of the argument.

According to Habermas, democracy operationalizes the discourse principle in the form of law. Just as democracy cannot be achieved without the form of semantically and procedurally general law, a democratic legislator must produce the very form of law. The principles of the *Rechtsstaat* thus ensure the stability of the system of rights and of democratic law-making, especially by taming political technology. Consequently, the relationship between *Rechtsstaat* and democracy is not one of antinomy; rather, they refer to each other systematically. For Habermas, the systematic link between law-rule and democracy becomes apparent if one folds self-regulating legal arguments into legal procedures.[125] He therefore combines the principle of enactment with the principle of justification in order to ensure impartiality as the valid basis for modern law. The democratic *Rechtsstaat* is thus introduced in

---

123 Habermas, *Between Facts and Norms*.

124 Cf. Günther, 'Welchen Personenbegriff braucht die Diskurstheorie des Rechts?'

125 Habermas, *Between Facts and Norms*. For details, see Günther, *Der Sinn für Angemessenheit*.

opposition to traditional statist accounts and justified regardless of the specific features of its actual institutionalization. The concept of the *Rechtsstaat* is based on processes of public and parliamentary deliberation as well as on a system of rights that make it possible to at least scandalize, if not prevent, executive encroachments on powers under emergency law.

3.8 *RECHTSSTAAT*: ALL FORM – NO JUSTICE?

Law-rule has always been shadowed by the question of its relationship with justice. Again, this raises the issue of how form and substance are related. The Basic Law seems (and is doctrinally argued) to have answered the question of justice once and for all. Overall, it largely resisted the initial renaissance of natural law – despite the substantive designation of 'its' *Rechtsstaat* as a social one.

Opponents of opening the constitution to extra-positive law always insist that the *Rechtsstaat* only contains an ethical minimum.[126] They try to avoid the notion of justice and thus the paradox of positivized extra-positive law with reference to the fundamental rights that bind all state powers: the principles of equality and legality as well as the principle of the welfare state. The question of how one can prevent indeterminate notions of justice entering the Basic Law through the channel of a vague and open principle of justice is passed on to this very constitution – while no clear position on justice is actually taken.[127] The above-mentioned principles are in fact somehow captured by a substantive concept of the *law-rule*, although not necessarily by paradoxically positivized extra-positive legal acts.

---

[126] For this controversy, see Dreier, *Rechtsbegriff und Rechtsidee*; Sobota, *Das Prinzip Rechtsstaat*, 90 ff. Cf. also Forsthoff, 'Die Bindung an Gesetz und Recht (Art. 20 Abs. 3 GG)' and recently Dieckmann, *Überpositives Recht als Prüfungsmaßstab im Geltungsbereich des Grundgesetzes?*

[127] Constitutional doctrines might open themselves up to the vivid and constitutionally relevant debate about theories of justice which has continued in philosophy for more than two decades now: Rawls, *A Theory of Justice*; Dworkin, *Taking Rights Seriously*; Forst, *Kontexte der Gerechtigkeit*; Honneth, *Das Andere der Gerechtigkeit*; Young, *Justice and the Politics of Difference*; Frankenberg, *Auf der Suche nach der gerechten Gesellschaft*; Derrida, 'Force of Law'.

'Hours of Pure Justice'?

While the formula that the executive and the judiciary shall be bound by 'law and justice' in Article 20(3) initially ignited some scholarly debate and led to a peculiar wavering exegetic course in the Federal Constitutional Court's case law, ultimately it remained virtually without consequences. This began to change when, after German unification, the conflict between *law-rule* and justice emerged again in the context of criminal proceedings that dealt with the history of the GDR.[128] 'We expected justice and got the *Rechtsstaat*', complained the civil rights activist Bärbel Bohley.[129] Her dictum revealed both the painful experience of supposedly 'true justice'[130] in the 'socialist *Rechtsstaat*' and the disappointment of victims of the dictatorial GDR regime with the supposedly social *Rechtsstaat* of the Federal Republic. Their lack of familiarity with the formal rationality of a sober and 'distanced form of state', and with its corresponding techniques of governing, led them to demand that this distance should be overcome by greater care for the victims and by sacrificing formal provisos, in particular the prohibition of retroactivity (Article 103(2) BL), on the altar of substantive-emphatic notions of justice.

The case law on GDR micro- and macro- or government criminality[131] illustrated a specific feature of the *Rechtsstaat*, criticized by the activist Bärbel Bohley: despite – or perhaps because of – its ethical minimum and its range of extra-positive concepts of law, the *Rechtsstaat* turned out primarily to be a *defence* against legal wrong. And the latter was based on the – admittedly, not very determinate – principle of proportionality.

---

[128] Isensee, *Vergangenheitsbewältigung durch Recht*; the contributions by Starck, Berg and Pieroth regarding the topic: 'Der Rechtsstaat und die Aufarbeitung der vor-rechtsstaatlichen Vergangenheit'; Schlink, 'Rechtsstaat und revolutionäre Gerechtigkeit'. For the controversy about the rule of (un-)law in the 'socialist *Rechtsstaat*' GDR, see Klein, 'Vom sozialistischen Machtstaat zum demokratischen Rechtsstaat'; Müller, 'Die DDR – ein "Unrechtsstaat"?', as well as Denninger, 'Die Wirksamkeit der Menschenrechte in der deutschen Verfassungsrechtsprechung', 1131 ff.

[129] Cf. von Münch, 'Rechtsstaat versus Gerechtigkeit?', 165 ff., and Steffen Heitmann, 'Die Revolution verkommt zur Wende', *Frankfurter Allgemeine Zeitung* 13 (12 September 1994): 'The rule of law is objectively unable to rectify missed revolutionary acts'.

[130] So Walter Ulbricht at the end of his political career as Chairman of the GDR State Council, cit. in Heuer, *Die Rechtsordnung der DDR*, 59.

[131] *BVerfGE* 92, 277/316 ff. (criminal liability of GDR spies) and 95, 96/127 ff. ('Mauerschützen' – criminal liability of GDR soldiers).

Even where legal wrong had to be compensated, the provisos of the *method Locke*, under both positive law and the *Rechtsstaat*, remained in place. Accordingly, justice had to be implemented in two ways, (1) *institutionally*, primarily through the separation of powers and the binding force of the constitution and statutes for public authorities plus (2) *procedurally*, especially through formalized procedures, judicial independence, public proceedings and the effective protection of fundamental rights.

This means that the 'hour of pure justice' would be nothing more than a state of exception to be had at best during a revolution, in which neither legal certainty nor fundamental rights nor procedural guarantees could be expected to protect tyrants and their staff (as was experienced by the Romanian dictator Ceauşescu and his wife).

Consequently, outstanding and deserving civil rights activists also had to learn that the infringement of constitutional normality and normativity in favour of a higher legitimacy – notably justice – invariably follows the logic of arbitrariness, which is bound to seek justification for extraordinary measures in an extra-constitutional state of exception.

3.9 THE PREVENTIVE STATE – A GLOBAL FORMULA

The formula *law-rule versus the preventive state* marks a conflict constellation that leads directly to the key concept of security and thus to the precarious legal relationship of dangers in normal situations, with exceptional dangers in extreme cases. As such, the formula transgresses the confines of the idiosyncratic trajectories of national constitutions and laws. Since the 1970s, two main secular developments have urged Western regimes of law-rule to exceed the reasonably secure confines of danger prevention by police and politics. First, rapid scientific-technological progress in the risk society[132] gave rise to potential novel hazards that are difficult to control; they were accompanied by a dramatic loss of public confidence and fostered demands for new concepts of security.[133] Second, criminal phenomena and practices, such as cross-border criminality and especially terrorist organizations, provoke the state apparatus and public officials to design a new 'security architecture'.

[132] Beck, *Risk Society*; Giddens, 'Risk and Responsibility'; Bonß, *Vom Risiko*.

[133] Ericson and Haggerty, *Policing the Risk Society*.

Behind the façade, the tamed Leviathan under the rule of law mutates into a hardly (or at least: less) tamable one.[134]

In this way, the *method Hobbes* moves right next to the *method Locke*. It turns out that both methods of governing are intertwined in a highly problematic way. As a result, the illiberal valency of both methods comes to the fore and is conjoined in the *method Foucault*.[135] In the actual practice of political power (in developed capitalist countries) within and without the context of counter-terrorism[136] – eavesdropping on conversations, registering movement and travel, video observation of public places, controlling email traffic, and other state interventions with extreme areal extension – the problem areas of the 'risk society' and the 'preventive state' are linked via the information technology of the 'surveillance state'.[137]

From the Prevention of Dangers to the Hyper-Preventive Management of Risk

In the classical field of danger prevention by the police, the preventive and security state triumphs overall in a special police law, whose key terms and powers lose their contours under the rule of law, as is shown in the following chapters.[138] This special police law follows the rhetoric and logic of a 'combat law'. Its hyper-preventive approach leads to the linking of the prevention of danger and law enforcement with the help of supposedly innocent categories, such as 'multitasking', 'operation' or 'pre-emption'; according to this perspective, the security agencies are also responsible for the 'preventing of crime'.[139] With extremely precarious consequences, this concept exceeds the confines of the *method Locke*. The characteristics of the new amalgamation of political-technological styles are: the mingling of police and intelligence powers,

---

[134] Cf. Denninger, 'Der Präventionsstaat'; id., *Der gebändigte Leviathan*; Janus, 'The Preventive State, Terrorists and Sexual Predators'.

[135] See Chapter 1, Sections 1.3 and 1.4.

[136] E.g. Cole et al., *Secrecy, National Security and the Vindication of Constitutional Law*.

[137] See Ericson and Haggerty, *The New Politics of Surveillance and Visibility*; Lyon, *Surveillance Society*; id., *Surveillance after September 11*; Ball and Webster, *The Intensification of Surveillance* and Monahan, *Surveillance and Security*.

[138] For a more detailed account, see already Frankenberg, 'Kritik des Bekämpfungsrechts' and Chapter 6 below.

[139] Denninger, in: Lisken and Denninger, *Handbuch des Polizeirechts*, E Rn. 193 ff.

the abolition of the alternative between the prevention of danger and law enforcement as well as data sharing between the various security agencies and state authorities which have a different security agenda, such as the welfare bureaucracy. Moreover, the surveillance state in particular intervenes by collecting data – long before a concrete danger emerges or concrete suspicion of an offence exists.

The preventive state borrows its structures from the rather infant technology law and from classical police law. The powers of the security agencies no longer follow the ideal of an effective yet at the same time freedom-conscious prevention of danger, constrained by democratically generated intervention statutes under the rule of law. Rather the latter are replaced by an emergency regime under security imperatives, containing comprehensive measures for the prevention of dangers as they develop, or, more precisely, what governs now is anticipatory risk prevention on the basis of vague mandatory norms and objectives.[140]

The notion of prevention as such is not new. The averting of dangers by the police has always been preventative; police decisions have always entailed a prognostic element. However, what can be seen as innovative is the shift from a prevention of dangers to a hyper-preventive risk management that clearly exceeds the limits and rationale of the traditional forms of rule-law and of the *method Locke*. In the security state, political technology bases its legitimacy not on success in terms of legal certainty, but increasingly on achieving the common good by avoiding risks for civilization. Under the umbrella of a broadly defined protection of legal interests,[141] state responsibilities increase in number and are reinterpreted. They now include the production of security in general. Accordingly, the apparatus of the security agencies and the military, with the help of pre-emptive strategies and measures,[142] expands in accordance with the effective prevention of risk. In turn, civil liberties are restricted, sometimes with the approval of the courts; yet in cases of extreme interventions, they distance themselves from the claim to powers and the hunger for data of the security bodies.[143]

---

[140] Instead of the vast literature, see here Ericson and Haggerty, *Policing the Risk Society*; Roßnagel, *Digitalisierung der Grundrechte*; Di Fabio, *Risikoentscheidungen im Rechtsstaat.*

[141] Denninger, *Der gebändigte Leviathan*, 33 ff. and 219 ff.

[142] See Kegley and Raymond, 'Global Terrorism and Military Prevention'; Shue and Rodin, *Preemption: Military Action and Moral Justification.*

[143] The Federal Constitutional Court has recently denied unconditional approval for some particularly extreme measures, such as the 'rescue downing' of renegade aircraft in control of suspected terrorists (*BVerfGE*) as well as broad

In technology law, particularly also in environmental law, atomic energy law, the law of genetic engineering and health law, this shift in favour of a generalized risk prevention and resource management becomes manifest in extremely indeterminate legal concepts – such as social acceptability, proportionality, reasonableness and reliability – or in indefinite hardship clauses. They institute the transition from imperative, legal-formal and direct regulation of behaviour to the control of social communication and processes, put into effect by highly flexible and open-textured provisions and an information management beyond judicial review.[144]

surveillance procedures and measures of data retention. *BVerfGE* 120, 274 (Online-Durchsuchung); *BVerfGE* 120, 378 (automatische Kfz-Datenerfassung); *BVerfGE* 121, 1 (Vorratsdatenspeicherung).

[144] Di Fabio, 'Grundrechte im präzeptoralen Staat am Beispiel hoheitlicher Informationstätigkeit' (with further references).

4. The state of exception as mindset and doctrine

4.1 THE AMBIVALENCE OF THE LIBERAL PARADIGM

Democratic law-rule and the *method Locke* as its corresponding technique of governing entail two projects linked to the liberal paradigm. The first is the ambitious attempt to legally programme state practice with acts of parliament. Accordingly, the legislature has to define what is right and what is wrong, what should be done and what can be expected by dint of general statutes. The statutes, and in the final analysis constitutional law, are charged with regulating all essential aspects of life in society. For this purpose, state authorities are given powers that allow them to intervene in the citizens' spheres of action demarcated by civil and political liberties – or, to put it technically, to coordinate actions and their consequences.

First under the banner of rule of law, then of democracy, self-government through self-legislation was to resolve everyday conflicts once society had entered into the civic state (Kant). Consequently, the techniques of governing that are oriented towards the expedient become in the liberal paradigm – theoretically – less important as rationalist concepts of the state gain acceptance, and always have an interest in effective legal steering and the smooth functioning of the executive within legal barriers. In this way, effectiveness and normativity enter a tension-ridden relationship as standards for the resolution of societal situations of conflict.

Linked to the first, the second project of liberal political technology is to replace all previous references to powers outside the legal realm: from the *arcana dominationis*, the prerogatives of the monarch, martial law and extra-legal emergency law to more recent forms of princely prerogatives, like the executive or administrative discretion widely exempt from judicial control. In theory and practice, law-rule is meant to banish the nightmare of the state of exception. For that purpose different options are available: the state of exception can, first, be made subject to the judiciable discretion of the executive prerogative[1] or, second, vanish from the civil legal order. Third, it can be given the normal features of modern law.[2] The following considerations focus upon these three options.

Against the backdrop of the opposition between the ordinary (rule, normalcy, regular law) and the extraordinary (exception, emergency, extreme case) and conceptionalized as an alternative to monarchist absolutism, the form of the rule of law and its other – war and siege, the arbitrary use of power, civil rebellion, etc. – takes legal shape. Martial law, the legal regime of the state of siege and emergency powers of any kind show themselves for the first time as a variety of the law-oriented – either illegal, extra-legal or legally regulated – exceptional situation. In accordance with the norms and standards of law-rule, which establish the criteria for assessing the handling of everyday 'normal' conflicts, the usurpation of special powers that exceed the legal framework and their exercise can be recognized and criticized. Such criticism sharpens awareness of the dangers of the exceptional. Whether criticism can also tame its mythical attraction and block the way for all temptations to turn to exceptional measures in times of crisis is a quite different matter. The thorough success of the liberal paradigm is rendered doubtful, as will be shown, by its ambivalence towards phenomena of the extraordinary.

This ambivalence vis-à-vis situations of crisis rests on liberal regulatory rationalism.[3] Hyped up into the euphoric, it encourages the representatives of the optimistic version of the liberal project to ignore the need for regulating riots, coup attempts, wars or disasters. In this vein, the 1831 Belgian Constitution stated that the constitution could neither completely nor in part be suspended (Article 130);[4] similarly the 1830 French Constitution forbade the monarch to suspend laws or interrupt their enforcement.[5] One may infer from this optimistic point of view that

---

1 According to John Locke's *Two Treatises of Government*, Second Treatise, ch. 14, in case of a state of exception the executive has the discretionary power to act contrary to the law but afterwards has to first acknowledge any illegal action and then take responsibility. These extra-legal powers should not be given the weight of precedents and encourage the expansion of executive powers in normal situations.

2 For a different modelling of emergency powers see Gross and Ní Aoláin, *Law in Times of Crisis*. See also Dyzenhaus, *The Constitution of Law*.

3 Instructive, also for criticism of Schmitt's critique of liberalism, Casson, 'Emergency Judgment'; McCormick, *Carl Schmitt's Critique of Liberalism: Against Politics as Technology*, ch. 3, and Dyzenhaus, *Law as Politics*.

4 The current Belgian Constitution includes a corresponding provision in Art. 108.

5 Schmitt, *Die Diktatur*, 195.

the state of exception does not take place. Or better, it is not allowed to take place under law, because, as the epitome of what cannot be regulated, it resists every attempt at typification and standardization – or would drive a wedge between normalcy and normativity.

In spite or because of the Jacobite trauma and the ubiquitous shying away from the situation of civil war, the state of exception was anathema not only in early constitutionalism. Also at the end of the 19th century – when liberal theories of law-rule repeatedly tried to achieve the impossible, namely to protect civil liberties and at the very same time limit them in emergency situations in favour of the state – and in the following decades, prominent theories of the state kept silent about the state of exception while still implicitly assuming it.[6]

In contrast, realist-rationalist theories of the *Rechtsstaat*, notably Georg Jellinek's general theory of the state, held that

> the law … never has the power to determine the course of national life in times of crisis. In order to gloss over blatant violations of the legal order of the state [*Staatsordnung*], one applied the category of state emergency law [*Staatsnotrecht*] which is only another expression for the dictum that might overrides right [*Macht vor Recht*].[7]

Accordingly, some authors followed the rationalist vision that all aspects of societal life, and hence also all situations of emergency, can be regulated; they therefore embarked on the precarious, if not paradoxical, 'registering' of the state of exception in the constitution.[8] Since the second half of the 19th century and even more so after World War II, in the actual practice of this variant of the liberal project, numerous legal systems tied the state of siege to a formal declaration as well as to time limits and norms that all aim at ending their very own use. This approach achieved perfection in legal positivism. Here '[the state of exception] exists formally as a general norm' as the epitome of the relevant provisions under emergency law provided by a legal order.[9] Contrary to the dictum *necessitas legem non habet* attributed to Gratian, extreme necessity was not meant to remain unregulated and free of any legal constraints.

---

[6] The leading *Staatslexikon* (state encyclopaedia) of the 19th century includes only half a page on the 'state of siege' but not on the *Rechtsstaat*; see von Rotteck and Welcker, *Staats-Lexikon*, 281.

[7] Jellinek, *Allgemeine Staatslehre*, 349.

[8] Boldt, *Rechtsstaat und Ausnahmezustand*, 162.

[9] Ibid., 86 and 166 ff.

While the legal regime of the state of siege can be traced back to a decree of the French Constitutional Assembly of 8 July 1791, constitutional monarchy and the *état de siège fictif* or *politique*, dating back to the restoration period, remained its reference point and model in the 19th century. In principle, this applies also to Article 68 of the 1871 German Imperial Constitution. This gave the Emperor the power to declare a state of war for those parts of the Federal territory where public security was under threat. While of war indicates that the state of exception has a military pedigree and dates back for quite some time, the protection of public security points to a modern trajectory.

Only at the end of the 19th century and increasingly after World War I did a threefold change occur: first, a semantic shift from the state of siege to the internal and external state of exception accompanied the transition from constitutional monarchy to constitutional democracy. Second, emergency law changed its strategic orientation. No longer did the supposed 'lessons of the French Revolution' (actually the Jacobite trauma) dictate its primary aim, namely the prevention of feared leftist coups. The provisions functioned rather as an apparatus for averting political dangers, and were meant to maintain or restore constitutional conditions. After all, the constitutionalized emergency legislation that combated political and economic crises was characterized by certain formal requirements: formal declaration, temporary application, reference to a system of powers under the rule of law and its aim of re-establishing normal constitutional conditions.

These regimes under emergency law suggest that liberalism made its peace with the state of exception and apparently succeeded in resolving the paradox of regulating the unthinkable and of standardizing what resists standardization. Once one takes a closer look at the executive-professional and intellectual romantic relationships with the state of exception, this peace reveals itself as a very volatile truce.

4.2 APOCALYPSE AND THE POLITICS OF FEAR: ABOUT SCHMITT

The state of exception as executive project, scientific enthralment and worst-case scenario regularly points to intense fears and threat perceptions, which cannot be neutralized by law-rule and still fuel both theoretical-dogmatic fantasies as well as state practice utilizing the repository of arguments prevalent in an emergency mindset. The following focuses only on those preferences for the state of exception caused by fear.

Incumbents of executive positions, primarily those responsible for internal security, tend to routinize this preference and often argue against supposedly existing exceptional situations of danger. Since internal and external threats to society potentially jeopardize their reputation as competent office-holders and thus their chance of re-election, they need to be wary of being misperceived and ill-prepared. To counter such criticism, they routinely anticipate and take precautions for extreme cases. A kind of office preservation and legitimation reflex causes them to invoke the exceptional situation, when, in the face of supposed or actual new threats, they claim emergency powers to initiate exceptional countermeasures.

While governmental threat scenarios lack the element of sensationalism, it may well create a stir when political theorists and legal scholars, whose professional socialization and dealing with doctrinal law production implies some distance from everyday politics and passions, succumb to the fascination of the exceptional. However, it would be historically questionable and actually mistaken to accuse political theory and legal scholarship in general, or only their conservative proponents, of cultivating a focus on the state of exception, and hence a preference for the extraordinary, or of showing symptoms of disenchantment with the normal everyday of democracy and law-rule. Nevertheless, there is historical and current evidence that more than a few legal scholars are tempted to perceive the world as revolving around the state of exception and to reserve regular law for issues of lesser importance. This might be caused by fears triggered by a feeling of homelessness in secularized systems,[10] societal crises or confrontation with alien phenomena.[11]

Carl Schmitt's Apocalyptic Scenario

Certainly, one of the most prominent inhabitants of this island of fears is Carl Schmitt. Now, it would be quite absurd to reduce Schmitt's substantial work to his mental state. His apocalyptic *Weltangst* is therefore utilized here as only one possible hermeneutic lens to shed light on the core elements of his theory of the political and law: namely, the state of exception and sovereignty, both inherently linked to *The Concept of the Political*. The following considerations are guided by the thesis that

---

[10] This applies especially to Carl Schmitt and his current-day proponents as will be shown below.

[11] Isensee, 'Normalfall oder Grenzfall als Ausgangspunkt rechtsphilosophischer Konstruktion?', refers among others to waves of secularization, the import of foreign religions (Islam), crises and chaos.

Schmitt mystifies the exception in the face of what he regards as the apocalypse in order to play the corresponding concepts of the political and the sovereign decision off against the (liberal) law as well as its normativity.

Theoretical prompters for his fears were primarily Thomas Hobbes and the Catholic counter-revolutionaries of the 19th century. In his one-sided (mis)reading, Schmitt presents Hobbes as a theorist of state security.[12] As a matter of fact, Hobbes, who was a major influence on Schmitt, wrote shortly before his death: 'I was born as the twin brother to fear.'[13]

Thomas Hobbes' theory of the state was indeed profoundly, although not exclusively, shaped by the fear of an unnatural, violent death. In the anarchical state of nature, this fear is generated by the right of everyone to everything that entails an excessive tendency to drift towards a war of all against all, given the wolfish human nature. The 17th century's seemingly endless chain of revolts, rebellions, civil and religious wars was experienced by Hobbes as a quasi state of nature, and perceived by him as a ubiquitous threat caused by competition, mistrust, envy and lust for power and glory – a scenario reflected in his political writings.[14] According to his own statements, Thomas Hobbes engaged with his dramatic and rapidly changing environment not without fear but in a productive, even revolutionary manner[15] by risking a transition from an absolutist to a post-absolutist period via a contractualist justification of abstract sovereignty.

In contrast to Hobbes, the 19th century Catholic counter-revolutionaries, whose political theology and approval of dictatorship Schmitt adopted without hesitation, reacted to the revolutionary era from the beginning to the middle of the century with fear of the apocalypse. Schmitt cited his philosophical favourite, Donoso Cortés, with the apocalyptic vision of a godforsaken society, after secularization, Enlightenment and revolutions:

> [H]umanity reels blindly through a labyrinth that we call history, whose entry, exit, and shape nobody knows; humanity is a boat aimlessly tossed about on the sea and manned by a mutinous, vulgar, forcibly recruited crew that howls

---

12 A differentiated reading of Hobbes is proposed by Loughlin, *The Foundations of Public Law* and Skinner, *Hobbes and Republican Liberty*.

13 Hobbes, *Thomae Hobbesii Malmesburiensis Vita*, 2. Cf. Ginzburg, 'Welt der Leviathane'.

14 Thomas Hobbes, *Leviathan*, chs. 10 and 13.

15 Schmitt's account makes a comprehensive effort to avoid portraying Hobbes as a revolutionary. He wrongly turns him into a proponent of his decisionism and his doctrine of sovereignty, developed in his *Political Theology*.

> and dances until God's rage pushes the rebellious rabble into the sea so that quiet can prevail once more.[16]

To characterize the political and intellectual situation of his time, Schmitt added in 1922 a brief update for the 20th century:

> But the typical picture is a different one: the bloody decisive battle that has flared up today between Catholicism and atheist socialism.[17]

This is only one aspect[18] of the frightening scenario drawn by Schmitt. It shaped his thought, gave him the impression that the world was on the brink of the abyss and robbed him of the confidence that the Weimar Republic was a new order he could trust.[19] Only the National Socialists seemed to him authoritarian and unscrupulous enough to convince him of their capability to establish order.[20] Hobbes, who had to go to exile because of his works, in his theory dared to perform a balancing act between tradition and modernity and moved from personal sovereignty to abstract sovereignty. By contrast, Schmitt's political theory took a trajectory from the authoritarian German Empire to the totalitarian *Führerstaat*; bridging the fragile democratic-republican interregnum of Weimar was not really a risk.

For Schmitt, the apocalyptist, the world became accessible through his fears,[21] as shown by his critique of political romanticism (actually: of liberalism again). He repeatedly articulated his fear that the strong state was doomed to be destroyed by neutralization, de-politicization and secularization. And anxiety is also manifest in his concept of a state of nature (which he cultivated emphatically), entered into by nation-states since the crisis of religious civil wars, and provoking the danger that

---

16 Cortés, *Obras I*, 192, and id., *Obras IV*, 102.

17 Quoted by Schmitt, *Political Theology*, 59. See, by way of comparison, Schmitt, *Political Theology II*.

18 In *The Concept of the Political*, he addresses another facet of the scenario: the angst caused by the 'neutralization' of the state, which ends in a 'religion of technology' (pp. 80–96).

19 Also instructive is Noack, *Carl Schmitt*; Laak, *Gespräche in der Sicherheit des Schweigens* and Groh, *Arbeit an der Heillosigkeit der Welt*.

20 A similar assessment of Schmitt can be found in Philipp Reemtsma, *Vertrauen und Gewalt: Versuch über eine besondere Konstellation der Moderne* (Hamburg: Hamburger Edition, 2008), 436.

21 For the psychology of apocalyptic views, see Körtner, *The End of the World*; Vondung, *Die Apokalypse in Deutschland*. Cf. also Schumacher, *Die Angst vor dem Chaos*.

> every people will perish without mercy, which does not prove able to cope with its concrete situation and lets itself be persuaded, if only for a moment, to forget its most natural, self-evident and first right to a free, independent, united and undivided existence.[22]

The triad of state of exception, sovereignty and decision served Schmitt as a magic formula to placate his *Weltangst* and to get rid of the evil of the liberal-democratic interregnum between the Empire and the *Führerstaat*, as well as being a vehicle for leaving the realm of law for the realm of politics without legal constraints.

The Primacy of the Exception

How little Schmitt was able to accept a dramatically changing, socio-political reality and how much he perceived these transformations as anarchy and chaos becomes obvious in his *Political Theology*, which offers a good entry point into his thought. Due to his longing for order, aggravated by fear, he mystified the empty place of the sovereign, the ultimate decision as a *creatio ex nihilo* and the state of exception as a 'miracle' to deny the despised modern age any legitimacy.[23] Thus he countered the scares of autonomy (*Schrecken der Autonomie*)[24] with his imagination of (rather mythical) concrete orders. In the abnormality of the big crisis, he enthroned the acting, order-creating sovereign, equipped with absolute power, as saviour and ultimate executive decision-making authority, when it comes to the realization of the law.

Driven by a vicious, in places paranoid, anti-Semitism[25] and guided by his militant anti-democratic mindset, Carl Schmitt crusaded passionately against all consequences of revolution and secularization – liberalism, law-rule, parliamentarianism, socialism, 'anti-Roman attitudes', the 'age of bourgeois security', etc. With this campaign, Schmitt made his name as the main inspirator of preferences for the state of exception grounded

---

22 Schmitt, 'Völkerrechtliche Probleme im Rheingebiet', 108.

23 Against this, Blumenberg, *The Legitimacy of the Modern Age*.

24 Habermas, 'Die Schrecken der Autonomie'; id., 'Sovereignty and Führerdemokratie', *The Times Literary Supplement* (26 September 1986). See also McCormick, *Carl Schmitt's Critique of Liberalism*, 122–56; Dyzenhaus, *Law as Politics*.

25 Schmitt's anti-Semitism can be traced from his diaries to the 1934 '*Judenveranstaltung*' organized by him. See Reemtsma, *Vertrauen und Gewalt*, 396, for an instructive assessment of anti-Semitism: 'The Anti-Semitism is the offer of a collective psychosis, which can spare to develop an individual one.'

on a normatively unleashed political technology. Still, there are precursors to his doctrine of the priority of the exception.[26] And the state technology informed by this priority was certainly so much the rule before the advent of law-rule theories that both the concept and idea of such exceptional situations were lacking. But Schmitt only enters the history of state theory as spokesman of the exceptional case via his 'small study' about *Political Theology*, consisting of *Four Chapters on the Concept of Sovereignty.*[27] In his work *The Concept of the Political*,[28] he reveals the explosive political implications of his theory of the state of exception, with the emphasis on the existential 'decision about war and enemy'.[29]

In a key passage of his *Political Theology*, which from time to time cannot avoid coming close to pompous kitsch, Schmitt displays his unconditional preference for the exceptional:

> Precisely a philosophy of concrete life must not withdraw from the exception and the extreme case, but must be interested in it to the highest degree. The exception can be more important to it than the rule, not because of a romantic irony for the paradox, but because the seriousness of an insight goes deeper than the clear generalization inferred from what ordinarily repeats itself. The exception is more interesting than the rule. The rule proves nothing; the exception proves everything: It confirms not only the rule but also its existence, which derives only from the exception. In the exception the power

---

[26] Vico, *De antiquissima Italorum Sapientia ex linguae Latinae originibus eruenda*; id. (in English), *On the Most Ancient Wisdom of the Italians*, ch. II: 'Similarly, in jurisprudence it is not the jurist who because of his strong memory masters "thetic" or positive law, the highest and most general law, who is well thought of, it is, rather, the jurist who can see with acute judgment the distinctive characteristics in his cases, the circumstances through which they deserve the application of equity, or the exceptions through which they escape from the general law.'

[27] Schmitt had already explored their patterns of argument – norm vs decision and normalcy vs exception – in his studies *Gesetz und Urteil* and *Die Diktatur*.

[28] Carl Schmitt, *The Concept of the Political*, based on the text of 1932.

[29] Impressive analyses of Schmitt's work and impact can be found in Maus, *Bürgerliche Rechtstheorie und Faschismus*; Hofmann, *Legitimität gegen Legalität*; Habermas, 'Die Schrecken der Autonomie'; Preuß, 'Zum Begriff des Politischen bei Carl Schmitt'; Dyzenhaus, *Legality and Legitimacy*, ch. 2, and McCormick, *Carl Schmitt's Critique of Liberalism*.

> of real life breaks through the crust of a mechanism that has become torpid by repetition.[30]

As the staccato of Schmitt's sermon working itself up to 'the power of real life' shows, his romance – actually his state-theoretical marriage – with the exception is fed not only by an apocalyptic worldview but also by the myth of vitality he juxtaposes with the modern era he despises, its weakly *Rechtsstaat* and its meekly parliamentary democracy. Thus, Schmitt's criticism of the modern era and liberalism that accompanies his critique of law is mainly ignited by the fact that the secularization of the foundations of political legitimacy evades the big decision between 'god' and 'world' and in all seriousness leaves fundamental conflicts to public discourse and parliament. According to Schmitt, it is only from the viewpoint of the extreme case of civil war, i.e. the existential confrontation with the enemy, that political everyday conflicts can be grasped properly and be suspended by an ultimate decision but not by debate. The exceptional situation requires a decision, and this in turn 'generates' a sovereign decision-maker, who situates himself between chaos and legal order with the help of this very decision concerning the exceptional situation:

> Because the state of exception is always something different from anarchy and chaos, there exists in a juridical sense always an order, albeit not a legal order. [...] The decision liberates itself from any normative constraint and becomes absolute in the most genuine sense. In the exceptional case the state suspends the law owing to its right to self-preservation.[31]

Since the normatively empty state realizes law[32] according to its reasons[33] and in a sovereign manner, it stands at the same time outside and within the law.

In *Political Theology*, Schmitt derives the primacy of the exception from an unnamed 'protestant theologian'. This anonymous author is none

---

[30] Schmitt, *Political Theology*, 15. The quote implies that the *Political Theology* would more precisely be subtitled *Four Chapters on the Concept of the State of Exception*.

[31] Ibid., 18 ff.

[32] For Schmitt's theory of the realization of law, see Hofmann, *Legitimität gegen Legalität*, 41 ff.

[33] '[T]he often misinterpreted raison d'état ... does not rest in substantial norms, but in the efficiency with which it [the state] creates a situation, in which norms may at all have validity, because the state puts an end to the cause of all disorder and civil wars, the struggle for what is normatively right.' Schmitt, 'Die Wendung zum totalen Staat'; cf. Rüthers, *Die unbegrenzte Auslegung*, 99 ff.

other than Søren Kierkegaard.[34] Schmitt often uses other authors to present his critique of the modern era. Such a strategy is quite in accordance with his style of argumentation. It is, however, remarkable that he does not name Kierkegaard explicitly, in stark contrast to other authors he relies upon, such as for instance Bonald, de Maistre and Donoso Cortés. This fact tempts one to assume not only that he wanted to provide his decisionism with theological depth[35] but also that he wanted to avoid naming the non-Catholic philosopher of anxiety[36] in order to stop any conclusions being drawn about his own anxious mental state. Schmitt quotes Kierkegaard as follows:

> The exception explains the general and itself. And if one wants to study the general correctly, one only needs to look around for a true exception. [...] Endless talk about the general becomes boring; there are exceptions. If they cannot be explained, then the general also cannot be explained. The difficulty is usually not noticed because the general is not thought about with passion but with a comfortable superficiality. The exception, on the other hand, thinks the general with intense passion.[37]

On the quiet, Schmitt swaps Kierkegaard's 'justified' with the 'actual' exception celebrated by him[38] and ignores the latter's significant intermediate step, which neutralizes every apocalyptic effect:

> The justified exception is reconciled in the general. ... [T]he unjustified exception is exactly recognizable in that it wants to circumvent the general.[39]

It needs to be added that according to Kierkegaard the general also connotes the ethically right and divine.

Tired of the general, Schmitt as political romanticist celebrates[40] and ontologizes the very exception that 'wants to avoid the general'. He ascribes to the exception the power of 'thinking with intense passion' – despite the fact that it is not really the exception but its theoretical creator who does the thinking and aims at the normal case from the vantage point of the exceptional case. If one reads the above quote from *Political*

---

34 Kierkegaard, 'Repetition'.

35 Cf. Hofmann, 'Souverän ist, wer über den Ausnahmezustand entscheidet', 173.

36 Kierkegaard, *Concept of Anxiety*; id., *Fear and Trembling*.

37 Schmitt, *Political Theology*, 15.

38 Hofmann, 'Souverän ist, wer über den Ausnahmezustand entscheidet', 173.

39 Kierkegaard, 'Repetition', 79 ff.

40 McCormick, 'Irrational Choice and Mortal Combat as Political Destiny'.

Theology against the backdrop of Schmitt's scenario of an ultimate cultural struggle between Catholicism and atheist socialism, then it becomes readily apparent why the October Revolution, the Soviet Republics, revolts, general strikes and other upheavals of the early Weimar Republic did not calm the fears of the cultural- and national-conservative existentialist. Like Thomas Hobbes, Carl Schmitt turns out to be the twin brother of fear, although with a delay of more than a quarter of a millennium. This makes itself felt in Schmitt's criticism of parliamentary debates as useless and powerless 'permanent talk of the general'.[41] And the sovereign decision about the state of exception, the existential distinction between friend and enemy as well as the dictatorship as a concrete framework establishing order serve him as stable, calming fixed points to end the disintegration of the mortal god caused by pluralism and proportional representation.[42]

In Schmitt's theory of the state of exception, the 'vital intensity' turns out to be the rather dangerous 'supplement'[43] of the decision. It assists the decision. It needs to accompany and carry the decision. Without this passion, romanticized by Schmitt, the exception lacks the power to push the rule aside. However, those who share neither such energetic passion nor the dark worldview of the thinker of a Catholic counter-revolution can effortlessly keep their distance from the latter's sentimental-apocalyptic romanticization of the exceptional and, if required, they may also plausibly justify the primacy of the rule. Labelled with contempt by Schmitt as what repeats itself on an average level and 'talk about the general', the exception still borrows its dark glamour from the rule. The state of exception as a 'societal institution … is defined only in relation to what it is not, to its other'.[44] Without the rule the exception does not attract attention. It is only in contrast to the regular case that the contours and shape of the exceptional become apparent. This is proven by regimes that lack rules. Only from outside the safety of a normal situation and its normativity do they reveal themselves as regimes of the state of exception.

Like no other political theorist of the 19th century or of his own time, Carl Schmitt was obsessed with the exception. This obsession led him to

---

[41] This wording not only indicates the longing for an ultimate decision, but also Schmitt's anti-parliamentarianism and his contempt for the bourgeois *Rechtsstaat*.

[42] For Schmitt's anti-parliamentarianism and anti-pluralism, see Schneider, *Ausnahmezustand und Norm*, 119 and 139 ff.

[43] Derrida, *Of Grammatology*.

[44] Adorno, *Aesthetic Theory*, 3.

overlook that John Locke, one of the fathers of a 'government of laws and not of men' and often criticized by him, not only argued in the 'Second Treatise' that law gives authority but, in contrast to Schmitt's arch-opponent Kelsen, allowed the prerogative[45] of the executive entry into the 'well-framed government', where it has ever since haunted liberal theories of state and law. But if the exception stands alone and unconfined at the centre of academic interest, the political is given priority over the law. For a theorist of the political – its concept, theology and legitimacy – the law is at best of secondary importance.

The Aesthetics and Politics of Privileging the State of Exception

Other readings offer an explanation for why the state of exception became Schmitt's second nature, became a habit[46] of his apocalyptic thinking. The legal scholar Josef Isensee recognizes in this habit the attraction of 'belles-lettres'[47] for those who (have to) deal professionally with the dry prose of constitutional law. According to Isensee, Schmitt realizes his aesthetic affinities in his thinking on exceptions:

> The aesthete, however, feels attracted by the orgiastic cult of the exception and the intellectual play with fire. Carl Schmitt himself denies that a 'romantic irony for the paradox' guides him. But the exception, as he portrays it, is more interesting than the regular case, since in it the power of real life breaks through the hard shell of a mechanics paralysed by repetition.[48]

Isensee adds:

> A similar underlying trend runs through belles-lettres, which rather turns toward the borderline case than normalcy; which attaches more significance to a life on a knife's edge than to a life in bourgeois safety and which sees sin as more exciting than unchallenged virtue; which sees an attractive subject in illness rather than in chubby-cheeked health.[49]

The escape into the aesthetics of belles-lettres can, however, also be interpreted in a less superficial way: namely as an attempt by a legal

---

45 For a detailed account, see Casson, 'Emergency Judgment', 948–9, 953: 'Schmitt's critique [of Locke's conception of constitutional government – G.F.] is simply off the mark.' See also Pasquale Pasquino, 'Locke on King's Prerogative'.

46 As Bloch argued in *Natural Law and Human Dignity*.

47 Isensee, 'Normalfall oder Grenzfall als Ausgangspunkt rechtsphilosophischer Konstruktion?', 67.

48 Ibid., 67 with reference to Schmitt, *Political Theology*, 15.

49 Ibid.

scholar to obtain the legitimacy of an artist by his method of privileging the exception to dispense himself from the cold analysis of the legal order and to free himself from the 'tyranny' of legal normalcy – the law denounced as 'abstract', 'liberal', 'Jewish', 'without foundation' – and the 'struggle for law'.[50] This heroic-aesthetic gesture is based on the assertion of a rigid and static model of the legal order. Schmitt in fact sees law as a 'homogeneous medium'[51] and therefore fails to recognize, first, that this order is constructed[52] and, second, that its rules are continuously amended in a dynamic process of ever shorter intervals.[53] His lack of understanding or his misunderstanding of legal normalcy,[54] which suggests his escape into the world of the exceptional, could be caused by a deep unease about modern, permanently amended law and the accompanying struggles that are, after all, a permanent feature of pluralist societies. Such struggle was for him palpable after World War I and in the Weimar Republic. Herein, he thought, lay the 'cause of all disorder and civil wars'.[55]

His *Political Theology* and especially his decision about the state of exception, which comes like the big bang out of nowhere, out of the unoccupied place of sovereignty, therefore show the features of what is in fact a 'nostalgic project'[56] – namely an escape from democratic self-government to be achieved by immanent means[57] in a pluralistically polarized society. This escape leads Schmitt into the past of a transcendentally legitimized, unitary order of state and society.

Such a reading finds support in the fact that Carl Schmitt sees himself as the heir of the Catholic counter-revolutionaries. With his criticism of the 'discussing class', he adopts at the same time the *Weltangst* that the possibility of the transcendental legitimation of rule was lost with the guillotining of monarchs and that the principle of a superior legitimacy

---

[50] Von Ihering, *The Struggle for Law*.

[51] Schmitt, *Political Theology*, 13; id., *Der Hüter der Verfassung*, 75 ff.

[52] For the construction of normalcy, see Denninger, 'Normalfall oder Grenzfall als Ausgangspunkt rechtsphilosophischer Konstruktion', 5.

[53] Augsberg, 'Denken vom Ausnahmezustand her', 35 ff. with further references.

[54] Schmitt, 'Staatsethik und pluralistischer Staat', 141: 'There is no plurality of normal situations.'

[55] Schmitt, 'Die Wendung zum totalen Staat'.

[56] According to Augsberg, 'Denken vom Ausnahmezustand her', 36, it is characterized by the fact that the reference to the notion of the exception rests on the assumption of a correlated, fixed and homogeneous normalcy.

[57] Rödel et al., *Die demokratische Frage*, especially 128 ff.

had become obsolete as well. Unable to engage with notions of self-government, discursive legitimacy and the *method Locke*, Schmitt replaced theocracy and monarchy, in the spirit of the reactionaries de Maistre, Bonald and Cortés, with 'pure decision not based on reason and discussion and not justifying itself'[58] via his rearranged concepts of constitutional law. In this way, the Schmittian phantasmagoria of the exceptional turns out to be a (futile) attempt to combat fear and a vehicle for introducing a superior legitimacy,[59] allowing him – in contrast to the Catholic counter-revolutionaries, whose reference point was a theocracy – to hand over the democratic republic he despised to a concrete dictatorship: initially to a temporary dictatorship of the *Reichspräsident* based on Article 48 Weimar Constitution and later to a sovereign *Führerdiktatur*.

Schmitt sacrificed parliamentary democracy and law-rule on the altar of non-bourgeois security through his very own determination. His comment on Adolf Hitler's speech at the 1933 German Jurists' Forum (*Deutscher Juristentag*) – 'The *Führer* protects the law from the worst abuse, when by virtue of his *Führertum* he immediately creates law, as supreme master of justice, in the moment of danger.'[60] – therefore reads like a logical continuation of his theory of the state of exception: combining his critique of parliamentarianism with his apology for dictatorship.[61] With the help of his sovereign decision, the *Führer* ultimately *realizes* what he perceives as right.

There are no good reasons to follow Carl Schmitt into the darkroom of his fears and the supposedly ideal world of the past or to celebrate his *Political Theology*, let alone his preference for the state of exception.[62]

---

58 Schmitt, *Political Theology*, 66. For criticism, see Rödel et al., *Die demokratische Frage*, 128 ff. See also McCormick, 'Irrational Choice and Mortal Combat as Political Destiny'.

59 Schmitt, *Legality and Legitimacy*.

60 Schmitt, 'Der Führer schützt das Recht'. Cf. also id., *Staat, Bewegung, Volk*.

61 Concerning the controversy about the continuity or discontinuity in Schmitt's work, I follow those authors who do not see a turn between Schmitt's early works and his *Führerschriften*, e.g. Dyzenhaus, *Legality and Legitimacy*; Scheuerman, 'Legal Indeterminacy and the Origins of Nazi Legal Thought', 571 ff.

62 See Mouffe, *On the Political*. See in contrast the sober point made by Preuß: 'One does not become sovereign by having absolute and undivided power over others and also not by, as Carl Schmitt stated, by having the ability to decide about the exception, or in short: to disregard valid law. *Sovereign is rather he who possesses the authority to create sovereign right unilaterally.*'

4.3 FROM SCHMITT TOWARDS AGAMBEN: THE BARE STATE OF EXCEPTION

Theories that conceptualize normalcy through the lens of the extraordinary invariably liberate the exercise of power from legal considerations and constraints. They gear it towards the effective implementation of the reason of state and therefore stand in intellectual and operational proximity to Machiavelli's logic. In the tradition of constitutional theory, founded by Schmitt's *Political Theology* and his *Concept of the Political*, the philosopher Giorgio Agamben has recently gained prominence. The affinities and differences between his and Schmitt's work shall be briefly examined in the following.

A Philosophy of Strong Words

Giorgio Agamben follows Schmitt in the sense of moving from a philosophy in the strong sense of the word to a philosophy of strong words. He replaces Schmitt's apocalyptic vision with a negative utopia: for Agamben, the 'matrix' of Schmitt's approach reveals itself in the archetypical camps of the 20th century.[63] Methodologically, he too searches for the truth via the extreme. Substantively, he continues Schmitt's thinking about sovereignty and extreme critique of the modern era in *Homo sacer* and *State of Exception*.

Furthermore, Agamben also follows the concept of the state of exception à la Schmitt,[64] who abstracts the latter from states of siege, civil wars, emergency degrees as well as coups, and turns it into a general term, before in 1957 abandoning it somewhat bashfully as 'something old-fashioned' in the aftermath of the permanent state of exception during the time of Nazi terror.[65] Similar to Schmitt, Agamben's theory follows empirically historical models of classical antiquity and the classical, military and police state of siege in the 19th century, updated with, for instance, experiences of the Weimar emergency decree dictatorship.

('Souveränität – Zwischenbemerkungen zu einem Schlüsselbegriff des Politischen', 314; emphasis added).

[63] Agamben, *Homo Sacer*, and id., *State of Exception*.

[64] For this and the following, see Schmitt, *Political Theology*, 11 ff.; id., *Die Diktatur*, in particular pp. 95 ff., 127 ff., 168 ff., and id., *The Concept of the Political*.

[65] Stated by Schmitt in a subsequent comment on his study 'Die staatsrechtliche Bedeutung der Notverordnung', 261.

Agamben also moves the focus of attention to both the suspension of the constitution by the sovereign and the legal relationship vis-à-vis the enemy. The sovereign, who according to Schmitt 'need not be based on law',[66] stands according to Agamben outside the law. Consequently, the exceptional situation he outlines does not entail any powers derived from law-rule but only the sovereign decision. Both oppose a possible standardization of the state of exception by conceptualizing it as the 'not subsumable' (Schmitt), which eludes every factual description. While Schmitt claimed later, not without contradicting the 'general concept' of the state of exception he had earlier introduced, that it eludes 'general drafting', for Agamben (and his mentor) the state of exception reveals itself, somewhat mystically, as 'a specifically juristic element – the decision in absolute purity'.[67]

Whereas Schmitt conceptualizes the state of exception as the coronation hall of the sovereign, Agamben translates it into the dark phantasmagoria of the 'bare life that cannot be sacrificed yet may still be killed'.[68] Regarding the suspension of the legal order in the case of a totalizing exception, he thereby follows Schmitt's theory of sovereignty. However, since Agamben shares neither Schmitt's anti-Semitism nor his contempt for the *Rechtsstaat*, he can ignore the fact that Schmitt stylized his theory as the radical opposition to the law-rule he equated with legal positivism and a supposed 'Jewish liberalism'.

Following Walter Benjamin, Agamben locates the state of exception in the gloomy realm of purpose-free power, in the 'emptiness of law', in an 'anomic space', a 'space without law' – a morgue, so to say.[69] In the terminology of Walter Benjamin, this state of exception is determined not by the violence or power that generates or maintains law, but by a fearsome divine power. Beyond the liberal paradigm and the conservative tradition, Agamben undertakes a radical disjunction of law-rule, on the one hand, and the state of exception, on the other hand. With a rather vague metaphor, he describes the latter as 'a threshold at which logic and praxis blur with each other and a pure violence without *logos* claims to realize an enunciation without any real reference'.[70]

---

[66] Schmitt, *Political Theology*, 13.
[67] Schmitt, *Political Theology*, 13.
[68] For a detailed account, Agamben, *Homo Sacer* and id., *State of Exception*.
[69] Agamben, *State of Exception*, 6, 39, 51, and Walter Benjamin, 'Critique of Violence'.
[70] Agamben, *State of Exception*, 40.

For him, one paradox of the state of exception consists in the fact that 'it is impossible to distinguish transgression of the law from execution of the law, so that what violates a rule and what conforms to it coincide without any remainder'.[71] In contrast to Schmitt, who locates the state of exception somehow 'in-between', between law and chaos, Agamben, in, one might say, rather an agreeable move, insists on an enigmatic neither-nor of the totally different: he characterizes the specificity of the situation created by the state of exception as determined neither as a factual nor as a legal situation. Ultimately, Agamben seems, however, also to settle for the vague both-and of fact and norm:

> The state of exception is the device that must ultimately articulate and hold together the two aspects of the juridical-political machine by instituting a threshold of undecidability between anomie and *nomos*, between life and law, between *auctoritas* and *potestas*.[72]

The Mystery of the Exceptional

Agamben shares Schmitt's fascination with the extraordinary and his preference for the exception, which he intends to justify philosophically and not under constitutional law – even though on a rather soft foundation. Without hesitation, he shares Schmitt's misunderstanding that the merely 'suspended' legal order can be reinstated after the suspension is revoked. In the state of exception, he argues, only 'the application of law' is suspended: 'in order to apply a norm it is ultimately necessary to suspend its application', whereas 'the law as such remains in force'.[73] In this way, he neglects two very essential aspects. On the one hand, a legal order, once suspended, is unable to generate the same level of trust in its stability in case a future crisis arises. After all, it runs the risk of enjoying the reputation of a good-till-cancelled normalcy. On the other hand, the suspension also changes the foundation of its *validity*, when the decision-maker responsible for the state of exception revokes the suspension:

> The re-established or restructured order shows possibly strong similarities, potentially even a complete substantive congruence, with the suspended legal order. However, it possesses obviously a different reason of validity and can therefore not simply be celebrated as a mere re-awakening. If the decision that brings about and ends the state of exception emerges ex nihilo, then the same

---

[71] Agamben, *Homo Sacer*, 57.

[72] Agamben, *State of Exception*, 86; for the localization in the in-between, cf. also id., *Homo Sacer*, 28.

[73] Agamben, *State of Exception*, 40, 59, 62 ff. (emphasis in the original).

> needs to apply to the allegedly only re-established order. The old order may have been revived […]. But what exists there is merely a zombie.[74]

Both Agamben and Schmitt oppose projects to situate and regulate the state of exception within the confines of law-rule. They argue such a positivist endeavour would get hopelessly caught up in the paradox of regulating what cannot be regulated and would therefore be bound to fail. In this way, they remain true to their heroic philosophy, which mystifies the exceptional, while Schmitt also maintains his contempt for democratic legality. However, both miss the secular trend to juridify the extreme case in the 20th century. And concerning the concomitant, specific ambivalence of a 'normalization of the state of exception', they have nothing to tell us.[75]

4.4 SEARCH MOVEMENTS: THE REPRESSED STATE OF EXCEPTION

After the moral-political bankruptcy of the Schmittian theory of the state, constitutional theories of law-rule – even conservative ones[76] – could not be expected to emulate the public enemy of the *Rechtsstaat's* unrestrained preference for the state of exception in the historical context of a new German democracy in its infancy. Nevertheless, leaving aside concerns for political correctness and ethics, is it not necessary to ponder the exceptional to defend a legal order in the case of emergency and to gear its political technology towards the unthinkable?

The fact is that history offers an array of natural, social and political disasters that stimulate and steer (regulatory) phantasies and methods of political technology: from the destructive force of the 1755 earthquake in Lisbon to the devastating occurrences of the plague, fires, floods, bloody

---

[74] Augsberg, 'Denken vom Ausnahmezustand her', 29. Similarly, Rossiter, *Constitutional Dictatorship*, 295: 'No constitutional government ever passed through a period in which emergency powers were used without undergoing some degree of permanent alteration, always in the direction of an aggrandizement of the power of the state.'

[75] See Chapters 5–7 for a detailed account. Cf. Frankenberg, 'Kritik des Bekämpfungsrechts', 374, and Beck, *Risk Society*, 31: 'The risk society is a catastrophic society, in which the state of exception threatens to become the normal state.' For the normalization of exceptional emergency powers through case law in the USA, see Rossiter, *Constitutional Dictatorship* and Casson, 'Emergency Judgment', at 965.

[76] Forsthoff, 'Der introvertierte Rechtsstaat und seine Verortung', 397.

revolts, assassinations, revolutions and the murderous slaughter of two world wars.[77] Societies, regions, states and their security apparatus have always had to adapt to these security upheavals engraved in collective memory.

It seems therefore perhaps optimistic, yet not per se implausible, to integrate the exceptional into the legal order by dint of a general clause or to dissect the monumental aspect of a potential emergency into the prism of different exceptions and to standardize them according to the relevant provisions about both the distribution of powers and respective procedures. Against the backdrop of such approaches, one can outline attempts at the boundaries of law-rule that lead to a situational and punctual marking of exceptional situations and now and then document in the legal debate an 'intellectual pleasure in the anticipated state of exception'.[78]

Ernst Forsthoff, on his own admission, like Carl Schmitt himself once under Hitler's spell,[79] expressed this sentiment rather carefully:

> Historical experience teaches that the normal state has its time, legal experience seems to suggest that one should consider the normal state not without the exceptional case. The Federal Republic has of course a specific normal state but also a specific exceptional state, which can be outlined and described via the characteristics of the normal state.[80]

He was ambivalent about the emergency constitution (*Notstandsgesetze*), especially about Article 87a(4) BL introduced into the Basic Law in spring 1968. As a scarcely topical reminiscence of the 19th century, he was ironic about the power of the Federal Government to 'employ the Armed Forces to support the police and the Federal Border Police in protecting civilian property and in combating organized armed insurgents'. This statement refers vaguely to Forsthoff's never fundamentally revised position dating back to the Weimar Republic that the state

---

[77] Schmitt could at least look back on World War I. Today, the list of destruction needs to include the nuclear bomb and climate catastrophes.

[78] In the US-American context, a number of authors pursue similar arguments to Böckenförde's; see Rossiter, *Constitutional Dictatorship* (see below), and recently Ignatieff, *The Lesser Evil*, and Ackerman, *Before the Next Attack*. For voices from the German context see Di Fabio, 'Sicherheit in Freiheit', 423; Isensee, 'Normalfall oder Grenzfall als Ausgangspunkt rechtsphilosophischer Konstruktion?', 67. Cf. Denninger, 'Normalfall oder Grenzfall als Ausgangspunkt rechtsphilosophischer Konstruktion?'.

[79] Documented especially in Forsthoff, *Der totale Staat*.

[80] Forsthoff, 'Der introvertierte Rechtsstaat und seine Verortung', 397.

guarantees the legal order and therefore stands above the law; utterly in accordance with Schmitt's dictum: 'The existence of the state maintains here an undoubted superiority to the validity of the legal form'.[81]

The constitutional scholar and future judge of the Constitutional Court, Ernst-Wolfgang Böckenförde, approached the state of exception rather more carefully than Carl Schmitt in an essay in honour of the latter's 90th birthday. Even under the shadow of the murderous attacks by the terrorist Red Army Faction (RAF) in the 1970s and 1980s, he could not be tempted to celebrate an exceptional dictatorship. He rather started off his reflections on 'actions of the state in exceptional situations' by expressly dissociating himself from Schmitt's *Political Theology*: 'To maintain the law of the normal situation requires the recognition of the state of exception'.[82] Subsequently, Böckenförde examined the 'supra-legal state of exception' in detail, which had been evoked by analogy to the necessity defence (§ 34 German Criminal Code) not only by representatives of the executive but also by some constitutional scholars to justify anti-terror measures during the first crisis of the German *Rechtsstaat*.[83] While Böckenförde rejected such arguments as 'open general authorizations', the author of the almost simultaneously published 'considerations for the defence of the *Rechtsstaat* in extraordinary situations', adopted a different argument. Like Böckenförde, he led his readers to the 'boundaries of the *Rechtsstaat*';[84] however, in contrast to Böckenförde and in opposition to prevailing opinion, he derived from necessity as justification under criminal law 'the codified confirmation that emergency situations can be resolved by dint of evaluating the respective legally protected interests'. Paradoxically, however, he was nevertheless not prepared to sacrifice the unity of the *Rechtsstaat*.

Although with a different degree of decisiveness, both authors objected to a 'release or superordination of the measures of a state of exception' and denied themselves any preference for the extraordinary. Still, Böckenförde criticized – rather in the vein of Carl Schmitt – the repression of the state of exception and argued for its containment with the help of a provision under constitutional law that was to exceed the

---

81 Forsthoff, 'Der Ausnahmezustand der Länder', 139, and Schmitt, *Political Theology*, 18.

82 Böckenförde, 'Der verdrängte Ausnahmezustand', 1881. Critical of this, Lübbe-Wolff, 'Rechtsstaat und Ausnahmerecht'. Böckenförde replied to this criticism ('Rechtsstaat und Ausnahmerecht') and elaborated his position in even greater detail later ('Ausnahmerecht und demokratischer Rechtsstaat').

83 See Chapter 5 for a detailed account.

84 Meinhard Schröder, 'Staatsrecht an den Grenzen des Rechtsstaates'.

emergency law entailed in the Basic Law. His position is not free of contradictions: on the one hand, it is based on the assumption that the state of exception cannot be anticipated via juridification. On the other hand, this leads also to the claim to provide those provisions that are feasible within the framework of a constitutional state and *Rechtsstaat*. Against the backdrop of Schmitt's 'sovereignty epiphany'[85] and the regulatory deficit of the Basic Law, Böckenförde designed the 'model structure' of a positive-legal exceptional rule.[86]

In the aftermath of 9/11, the core substance of Böckenförde's project was taken up in other epistemic communities (less spellbound by Schmitt than the German), notably by US scholar Bruce Ackerman, a constitutional scholar of equal stature. Interestingly enough, very much like Böckenförde, he wants to prepare for the next terrorist attack, while preserving civil liberties. Both undertake to account for such extraordinary situations by extending executive powers and the danger of executive overreach.[87] Böckenförde offers a 'model structure' characterized by (a) the distinction between normal and exceptional state, (b) the constraint of emergency powers to purpose-dependent, proportional measures, which (c) suspend regular law only temporarily and are (d) always geared towards restoring the normal state of affairs. Ackerman wants to prevent overreaction and poor judgement (ostrich behaviour) in times of crisis (caused by terrorism) and therefore recommends a 'supermajoritarian escalator' through a 'framework statute' which controls the renewal and extension of presidential powers by requiring increasing numbers of congressional votes to extend emergency measures.[88] This proposal has been convincingly criticized for (1) its lack of realism as regards the executive's willingness to disclose information about its conduct to enable judicial or congressional oversight as well as regarding the willingness of Congress, not to speak of a minority party, to exercise independent and efficient checks on executive powers in addition to having (2) neither a workable concept of 'security' nor an adequate conception of how civil liberties can be protected.[89]

---

85 Hofmann, 'Souverän ist, wer über den Ausnahmezustand entscheidet' [Sovereign is he who decides on the exception], 179.

86 Böckenförde, 'Ausnahmerecht und demokratischer Rechtsstaat', 264 ff.

87 Ackerman develops in 'The Emergency Constitution' and *Before the Next Attack. Preserving Civil Liberties in an Age of Terrorism* the components of a 'framework statute'.

88 Ackerman, *Before the Next Attack*, 142–68.

89 See only Minow, 'The Constitution as Black Box During National Emergencies'.

Unlike Ackermann, Böckenförde had to follow the emergency legislation of the Basic Law and left the parliament largely in charge of the state of exception. In these considerations, the state as power, decision and peace unit therefore ranks higher than the constitution.[90] With his concept of emergency law, Böckenförde rejected the legacy of the radical aspects of Schmitt's decisionism (as did Ackerman). He also refrained from developing a threat scenario. Nevertheless, he situated himself within the statist tradition, since he conceptualized the protection of law with the help of the state. That aside, Böckenförde needs to be asked whether he is able to conceptualize the unforeseeable, if it is really unforeseeable, better with his 'model structure' for exceptional situations than, for instance, the emergency constitution of the Basic Law, which reveals its embarrassment about the phenomenon of the unthinkable in its categorization of imaginable, historically saturated exceptional situations, and the changes it stipulates for the normal distribution of power.

Against Böckenförde's project of standardizing the actually non-standardizable, at least in a comprehensive model, it can be argued that he assumes a gap in the constitutional order and its emergency law regarding its handling of factual exceptional situations. This gap is meant to be closed by his model law of the state of exception. It can, however, be assumed that there will be new exceptional situations in the future, whose foreseeability will reveal new gaps[91] in Böckenförde's model structure.[92] After all, the initial assumption of a patchy positive legal order leads consequently to an 'infinite regress of ever new meta-(emergency) rights'.[93] The objection of Gertrude Lübbe-Wolff can therefore hardly be refuted: she argues that it is not possible to effectively rule out the political temptation to use a vague general authorization in an exceptional situation following the model of necessity as justification in

---

90 Hofmann rightly argues that this conception still entails Schmitt's theses in weakened form ('Souverän ist, wer über den Ausnahmezustand entscheidet' [Sovereign is he who decides on the exception], 181).

91 The same objection can be levelled against the general clause of emergency law suggested by Enders, 'Der Staat in Not', 'which leaves also in a formally declared state of exception [...] the principles of Art. 1(1) and (2) untouched' (1045).

92 Cf., for instance, suggestions to extend the definition of defence in Art. 87a(2) BL to 'non-state attacks on the foundation of the polity' in Enders, 'Der Staat in Not', 1043 ff., or to end the separation of police/danger prevention and the military/defence and to allow 'the use of military means' in official assistance in cases of particularly serious accidents in Schäuble, 'Aktuelle Sicherheitspolitik im Lichte des Verfassungsrechts', 213.

93 Rightly so, Augsberg, 'Denken vom Ausnahmezustand her', 26.

criminal law. This is even more the case, if an emergency provision under constitutional law establishes conditions, even if they are only minimal – for instance, with regard to powers, procedures and purposes.[94]

4.5 FLIRTING WITH THE STATE OF EXCEPTION: IMAGINING WORST-CASE SCENARIOS

Challenged by terror networks and 'organized crime', law-rule in most Western industrial societies was significantly consolidated by the re-inforcement of the personnel and finances of their security apparatus at the end of the 20th century. At the same time, the legal regimes thus fostered invariably assumed features of preventative or security states respectively through the expansion of powers under legislation meant to avert danger.[95] Time, it seems, blurred the links, only outlined here,[96] between the early, middle and late works of Schmitt, while his involvement in the design of constitutional law under the Nazi regime seems to have faded into the background.

In general, geographical and temporal distance tends to make it easier for constitutional and legal scholars to refer to Carl Schmitt's vocabulary and argument affirmatively and to adopt his preference for the state of exception explicitly or at least substantively. Historico-political uninhibitedness and naïve variants on Schmitt's thought[97] emerge in accounts that indicate a – not entirely casual – romance with the state of exception, for example, by questioning the taboo of torture with reference to a self-designed ethics of rescue, by not questioning the special treatment of 'enemies' under criminal law, by justifying the domestic deployment of military forces (to down renegade airliners) and by reviving the theory of citizen sacrifice.

---

[94] Lübbe-Wolff, 'Rechtsstaat und Ausnahmerecht', 121.

[95] See Cole and Dempsey, *Terrorism and the Constitution.*

[96] As regards a dissection of Schmitt's preference for the exceptional case, a detailed systematic exegesis of his work was not possible in this context. For the trajectory of Carl Schmitt's philosophy, see Hofmann, *Legitimität gegen Legalität.*

[97] Posner and Vermeule, *Terror in the Balance*, claim to rely on Schmitt when they attempt to 'understand how this practice [of coercive interrogation etc. – G.F.] fits into legal norms and traditions and how it ought to be regulated' (at 183).

Ticking Bombs and other Worst-Case Scenarios

The legal scholars who come up with extreme cases and apologists for emergency powers respectively do not need to receive or independently re-imagine the fear-ridden worldview of a Carl Schmitt. With the *Clash of Civilisations*[98] and the 'war against Islamic terror', they are provided with a topical functional equivalent of a global apocalypse by politics, the media and academia. The consequently emerging worst-case scenarios of the 'ticking bomb' or the 'attack on the heart of the state' by international terrorism points – as did Schmitt's fascination with the exceptional – to intense perceptions of threat. Take, for instance, the statement of a constitutional scholar who otherwise argues with deliberate calm and differentiation:

> And today, the state is in peril, threatened by international terrorism. Terror attacks aim at destabilizing the state, in the long term even at its collapse. [...] The state seems to have reached the limits of its traditional course of action shaped by the regular case of the normal state. This is reminiscent of a drowning person who follows the principles of proper action in everyday life but in the situation of existential threat only survival counts.[99]

Much attention is given to the adverse consequences of these threats, while their actual likelihood is hardly discussed; the neglect of probability is apparently a significant aspect of worst-case scenarios.[100] However, the apologists can only figure as heirs of Schmitt, if they consider the normativity of the normal state from the perspective of the state of exception, copy his vocabulary or the structure of his argument and especially adopt both the suspension of law for the purpose of concretizing law in extreme cases as well as a dualistic legal status (applying to friend and enemy).

An 'Enemy Criminal Law' Without Schmitt?

Among the proponents of a mindset oriented towards the state of exception, the established scholar of criminal law, Günther Jakobs, has

---

[98] Huntington, *The Clash of Civilizations and the Remaking of World Order*; for a critical point of view, see Sen, *Identity and Violence*.

[99] Enders develops this scenario in 'Der Staat in Not', 1039.

[100] For the 'law' of probability neglect, see Sunstein, 'Probability Neglect'; id., *Gesetze der Angst*, 98. For criticism of the neglect of likelihood in the discourse about domestic security, see also Prantl, *Der Terrorist als Gesetzgeber*, especially 42 and 47 ff.

gained international prominence with his thesis of an 'enemy criminal law' dating back more than two decades. In numerous publications, he has presented an argument whose fundamental distinction between citizen and enemy appears to be indebted to Schmitt's concept of the political and the inherently connected theory of the state of exception. Unlike and also with more precision than Schmitt, Jacobs defined the 'enemy' as 'unperson', who will 'neither be forced under the civil constitution nor departs from it only partially'; rather he 'turned his back on the law permanently' 'in a not only casual manner' 'and hence cannot guarantee the cognitive minimum security of personal behaviour'.[101] 'Enemies' are accordingly not criminal citizens but 'dangerous human beings'. With their attribution to 'enemy criminal law', they get their comeuppance for the fact that liberal and rule-of-law principles cannot possibly govern them.[102] The prototypes of this category include all sexually compulsive criminals resistant to deterrence and reintegration as well as other habitual criminals, members of criminal gangs and especially terrorists – not envisaged by Schmitt in his *Concept of the Political.*[103]

Despite his statements to the contrary, Jakobs moves within the force field of Schmitt's vocabulary and within his apocalyptic scenarios not only because of the intensity of his distinction between citizen and enemy but also due to the war metaphor he uses, when he defines 'enemy criminal law' as war, whose containment and totality also depends on what is feared of the enemy.[104] His 'enemy criminal law' presents itself as a 'legal form of what', according to Agamben, 'can actually not assume a legal form' and which Schmitt would locate in the state of exception. Jakobs would hardly deny that 'enemy criminal law' has an extraordinary character.

At first glance, 'enemy criminal law' therefore seems a relatively clear case of Schmitt reception. However, Jakobs apparently wants to avoid such a categorization. He is consistent in not quoting Carl Schmitt. It is obvious that he does not see himself as an heir of the latter. He does not even feel that he needs to distance himself from Schmitt. Analysing

---

[101] Jakobs, 'Bürgerstrafrecht und Feindstrafrecht', 91 ff., and id., 'Terroristen als Personen im Recht', 841 ff.

[102] Foucault, *Schriften in vier Bänden*, vol. 3, 568 ff.

[103] Schmitt is concerned with a 'simple and elementary statement' of the state as a particular – political – state of a people, which he almost codes in a systems-theoretical binary scheme (*The Concept of the Political*, 20 ff.).

[104] Cf. Jakobs, 'Bürgerstrafrecht und Feindstrafrecht', and id., *Staatliche Strafe: Bedeutung und Zweck*, 41 ff.

among others state measures against the RAF terror in his first relevant publications, he assumed the position of an observer[105] who only diagnoses and criticizes system-incompatible 'sprinkles' of enemy criminal law in civil criminal law and the law of criminal procedures with the intention of rescuing the civility of criminal law.[106] Concerning the design for an 'enemy criminal law', in contrast, Schmitt would certainly have taken the opportunity to destroy the frail civil/liberal criminal law.

Moreover, Jakobs does not refer to the primacy of the exception or a concept of the political; rather he makes reference to a theory of the validity of norms informed by Fichte, Hobbes and Kant, but not Schmitt. This theory starts from the question of whether a norm and its underlying expectation of norm compliance are disregarded only as an exception or systematically. Following Hobbes, Jakobs advances his thesis, again in proximity to Schmitt, that actions taken against individuals 'who cannot be forced into a civil state', in short: against 'enemies', are legally meaningless, i.e. they do not de-individualize but only apply force:

> Civil criminal law *maintains* the *validity of norms*, enemy criminal law (in a wider sense including sentencing guidelines) *combats* dangers.[107]

There is no objection to building a theory of norm validity on the classics; however, it should be noted that Hobbes' theory of punishment[108] is embedded in the overall concept of an enlightened despotism – far removed from the actual regimes of law-rule. What the legislator fears regarding 'enemies' leads Jakobs to adopt a view in both material criminal law and the law of criminal procedures – apart from its general combative character – that follows the trajectory of police law in its shift from what has already happened to the future criminal act[109] without also arguing for a reduction in the punishment proportional to this predating[110] and to stress the strict observance of procedural guarantees.

---

[105] This also distinguishes him from Schmitt.

[106] Jakobs, 'Kriminalisierung im Vorfeld einer Rechtsgutsverletzung'; cf. Saliger, 'Feindstrafrecht'.

[107] Jakobs, 'Das Selbstverständnis der Strafrechtswissenschaft vor den Herausforderungen der Gegenwart (*Kommentar*)', 51 ff. (emphasis in the original).

[108] Hobbes, *Leviathan*, especially part II, ch. 28.

[109] Jakobs, 'Das Selbstverständnis der Strafrechtswissenschaft', 51.

[110] Jakobs lists, for instance, the offences of forming a criminal or terrorist organization (§§ 129, 129a StGB), and the organized cultivation of narcotics (§§ 30 Abs. 1 Nr. 1, 31 Abs. 1 Nr. 1 BtMG).

From Jakobs' examination of legislative measures, one does not necessarily need to derive an apology for 'enemy criminal law', particularly since he ignores Carl Schmitt persistently – in contrast to some Schmitt epigones[111] – and finally dares only to state diplomatically and ambiguously that 'a clearly defined enemy criminal law is less dangerous under the *Rechtsstaat* than a melange of all criminal law with sprinkles of provisions under enemy criminal law'.[112] Given a benevolent reading, which comes to the detriment of imitating followers,[113] his approach can be interpreted as an intervention to rescue civil criminal law under law-rule from infiltration by enemy criminal law.

However, if one examines Jakobs' later studies, which by the way were unimpressed by arising criticism, the reluctance to cite Schmitt turns out to be an empty gesture. After all, Schmitt stands shoulder to shoulder with him: semantically with his concept of the enemy and also substantively with the construction of a relationship of extreme intensity (here in criminal law, there warlike), although normatively and not existentially.[114] Substantively, Jakobs accepts as legacy the *Concept of the Political*, for which the distinction between friend and enemy is constitutive, and also the latest version of the theory of the state of exception, when he shifts from analysis and description to a legitimizing and

---

[111] The thesis of an enemy criminal law finds ardent approval in Depenheuer, *Selbstbehauptung des Rechtsstaates*, 55 ff., who has no issues with Carl Schmitt as main proponent; see nn. 67, 69, 72, 74 and 82 as well as the corresponding text.

[112] Jakobs, 'Bürgerstrafrecht und Feindstrafrecht', 95. He had concluded his first study of enemy criminal law with the sentence: 'The current criminal code obscures that the limits of a free state are violated at a number of places.' ('Kriminalisierung im Vorfeld einer Rechtsgutsverletzung', 784).

[113] Otto Depenheuer, for instance, introduces the enemy, enemy criminal law and enemy (combating) law in general affirmatively: 'The term enemy is in various ways contaminated, compromised and prone to abuse, but substantively it is without alternative. […] [T]he enemy is the negation of the citizen in *status civilis*; as human being; he stands outside of the social contract, out of which he cannot derive any rights. From the perspective of constitutional theory, the enemy is not a legal person, which generally observes the law but a threat which has to be fought for the sake of the force of law. […] As phenomenological sign for the lacking rights of the enemy and the priority of pure reasons of State, "Guantanamo" epitomises a place at which law is suspended as long as the threat continues. The prisoners do not have the status of legal subjects, they are only left with their "bare life"' (*Selbstbehauptung des Rechtsstaates*, 56–63).

[114] 'The distinction of friend and enemy denotes the utmost degree of intensity of a union or separation […]' (Schmitt, *The Concept of the Political*, 26).

prescriptive discourse in his publications since 1999. As soon as he follows his terror fears and realizes the necessity for anti-terror measures under emergency law, he abandons the position of an analytical-critical observer and decides to argue in favour of a suspension of regular criminal law in the relationship with the 'enemy'. He is no longer concerned about maintaining order under civil criminal law after irritations within society; rather his focus is on establishing bearable environmental conditions, which are meant to be achieved by 'putting all those out of the way, who do not offer a cognitive minimal guarantee necessary to be able to actually treat them as persons.'[115] Mark you: 'put out of the way'. With this step, Jakobs places his 'enemy criminal law' within the war against terror and takes up Schmitt's notion of the 'ever present possibility of combat'.[116]

In his most recent publication, Jakobs approves of a two-tier order of criminal law consisting of a (legal) civil criminal law and a (legitimate) enemy combating criminal law.[117] With the construction of such an apartheid system, he recapitulates the dichotomy of legality and legitimacy for criminal law which runs through Schmitt's constitutional law; this system extends, first, the penalization of 'predicate offences',[118] which are not punishable under civil criminal law; second, it makes the sanctions of criminal law more severe; third, it reduces guarantees under the law of criminal procedures; and, fourth, it marks and excludes a category of delinquents as 'enemies'. Just as Schmitt ascribes the 'normal state' the task 'within the state and its territory to create "tranquillity, security and order" and thereby establishes the *normal* situation which is the prerequisite for legal norms to be valid',[119] Jakobs claims he excludes and ostracises the 'enemy' in the defence of civil criminal law.

[115] Jakobs, 'Das Selbstverständnis der Strafrechtswissenschaft', 47 ff.; id., 'Bürgerstrafrecht und Feindstrafrecht', 92, and id., *Staatliche Strafe*, 41 ff. For a critical view see Prantl, *Der Terrorist als Gesetzgeber*, 150 ff.

[116] Schmitt, *The Concept of the Political*, 32.

[117] Most recently Jakobs, 'Zur Theorie des Feindstrafrechts'.

[118] Instructive in this context is a bill of the free states Bavaria and Thuringia of 27 November 2001 to improve the possibilities of combating terrorism and organized crime under criminal law, which among other things takes the 'support and promotion of terrorist organizations as predicate offences' (*BR-Drucksache* 1014/01) as well as the bill of an 'Act for the prosecution of the planning of serious acts of violent subversion' (*BT-Drucksache* 16/11735); worth reading and informative is the convincing criticism of Walter, 'Der Rechtsstaat verliert die Nerven'.

[119] Schmitt, *The Concept of the Political*, 46.

However, there remains an important difference compared with Carl Schmitt. Whereas the latter entertains the phantasmagoria of the extreme case so as to realize actual law, whatever that may be, through suspension and to contain the fight against the enemy legally; Günther Jakobs, following Agamben's concept of the state of exception, declares the 'enemy' he wants to put out of the way, by dint of special treatment under criminal law, as without rights. Thus, Jakobs finally serves up an updated version of the Hobbesian political technology, which maintains, on the one hand, the rationality of civil criminal law and, on the other hand, is freed from the usual legal constraints and follows the supposed security imperatives of an effective fight against terror in criminal law.

Schmittian Approaches to the Exception in the 'Torture Discourse'

Manifest in a repressed manner in the logic of averting danger, 'enemy criminal law' finds an echo in the discourse about torture in preventative law. This applies not only to attempts to introduce the institution of 'rescue torture' into laws designed to avert dangers but also to attempts under criminal law to mask the fact of torture as self-defence, necessity or assistance in an emergency (*Nothilfe*).

It would, however, be a rather hopeless enterprise to try and smuggle torture into the array of instruments available to the *method Locke* in the name of a *Political Theology* or a *Concept of the Political* à la Schmitt. Whoever wants to allow the use of brutal force in extreme cases within law-rule in order to extract information therefore needs willy-nilly – at least in the German context – to avoid any association with Gestapo methods and therefore also any link to the works of the 'crown jurist' of the Third Reich.[120] In other national contexts too, justification of torture requires nothing less than the squaring of the circle, namely to meet the obligation of democratic law-rule, while at the same time taking out a mortgage with a lawless state. Translated into legal doctrine under constitutional and police law, from the above follows the paradoxical enterprise to relativize both the strict ban on torture under human rights legislation and the protection of human dignity, but without starting the trajectory into the state of exception.

As resistant to criticism as Günther Jakobs, the legal philosopher and scholar of public law Winfried Brugger engaged with this paradox in a

---

[120] Brugger expressly distances himself from the Nazi regime and its methods in his article 'May Government Ever Use Torture?' and refers to Jean Améry as an opponent of torture. Chapter 7 locates the justifications for torture historically.

number of publications and continued with this enterprise accompanied by support and criticism.[121] Guided by a – perhaps well-meaning – ethics of rescue, he considered authorizing the state to torture in exceptional circumstances, long before the terror attacks on the World Trade Center and the declared 'war on terror' motivated quite a few legal scholars globally to pursue the same or a similar line of reasoning. From an 'unconditional ban of torture' he proceeded to finally argue for 'a conditional right to torture'.[122] Brugger set off with an almost everyday speech act, what would shortly turn into the 'torture discourse': 'May Government Ever Use Torture?' It is not Carl Schmitt he turned to for an answer. Rather he consulted Niklas Luhmann, the father of systems theory, to disinfect his emergency torture theoretically. Following 'good legal tradition', the latter had discussed the following case in a 1993 lecture in Heidelberg, which was concerned with the question of whether there are still indispensable norms in our society:

> You are a high-level law-enforcement officer. In your country – it could be Germany in the not-too-distant future – there are many left- and right-wing terrorists – every day there are murders, fire-bombings, the killing and injury of countless innocent people. You have captured the leader of such a group. Presumably, if you torture him, you could save many lives – 10, 100, 1000 – we can vary the situation. Would you do it?[123]

Of course, Luhmann was totally indifferent as to whether they would 'do' it. The systems theorist was merely interested in the issue of whether functional differentiation, here between law and ethics, could be maintained in exceptional cases. Strangely, Luhmann concluded with considerations that were 'regardless of all legalistic considerations', rather unsatisfying and totally outside of his usual systems-theoretical approach; he contemplated allowing torture performed by internationally supervised courts, with closed-circuit surveillance of the scene in Geneva or

---

[121] There is a plethora of critical literature. See, for instance, Enders, 'Der Staat in Not'; Poscher, 'Die Würde des Menschen ist unantastbar'; Marx, 'Folter – eine zulässige polizeiliche Präventionsmaßnahme?'; Hecker, 'Relativierung des Folterverbots in der BRD?'; Kretschmer, 'Folter in Deutschland'; Frankenberg, 'Torture and Taboo' and Chapter 7 below.

[122] Brugger, 'May Government Ever Use Torture?'; and id., 'Vom unbedingten Verbot der Folter zum bedingten Recht auf Folter'. Recently Brugger refers to the 'extraction of life-saving statements' (*lebensrettender Aussageerzwingung*) – id., *Freiheit und Sicherheit*.

[123] Luhmann, 'Are There Still Indispensable Norms in Our Society?' 8.

Luxembourg, long-distance supervision via telecommunications in order to avoid 'sacrific[ing] innocent-bystanders to the fanaticism of terrorists'.[124]

Substantively and perhaps against his conviction, Brugger, who had attended Luhmann's lecture, linked the exceptional situation of the 'ticking bomb' with Schmitt's argument about the state of exception as a situation of the *realization* of law. He adopted the structure of the *Concept of the Political* with his own design of a two-tier legal status for victims, on the one hand, and culprits/dangerous persons, on the other hand. In Brugger's justification scenario of the 'ticking bomb', the prototypical terrorist/bomb planter/hostage taker functions implicitly as the enemy of law-abiding citizenry. Unlike Schmitt's friend/enemy conception and Jakobs' apartheid system under criminal law, Brugger temporarily suspended regular law, which bans torture, protects dignity and bodily mental integrity, for those who knew the hiding place of the 'ticking bomb'. But to the detriment of the terrorist or the hostage taker, who abuses innocent victims as mere objects, with his argument he relativized the thesis that every intervention (by torture) into human dignity equates to a human rights violation.[125] In fact, he concluded:

> The legal assessment of the behaviour of the blackmailer (unlawful) and the situation of the victim (law-abiding) is unambiguous. Only the blackmailer can free himself from intervention, the victim cannot. Only he can be expected to withdraw into the sphere of lawful behaviour; unreasonable for the threatened person is flight or the handing over of the hostage. From the perspective of proportionality, it cannot be ruled out that the use of force is an appropriate means. Appropriateness can therefore be affirmed. Despite the ... rightly emphasized objections against the state extorting statements, an exception is possible in the given case.[126]

Arguing similarly but more succinctly, a commentary on the Basic Law arrived at a two-tier legal order, in which torture can be justified: 'The life of the attacked or the prevention of a massive attack on his bodily integrity is ranked higher than the life of the attacker'.[127]

---

[124] Ibid., 33.

[125] Brugger, 'Darf der Staat ausnahmsweise foltern?', 70 ff.

[126] Ibid., 81.

[127] Starck, in von Mangoldt et al., *GG I*, Art. 1 Abs. 1 Rn. 78. Similarly, Kirchhof, 'Die Zulässigkeit des Einsatzes staatlicher Gewalt in Ausnahmesituationen', 114: 'The victim which remains within the confines of the legal order deserves primarily the protection of the state'. Pawlik, '§ 14 Abs. 3 des Luftsicherheitsgesetzes – ein Tabubruch?', 1048, argues in a similar vein, albeit

Following the concept of a two-tiered legal protection,[128] other authors also did not openly weigh up the dignity of the victim and the perpetrator; rather they reduced human dignity, which is from the outset conceptualized as immune to balancing, to a two-class system of the protection of dignity, against the backdrop of a Manichean distinction between good and evil. The guilty bomb planter is therefore, due to his behaviour, himself responsible for the second-class dignity ascribed to him and the torture that may ensue. He loses his status as legal subject insofar as the state 'sends him back into the legal sphere he has unlawfully left'[129] by means of torture. This argument ignores the objection that the state, which reaches the limits of the duties it can perform in a doubtlessly difficult situation, makes the tortured 'as depersonalized object subject to external control', integrates him directly into the state function of danger prevention and subjects him unconditionally to external purposes by constructing a state duty to protect, which comes to his detriment.

However, these authors cannot seriously be accused of taking legal reason to court, following Carl Schmitt, to indulge in their preference for the exception and celebrate the ultimately unfounded, because unsubstantiated, decision. Without Schmitt's 'energetic passion' and sympathy for the solitary deciding sovereign but instead driven by the concern to protect a citizenry threatened by particularly 'dangerous persons', they open the way to emergency law with their meticulous justifications: those who are the subject of 'enemy criminal law' in Jakobs' account and those who are tortured for rescue purposes pay with their deprivation and exclusion from the community of law for the fact that, due to their criminal or dangerous actions, they cannot be treated according to the commands of law-rule.

Although Jakobs, Brugger and their seconds may be intent on keeping their distance from Carl Schmitt, they still need to assume responsibility for the significant 'harm' done to the discourse resulting from their romance with the exception – or more specifically, from the adoption of Schmitt's vocabulary and mindset privileging the state of exception. Where Schmitt leaves the sphere of the law to turn wrong produced by decision into 'law' and to exclude 'enemies', today more than a few followers in academia and state practice can be found who also pursue

more cautiously: 'Those who participate in generating a danger they are meant to avert afterwards possess a comprehensive duty to self-sacrifice'.

[128] For detailed references, see Chapter 7.

[129] Enders, 'Der Staat in Not', 1041.

the exclusion of 'enemies' from law-rule or advocate the legal normalization of torture.[130]

The 'Final and Fatal Rescue Downing' (*Rettungsabschuss*)

Constructions of a two-tier legal status manifest themselves also in considerations about the life- and law-eradicating shooting down of airliners. After 11 September 2001, the apologists of the downing of passenger airplanes taken hostage by alleged terrorists (renegade airplanes) tried to semantically mask the doctrines they provided for the extreme case. The masquerade of the exceptional usually starts with the introduction of euphemistic terms. In this way, the agony of torture is trivialized into a 'life-saving extraction of a statement', which turns a human being 'usually … into an object',[131] while the destruction of life in the case of a downed airliner becomes almost casually a 'final rescue downing'[132] for the purpose of averting danger. Both the ethics of rescue indicated by the term as well as the normalization of such interventions as preventative measures obviously have the purpose of veiling the use of emergency powers in extreme situations in order to facilitate their acceptance.

The German Aviation Security Act (LuftSiG) of 11 January 2005 and its apologists initially followed the logic of emergency law, as suggested by the justification for torture: the state offers protection to individuals by withdrawing its protection from others.[133] In this vein, § 14(3) Aviation Security Act states:

> The direct use of armed force is only permissible, when, according to the specific circumstances, it can be concluded that the airplane is going to be used against the lives of individuals, and it is the only means to prevent this imminent danger.

Obviously informed by the attack on the World Trade Center, the authorization of the shooting down, however, moves a significant step

---

[130] The discussion of 'enemy criminal law' continues in Chapters 6 and 7 from another angle.

[131] This is the extenuating argument in Brugger, 'May Government Ever Use Torture?', 88.

[132] The euphemism for torture can be found in Brugger, *Freiheit und Sicherheit*; Lindner refers to the 'final and fatal rescue downing' (*finaler Rettungsabschuss*) in 'Die Würde des Menschen und sein Leben', 579.

[133] Merkel, 'Wenn der Staat Unschuldige opfert' and id., '§ 14 Abs. 3 Luftsicherheitsgesetz'.

further. It ignores fundamental principles of the law covering the averting of danger and the state of exception. Up until this authorization to down an aircraft and kill its passengers (which was later found unconstitutional by the Federal Constitutional Court[134]), it was undisputed that, first, the balancing of life against life was not permissible, because the *Rechtsstaat* does not allow the offsetting of life and quantities of life.[135] Second, 'innocent individuals' should only be taken out by police in emergency situations, if other remedies are not available, and only if they are not exposed to a serious threat. These restrictions of liability under police and criminal law applied to all normal situations, hence, even to cases of averting mortal danger.

With reference to the 'common topos of averting danger',[136] the legislator introduced with § 14(3) LuftSiG an extraordinary utilitarian security calculus, which, according to military logic, qualifies 'innocent' passengers as unaffected third parties or as a functional component of the offensive weapon,[137] whose prematurely ended lives could be accounted for as collateral damage: 'To save life, life can be destroyed'.[138] While the distinction between innocent and guilty was in the context of 'rescue torture' significant for the downgrading of the legal status of the terrorist/hostage taker, it vanished in the case of renegade aircraft. The Air Security Act was meant to open the way to sacrificing citizens, if given the asymmetrical chances of rescue – doomed passengers versus threatened population on the ground – a bigger number or only those potentially threatened could be saved. For the time being the Federal Constitutional Court has ended this ghostly spectacle; but only for the time being, since it can be foreseen that the debate will re-emerge once another airborne terror attack occurs.

---

134 *BVerfGE* 115, 118/139 ff.

135 For the theory of the state of exception in criminal law, see Stratenwerth and Kuhlen, *Strafrecht Allgemeiner Teil I*, § 9 Rn. 113, and Pawlik, '§ 14 Abs. 3 des Luftsicherheitsgesetzes – ein Tabubruch?', with many further references.

136 *BT-Drucksache* 15/2361, 14 – critical of this, Pawlik, '§ 14 Abs. 3 des Luftsicherheitsgesetzes – ein Tabubruch?', 1055, and Merkel, 'Wenn der Staat Unschuldige opfert'.

137 One is tempted to take the cynical argument of Isensee as a faux pas, see Isensee, 'Menschenwürde – die säkulare Gesellschaft auf der Suche nach dem Absoluten', 193. In contrast, Lepsius, 'Das Luftsicherheitsgesetz unter dem Grundgesetz', 60 f., and Enders, 'Der Staat in Not', 1042.

138 In this way, Pawlik, '§ 14 Abs. 3 des Luftsicherheitsgesetzes – ein Tabubruch?', 1055, describes this logic aptly. See also Roellecke, 'Der Rechtsstaat im Kampf gegen den Terror', 266.

Apart from the different treatment of innocent individuals, 'rescue torture' and 'final rescue downing' show the same structure: in both cases, the legal doctrines of the normal state give way to the doctrines of the borderline situation, behind which nothing else hides than the unruly doctrines of the state of exception. And in the case of an emergency, the human dignity and right to life of culprit and victim are – in advance – differently assessed and submitted to a mock weighing, privileging the latter and integrating the rights and duties into a tiered legal status.[139]

The State of Exception as a Mindset

The mindset informed by privileging the state of exception does not always reveal itself openly. At times, it hides in a 'dogmatics of the borderline situation'. More often, however, it is situated in the sphere of 'tragic choices', in which the 'gaps' between the doctrines of the normal state and the doctrines of the exceptional case, or, as is sometimes said, the 'realm free of legal assessment' are fathomed.[140] Alternatively, it is stated more carefully that 'assessment gaps' are meant to be closed at the boundaries of law-rule. Similarly to Schmitt's *Political Theology*, the destruction of law, although at least limited to one case, here serves the supposed concretization of law. The mindset of the extraordinary becomes particularly apparent in the extreme thought experiments[141] that operate in the 'ticking bomb' scenario. Here is an instructive example:

---

[139] For the theory of pre-evaluated balancing doctrines (*vor-gewichteten Abwägungsdogmatik*), see Starck, in von Mangoldt et al., *Grundgesetz I*, Art. 1 Rn. 79 ff.; Brugger, 'Vom unbedingten Verbot der Folter zum bedingten Recht auf Folter', especially 168 ff.; Hillgruber, 'Der Staat des Grundgesetzes – nur "bedingt abwehrbereit"?'. In contrast, Horst Dreier formulates it more cautiously (in von Mangoldt et al., *Grundgesetz I*, Art. 1 Rn. 133): 'In fact, state authorities can be confronted with individual cases in which two principally equivalent legal obligations contradict each other, both derived from 1 BL: after all other measures have been taken, there is only the choice between violating the human dignity of the victim or the perpetrator.' More critical than authors who assume the 'certain death' of the passengers of a renegade aircraft is the argument of the *BVerfGE* 115, 118/140 ff. (Air Security Act).

[140] Lindner, 'Die Würde des Menschen und sein Leben', with further references; id., *Frankfurter Allgemeine Zeitung* (15 October 2004), 8; cf. also Merkel, 'Wenn der Staat Unschuldige opfert', for the downing of aircraft.

[141] See, for instance, in Brugger, 'Vom unbedingten Verbot der Folter zum bedingten Recht auf Folter'; Merkel, 'Folter als Notwehr', 46, and Pawlik, '§ 14 Abs. 3 des Luftsicherheitsgesetzes – ein Tabubruch?', 1053: 'One should imagine that an enemy state occupies a part of the territory of the Federal Republic'.

> Policeman P is in the same room as terrorist T, which both cannot leave in the near future, let us say they sit in an airliner 10,000 meters above the Atlantic Ocean. There is also a bomb on board, which T smuggled into the airplane and which is equipped with a time fuse. T (a suicide bomber) refuses to defuse the bomb with the help of a code only known to him. P knows that the bomb will explode in about 20 minutes' time. An emergency landing is not possible. The only chance for P's survival is that he ties up the physically inferior T, threatens him with pain and, if necessary, causes him pain until T gives in and defuses the bomb.[142]

The author provides as explanation to his readers that those who argue for an absolute ban on torture have to deal with all imaginable examples and still need to remain consistent or change position after all.

What characterizes scenarios like these as concepts of emergency law, and in what respect do they need to be criticized? This line of action or rather thinking invites criticism, because the authors of such scenarios, for example Niklas Luhmann in his Heidelberg lecture, outline an extreme situation for logical or academic purposes and then ask whether a principle or strict ban, which is embedded in the normativity of regular law, can be maintained or has to be given up in the extreme situation. Due to the pressing suggestive effect of the example, a negative answer suggests itself immediately: to defend the principle would be even more extreme than the hypothetical case. With this insight informed by the exception, logicians and legal scholars (as well as systems theorists) return to normal law-rule and argue here that the experiment shows: the principle does not withstand the extreme stress test. Consequently, it was designed faultily, they argue, and needs to be abandoned or modified. As a result, the thought experiment justifies the use of the strictly forbidden (torture) in situations of self-defence or at least the balancing of human dignity, originally conceived as inviolable and non-balanceable.

The mindset informed by extreme scenarios claims for itself the charm of cold logic, and borrows from Hobbes, Hegel, Rousseau, Kant and other philosophers their respective categorical imperative or rationale for the justification of extraordinary violence and killings implemented by the state or rather its political technologists, the experts in cruelty. The philosophically charged logic then exposes regular law by rejecting normative and empirical objections and by suspecting the defenders of regular law to be cynics or overgeneralizers. The broad nature of their suspicion relieves them from taking seriously, for instance, the regular

---

[142] Merkel, 'Folter und Notwehr', 392. The author himself mentions the '(moderate) empirical unlikeliness', but ignores it since he only wants to 'depict the logical structure of problems'.

principle of proportionality and from finding out whether torture or shooting down is the apposite means of achieving rescue in the individual case to be assessed; whether there are less interventionist but similarly effective means available; and which effects 'legitimized' torture or the 'legitimized' downing would have on the *Rechtsstaat* and the self-respect of a society.

Finally, it is also a strategy of the legally extremist mindset to introduce the state as a victim:

> The state seems to have come to the limits of its traditional scope of action shaped by the regular case of the normal state. It therefore is reminiscent of a drowning person, who might follow in everyday life the principles of proper action – in the situation of existential peril, however, only mere survival counts.[143]

Terrorist attacks need therefore primarily to be repelled not because they endanger innocent citizens but because they attack 'the very heart of the state'; they in fact aim at

> [the state's] role as the monopolist on the use of force, which enables it to guarantee a legal order of peace in the first place. This capability is a necessary condition for its legitimacy. Only to the extent that it can sufficiently guarantee the protective function of his norms, it can demand obedience for them and before them. Attacks, which cast principle doubt on this capability of the state, threaten therefore the normative foundation of its existence.[144]

'[I]n the emergency case of self-preservation'[145] against an 'attack on the heart of the state',[146] that is to say, if the Hobbesian duty to protection is in jeopardy, state officials are allowed to transgress the boundaries of the law of the normal state. Via this argumentative detour, the doctrines of police law and criminal law establish again a link to Carl Schmitt and the post-Schmittian theory of the state of exception: 'The state guarantees the

---

143 Enders, 'Der Staat in Not', 1039.

144 Merkel, 'Wenn der Staat Unschuldige opfert', 33. The Federal Constitutional Court argues similarly in its decision on the Communication Ban Act – *BVerfGE* 49, 24/56 ff.; cf., however, Hillgruber, 'Der Staat des Grundgesetzes – nur "bedingt abwehrbereit"?', 218.

145 Depenheuer, *Selbstbehauptung des Rechtsstaates*, 55. See also Gramm, 'Der wehrlose Verfassungsstaat'.

146 This metaphor with a critical connotation can be traced back to Hess et al., *Angriff auf das Herz des Staates*; it turns into an argumentative figure that justifies the sacrifice of citizens in Merkel, 'Wenn der Staat Unschuldige opfert'.

legal order. This is why it ranks above the system of legal norms.'[147] And the guarantor of the legal order has to be protected, if necessary, with the help of torture or the downing of innocent passengers.

In this context, it should be noted only that those crossing the boundaries of law-rule today operate, just like Carl Schmitt in his time, with concepts of emergency law, some them desperately seeking to re-imagine the legal form and to find some kind of legal regulation out there.[148] Whether they also share his decisive and unrelenting preference for the state of exception needs to be the subject of further investigation. Evidence against such a reading could be found in the crazy image of an erratic intellectual extremism which characterizes the doctrines relating to 'rescue torture', 'rescue downing' and 'enemy criminal law': Günther Jakobs, yesterday's critic and, arguably, today's apologist for the 'enemy criminal law' can remain silent about torture and downing, although these 'measures' would clearly be 'sprinkles of enemy law' in (civil) danger-averting law.[149] The opponents, and especially practitioners, of his thesis of a necessary exceptional law for 'enemies' do not share this point, because they take its phenomena as normal and feel comfortable handling them in practice. Whoever rejects with good reasons the integration of the 'rescue downing' into regular law, on the one hand, can with the help of this logic be led to the justification of the rescuing 'self-defence torture'.[150] Vice versa, others reject entry into the dark territory of torture, but find justifying reasons for the downing of renegade airliners.[151] And

---

[147] Forsthoff, 'Der Ausnahmezustand der Länder', 139. In a similar vein, Hillgruber, 'Der Staat des Grundgesetzes – nur "bedingt abwehrbereit"?', 218 tries via his respective interpretation of the constitution 'to give the state its [!] right back'. Other authors also ask citizens to sacrifice their life if it serves to protect the state as guarantor of the legal order and legal unity (see Baldus and Depenheuer below, Merkel above).

[148] As, for instance, Posner and Vermeule, *Terror in the Balance*, 183–205 and Dershovitz, *Why Terrorism Works*. See also the torture controversy (Chapter 7). For a critique see Waldron, 'Torture and Positive Law'; Ramraj, *Emergencies and the Limits of Legality*.

[149] Also Depenheuer, *Selbstbehauptung des Rechtsstaates*, who expands enemy criminal law into a general enemy law, is cautious regarding torture (72), but emphatically approves of the downing of renegade aircraft as a necessary sacrifice of citizens (87–104).

[150] Merkel addresses torture within but the downing of aircraft outside of the confines of law, see id., 'Folter und Notwehr'; id., 'Folter als Notwehr', 46, and id., '§ 14 Abs. 3 Luftsicherheitsgesetz'.

[151] Enders, 'Der Staat in Not', tries to show that 'the cases of rescue torture and the downing of hijacked passenger planes [... require] a differentiated

others consider neither torture nor shooting down permissible and situate them in the 'realm free of legal assessment', in which state violence 'is permitted in exceptional circumstances, but not considered to be lawful'.[152] This list of possible combinations could be continued, at will.

Instead of a systematic approach to the perspective of thinking about the state of exception, we are rather confronted with some penetration into the doctrines of regular law. Not without pleasure in the extraordinary, the doctrinalist of the exceptional gets involved with the darkly passionate Mr Hyde. However, one would hope that their legal love is still with the 'usually recurring' Dr Jekyll.

4.6 THE DECAPITATION OF LAW-RULE AND LOCKE

The constitutional lawyer Otto Depenheuer is oblivious about all these more or less careful dogmatic manoeuvres between rule and exception, assessment of gaps and tragic moments of decision-making. His passionate appeal for the 'self-preservation of the *Rechtsstaat*'[153] borrows consistently from Carl Schmitt's key points and follows unreservedly his well-known preference for the exception. Without hesitation, he expands Brugger's torture thesis into a general theory of citizen sacrifice and turns Jakobs' 'enemy criminal law' into a comprehensive 'enemy law'. A highly selective reading allows him to decontextualize Schmitt's theory of the political and the state of exception and to turn it into a pillar of his not even differentiated concept of a militant state and a citizenry prepared to make sacrifices.

His polemical paper is interesting as a symptom of a new 'innocence' and for its use of the term self-preservation. As a functionally equivalent scenario to Carl Schmitt's fear of the destruction of occidental culture through socialism under the accidental support of a weak liberalism, the author mobilizes the additionally darkened, fear-ridden vision of a *Clash*

---

perspective'. For a similar but less careful argument, see Depenheuer, *Selbstbehauptung des Rechtsstaates*.

[152] Lindner, 'Die Würde des Menschen und sein Leben', 588.

[153] Depenheuer, *Selbstbehauptung des Rechtsstaates*. Augsberg criticizes this suggestion aptly as the 'self-decapitation of the *Rechtsstaat*' (id., 'Denken vom Ausnahmezustand her', 26). For criticism of this position, see also Hetzer, *Rechtsstaat oder Ausnahmezustand?*, 185 ff.

of Civilizations.[154] In this scenario, the 'pagans of the secular rule of law and individual freedom', i.e. Islamist terrorists, appear as enemies equipped with weapons of mass destruction, which threaten our very existence. Depenheuer – just like the legal advisers to the Bush Administration[155] – harbours no doubt that for these enemies a significant part of regular legal relations and provisions needs to be suspended.[156] Without inhibition, he presents Guantánamo as the constitutional state's 'possible answer' to the Islamist threat – or at least as his theory's answer. He has no intention of objecting to the combination of 'the lawlessness of the enemy and the decisive significance of the mere reason of state'.[157] Certainly, he has to concede that 'thus far terrorist attacks have nowhere come near questioning the existence and constitution of the respective states'. However, this does not keep him from accustoming the citizenry of law-rule regimes – or as he states repeatedly and perhaps as a critique of contemporary culture: the 'hedonistic and affluent society' – to the exceptional. Entirely in the vein of his guiding intellectual force Schmitt, he celebrates himself and the executivist political technology he propagates as 'sovereignty of the act', which leads him to the 'enemy danger averting law' and finally to demand the citizen sacrifice characterized by the 'bloody struggles' in history.

It seems odd that, in justification of this sacrifice as an 'act of self-legislation', he gives in all seriousness Kant as one of his sources. A careful reading would have shown him that Kant does not aim at self-protection, and that he sees the citizen sacrifice only as permissible if the human being 'is not used as a mean, but seen as a purpose and recognized in her dignity, i.e., if she is asked whether she agreed or could have agreed to the act that requires the sacrifice'.[158] However, such a rather substantial agreement does not occur, since his political technology demands law to resign, just as Schmitt strived for in his time, in order to be prepared in the face of terror.

Therefore, protagonists of the self-preserving state, such as Depenheuer, need to stick to not even unsuspicious sources like Carl

---

[154] Huntington, *The Clash of Civilizations and the Remaking of the World Order*. For criticism of Depenheuer's vision of fear, see Stolleis, 'Angst essen Seele auf'.

[155] Sands, *Torture Team*.

[156] Depenheuer, *Selbstbehauptung des Rechtsstaates*, 12 ff., 14, 24.

[157] For this and the following, see ibid., 40 ff., 53 ff., 63, 70 ff., 75 ff. and 104. Cf. also Schmitt, *Legalität und Legitimität*, 70 ff., for the sovereignty of the act.

[158] Schlink, 'Das Opfer des Lebens', 1026.

Schmitt, Martin Heidegger and Ernst Jünger. They agree with the rejection of any kind of self-legislation. They favour the authoritarian sovereign and see fulfilment in sacrifice, if necessary also in the sacrifice of life:

> The most profound happiness of man consists in being sacrificed, and the highest art of commanding consists in showing goals that are worthy of sacrifice.[159]

Carl Schmitt had already noted that such happiness could not be provided by liberal individualism:

> Such a demand [to sacrifice one's life – G.F.] is in no way justifiable by the individualism of liberal thought. [...] For the individual as such there is no enemy with whom he must enter into a life-and-death struggle if he personally does not want to do so. To compel him to fight against his will is, from the viewpoint of the private individual, lack of freedom and repression.[160]

Abandoned by a constitutional theory that 'has lost sight of the state', Depenheuer writes boldly against the 'emerging catastrophe' as the escapologist of the *Rechtsstaat*. Unimpressed by the 'perversion of legal thought' and the 'constitutional autism' he seems to notice in the decision of the Federal Constitutional Court that struck down the Aviation Security Act,[161] he entertains himself with the 'erotic of the thinking in exceptions' and his 'intellectual pleasure in the anticipated state of exception'.[162] Although he conceptualizes the emergency situation not with 'energetic passion' like Schmitt, he still himself is driven by a significant security autism with 'norm-oriented seriousness'. For him, it seems unproblematic that his mindset implies sacrificing significant values on the way towards the self-preservation of the state. In this way, the apocalypse, political fears and the state of exception can be short-circuited, very much as in Schmitt's case.

---

[159] Jünger, *Der Arbeiter*, 74. Jünger's and Schmitt's theory of sacrifice is quoted approvingly by Depenheuer (*Selbstbehauptung des Rechtsstaates*, nn. 106, 111).

[160] Schmitt, *The Concept of the Political*, 71.

[161] Depenheuer's accusation of autism was criticized by the Constitutional Court Judge Udo Di Fabio (id., 'Sicherheit in Freiheit').

[162] Di Fabio, 'Sicherheit in Freiheit', 423.

Before the altar, at which fundamental rights and, if necessary, life have been sacrificed,[163] the last piece falls into place, when Depenheuer joins other romantics in the defence of the monosyllabic state. However, in the context of a *law-rule*, this can only be achieved as a result of preference for the exceptional case.

4.7 STATE IMPOTENCE AND ABUSE AS FIXED POINTS IN THE MINDSET OF EMERGENCY TECHNICIANS

In theory and practice, law-rule and the state of exception entertain rather different relationships, as can be gleaned from the global responses to terrorism and organized crime.[164] The applied perspective significantly determines them. Embedded in these perspectives are specific fears about state impotence (perspective 1) or state abuse of emergency powers (perspective 2); both in turn shape different ideas of – state- or constitution-centred – techniques of governing. Fears of an emergency situation that cannot be handled with regular law lead the way to written and unwritten *state emergency law*. Fears of the abuse of such law suggest an agnosticism concerning emergency law or a fixation on constitutional law and a constraint of powers for emergency situations.

State Impotence and Lawless Necessity

State-centric approaches[165] always focus their fears on state necessity or a crisis of the state respectively. They argue that their option for an unwritten emergency law was based on a differentiated perception of normalcy and crisis. In this perception, rule and exception are taken as different politico-legal modes of aggregation. This model knows no

---

[163] Haltern, 'Internationales Verfassungsrecht?', 533 ff., 537 ff., needs to be mentioned as seconder, who – like Schmitt – accused the liberal political theory 'to be speechless in the face of the victims'. He continues: 'It is a central feature of a political community that it expects sacrifices from their members. In a state this can concern a question of life and death.'

[164] See e.g. Ramraj, *Emergency and the Limits of Legality*; Ramraj et al., *Global Anti-Terrorism Law and Policy*; Özbudun and Turhan, *Emergency Powers*; International Commission of Jurists, *States of Emergency and their Impact on Human Rights*.

[165] For a somewhat different characterization of the state-centric model, see Jakab, 'Das Grunddilemma und die Natur des Staatsnotstandes'.

positive-legal provision for the case of exception, because it is beyond any legal containment. In the spirit of Schmitt, the political technologist is enthroned as a legally largely independent, quasi-dictatorial commissioner for averting extraordinary dangers.

With the declaration of the state of exception, one leaves the realm of regular law. To avoid the abuse of extra-legal emergency powers, if this is intended at all, it requires, similar to the *method Machiavelli*, a reason of state, which can be expected from an astute sovereign interested in staying in power.[166] In contrast, more careful authors find orientation in extra-legal notions of an ethical state or see the effect of divine law, natural law, state ethics or finally constitutional ethics as a means to prevent the abuse of power.[167] Since they want to operate without a written state emergency law, they derive from the right to self-preservation of the state legitimacy geared towards the effective averting of danger, which provides the holder of state authority with emergency powers to operate in all situations of necessity regardless of the law of normalcy. In the handling of exceptional crises, the concept of necessity beyond (constitutional) law, informed by the self-preservation of the state, is often used as a normative source. It justifies the 'technicity of dictatorship', which 'is principally independent from the consent or understanding of the addressee and does not expect his agreement',[168] as well as all measures necessary for the self-preservation of the state. The defence of the interests of the state per se occurs *hors la loi*. Strictly speaking, both the state's right to exist as well as the emergency powers of the dictator stand outside of the law of normalcy.[169]

---

[166] For Machiavelli as father of the pre-*Rechtsstaat* state technology, see Machiavelli, *The Prince*; cf. Kersting, *Niccolò Machiavelli* and Münkler, *Machiavelli*. The argumentative figure of the 'extra-constitutional state of exception' introduced above and the polemical treatise by Depenheuer, *Selbstbehauptung des Rechtsstaats*, especially 52 ff. and 62 ff., reveal that a model à la Machiavelli is also of significance for the academic discourse.

[167] For this distinction, see Stolleis, '"Staatsethik" oder Vom sittlichen Staat zu den Bürgertugenden'; id., *Staat und Staatsräson in der frühen Neuzeit*; Schmitt, 'Staatsethik und pluralistischer Staat'; Böckenförde, *Der Staat als sittlicher Staat*.

[168] Schmitt, *Die Diktatur*, 13.

[169] Heller, *Staatslehre*, 281 ff.

State Impotence and Written State Emergency Law

Unlike inherently tyrannical regimes, like a 'lawless state' following a fascist, Stalinist or similar pattern, in state-centric approaches the emergency law, which is also shaped by perspective 1 of impotence in extreme situations, takes the emergency as normalcy. The state-centric inclusion of the state of exception in the regime of law negates the contradiction between rule and exception.[170] The state of exception becomes the rule, as Walter Benjamin observed in his comment on contemporary developments in Germany.[171] It is not repressed but standardized and normalized. The key element and cornerstone of this concept is again the right to self-preservation.

Legal positivists in particular sharply criticize the reference to state self-preservation in written and unwritten concepts of state emergency law:

> All speculating about a 'necessity beyond constitutional law' as permission for measures that are not justified by the written constitution are nothing else than a reprehensible glossing over a breach of the constitution, the betrayal of the constitution.[172]

The Fear of Abuse and the Renunciation of an Emergency Law

The fears of perspective 2 inspire alternative constitution-centric options: they try either to avoid abuse by refraining from legal emergency provisions or to stop it with the help of the positive provisions of an emergency constitution. The options for the law of normal situations or for an emergency constitution need, however, to consider whether emergencies can in fact be handled with the tools of the law of normalcy or of a necessarily limited emergency constitution. For liberal regulatory optimists, who take their orientation from normal law and refrain from regulating the emergency case, the first should not be questioned. It is exactly in the abstinence from emergency law that they see the very

---

[170] E.g. Posner and Vermeule, *Terror in the Balance*, reject 'robust judicial review' of governmental measures that qualify as emergency measures and argue instead for 'judicial and legislative deference to governmental decisionmaking in times of emergency' (p. 15).

[171] Benjamin, 'Über den Begriff der Geschichte, These VIII', 697.

[172] Arndt, 'Demokratie Wertsystem des Rechts', 13 (quoting Kelsen, *Allgemeine Staatslehre*).

moral capital of law-rule.[173] Fatalist observers take the supposed 'defencelessness' of the *law* as fate to be overcome at best by war-like measures.[174]

Their critics see the non-regulation of the state of exception as a symptom of the weakness of an 'introvert *Rechtsstaat*'.[175] They accuse those who do not or only partly regulate the case to understand 'the principle of rule of law only from the vantage point of the normal state' and therefore to rashly and carelessly do without 'considering a modified use of the principle in exceptional circumstances'.[176] According to the more strongly phrased criticism, the regulatory optimists were victims of a twofold error concerning both the extent of possible dangers as well as the 'function of legality in times of crisis'[177] and, instead of relying on the Hobbesian political technology necessary in an emergency situation, would rather depend on the impotent legal techniques of governing aligned with the *method Locke* – geared towards the normal state of a 'fair-weather constitution'.[178]

The Legalization of Emergency Powers as Abuse Prevention

In contrast to both classical state-centric models as well as the related notions of Schmitt and Agamben about the lawlessness of the state of exception, the proponents of constitution-centric models argue from the perspective of the regular case – to the extent that, following a positivist vein, they demand the integration of the exceptional case into the regime of law-rule. Their demanding but delicate attempt to contain the state of exception within a constitutional framework[179] is meant to prevent

---

[173] Kägi, *Die Verfassung als rechtliche Grundordnung des Staates*, 115 ff. Perhaps also Borgs-Maciejewski, 'Parlament und Nachrichtendienste'; id. and Ebert, *Das Recht der Geheimdienste*.

[174] Isensee, 'Wehrhafte Demokratie'.

[175] Forsthoff, 'Der introvertierte Rechtsstaat und seine Verortung', 397 ff.: 'Those who have accustomed themselves to the constitutional movements of this century, its revolutions, turning points, civil wars and dictatorships will not doubt that current political theory can less and less afford to only think in normal situations and to still believe in the end of power and politics.'

[176] Schröder, 'Staatsrecht an den Grenzen des Rechtsstaates', 147 ff.

[177] Forsthoff, 'Der introvertierte Rechtsstaat und seine Verortung', 397.

[178] This is the scarcely surprising thesis of Depenheuer, which lays the groundwork for his theory of the enemy and sacrifice; see Depenheuer, *Selbstbehauptung des Rechtsstaates*, especially 26 ff.

[179] From the plethora of 'constitution-centric' literature about the state of exception, see only Thoma, 'Der Vorbehalt der Legislative und das Prinzip der

recourse to both the state's right to self-preservation under a quasi-natural but in any case supra-positive law and necessity beyond (constitutional) law.

With the inevitable constitution-centric juridification, the *raison d'état* is meant to be turned into and civilized as a constitutional reason, and at the same time potentially exceptional situations of crisis are to be addressed by means of regular law. The variations of a state of exception integrated into the rule of law is considerable. They range from 'constitutional dictatorship', the 'militant *Rechtsstaat*' or 'militant democracy' to an 'emergency constitution'. In the following, the fluid transition between state- and constitution-centrism and their specific answers to the issue of abuse prevention is briefly outlined in the example of the influential conception by Clinton Rossiter and Carl J. Friedrich as well as the internalization and normalization of the state of exception.

Following the 'ordinary dictatorship' in the Roman Republic and the disorderly Weimar experience, the theories of a 'constitutional dictatorship'[180] by Rossiter and Friedrich assume that extraordinary crises cannot be managed with the tools of regular constitutional law. As a result, the dictatorial state of exception is permissible, but only for legitimate purposes, especially for the protection and restoration of constitutional conditions:

> The complex system of government of the democratic, constitutional state is essentially designed to function under normal, peaceful conditions, and is often unequal to the exigencies of a great national crisis. [...] Therefore, in time of crisis a democratic, constitutional government must be temporarily altered to whatever degree is necessary to overcome the peril and restore normal conditions.[181]

Clinton Rossiter developed eleven criteria of a constitutional democracy, so as to develop and control executive power in crisis situations. He was well aware of the paradox of this concept as well as of the risk involved

---

Gesetzmäßigkeit von Verwaltung und Rechtsprechung', 232; Hesse, 'Grundfragen einer verfassungsmäßigen Normierung des Ausnahmezustandes'; Arndt, 'Der Rechtsstaat und sein polizeilicher Verfassungsschutz'; Koja, *Der Staatsnotstand als Rechtsbegriff* and Schneider, *Ausnahmezustand und Norm*, 264 ff.

180 This term was coined by Rossiter, *Constitutional Dictatorship*. Earlier, Tingsten, *Les pleins pouvoirs*, and at about the same time Friedrich, *Constitutional Government and Democracy*. Instructive is the differentiated, comparative analysis of Lietzmann, 'Von der konstitutionellen zur totalitären Diktatur' and id., *Die Entwicklung der Totalitarismustheorie Carl J. Friedrichs*.

181 Rossiter, *Constitutional Dictatorship*, 5.

in the partial suspension of a constitution; but he deemed these measures indispensable in view of big economic crises and the emerging nuclear era: 'No sacrifice is too great for our democracy, least of all temporary sacrifice of democracy itself.'[182]

Carl J. Friedrich too could not imagine institutional safeguards that might effectively guarantee the application of emergency powers only to rescue or safeguard the constitution.[183] He feared that a concentration of power not properly controlled could turn into a totalitarian system, given the 'right' political and social conditions. In order to contain this residual risk, he wanted to equip the 'organizational minimum' of the constitution with a dictatorship-proof protection belt. In contrast, Rossiter stressed that emergency law itself had to be subject to checks under constitutional law and codified time limits. With their suggestion to unleash the executive constitutionally in times of crisis, both authors operate in obvious proximity to Schmitt's 'commissarial dictatorship'. This applies particularly to Carl J. Friedrich, whose works before his turn to the critique of totalitarianism testify to a rather negative attitude to pluralism, mass democracy and parliamentarian legislators, and invoke the political imagery of a 19th century constitutional monarchy.

The idea of an 'emergency constitution', which worked as the model for the emergency provisions in the German Basic Law, conceptually goes much further in the direction of a legalized state of exception. It characterizes the precarious and highly ambivalent project to anticipate the crisis-prone reality of exceptional situations and to accept the challenge to regulate them at the level of the constitution as comprehensively as possible without compromising the rule of law.[184]

Since the mid-19th century and even more so after World War I, one may note a tendency to integrate different regimes of emergency under public law into the *Rechtsstaat* as law-maintaining violence – to return to Benjamin's terminology. In legal theory and in the practice of legislation, attempts are undertaken to establish an internal link between law-rule and state of exception, between rule and exception, something which

---

182 Ibid., ch. XIX and 314.

183 Friedrich, *Constitutional Government and Democracy*.

184 This corresponds largely to the nature of the task outlined in Böckenförde, 'Der verdrängte Ausnahmezustand', especially 1885 ff. Its implementation in Western democracies and the amendments of the law of domestic security is seen by Agamben as 'an unprecedented generalization of the paradigm of security as the normal technique of government' (Agamben, *State of Exception*, 14).

becomes structurally manifest in conditional programmes under constitutional or statutory law as well as particular institutions and power distributions geared towards the exceptional situation.

General definitional elements of the legalized state of exception are its formal declaration and limited validity as well as its substantive design that is geared towards a particular predetermined aim, such as the defence of democracy, law-rule or domestic peace. The rationality of law-maintaining violence becomes obvious in the shift of powers from the legislature and judicature to the executive as well as from the police to military forces and secret services. On the other hand, it becomes apparent in the violation or restriction of fundamental rights as negative competences of state agencies in favour of executive powers to intervene in social processes and spheres of freedom. These changes in the regular system of competences and jurisdiction are linked to shifts at the level of institutional organization as well as a turn away from the public to the arcane exercise of state power.

With the constitutional internalization of the exception, law-rule and the state of exception develop a mutually parasitic relationship. Law-rule integrates the extraordinary – one may assume: not carelessly but guided by concerns about power abuse and the averting of dangers. On the one hand, law-rule lends the exception legal structure; on the other hand, law-rule receives an extraordinary power bonus not to be had within the confines of ordinary law. In this way, the constitution spreads into a legal order covering as many exceptional situations as possible to rescue this order from chaos, revolt, coups and disaster. Like a shadow, emergency law from now on accompanies regular law. According to its functions, regular law makes itself available to the engineers of power and can be used by them, outside the confines and liberated from the constraints of the *method Locke*, in whatever crisis situation may occur.

But this is not all. The legal regime of the state of exception develops in the course of its standardization an excess domestic tendency, as will be elaborated in the following chapters. Its legal internalization triggers a dynamic and a habitual process. Part of the dynamic is that the legal institutionalization of the anticipated necessities and emergency powers grants the state authorities, especially the executive, a general responsibility on the quiet for establishing desired security situations of all kinds. The political class reacts to crises of security with almost ritual promises of security and increases thereby the security demands of the population. Just as society mutates into a 'security society'[185] in the shape of a new form of social control and constellation of heightened security expectations, on the one hand; the *Rechtsstaat* turns into a 'security state',[186] on the other hand.

The habituation starts with the integration of the exceptional into law-rule's regular security architecture. The habituation effect is deepened and made permanent by ever new state intervention powers, widely demanded and mostly granted due to given or anticipated events. Exceptional surveillance – be it bugging, dragnet investigations and controls, video and online – or the screening of online communication, racial and ethnic profiling, detention without minimal due process or deportation, guilt by association[187] or the deployment of the armed forces domestically – is gradually, measure by measure, normalized as a regular technique of governing. Regarded as 'not really important' or 'not extraordinary' measures that can be legally justified, exceptional and drastic answers to exceptional circumstances thus move out of sight as threats to democratic law-rule and, more importantly, as threats to society and all ordinary or extraordinary people.

---

[185] For this term, see Singelnstein and Stolle, *Die Sicherheitsgesellschaft*, who follow Garland, *The Culture of Control*; Foucault, *Geschichte der Gouvernementalität I*, especially 52 ff.

[186] Robert, *Le citoyen, le crime et L'État* (Genf: Droz 1999); Denninger, 'Freiheit durch Sicherheit?'

[187] For an overview of US anti-terror measures after 9/11, see Cole and Dempsey, *Terrorism and the Constitution*, 147–75; for a more global perspective, see Cole et al., *Secrecy, National Security and the Vindication of Constitutional Law*.

5. Political extremism and the militancy of law-rule

5.1 PROTEST, LAW-RULE AND FEAR[1]

The 1960s student revolt, protest movements against nuclear armament and, in the Federal Republic of Germany, opposition to emergency laws triggered the first crises in many Western countries after World War II. The situation was dramatically aggravated in the confrontation with terrorist groups, such as the militant separatists of the IRA in Ireland, 'Weathermen' in the United States, the 'Red Army Faction' (RAF) in Germany, the 'Red Brigades' in Italy, the Basque independence movement ETA in Spain and the 'Action Directe' in France.[2]

The escalation of conflicts did not follow the same trajectory everywhere, but showed comparable patterns. Initially confronted with an anti-hegemonic, extra-parliamentary movement that at first resorted to provocation, the police in many European cities reacted as if they were facing real revolt and not (still) non-violent, limited rule violations.[3] This 'cultural-revolutionary' agenda and its outrageous forms of protest, along with the techniques of governing used in response by the somewhat unprepared security services in Germany, France and Italy, have been etched into the collective memory as signs of a new 'militancy'.

In the Federal Republic of Germany, this militancy became for the first time apparent during the unrestrained police operations against young

[1] Some of the following considerations were published in the essay 'Angst im Rechtsstaat', Kritische Justiz (1977), 353 ff.; they were considerably revised for this publication. I have drawn valuable insights from Bung, 'Terror als Gegenstand einer Phänomenologie der Angst'.

[2] Varon, *Bringing the War Home*; Dartnell, *Action Directe*; Cerella, *Il ritorno della violenza*; Engene, *Terrorism in Western Europe*; Hoffmann, *Right wing Terrorism in Europe since 1980*; and Waldmann, *Terrorismus*.

[3] For an instructive and thoughtful analysis of student protests and RAF terrorism, see Scheerer, 'Deutschland: Die ausgebürgerte Linke', 193 ff. Instructive also are Hess, 'Terrorismus und Terrorismus-Diskurs'; Aust, *The Baader-Meinhof Group*.

buskers in Munich, which triggered the so-called *Schwabinger Krawalle*,[4] student riots reacting against police militancy in 1962, and demonstrators protesting against a state visit of the Persian Shah in Berlin. That the student Benno Ohnesorg was killed by police with a shot to the head during such a demonstration on 2 June 1967 matches – despite recently unearthed SED/Stasi connections – the perception of excessive police action and reaction, which resulted in an escalation of the protests.

Confrontation not only with slogans but also through 'direct action' by terrorist groups caused an escalation of violence and prosecution measures on the part of the government, which the scholar of criminal law, Günther Jakobs, as mentioned above, characterized as 'enemy criminal law' with respect to some of the German anti-terror laws. In other states too, methods of governing were stepped up as a secular tendency and shifted from legal to political techniques, frequently analysed as elements of a 'militant democracy'.[5] Under the impression of terrorist attacks, a differentiation took place at both the semantic as well as the operational level. In the fight against 'political extremism', there was a blurring of the significant differences between the actions of self-declared social revolutionary or neo-fascist terrorist groups, on the one hand, and radical student and extra-parliamentary protest, on the other hand, which, in the course of radicalization, moved further and further away from provocative rule violations or the 'market-place' of ideas and arguments.

After the demonstrations and street battles at the end of the 1960s, those state reactions that were etched into the collective memory in the Federal Republic were especially the 1972 'Radicals Decrees' (*Radikalenerlasse*), wiretapping and systematic political snooping, occupational bans, bans on visits and letters for terrorists in prison and dragnets; here, for the first time, *indirect* interventions in social processes – monitoring and surveillance as phenomena of the *method Foucault* – emerged.[6] These techniques of social control in the declared struggle against 'political extremism' pointed for the first time to a normalization of instruments usually classified as emergency law and brought to the fore the problem of fear.

---

4 For a thorough analysis see Fürmetz, *Schwabinger Krawalle*.

5 Cf. Sajó, *Militant Democracy* and the seminal article by Loewenstein 'Militant Democracy and Fundamental Rights'.

6 See, in detail, Gladstone and Brinkmann, 'Militant Democracy and Radicals in the West German Civil Service'; Dyson, 'Anticommunism in the Federal Republic of Germany'; Monson, 'Political Toleration versus Militant Democracy' and Braunthal, *Political Loyalty and Public Service*.

The then Federal President Gustav Heinemann, an observer of the political landscape and certainly not suspected of being close to ultra-leftism, as well as two liberal holders of the Peace Prize of the German Book Trade, the writer Max Frisch and the publicist and political scientist Alfred Grosser, identified the link between fear and political rule as the problem that stands at the centre of the following considerations:

> The development in recent years forces us to carefully investigate these methods [used by the security services – G.F.]. For what we can observe is that the frank and certainly often also unruly behaviour of the young generation, which we saw at the end of the 1960s, has given way to an anxious attitude. Instead of political alertness and the rigorous moral assessment of the political daily routine, it is obvious that conformity and silence spread, as if the only essential thing left is to rescue one's own skin and career. […] The courage decreases to answer for one's own opinion. Amnesty International, for instance, complains that even less and less people are willing to sign a protest against torture.[7]

> Schoolchildren and apprentices, even university students, when asked their thoughts about the tasks of democracy, shrug their shoulders today. They know what the cost can be if they make use of the constitutional right to freedom of expression. The fact that even young people have been successfully coerced into resignation is no triumph of democracy.[8]

In the 1970s and 1980s, the discourse on 'enemies of the state' and 'militant democracy' in numerous countries under law-rule was aimed in the beginning at radicals, then at self-declared social-revolutionary terrorists, including their 'sympathizers' and 'intellectual forerunners'. The strategy of the West German security services stood out only for its hard as well as bureaucratic approach, which levelled the difference between political radicalism and terrorism under the label of anti-extremism.[9] In the measures applied in the fight against radicals and terrorism – and not only in West Germany – a political technology succeeded that was shaped by the imperatives of internal security, freed itself more and more from legal restraints and moved from indirect to direct behavioural control, safeguarded by a wide surveillance regime monitoring extensive loyalty obligations. Anti-extremism as an amalgam of semantics and

---

7 Heinemann, 'Freimütige Kritik und demokratischer Rechtsstaat', 61 ff. Similarly, Grosser, 'Die Bundesrepublik, der internationale und der innere Friede'.

8 Frisch, 'We Hope', 536.

9 See Cobler, *Law, Order, and Politics in West Germany*; Dyson, 'Anti-communism in the Federal Republic of Germany'; and Dobbelstein and Gellert, 'Shades of a New McCarthyism in West Germany?'.

operations resulted in a politics of fear that pointed to a structural change of law-rule and the techniques of governing in quite a few Western industrialized societies, but not only there.[10]

5.2 HOBBES, LOCKE AND THE FREEDOM FROM FEAR

Constitutionally, in a state governed by law-rule, law and freedom are expected to prevail. Freedom under law-rule always implies (which is not to say: guarantees) freedom from fear. Demanded by both conservative and liberal theories, the struggle for freedom from fear accompanied the development of law-rule from its very beginning.[11] In the Hobbesian concept of a semi-government of laws, the fear of an unnatural death rampant in the state of nature is replaced by the fear of punishment meted out by the Leviathan, following the contractual waiver in favour of this legally unrestrained new authority:

> A Punishment, is an Evil inflicted by publique Authority, on him that hath done, or omitted that which is Judged by the same Authority to be a Transgression of the Law; to the end that the will of men may thereby the better be disposed to obedience.[12]

Apart from its deterrent effect, the predictability of a punishment according to the principles *nullum crimen sine lege* and *nulla poena sine lege*[13] already played a significant role in Hobbes' thought. Within the

---

[10] See only Hoffmann, *Right-Wing Terrorism in Europe*; Tan, *Politics of Terrorism*; Engene, *Terrorism in Western Europe*.

[11] Montesquieu, *The Spirit of the Laws*, Book 12, ch. 1 (of the laws that form political liberty in relation to the subject); Hobbes, *De Cive*, ch. I; id., *Leviathan*, ch. 13; preamble of International Convenant on Civil and Political Rights, 16 December 1966; Neumann, 'The Concept of Political Freedom', 195; Arndt, 'Der Rechtsstaat und sein polizeilicher Verfassungsschutz', 898: 'in order to grow democracy from the roots, for everyone, who is an individual also, the freedom from fear is the very first requirement'. Similarly also Denninger, 'Verfassungstreue und Schutz der Verfassung', 27 ff.; Bung, 'Terror als Gegenstand einer Phänomenologie der Angst', 64 (loss of rationality and autonomy caused by fear).

[12] Hobbes, *Leviathan*, part II, ch. 28; see remarks concerning punishment in ch. 17.

[13] 'No crime without law' and 'no punishment without law'. See the Bavarian Criminal Code of 1813. Almost all constitutions prohibit ex post facto (criminal) laws, see for instance Art. 11(2) Universal Declaration of Human

framework of a semi-law-rule he reserved the 'legal punishment imposed by the authorized judge' after 'a preceding public conviction' for the relationship between state and citizen that had to be free from arbitrariness. Due to their 'conscious revolt against the sovereign power', he allowed arbitrary sanctions against 'declared enemies', especially persons guilty of high treason and lese-majesty,[14] and thereby designed the basic features of a lawful enemy criminal law.

Other philosophers also deal with fear in the state of nature. The right to everything,[15] described as follows by John Locke, releases such fear:

> [M]an being born [...] hath by nature a power, not only to preserve his property, that is, his life, liberty, and estate, against the injuries and attempts of other men; but to judge of and punish the breaches of that law in others, as he is persuaded the defense deserves, even with death itself, in crimes where the heinousness of the fact, in his opinion, requires it.[16]

Hobbes' extremely dangerous 'right to everything' is defined more narrowly by Locke, however. Where an authoritative way of conflict resolution is absent, the defence of the natural rights to life, property and freedom is 'very insecure and uncertain'. With the contractual bond of all individuals establishing a community, 'putting themselves under government, is the preservation of their property', an end is found for a situation that is 'full of fears and constant dangers'. From then on, the rule of force and self-help vanish[17] – and concomitantly the ubiquitous fear of the arbitrary use of individual power. Unlike Hobbes, Locke and also Rousseau refrain from using the category of fear in their concepts of the state of the social. Strictly speaking, Locke makes it disappear in the liberal paradigm of the relationship between ruler and the ruled – *limited government* and *rule of law*. Rousseau neutralizes it with the help of the general will of the law-governed republic.[18] One may conclude that this promise of freedom without fear might have been a significant factor in the success of the liberal paradigm and the proliferation of the *method Locke*.

Rights; Art. 103(1) German Basic Law or Art. 1, sec. 9 US Constitution, which prior to the Fourteenth Amendment prohibited the passing of ex post facto laws.

[14] 'Lastly, Harm inflicted upon one that is a declared enemy, falls not under the name of Punishment.' Hobbes, *Leviathan*, part II, ch. 28.

[15] Rousseau, 'Social Contract', Book I, ch. 8.

[16] Locke, *Two Treatises of Government*, Second Treatise, ch. 7.

[17] Ibid., Second Treatise, ch. 9, 154.

[18] Rousseau, 'Social Contract', Book II, ch. 6.

5.3 PRELIMINARY CONSIDERATIONS ON THE ANALYSIS OF POLITICO-LEGAL FEARS

If one can rely on the numerous statements about the state of the German citizenry – at least its active, socially engaged part – before, during and after the *Deutsche Herbst* (German autumn) in 1977, a feeling of fear was predominant. In the then common parlance, it became manifest (also in other European countries) as 'moral cowardice', 'political apathy', 'pussyfooting' and as 'a retreat into the private domain'. This raises the question of what social conditions and changes in normalcy and normativity made virulent 'the danger of devastating the natural, youthful self-confidence'.[19]

An inquiry into the reasons for these frequently debated and certainly not unsubstantiated fears (not only of young people), points far beyond the distinction between law-rule and the state of exception. In this context, it is condensed into the interplay between the institutional and 'pre-institutional elements' of a constitutional democracy.[20] Terms like regressive law-rule and 'fear in the *Rechtsstaat*' indicate that this inquiry confines itself to the psychological dimension of legal forms and structures of political rule. Unlike normative and sociological analyses of law-rule, the following considerations start from the assumption that in the respective historical context there is a demonstrable empirical correlation between legal forms, procedures and structures, on the one hand, and certain types of fear, on the other hand, which can be observed in the behaviour of subjects.

Such an analysis of the politico-legal mechanisms of state technology generating fear and of their manifestation in psychical structures and political behaviour cannot fall back on systematic theoretical studies and solid empirical analyses. Therefore, such an enterprise moves on rather thin ice and needs to reflect an appropriate methodological-theoretical framework in the first place. When addressing the issue of 'fear in the context of law-rule', I am therefore primarily concerned with offering a first path through the psychological dimensions of law-rule and the corresponding political technology handling normal situations. Inevitably, the social and economic fears typical of industrialized/capitalist societies fade into the background, especially fears of failing professionally, of

---

19 Heinemann, 'Freimütige Kritik und demokratischer Rechtsstaat', 61.

20 Denninger, 'Verfassungstreue und Schutz der Verfassung', 26 ff., mentions the freedom from fear as a 'pre-institutional element of a free democratic order'.

losing employment or social status. However, this neither suggests the primacy of the relations between the state and its citizens in the analysis of fear nor does it imply a misleading politicization of the fear *problématique*.

The Fear of the Frighteners

The fear of the frighteners can only be addressed rather briefly here, although it needs theoretical clarification and is of empirical relevance. In the theories of monarchy and tyranny, there are numerous references to the fear-ridden mental state of the ruler. Francis Bacon described such fear as a 'deplorable mental state' if one has little to desire and much to fear. He believed this to be in general the fate of kings who are surrounded by imagined dangers and threatening shadows.[21] For Jean Bodin, fear is an important criterion for distinguishing legitimate monarchy and tyranny:

> Love of the subject for his sovereign is much more conducive to the preservation of the state than fear, for love always has an element of fear in it, the fear of offending the object of one's love.[22]

During the first crisis of the West German *Rechtsstaat* after World War II, the fear of the rulers became manifest in the call for increased protection of the state and in exaggerated threat scenarios suggested by the police. It showed itself in demands for extended powers to intervene, especially by police and security services, and became manifest in the significant growth of available personnel and financial resources in the period from 1968 to 1978. In 1969, the Federal Office for the Protection of the Constitution had 1,016 statutory posts; by 1985 this figure had grown to about 2,200. Its annual budget grew from 4.4 million D-Mark in 1950 to about 210.3 million D-Mark in 1985.[23] The staff of the Federal Criminal Investigation Agency was increased from 500 in the 1960s to 1,500 in the 1980s. In a speech to members of the Federal Criminal Investigation

---

[21] Bacon, 'Of Regiment'.

[22] Bodin, *Six Books of the Commonwealth*, Book II, ch. 4, no. 290 and Book IV, ch. 6, no. 616.

[23] For references, see Schwagerl, *Verfassungsschutz in der Bundesrepublik Deutschland*, 37. Concerning the development of the secret service for the protection of the constitution see: Droste, *Handbuch des Verfassungsschutzrechts* and Foschepoth, *Überwachtes Deutschland*, chs. 4–5. Cf. also Merk and Werthebach, *Innere Sicherheit*; generally, also Scheerer, 'Deutschland', 395 ff., and Hess, 'Terrorismus und Terrorismus-Diskurs', 69.

Agency, Federal Chancellor Helmut Schmidt talked about 3,200 staff and a budget of 270 million D-Mark.[24] The number of police personnel grew from 113,124 in 1960 to 194,203 in 1980. Accordingly, expenditure on public security grew and was repeatedly topped up with additional funds for 'immediate measures to combat terrorism' from 1977 onwards. In 1985 alone, they amounted to 294 million D-Mark.[25] The security apparatus' constant growth in personnel and financial resources continued throughout the period of crisis until the present.[26] In the years of the fight against terror, the fear of attacks had therefore quite significant legitimizing effects and triggered marked phases of repression, which is a reason for pointing to Bodin's dictum that the legitimate monarchy(!) would be more secure if it had fewer security forces than it has.[27]

The theoretical-methodological issues linked to the aspect of rule in an analysis of fear cannot be solved *en passant*. Government and semi-official statements suggest, however, that it was not only terrorist attacks and political extremism that were perceived as dangerous phenomena by the political class but also the 'growing political awareness of the population', a spreading 'intellectual unrest', radically oppositional agendas and the working conditions frequently raised by workers.[28] Social scientific and especially legal studies of political rule have rather tried to

---

24 Boldt and Stolleis, 'Geschichte der Polizei in Deutschland', A Rn. 82, and Schwagerl, *Verfassungsschutz in der Bundesrepublik Deutschland*, 37 with further references.

25 Schwagerl, *Verfassungsschutz in der Bundesrepublik Deutschland*, 37 with further references and Boldt and Stolleis, 'Geschichte der Polizei in Deutschland', A Rn. 79; Bulletin der Bundesregierung No. 31, 6 April 1982.

26 For references, see Lange, *Wörterbuch zur Inneren Sicherheit*; Deutscher Bundestag – 14. Wahlperiode, *BT-Drucksache* 14/4113, 7–8.

27 Bodin, *Six Books of the Commonwealth*, Book IV, ch. 1, no. 519.

28 The then Interior Minister Genscher stressed in a 1972 speech about the state of domestic security that the overall concept of the Federation and federal states 'was the result of a lengthy, meticulous, objective and dispassionate consultation by the Interior Minister of all democratic parties'. Deutscher Bundestag, debate of 22 June 1972. The fear that the labour movement could engage in political protests was articulated by the President of the Federal Intelligence Agency, Günther Nollau, *Wie sicher ist die Bundesrepublik?*, 189: 'The masses will one day become aware that their working conditions, especially the consequences of the division of labour are inhumane, i.e. they do not accommodate their entire human being comprehensively. If this sentiment can be turned into broad outrage against this injustice by a political movement, the situation becomes critical. Our society can use coercive means against terrorist actions committed by small groups. Whether our democracy had the strength to

evade the subject of fear, not least due to reservations about this 'existential term':[29]

> In the regulated language game of the taking and giving of reasons, the confession to emotions is no regular move. Emotion has no relation to truth but at best to truthfulness. But truthfulness is no decisive aspect in science.[30]

Nevertheless, fear is a societal and politico-legal problem that is both susceptible to and in need of analysis. The following considerations use this thesis as a point of orientation,[31] which I would like to illustrate at the trajectory of the German *Rechtsstaat* and political technology in the 1970s and 1980s.

Fear as a Category of Politico-Legal Analysis

Fear may generally be described as

> the totality of the human experience of being threatened, if they are associated with emotional and bodily misery: the motiveless and seemingly motiveless, the real and appropriately motivated as well as the unreal and inappropriately motivated, those related to current as well as future danger, the qualitative and quantitative shadings of permanent anxiety up to acute fear, the dispositional as well as the current conditions.[32]

Fear is consequently an individual but not only subjectively experienced phenomenon insofar as objectively measurable correlates exist.

For heuristic purposes, I differentiate between *real* and *neurotic* fears here. This distinction can be traced back to Søren Kierkegaard, who kept apart fear related to an object, a threat, on the one hand, and objectless diffuse *angst*, on the other hand.[33] In the psychoanalytical theory of Sigmund Freud, this contrast is represented in the very distinction between real and neurotic fear. The distinguishing criterion used is

---

turn machine guns against revolting working masses, I doubt it. A. Noske, who stated in 1919 that "someone has to be the bloodhound", seems not to be in sight.'

29 Similarly, Preuß, 'Gesellschaftliche Bedingungen der Legalität', 30.

30 Bung, 'Terror als Gegenstand einer Phänomenologie der Angst'.

31 Cf. also the studies by Neumann, 'Anxiety and Politics'; Duhm, *Angst im Kapitalismus*; Horn, 'Über den Zusammenhang zwischen Angst und politischer Apathie'; id., *Psychoanalyse – Kritische Theorie des Subjekts* and Wiesbrock, *Die politische und gesellschaftliche Rolle der Angst*.

32 Von Baeyer and von Baeyer-Katte, *Angst*, 26.

33 Kierkegaard, *The Concept of Anxiety*.

initially knowledge about the danger, later it is the appropriateness of fear with regard to the event that triggered it.[34] At first, Freud proceeds on the assumption that a realistic fear is a fear of danger that is actually impending.[35] Furthermore '[t]here are plenty of neuroses which exhibit no anxiety whatever'.[36] Later Freud introduces a distinction between the readiness to feel anxiety (*Angstbereitschaft*) and the development of fear (*Angstentwicklung*), for which the appropriateness of a reaction is decisive and not the origin, i.e. the triggering event, of fear.

If one turns to the rationality (or appropriateness) of the reaction, one can say that real fears warn against concrete danger and threats. They can trigger protective action, like the flight reflex or some avoidance behaviour, and therefore principally allow a conscious or at least near-conscious – in other words, rational or appropriate – engagement with concrete threatening or dangerous phenomena. In contrast, neurotic fear is motivated inappropriately. It is triggered by events that present no serious or no concrete danger and prevents possible protective action in the form of fear paralysis.[37] Decisive for the emergence of neurotic fears is less the actual danger of a situation or event, but rather past experiences and perceptions of threats triggering them. Freud denotes such a form of free-floating fears as 'anxious expectancy' or 'expectant anxiety', which 'lies in wait for any opportunity that will allow it to justify itself'.[38]

Despite the problem of maintaining the ideal-typical distinction between real fears and neurotic fears (or: anxieties or *Ängste*), especially in view of their inherent anticipatory elements and the unsolved question

---

[34] Freud's two theories of fear and its contradictions or tensions respectively are not reconstructed here but used to elucidate the problem of rationality. See, for more detail, Körtner, *The End of the World*, 108.

[35] Freud, 'Inhibitions, Symptoms and Anxiety', 108.

[36] Ibid.

[37] The interplay of real and neurotic fears is outlined by Neumann ('Anxiety and Politics', 275) as follows: 'The external dangers which threaten a man meet the inner anxiety and are thus frequently experienced as even more dangerous than they really are. At the same time, these same external dangers intensify the inner anxiety. The painful tension which is evoked by the combination of inner anxiety and external danger can express itself in either of two forms: in depressive or in persecutory anxiety'.

[38] Freud, 'Introductory Lectures on Psycho-analysis', 398. I owe this reference to Freud to Jochen Bung, who problematizes the conflating of real and neurotic fears in Freud's second theory of fear.

of their emergence,[39] I nevertheless try to apply them to the realm of the *Rechtsstaat* and transfer them to cognitive safety. Cognitive safety implies more than a vague feeling of safety, namely the certainty of individual actors, resulting from the 'cognitive underpinning' of the validity of norms,[40] that they can take their scope of action as relatively secure and, hence, assume – rightly or not – that the use of freedom protected under (constitutional) law comes usually with no nasty surprises or incalculable risks. In particular, those principles of law-rule work towards cognitive safety – or one might say: secure insecurity – that are meant to demarcate a civil level of expectations: determinacy, clarity of norms and effective, proportional protection of (fundamental) rights. In this respect, cognitive safety can be seen as a result of the freedom from fear and is, like the latter, a necessary condition for the normativity of normalcy. In contrast, any cognitive insecurity on the part of citizens generates a 'chilling effect'[41] that becomes among other things manifest in their lacking willingness to publicly present their interests and demands and to utilize their freedom for this purpose. Marcel Gauchet characterized this phenomenon aptly as 'civil desertion' from the public arenas.

In regimes of law-rule, politico-legally dangerous situations, which may trigger real fear, typically come from statutory prohibitions or requirements and such provisions that allow state interventions, like the restriction of freedoms or censorship. Whoever violates or does not meet such a norm can feel fear of punishment or a loss of gratification, if a sanction has to be reckoned with. Whoever, for instance, 'kills a person deliberately' is punished for manslaughter or murder with imprisonment. Consequently, most perpetrators will feel real fear during the violation of a sanction-equipped legal norm, provided they experience 'the custodians of the law as a representative of their rule conscience but also as an authority implementing these rules'.[42] The clearer the formulation of a legal command and its sanctions, the more comprehensive is their threat to the addressees of the norm.

The situation is different, when the semantics and substance of behavioural rules remain vague or ambiguous and entail only unclear or implicit threats of sanctions. Rather than instilling fear of a fairly

---

39 See Bung, 'Terror als Gegenstand einer Phänomenologie der Angst' with further references.

40 Jakobs, 'Das Selbstverständnis der Strafrechtswissenschaft'.

41 See Furedi, *The Politics of Fear*; Robin, *Fear: The History of a Political Idea*.

42 Von Baeyer and von Baeyer-Katte, *Angst*, 94.

concrete threat, they generate behavioural uncertainty: they increase the feeling of cognitive insecurity with the effect that the fear of the state's use of force intensifies and is made permanent, because diffuse threats hinder or prevent all measures to deal with them 'appropriately', such as especially the assessment of the danger, the influencing of the threat, flight or a change in behaviour. This means that real fear becomes secondarily neuroticized and can establish itself as a syndrome of ubiquitous anxieties in the structures of behaviour. These anxieties can coagulate into 'structural anxiety', since diffuse fears no longer relate to a concrete triggering event or person, but turn into and become permanent as a general undefined feeling of endangerment. The latter has a paralysing effect on the autonomy of decision-making and willingness to take action.

It is not only vague legal elements of an offence but also vague structures of norms authorizing covert or highly pre-emptive and incalculable police measures – such as wiretapping, 'consultations' without legally determined procedures, political snooping by anonymous authorities and the defamation of criticism – that nurture the notion of a Leviathan, a ubiquitous and largely unrestrained authority, which registers and sanctions potentially every anomalous and deviant behaviour that may violate the ambiguous norms. In the course of this development, the general relationship between citizen and state is increasingly experienced as 'organized peacelessness',[43] as a domestic system of surveillance and repression, if and to the extent that civic freedom does not sufficiently guarantee the necessary cognitive security of the individual – or at least the conviction of one's own safety already demanded by Montesquieu.

Fear Reactions

Aiming at indirect behaviour control, a diffuse threat on the part of the addressees or the public respectively may result in far-reaching behavioural changes: intangible threats may, for instance, cause the feeling of intimidation and fear paralysis, which become manifest in the over-adaptation to what is supposedly required ('fearful people are more conservative'[44]) and the attempt to remain unnoticed at any cost. Over-adaptation also becomes apparent in the hasty voluntary waiver of legal

[43] For this issue at the level of interstate threat, see Senghaas, 'Zur Pathologie organisierter Friedlosigkeit'.

[44] Hatemi et al., 'Fear as a Disposition and an Emotional State'.

positions.[45] This reaction fits in with education in the family and at school that is based not on trust but on sternness, accompanied by punishment, and produces the 'authoritarian personality' type.[46] Incapable of understanding the conditions, i.e. a threatening situation, this type is pressed towards depending on the authorities due to its underdeveloped ability to decide.[47] This is meant to offer a simple interpretation of the threat and to provide the certainty that everything necessary is being done to avert the danger. The self-weakness of the authoritarian personality causes a diminished tolerance for fear. Such a disposition is reinforced by specific adaptation requirements in professional life and the 'politically and economically manipulated exclusion from responsibility'.[48] To exaggerate somewhat, one could therefore argue that diffuse politico-legal threat situations encourage the emergence of neurotic forms of fear, which take on the dispositional anxiety of a child and infantilize the sovereign citizen, who is at least conceptionally and in theories of democracy meant to be an active participant.

The awareness of an intangible ubiquitous threat can, however, also provoke proactive reactions instead of a retreat. Less common than fear paralysis and political quietism, such activism finds expression, for instance, in the flaunting of illegal actions, kamikaze operations, rampages and martyrdom. Political murder, terror attacks and declarations of domestic war against a state perceived as threatening can be interpreted as mad and fatal attempts to give one's own threat scenarios a sharp outline in order to master them in this way – be it at the price of destruction or self-destruction.[49]

The *via media* between quietism and actionism and their respective variants, however, does not represent the line of least resistance. Focusing on rational protective action, an alternative presupposes that one remains within the tension-ridden realm of a diffuse threat and does not repress vague fears in order to manage inner conflict and, ultimately, the reasons

---

45 Such as, for instance, the common reaction to intervention into data privacy: that one had nothing to hide.

46 See, for a seminal work, Adorno, *The Authoritarian Personality*; Fromm et al., *Studien über Autorität und Familie*; Richter, *Eltern, Kind und Neurose*.

47 According to Neumann, persecutory fears lead to political alienation and apathy, 'because the individual sees no possibility of changing anything in the system through his efforts' ('Anxiety and Politics', 290).

48 See, for more detail, Horn, 'Über den Zusammenhang zwischen Angst und politischer Apathie'; and Robin, *Fear.*

49 For a theory covering these phenomena, see Hess, 'Terrorismus und Terrorismus-Diskurs'; and Scheerer, 'Ein theoretisches Modell zur Erklärung sozialrevolutionärer Gewalt'.

for such fears. To stand firm requires a high degree of fear tolerance, courage, intelligence and discipline so that the necessary warning function of fears is neither switched off nor turned into ubiquitous anxieties, which paralyse the willingness to decide and act. This can be illustrated with the help of some examples. Whoever participates in a 'wildcat strike' should accept the risk that this might jeopardize his employment. Those who want to participate in a banned demonstration or become a member of an organization labelled 'anti-constitutional' should also accept such a risk. In these situations, fear is not a sign of cowardice, nor a neurotic reaction, but initially an appropriate warning about concrete danger.

However, if fear is so intense that those concerned cannot take advantage of their scope of action, refrain from political protest or do not dare to imagine, let alone to express, ideas about societal alternatives, the warning about the danger becomes itself a danger. For the governors who frighten and intimidate gain ever-new possibilities, if civic action is not taken due to fear or cognitive uncertainty respectively. The less the subjects, who are meant to be the authors of the law, make use of their rights, the more likely it is that these very rights are taken away from them. The more they recede from the danger of being labelled as 'enemy', the larger is the scope for the state authorities to define 'enemy' and 'friend' and to turn 'the orientation toward the friend'[50] under the rule of law into a focus on the enemy. The more emphatically they keep silent about the intimidation, the more isolated they remain within the 'silent majority' – even if they might have contemplated a more courageous part.

5.4 THE FREEDOM FROM FEAR AND RATIONALITY UNDER LAW-RULE

The constitution of the civic state as a state subject to law-rule or as 'limited and lawful government' emerged, as outlined above,[51] in the theoretical and practical engagement with princely-monarchic sovereignty and the privileges claimed by nobility and clergy. On the eve of the democratic revolutions, the term '*Rechtsstaat*' emerges in political theory as a polemical term, which reckons with the absolutist practices of

[50] See Neumann, 'Anxiety and Politics'; Schneider, *Ausnahmezustand und Norm*, 244.

[51] See Chapter 3 above.

rule. And this was the revolutionary achievement of the aspiring bourgeoisie: it rationalized the state's monopoly on force, which became subordinated to economic purposes and was civilized, or rather transformed, into a bourgeois arrangement by law-rule.

Formal Rationality, Legislative Political Technology and the Freedom from Fear

This transformation initially becomes manifest in the formal rationality of the rule of law and the *Rechtsstaat* accompanied by the legislative state technology of the *method Locke*. Formal rationality turns societal relationships and conflicts into legal relationships by introducing and safeguarding universal forms of intercourse.[52] On the one hand, social asymmetries and violence vanish behind the mutual and non-violent forms of intercourse (contract) and formal rules (law) for the private pursuit of interests so as to ensure peaceful competition among citizens. On the other hand, the peaceful coexistence of citizenry and state is guaranteed in the concept of the *Rechtsstaat* mainly through civic freedoms and participatory rights, the separation of powers, the binding of executive power to acts of parliament as well as due process, fair trial and other legal guarantees in criminal procedures. Its obligation to the principle of legality is meant to prevent the executive power from intervening in societal and private life by way of personal orders, biased contracts with subjects or arbitrary actions, just like the prince previously. Ideal-typically, the expectation that sanctions under criminal law among other things refer only to external behaviour and not to supposed convictions is moreover geared towards substantively defined and therefore calculable laws.[53]

In this model of rule, political technology gains the contours of formal rational legality. Sovereign interventions are both predictable as well as calculable, as far as they follow the *method Locke*. Only those who violate laws need to fear sanctions. To the extent that rule is by semantically and substantively determined general laws, which prohibit or allow concrete behaviour, have no retroactive effect and are at least on

---

[52] For the significance of universal forms of intercourse, see Preuß, *Bildung und Herrschaft: Beiträge zu einer politischen Theorie des Bildungswesens*, 54 ff.

[53] Montesquieu, *The Spirit of the Laws*, Book 12, chs. 11 and 12; see also Denninger, *Verfassungstreue und Schutz der Verfassung*, 28, for further references.

average respected by the state, one can say that real fear is institutionalized.[54] For the regime of formal rationality claims to stop arbitrary acts of government and to ensure thereby freedom from fear and cognitive safety to the (economically?)[55] required and tolerated extent.

In principle, however, the project of a formal rational state governed by the rule of law and its primarily legislative state technology can only be successful if it is possible to define what is general law and, hence, what lawful is meant to mean, based on harmonious or harmonizable societal interests. This enterprise fails if the particular interests of an elite, group or class gain general validity by legislation or by enforcing state measures even against applicable law, when required.

However, civil society has never experienced a socio-economic equilibrium and the corresponding politico-legal repose required by the logic of formal rationality. The bourgeoisie had barely gained its freedom from princely sovereignty and estate-based privileges, when it had to defend itself again against the emerging industrial proletariat. The latter took 'the bourgeoisie at its word'[56] and demanded the redemption of freedom and equality. In early constitutionalism too, whose idealized conception was the model for the liberal twin project of a free competitive economy plus a minimal state, there could be no talk of both a socially balanced and peaceful situation as well as a state free market economy. There is certainly evidence of direct regulatory sovereign interventions in societal relationships, such as, for instance, the compulsory introduction of wage employment or the disciplining of the population and workers by a ban on association and strikes.[57] These interventions point to another rationality.

Material Rationality, Executive Political Technology and Freedom from Fear

Consequently, one always has to add to the formal rationality of law-rule and the legislative style of legal techniques of governing also their

---

[54] Neumann ('Anxiety and Politics', 291) distinguishes real fears in a 'halfway liberal' and 'depressive and persecutory anxiety' in a 'totally repressive' system. See also Shklar, 'Liberalism of Fear'.

[55] See Robin, *Fear.*

[56] Engels, *Anti-Dühring.*

[57] Cf. van Creveld, *The Rise and Decline of the State*, especially part IV; Reinhard, *Geschichte der Staatsgewalt*; Gerstenberger, 'Zur Theorie der Konstitution des bürgerlichen States'; Kühnl, *Formen bürgerlicher Herrschaft Liberalismus – Faschismus*.

(hidden) material rationality. Its aim is not legal certainty but rather is shaped in terms of content, especially socio-economic content. The instruments of a primarily executive style of governing, which leaves the ideal type of the law as a form of action and becomes manifest in *measures,* especially to ensure the distribution of public goods, rather than laws, point to this content. In the institutional shape of the welfare and interventionist state, the material or social *Rechtsstaat* respectively re-shapes the liberal construct of a government of laws and not of men. The new state technology appears in systematic interventions to regulate markets and production, to provide human resources, infrastructure and fundamental services (services of general interest), to correct market results through the secondary distribution of income, to provide risk management in an industrial society and also to ensure the primary distribution of public goods.[58]

Of interest here is whether and how the numerous tasks of the interventionist state and its strategies and practices have always modified and compromised the formal rational promise of freedom from fear by law-rule. I therefore address those mechanisms first that undermine the freedom from fear and lead to cognitive uncertainty. At the level of regulatory technique, they show in the porous structure and gaps of norms, notably indeterminate concepts and general clauses[59] as well as in blanket norms and legal dummies.[60] Such structurally 'undone' laws grant ample discretion to the agencies they empower and, by the same token, deprive their civic addresses of legal certainty,[61] yet keep up the appearance of both the form of law-rule and the legitimizing commitment to law. However, they extend the scope for governmental and administrative intervention and replace the general laws by or align them with concrete ad hoc measures, lacking in predictability and legal certainty.

---

[58] For the burgeoning literature on the welfare and interventionist state, see Polanyi, *The Great Transformation*; Ritter, *Der Sozialstaat – Entstehung und Entwicklung im internationalen Vergleich*; Ewald, *L'État providence*; Stolleis, 'Die Entstehung des Interventionsstaates und das öffentliche Recht'; Obinger and Zohlnhöfer, 'Abschied vom Interventionsstaat?'.

[59] See, already, Neumann, *The Democratic and the Authoritarian State*, ch. 2, 22 ff.

[60] Maus, *Rechtstheorie und Politische Theorie im Industriekapitalismus*, and id., 'Perspektiven "reflexiven Rechts" im Kontext gegenwärtiger Deregulierungstendenzen'.

[61] For these different readings, see Schmitt, *Constitutional Theory*, § 1; and Alexy, *A Theory of Constitutional Rights*, 80.

Violence, Legal Certainty and the Politics of Fear

The general nature and structure of law as a necessary condition for the institutionalization of realistic fear is also undermined so long as the exercise of power operates in the modality of force/violence.[62] In a society that cannot dispense with violence as a principle, 'complete generality of law is impossible'.[63] Genuine – semantic, structural and procedural – generality is undermined to the extent that governments resort to violence because of its ad hoc nature and inherent dynamics. Therefore violent interventions have to be limited, for reasons of legitimacy and the economics of power, in scope and intensity and with regard to its addressees. The residual formal rationality requires to threaten with and delay its use, as far as possible, to deploy it only when absolutely necessary. The logic of the situational confining of violence, its delaying and gradual use according to occasion finds expression among other things in the provisions of criminal law and penal law, police and other regulatory law, compulsory enforcement and particularly clearly in the rules for the use of direct coercion.

The appearance of formal rationality is likely be destroyed when and where the state is situationally and visibly present as an 'extra-economic coercive force', and whenever techniques of government are used to protect a private property regime or exploitative economic processes, or to intervene in conflicts between antagonistic groups and associations. In normal everyday conflicts, the intervening power is less visible; and they can routinely be transferred from the social to political, parliamentary or judicial arenas. In this way, they can be deferred and displaced, submitted to parliamentary or judicial routines and domesticated.[64] Thereby, it is possible to sublimate violence and to establish the state as neutral guarantor of the 'public interest'.[65] The sublimation of violence and civilization of conflicts is in danger, once the intervention (welfare) state turns into the real addressee of all sorts of societal demands and is

---

[62] See Benjamin, 'Critique of Violence'; Derrida, 'Force of Law'. For a phenomenology of violence, see Reemtsma, *Vertrauen und Gewalt*, 101 ff., 256 ff.

[63] Neumann, *The Democratic and The Authoritarian State*, ch. 2, 66.

[64] See Rödel et al., *Die demokratische Frage*; Frankenberg, *Die Verfassung der Republik*, esp. ch. VII.

[65] For a Marxist perspective, see Gerstenberger, 'Klassenantagonismus, Konkurrenz und Staatsfunktionen Gesellschaft – Beiträge zur Marxschen Theorie 3', 10; from the perspective of conservative statism, see Forsthoff, *Der Staat der Industriegesellschaft*.

expected to manage economic crises, answer the social question and ensure social peace by readjusting the unequal distribution of wealth and opportunities. With law-rule being transformed into an interventionist regime of policy measures, the claim that social relations can be regulated by general laws and within formal legal procedures is dropped.[66]

A modicum of legal clarity and legal certainty, established by general norms, can only be maintained in those areas of conflict where the configuration of interests is relatively clear and legally operationalizable, because no social group or class is denied the opportunity to live, gain wealth or learn in a particularly blatant manner. Structural poverty, unemployment, 'bottlenecks' in the education system, cost explosions in the health system, environmental degradation, problems with energy security, financial crises and other phenomena of crisis call for problem-solving strategies by the state and techniques of governing that transgress the confines and forms of ordinary law-rule. Formal rational law with its accompanying long-winded legislative procedures turns out to be too cumbersome. Legislation that meets the criteria of generality is in rapid succession replaced by hastily cobbled together legislative measures barely debated in parliament, by executive orders, decrees and guidelines, which ensure quick and flexible decision-making. The 'prerogative state'[67] installs a regime of measures with only a very thin legal veneer and operates with the instruments of political technology liberated from Lockean forms and constraints.

With the transition from formal to material rationality, policies tend to be legitimized by what they achieve rather than their legality. For this transformation, however, a high price has to be paid in the long run. The complexity and costliness of these extended state responsibilities pave the way for failures of crisis management that render legitimation based on achievement precarious. Formulas such as 'equal opportunity', 'social symmetry', 'full employment' or 'improvement in the quality of life' reflect attempts to align certain policies with a utility value. These legitimizing aims, however, institutionalize a pressure to act and perform accordingly. If those affected are dissatisfied with their particular situation, then they are likely to *politically* enforce the alleged utility value of policy and will not easily be pacified with *legal* answers.

---

66 Preuß, 'Gesellschaftliche Bedingungen der Legalität', 20.

67 This term was coined by Ernst Fraenkel in contrast to the 'normative state' (see Fraenkel, *The Dual State*).

Since the visibility and frequency of the use of physical violence as well as the intensity of coercion are critical variables for the legitimacy of political power and the stability of a political regime, political technology, as a rule, eschews violent means – be it even as *ultima ratio*. In contrast, structural violence is less conspicuous and more effective[68] because institutionally mediated power relations may appear as natural environment. If structural violence does not suffice, it may be efficacious to use violent means against out-groups as 'internal enemies' or peace-breakers and offenders, singled out and criminalized as 'hostile elements', preferably of foreign origin.

In a flanking move, official concepts of the enemy and threat scenarios provide the public with interpretations of societal conflicts and the background for threatening phenomena; they also produce an increased need for appeasement and harmonizing authoritative symbols.[69] As a result, the politics of fear generates a momentous tension between threats and appeasement. Whether intended or not, it mobilizes latent fears and needs for security on the part of the addressees. Precaution becomes the only value that finds general recognition; freedom, courage and dignity are sacrificed to the prejudice that 'our' security is the only issue that counts.[70] At the same time, it overtaxes – due to the excessive scope of security promises, fears and security needs – a state that regresses as *Rechtsstaat* by withdrawing promises of freedom and law-rule, while it presents itself as a security state – though unable to compensate for loss of freedom with gains in security under a political-legal regime of fear.

5.5 MANIPULATIONS OF THE LEGISLATIVE TECHNIQUES OF GOVERNING

The extent to which politics is able to regulate and reinterpret conflicts of interests and power struggles authoritatively and without loss of legitimacy depends generally upon whether (a) societal conditions are opaque, (b) threats are perceived clearly and immediately, (c) strong counter-positions exist, and (d) to what extent alternative interpretations stemming from other societal interactions are available. However, whether a state, under the obligation to maintain at least the allure of law-rule, is

68 For this term, see Galtung, 'Violence, Peace and Peace Research'.

69 Cf. Edelman, *The Symbolic Uses of Politics*, 10–19 and 34, and the introduction by Claus Offe, ibid.

70 Similarly Bung, 'Terror als Gegenstand einer Phänomenologie der Angst', 72.

able to exceed the legal confines of its authority with concrete interventions and symbolic mystifications and to manipulate fears as well as concepts of the enemy without losing its mandate to act with the (unquestioned) authority of law depends to a great extent on its ability to disguise such violations or to justify them as necessary to cope with an extraordinary crisis.

This issue is illustrated by three politico-legal tendencies in the 1970s and early 1980s, which brought the German Basic Law and the *Rechtsstaat*, as in some neighbouring countries, close to a regime of emergency law. These events and the reactions they provoked on the part of the governments involved significantly shifted the techniques of governing from the legal to the political and changed the conditions for freedom from fear by giving state authorities extraordinary powers and additional leeway in operations against 'extremists' and 'terrorists'. In the following I discuss three structural changes of law-rule that had adverse effects on the political climate in Germany.

The Return of the 'Enemy'

According to the liberal paradigm, the separation of powers is not only a question of how labour is divided among the branches of government but has always been considered as a mechanism to ensure freedom. Locke made this point in his *Second Treatise of Government* and Montesquieu in *Spirit of the Laws*. The French Declaration of the Rights of Man and of the Citizen dignified the separation of powers in 1789 as constituent of a democratic constitution.[71] Since then it has been regarded as modernity's promise of coherence and transparency for the benefit of citizens.[72]

Like many other constitutions, the German Basic Law also follows the classical path, although it replaces the classical model of separation of powers with a complex system of separations and entanglements,[73] allocating specific competencies to the different branches of government. One aspect of this system is the so-called 'privilege' of political parties to be declared unconstitutional *only* by the Federal Constitutional Court. Therefore no other state agency or agent may officially establish a party's unconstitutionality. By the same token, it was a given that, in terms of the

---

[71] Art. 16 of the 1789 Declaration of the Rights of Man and the Citizen: 'Any society in which the guarantee of rights is not secured, or the separation of powers not determined, has no constitution at all.'

[72] See Reemtsma, *Vertrauen und Gewalt*, 167.

[73] See Hanebeck, *Der demokratische Bundesstaat des Grundgesetzes* and Oeter, *Integration und Subsidiarität im deutschen Bundesstaatsrecht*.

constitution and the laws, internal 'enemies' – in the Schmittian sense or as defined by Günther Jakobs – do not exist. Such was the 'lesson' drawn from the Weimar Republic, and indeed most legal scholars assumed that the Weimar practice of politically bringing into disrepute parties or their members as 'anti-constitutional' or 'constitutional enemies' had been ruled out.[74]

Nevertheless, state practice and especially the Offices for the Protection of the Constitution began to operate, notably in the 1970s, quite unabashedly with the term 'constitutional enemy'. In its decision concerning the 'Radicals Decree', the Constitutional Court did not only refrain from opposing this executive practice inaugurated by the security and intelligence services but explicitly sanctioned the violation of the 'party privilege' as well as the separation of powers it implied:

> Affiliation with or membership in an anti-constitutional party, whether or not the Federal Constitutional Court has declared it unconstitutional, is an admissible factor in evaluating the credentials of an applicant.[75]

This decision granted the executive power official permission to refer to and politically defame 'anti-constitutional' parties or 'constitutional enemies'.[76] So, during the first crisis of law-rule, this practice of political defamation of parties (and also associations and individuals) was informed by the secret service (the Federal Office and the State Offices for the Protection of the Constitution), then translated into the politics of loyalty oaths and tests, and finally received constitutional blessing from the Federal Constitutional Court. Thus was installed and spread a regime of political suspicion, which favoured the perception of the executive and judiciary (and, as we will see later, also the legislature), against the backdrop of a Hobbesian concept of political technology, as a unitary association for the mutual generation of political distrust. In state practice it seems to be irrelevant that this view turns the relation of law-making

---

[74] This conclusion is also supported by the fact that the concept of an internal 'enemy' in the Schmittian sense does not appear in the Basic Law.

[75] Decision of the Federal Constitutional Court, 22 May 1975 (*BVerfGE* 39, 334/8). Using the term 'enemy of the constitution' was rather unnecessary, since in the context of civil service law radical opposition to the Basic Law or its rejection would have to be qualified as a violation of the duty of loyalty in view of the special constitutional loyalty required from civil servants.

[76] For the principally admissible reference to 'anti-constitutional' tendencies in the Annual Reports on the Protection of the Constitution, see the recent decision of the Federal Constitutional Court (*BVerfGE* 113, 63/74 ff.).

and law-execution on its head and, thus, neutralizes the effective control of executive and administrative agencies.

Legalizing Ex Post Facto

Where the executive may act with impunity on the basis of self-authorizations, the parliamentary legislator and especially the rulings of a constitutional court are relegated to legalizing post hoc the already executed political necessities. In the context of the defence against radicals in the 1970s, originally not necessarily related to counter-terrorism, the extra-constitutional discourse about 'constitutional enemies' was translated from an executive-bureaucratic practice into the legislative vocabulary. As a matter of fact, in a reversal of what Locke and Montesquieu may have had in mind, parliaments executed the counter-extremist policy defined by the executive power and legalized ex post facto an already ongoing practice, very much in the vein of methods of illiberal governmentality.[77] First, proposals for the amendment of the Civil Service Act assumed more or less without hesitation that 'constitutional enemies' exist not only in the militant executive rhetoric but also *by law* and that the screening of political convictions is necessary, possible and can be done correctly – *lege artis* – under law-rule.[78] Second, informed by the 'Radicals Decree' issued in 1972 by the heads of the Federal Government and the States,[79] various amendments to the Constitution Protection Acts of the Federation and the *Länder* provided a retrospective legal basis for the hitherto common but extra-legal collaboration of the Offices for the Protection of the Constitution with the administration (and later also with the private sector) in background checks for employment.[80]

---

[77] Cobler, *Law, Order, and Politics in West Germany*.

[78] For references, see Denninger, *Freiheitliche demokratische Grundordnung*, 568 and 571.

[79] In 1976 the coalition government of Social Democrats and Liberal Democrats decided to discontinue the practices based on the 'Radicals Decree' for the federal civil service.

[80] For instance, Art. 2(2)(No. 4) Bavarian Act on the Protection of the Constitution (*Verfassungsschutzgesetz*) of 8 August 1974: 'The Bavarian Office for the Protection of the Constitution collaborates on […] 4) the background check of individuals that have applied to join the civil service.' Cf. Denninger, *Freiheitliche demokratische Grundordnung*, 660 ff.

Third, other examples of the ex post legalization were the shoot-to-kill provisions in some of the *Länder* police statutes,[81] and also, after wiretapping operations had been revealed, provisions that would cover actions like the 1975 break-in and installation of a mini-transmitter behind the edge of the writing desk of a nuclear manager (who had turned into an anti-nuke activist).[82]

Legality in Advance

Where particular practices of state authorities are not sanctified by positive norms, the legislator occasionally closes this supposed gap to provide *future*, politically expedient actions with a legal basis – as, one might say, a kind of danger prophylaxis. In this vein, the interior ministers of the federal and state governments passed a number of measures, for instance, allowing shoot-to-kill also against persons 'who appear not to be 14 years old, if the use of firearms is the only means to avert danger for life and limb'; furthermore the use of firearms was also legalized 'against a crowd', 'if it undertakes or emanates acts of violence and coercive measures against individuals promise no success'.[83] Following the 1976 model draft of a unitary police law for the Federation and *Länder*, a number of the latter indeed introduced such provisions.[84] Heads of the executive believed that it was 'one of the most important tasks of politics … to legalize necessary police action'. And they also solved the problem of how the legalized killing of innocent bystanders could be avoided and the principle of proportionality of police action could be maintained: 'I can throw the hand grenade far enough to one side'.[85]

In other areas, the executive power received a legislative 'advance' for future security operations. The Federal Border Police Act, originally limited to operating within a 30 kilometre zone along the wide border,

---

[81] See, for instance, the provisions of the model draft for a unitary police law; for references, see Denninger, *Freiheitliche demokratische Grundordnung*, 718 ff., and Funk and Werkentin, 'Der Todesschuß der Polizei' for further references.

[82] See *Frankfurter Allgemeine Zeitung*, 21 March 2011.

[83] See §§ 41, 43, 44 of the model draft for a unitary police law passed by the Conference of Interior Ministers 1976. See Funk and Werkentin, 'Der Musterentwurf für ein einheitliches Polizeigesetz – ein Muster exekutiven Rechtsstaatsverständnisses'.

[84] For references, see Pieroth et al., *Polizei- und Ordnungsrecht*, 422 ff.

[85] Interior Minister of Rhineland-Palatinate, Heinz Schwarz, quoted by *Der Spiegel* No. 32, 2 August 1976, 31.

was in 1972 allowed to leave such a strip not only in emergency situations but also in order to support regular police forces (of the States) 'to maintain or restore public security or order in cases of particular significance'. This advance official assistance was meant to improve the chances 'to squash an armed revolution [...] in a pre-revolutionary situation'.

In a comparable manner, the closure of supposed gaps in political criminal law led to an extreme 'forward strategy' in the fight against extremists and terrorists. For example, the provisions to protect 'communal peace' were meant as a 'necessary complement' to fill the gaps in political criminal law;[86] they also sanctioned the 'advocacy of violence'.[87]

The practice of closing legislative gaps reveals two reality levels of political decision-making: first, at the instrumental and operative level, new types of offences and offenders were introduced and the state security apparatus was extended so as to be able to manage all kinds of social conflicts with authoritative force. According to the preventive logic and strategy of anti-extremism, the police were authorized, for example, to monitor lawful strikes, assemblies and demonstrations.[88] Second, at the symbolic level, the *legislative* provisions for protecting 'communal peace', public security and order as well as *executive* decrees and statements concerning extremism (promising that revolutions would be prevented etc.) conveyed to the public that the situation was serious but that the determination and vision of the political leadership could be relied upon.

---

86 The elements of offences in political criminal law seem to leave hardly any gaps, however: defamation of the state and its symbols (§ 90a StGB), anti-constitutional defamation of constitutional organs (§ 90b StGB), breach of the public peace by threatening to commit offences (§ 126 StGB), incitement to hatred (§ 130 StGB), dissemination of depictions of violence (§ 131 StGB), rewarding and approving of offences (§ 140 StGB) and threatening the commission of a felony (§ 241 StGB).

87 § 88a StGB (advocacy of violence) was later struck from the code due to massive public criticism. See Wiggershaus and Wiggershaus, 'Was schützt das "Gesetz zum Schutz des Gemeinschaftsfriedens"?'. Today § 130a StGB only sanctions the 'instructing of unlawful acts'.

88 In response to a go-slow of air traffic controllers, the phone conversations of the President of the Association of Air Traffic Controllers, Wolfgang Kassebohm, were bugged by judicial order. The bugging was ordered on suspicion of blackmail, *Süddeutsche Zeitung*, 14/15 May 1977, 5. The surveillance of demonstrations is regulated under §§ 12a, 19a Assembly Act.

Blanket Legality

In the case of retrospective or prophylactic legalization of repressive or preventive techniques of governing, the legislator is often provided with carte blanche instead of a clear and substantively precise authority to intervene. Vague legal concepts, such as, for instance, 'advocacy of violence', 'public order', 'necessary measures', etc., increase the porosity and flexible manipulability of authorization norms, even more so if these terms appear in combination. This development is further aggravated through the coupling of indeterminate legal concepts and general clauses, for example, authorizing the Federal Border Police 'to adopt the necessary measures after due consideration' and the Office for the Protection of the Constitution 'to use intelligence measures' – both authorized to fulfil their respective tasks.[89]

Blanket norms and legal dummies[90] liberate the legislator from the requirements of a proper legislative style: namely, to pass syntactically transparent, substantively determined elements of offences, which opens up or closes down the calculable scope of action for norm addressees to ensure a minimum of legal certainty as well as judicial 'density' of controls and thereby institutionalizing real fear rather than anxiety. Instead, the legislator issues totalizing, overbroad authorizations to let the political have its way at the expense of the legal. During the 1972 amending of the Constitutional Protection Act the parliamentary committee openly declared its self-emasculation and deference to the executive power:

> A substantive clarifying of the term 'intelligence means' [in § 3 of the Act – G.F.] turned out to be impractical. For the definition of legally permissible

---

[89] Cf. § 10(1)(1) Federal Border Police Act with its successor regulation § 14(1) Federal Police Act: 'To fulfil its functions under the §§ 1 to 7, the Federal Police can adopt the appropriate measures to avert dangers as far as this Act does not regulate the powers of the Federal Police differently.' For the expansion of the general clause applicable to the protection of the constitution, cf. § 3(3)(2) Act on the Protection of the Constitution (previous version) with the current § 3 ff. Act on the Protection of the Constitution.

[90] As an example of a legal dummy outside of the averting of danger, a key norm of civil service law is remarkable: 'An act of a civil servant off duty is misconduct, if it diminishes, given the circumstances of the individual case, to a particular extent the authority and trust into his position or the reputation of the civil service in a significant way.' (§ 45(1)(2) Civil Service Framework Act). In 2008, this provision was replaced by § 47(1) Civil Service Status Act – without any palpable semantic benefit.

intelligence means as well as the manner of their use, the Interior Minister is responsible.[91]

While the legislature explicitly declares its bankruptcy here, the silent abdication of law-rule and of the parliamentary legislator more commonly hides behind apparently successful legislative operationalizations.

The spirit of the counter-extremism agenda of the 1970s and 1980s is captured by the convoluted provisions for criminal offences under the Narcotics Act (§ 29) or the following definition of the criminal offence 'advocacy of violence' (later struck down as unconstitutional):

Those who

1. distribute,
2. exhibit publicly, put up, show or make otherwise available or
3. produce, order, store, offer, announce, extol, import or export into the spatial scope of this Act in order to use entirely or partially in the sense of number 1 and 2 or to allow someone else to use a work that contains the advocacy of an unlawful act listed and defined in § 126(1) (No 1 to 6) and is able, under given circumstances, to foster the willingness of others to engage in acts against the existence or security of the Federal Republic of Germany or against constitutional principles is punished by a term of imprisonment of up to three years or a fine.

If one inscribes this monster of censorship ('advocacy', 'to foster the willingness', 'security', 'make otherwise available', etc.) into the context of a still utterly vague doctrinal concept of violence,[92] which according to many courts encompasses strikes or passive resistance[93] as forms of violence, then the contours of an incalculable situation of danger – punishing failed self-censorship – generated by the legislator becomes apparent.

The genesis and consequences of the illustratively introduced blanket norms would need to be complemented by provisions to avert danger in political criminal law, the law of criminal procedure,[94] the Aliens

91 Report of the Committee for Internal Affairs of the Federal Diet concerning the amendment of the Statute for the Office for the Protection of the Constitution, 15 June 1972, quoted by *Frankfurter Rundschau*, 9 March 1977, 4

92 See Brink and Keller, 'Politische Freiheit und strafrechtlicher Gewaltbegriff'. See also Imbusch, 'The Concept of Violence'.

93 For the case law on sit-ins in lower courts, see Frankenberg, 'Passive Resistenz ist keine Nötigung'.

94 See Denninger, *Freiheitliche demokratische Grundordnung*, 991 ff.

Act[95] and also the so-called tapping act G 10.[96] They document that, during the first crisis of law-rule, indeterminate legal concepts and blanket norms help to normalize extraordinary powers in the national combat against political extremism and terrorism.

By defining only in retrospect or in the form of blanket norms what is permitted and forbidden, laws degenerate into legitimizing formulas, which immunize the government and administration against a halfway rigorous control of their practices. Blanket norms, especially with regard to state powers in the field of domestic security, allow the executive to advance its line of defence far into the political dispute, to undermine cognitive safety and the institutionalization of real fear.

5.6 METALEGALITY AND THE LAW OF FEAR

Those unfamiliar with law-rule, who believe, according to a widespread understanding, that what is not forbidden must be allowed, might be in danger of failing to decipher the following statement that captures the first crisis of the *Rechtsstaat*: the Federal Republic of Germany is (not only according to the opinion of the Federal Constitutional Court) a democracy 'which does not tolerate enemies of this fundamental order, even if they formally operate in the context of legality'.[97] After all, the liberal paradigm states that those who act lawfully cannot be an 'enemy'. 'Legality' in turn can ideal-typically be defined as

---

[95] Especially §§ 6(2), 7(2) and 4, 13(1) and 16 Aliens Act. In the meantime, the Aliens Act has been replaced by the provisions of the Residence Act of 25 February 2008, BGBl. I, 162.

[96] The Act on the Restriction of the Secrecy of Correspondence of 13 October 1968, BGBl. I, 949, last changed by dint of the Anti-Terrorism Act (*Gesetz zur Bekämpfung des internationalen Terrorismus*) 2002. Cf. the anti-terrorism legislation in the United States: Cole and Dempsey, *Terrorism and the Constitution*, 107–88; see also Charvat, 'A Study of UK Anti-Terror Law'.

[97] The Higher Administrative Court Lüneburg, *Deutsches Verwaltungsblatt* (1972), 961, in anticipation of the Federal Constitutional Court's decision about the 'Radicals Decree' and due to the heightened state loyalty of civil servants demanded by other courts. For a critique of the respective case law, see Frankenberg, 'Staatstreue' and Blanke and Frankenberg, 'Zur Kritik und Praxis des Radikalenerlasses'. Cf. also Cobler, *Law, Order, and Politics in West Germany*.

> the epitome of a legal structure, whose elements show a degree of precision so that their existence can be established in a verifiable manner within the framework of proven methods, and certain behaviour can be assessed with its help.[98]

Consequently, the ensemble of visible, not always coherent nor determinate, provisions constitutes the norm, i.e. legality. And legality, according to the liberal paradigm, starts off with external behaviour. Therefore such acts are lawful that are in congruence with the relevant norms. This is all that is expected from legal addressees. In contrast, the above-cited decision, its supporting case law and administrative practices play the norm off against the exception. And the level of legitimacy or super-legality[99] is smuggled into legality or (normal law-rule) as a state of exception that comes in small change.

It might be commonsensical, yet with regard to state practice a mistake, to suggest that the law sufficiently and ultimately determines what is forbidden or allowed. As can be learned from the above dictum and its variants at the time of German McCarthyism in the 1970s and first half of the 1980s,[100] this aspect is only decided upon at the level of legitimacy, i.e. super-legality. Strictly speaking, we are here confronted with *metalegality*, because the higher level it marks decides upon the principal question of the validity and interpretation of regular law at the lower level.

Metalegality therefore denotes the epitome of the value system that precedes law/rights and has a higher rank than the legal order. Its elements – supra-positive principles (natural law), norms and interpretations – decide about the substance and scope of a legal command in the individual case and about the validity of law in general. The heightened indeterminacy of this system of values prevents the courts with the help of reasonably established methods from determining its components in a verifiable manner and citizens being able to orient certain behaviour towards them. If a court, therefore, argues that the active membership in a permitted, publicly subsidized party or organization were lawful in the sense of the legal order but not legitimate in the sense of the metalegal system of values, then the true nature underlying the individual norms

---

98 Preuß, 'Juristen', 122.

99 Seminal, although not contradictory, is Schmitt, *Legality and Legitimacy*; Kirchheimer, 'Legalität und Legitimität' and Preuß, *Legalität und Pluralismus*.

100 See Gladstone and Brinkmann, 'Militant Democracy and Radicals in the West German Civil Service'.

comes to the fore – their deeper (or rather higher), supra-positive meaning and purpose.

What, at a superficial glance, seems to reflect the normal tension between legality and legitimacy (or ethics or, for that matter, politics) turns out to be the separation of a self-invented and judicially sanctioned metalegality that loosens the constraints of the *method Locke* (setting free its illiberal valence) and operates in favour of a Hobbesian security imperative. In this way, the state can object to behaviour by qualifying it as *lawful* but *not legitimate*. Consequently, citizens have to live with a state measure that is *not lawful* but *legitimate* – which is to say: opportune and effective in the sense of the averting of political dangers. The amazed citizenry witnesses the birth of normative Siamese twins: the 'law-abiding constitutional enemy' and 'legitimate legal abuse' by state authorities.

Key concepts for understanding such a system of values as the normative substance of illiberal governmentality are still the 'free democratic basic order', 'militant democracy' and the 'militant *Rechtsstaat*'. In its first decision about a party ban, the Federal Constitutional Court had initially defined the 'free democratic basic order' formally as a kind of umbrella term for essential aspects of the liberal paradigm geared towards political stability.[101] In the course of the first crisis of law-rule, this formal term turned into a substantial one: an 'existential value decision' for 'militancy', visible in administrative practice and case law informed by the 'Radicals Decree'. The instruments of the 'free democratic basic order' are – in rather a Schmittian turn – redefined as a fundamental constitutional value decision about militancy covering political behaviour, which can be applied universally and not only at the boundaries of the *Rechtsstaat*.[102]

The breakdown of the Basic Law and the construction of a metalegality lead to a structural deformation of political rule under the rule of law. 'Liberality' and 'militancy' are seen as preceding all legally standardized opportunities and limits for action. Consequently, the behaviour of all members of society has ultimately to be oriented towards these highly indeterminate value decisions. This is particularly true for civil servants.

---

[101] Decisions of the Federal Constitutional Court (*BVerfGE 2*, 1/2 – SRP decision); for a negative assessment, see Hesse, *Grundzüge des Verfassungsrechts der Bundesrepublik Deutschland*, Rn. 127 ff.

[102] See the decision of the Federal Constitutional Court (*BVerfGE* 28, 36/48). For a critical view: Denninger, 'Verfassungstreue und Schutz der Verfassung', 17; Preuß, *Legalität und Pluralismus*, 9 ff.; Blanke and Frankenberg, 'Zur Kritik und Praxis des Radikalenerlasses'.

Embedded in a special relationship of subordination (*besonderes Gewaltverhältnis*), which is characterized by 'traditional principles' with pre-democratic habits, civil servants are mysteriously integrated into the 'substantive constitution' via their regressively personalized duty of loyalty.[103] So, the 'free democratic substance' stands outside of societal conflicts and towers over law-rule as an 'absolute value'[104] – entrusted in good German tradition to the state. As a standardized order of values and life (inspiring a militant political technology), it 'cannot be subject to discussion; one cannot recognize it or reject it with any legal relevance; one can only follow it'.[105] Otherwise prosecution is the consequence.

If the liberal democracy is in essence militant, it can, if need be, generate cases of application not foreseen in the Basic Law. 'Wire-tapping' as actually(!) unlawful intelligence operations, surveillance measures and the screening of political convictions (as a precondition for acceptance to the civil service) demonstrated the carefree militancy of the 1970s and 1980s. The 'democracy ready for defence' turns into a 'super-defence system'.[106] In the shadow of law-rule, one learns, permanently lurks the protective proviso of a 'prerogative state',[107] which executes the highest fundamental values in a metalegal manner and for that purpose frees itself from the principle of legality to the extent necessary. And metalegality develops into a regime of extraordinary repressive instruments, a normalized emergency law, which manoeuvres the members of society into a kind of *double-bind* situation: at the level of positive law, citizens are invited to be politically active and use their freedom. At the meta-level, however, the message is: Don't!

---

[103] See the decision of the Federal Constitutional Court concerning the Radicals Decree (*BVerfGE* 39, 334/366); similarly Lerche, 'Grundrechte der Soldaten', 475.

[104] In its decision about the ban on the neo-Nazi SRP (1952), the Federal Constitutional Court defined the 'free democratic basic order' (*BVerfGE* 2, 1/12–13); the Court argued in its ban of the Communist Party KPD (1956): 'These highest basic values are an inalienable element of the free democratic basic order; the Basic Law sees them as a key part of the overall state order, as a system of principles for the layout of the state, which are excluded from the pluralism of aims and opinions generated by the political parties, and if democratically accepted once, they are recognised as absolute values and shall therefore be defended resolutely against all attacks.' (*BVerfGE* 5, 85/139).

[105] Quaritsch, 'Kirchen und Staat', 184 ff.

[106] Schuster, 'Relegalisierung der KPD oder Illegalisierung der NPD?'.

[107] For this term, see Fraenkel, *The Dual State*. Blanke, 'Der Deutsche Faschismus als Doppelstaat'.

'Liberality' and 'militancy' also mark a Janus-faced image of the state as a just political order and an institutional arrangement producing decisions that generate loyalty and concepts of the enemy. Elevated by the custodians of law into a doctrine, society is divided into the 'defenders of freedom' and the 'enemies of freedom' with the help of the official notion of 'liberality'. This polarization captures the contrast between political orthodoxy and heresy unrelentingly and legitimizes at the same time the role and practice of the security services. Whoever criticizes the state or the Federal Constitutional Court is suspected of being a fundamental 'opponent of the *Rechtsstaat*'.[108] Only the Office for the Protection of the Constitution is allowed to have evidence. Ultimately, what remains is a good-till-cancelled legality, an institutionalized hotch-potch of threats and appeasement beyond the constitution, which denies the citizenry cognitive safety. Reminiscent of Hobbes, such a law of fear accommodates state technology as security technology.

The next step leads from the law of fear to a political culture of precaution. An ambiguous legal situation tends to make norm addressees insecure and encourages them to refrain from exploring their legal scope for action, because they cannot be sure whether the security services have not already changed the boundaries of legality and may gather some 'evidence' via their intelligence methods which might be used in future 'job interviews' – not lawfully but legitimately. Who can guarantee that the data stored in bureaucratic everyday life is not passed on, despite data protection law, and ultimately reinterpreted to restrict fundamental rights? How shall 'constitutional enemies' be distinguished from 'constitutional friends', if reliable legal criteria are not available and one can only rely on the notion of militant liberality as a replacement for legality? Which organization is officially seen as lawful, but secretly regarded as 'anti-constitutional' or subversive? 'Friends of Nature', environmentalists, opponents of nuclear energy, democratic lawyers, active Christians, Young Democrats, Social Democrats and trade unionists, in cases of doubt are – or, more precisely, were then – all suspect.

---

[108] 'However, such reactions need to be heavily criticised that scold the Court [the Federal Constitutional Court – G.F.], because it had supposedly come to a political decision or intervened in the process of law-making. Constitutional law is any time political law [...]. Who criticises the Constitutional Court in the mentioned manner exposes himself to the suspicion [...] that he is an opponent of the *Rechtsstaat*.' Thus argued the scholar of constitutional law and future judge of the Constitutional Court, H.H. Klein, *Göttinger Tageblatt*, 20 July 1973, 3.

5.7 THE LAW OF FEAR AND 'META-FUNDAMENTAL RIGHTS'

Metalegality as the level of reference for supralegal measures finds its continuation in the 'meta-fundamental rights' of the state as the level of reference for the validity and interpretation of individual and collective fundamental rights. Meta-fundamental rights are claimed by the state as authorization to constrict freedoms in order to impose on citizens the obligation to tolerate. They caused a structural change from the *Rechtsstaat* to a security state – a change in which the normalized elements of a regime under emergency law can also be found at the level of fundamental rights.

The Meta-fundamental Right to Maintain the Political Status Quo

In the debates about 'domestic security' and 'loyalty to the state' in the 1970s and 1980s, frequently the topos of a state's right to existence or self-preservation appeared.[109] To the extent that this points to the necessary averting of danger by use of sovereign force, the Basic Law guarantees to its subjects protection, such as the continued existence of the country, the integrity of territory or democracy under the rule of law.[110] The right to self-preservation, however, turns into a state meta-fundamental right, if citizens and civil servants are required to recognize the state in its current concrete manifestation as unchangeable empirical and normative fact; in other words, if the preservation of the political status quo becomes the supreme norm and the state's guarantee to continued existence, unbound by the Basic Law, erects a barrier against changes to political structures.

The meta-fundamental right to self-preservation recalls the citizens' (paradoxically constitutionalized) right to resistance (Article 20(4) BL), but mobilized in a reversed manner. While the latter, as rather questionable *ultima ratio* of the citizenry, is geared towards protecting the

---

[109] See, the documents in Denninger, *Freiheitlich demokratische Grundordnung*, 487 ff., and the decision of the Federal Constitutional Court concerning the 'Radicals Decree' (*BVerfGE* 39, 334).

[110] As concretization of the territorial and political guarantee of existence, one can see especially the instruments of 'militant democracy' (Arts. 9(2), 18 and 21(2) BL), disaster management (Art. 35(2) and (3) BL) and the provisions regarding the internal emergency (Art. 87a(4) BL).

democratic constitutional order, the former treats as a taboo the established and exercised practice of rule and repulses civic freedoms instead of concrete dangers.

The reference to an 'emergency above constitutional law', 'state necessity' or else the 'reservation of public welfare' in favour of the state and to the detriment of the citizens shows that the state is ascribed a guarantee of existence, which reshapes the catalogue of fundamental rights. Due to this reinterpretation of the Basic Law in the spirit of counter-extremism, emergency law legitimized unlawful wiretapping and surveillance measures back in the 1970s:

> To the extent required by outstanding aspects of the common welfare, a fundamental right is not unrestrictable, even if it comes without a statutory reservation or if the attached statutory reservation would be insufficient for certain laws. It has still to give way to the requirements of common welfare. [...] Even if the constitution did not provide for these restrictions through the weighing of public dangers and the reservation of public welfare, the possibility to intervene would still have arisen out of the aspect of the 'extra-statutory necessity' to justify the averting of the incalculable dangers here present.[111]

The domestic legal order resembles the situation of international law. The validity of all state obligations is restricted by the reservation that the state can renounce them, if its existence is threatened. To protect its meta-fundamental right, it leaves the realm of law-rule and pursues its own purposes. In concrete cases, a supposedly extreme situation or an imaginary danger could lead to the negation of the *Rechtsstaat*; state institutions claim extra-constitutional powers that transgress the boundaries of fundamental rights.[112]

---

[111] W. Maihofer, quoted in *Frankfurter Rundschau*, 10 March 1977, 13. For the practice of state security in this matter, cf. the comprehensive documentation in *Der Spiegel* No. 10-14/1977.

[112] How the state of emergency has to be handled constitutionally can be seen in Fraenkel's analysis of the dual state (*The Dual State*, 33). For a similar argument, see Schuster, 'Relegalisierung der KPD oder Illegalisierung der NPD?', 417: 'The provisos of the BL that are geared toward defence are of exceptional character – or, like Helmut Ridder stated: "emergency character". [...] They must not be interpreted as if the Basic Law entailed a guarantee of existence for the current political "establishment" of the Federal Republic.' Schuster concludes: 'The state of emergency must not become the rule due to convenience of opportunity' (429).

The Meta-fundamental Right to Loyalty to the State

Constitutional loyalty corresponds to the *method Locke.* Just as the *government of laws and not of men* is meant to extinguish the personal dimension of rule and politics, so loyalty changes a personal fealty owed to the ruler to the impersonal obligation of obedience to law. Once abstract legal obedience is reinterpreted as a loyalty bond, tying the citizens to the state, their relationship is refeudalized and re-personalized, turning the loyalty obligation into a 'meta-fundamental right' of the state – reminiscent of the personal bond of fealty between subject and monarch.[113]

The transformation of loyalty to the constitution and the law into loyalty to the *state* begins and is laid out in provisions under the Civil Service Act, which require the addressees 'to *provide* the guarantee that he/she stands up at all times for the free democratic basic order'.[114] In its interpretation of the loyalty of the civil servant in the 'Radicals Decision', the Federal Constitutional Court extended this formula to conviction and switched the referent of loyalty from the constitution to the state:

> What we do mean [by loyalty – G.F.], however, is the duty to be willing to *identify with the idea of the state* the civil servant is obliged to work for and with the free democratic, social, and legal order of the state based on the rule of law [*Rechtsstaat*]. This does not preclude the right to criticize certain phenomena of this state or to speak up for changes in the status quo within the framework of the Constitution, using constitutionally valid means, so long as the state and its constitutional basis are *not called into question* [...] Nevertheless, the civil servant has an irrevocable duty to take a *positive attitude toward the state* – regardless of its deficiencies – and the existing constitutional order. He *must consider them worth defending* ... and *actively stand up for them.*[115]

---

[113] Captured e.g. by the sermon of Drummond Percy Chase, 'Constitutional Loyalty: A Sermon Preached Before the University of Oxford on Saturday, June 20, 1857, Being [the anniversary of] The Day on which Her Majesty Began Her Happy Reign'.

[114] This clause in § 7(1)(No. 2) BBG has continued to be valid in § 7 I (No. 2) Civil Service Status Act since 2008.

[115] Due to its broad significance, here only the Radicals Decision (*'Radikalen'-Beschluss*) is referred to (*BVerfGE* 39, 334) – emphasis added. Cf. also the positivization of the duty of loyalty in the Civil Service Act, such as e.g. §§ 35, 36

And the Court's argument that '[n]either the state nor society is interested in an "uncritical" civil service and therefore permitted criticizing "aspects of the state"'[116] remained empty phrases without consequences. How and to what extent a civil servant, despite her extended obligation to loyalty, is allowed to and should utter criticism without risking sanctions remains, however, a conundrum. Especially if the strength of the state is read off the loyalty on the part of its civil service[117] and criticism is taken to be an expression of a basically hostile attitude, the requirement of loyalty asks the civil servant de facto to refrain from criticism.

The meta-fundamental right to loyalty applied especially but not exclusively to the status as a civil servant but extended also, if to a lesser degree, to citizens.[118] On the one hand, the Federal Constitutional Court granted the 'normal' citizen in its decision 'the freedom to reject the constitutional order and fight against it politically, as long as he keeps aloof from unconstitutional parties and uses generally permitted means'. On the other hand, the Court stated that 'this democracy [expects] from its citizens that they defend the free order'.[119] Such a paradoxical task the citizens might expound for themselves and then execute with the full risk of illegality. In the 1970s and 1980s, citizens' loyalty was indeed a risky matter as it extended beyond respect for the constitution. University teachers of sociology had a 'particular obligation in maintaining and strengthening our free state-order through the respective instruction of students'.[120] The political loyalty of physicists was doubted, when they appeared on union-oriented lists of candidates.[121] For a bank employee, 'loyalty-breaching' activity on behalf of the German Communist Party was sufficient for a termination with immediate effect.[122] At the time,

---

[116] *BVerfGE* 39, 334/348.

[117] *BVerfGE* 47, 350; cf. also OVG Koblenz, *Juristenzeitung* 24 (1974) as one of the many decisions by administrative courts supporting the Federal Constitutional Court.

[118] Even the dissenting opinion in the 2003 headscarf decision of the Federal Constitutional Court contains echoes of the concept of 'the special relationship of subordination' (*BVerfGE* 108, 282/314 ff.).

[119] *BVerfGE* 28, 48; 39, 359.

[120] Quoted from the reasoning for a rejection by the Ministry of Education and Culture in the federal state of Schleswig-Holstein, *Demokratische Erziehung* 10 (1975).

[121] For further examples and references, see Engelmann, *Trotz alledem*, 409 ff.

[122] This and other 'cases' are included in the comprehensive documentation by Bethge and Roßmann, *Der Kampf gegen das Berufsverbot*. Cf. also Cobler,

citizens were asked to prove their loyalty by agreeing with governmental decisions, such as the 'Radicals Decree':

> Actually, already the circle of those involved should have guaranteed a democratic interpretation of this well-meant but failed attempt [the 'Radicals Decree' – G.F.]; on the basis of law, for decades unchanged in our country, and by decision of those responsible in the Federation and *Länder*, it should have guaranteed that they come to a unitary handling of discretionary decisions [concerning political loyalty – G.F.] when it comes to employment in the civil service.[123]

Instead of public criticism, the citizenry was ultimately advised to entertain a 'contented, slavish relationship'[124] with the state authorities. In this relationship the dogma of loyalty was underscored by the meta-fundamental right 'of ensuring the continued existence of the institution [of the state] and the belief system for which it stands'.[125]

5.8 META-FUNDAMENTAL RIGHTS, METALEGALITY AND MYTH

The generation of meta-fundamental rights, derived as it were by magic from the system of values or from constitutional goals or mandates, eroded law-rule and rights. In the 1970s and 1980s they became the décor of the executive powers' combat against political extremists and terrorists and were subordinated to the executive style of governing. Undermining the form of law, replacing formal rationality by material rationality in a regime of ad hoc interventions, legalizing ex post and in a blanket fashion, constructing a metalegality and meta-fundamental rights (of the state) strengthened the executive power during the first crisis of law-rule and mystified its role. Equipped with additional instruments, personnel and funds as well as powers to intervene, partly under

---

Law, Order and Politics in West Germany and Komitee für Grundrechte und Demokratie, *Ohne Zweifel für den Staat*, especially 144 ff.

123 Maihofer, 'Referat auf dem Bundesparteitag der FDP am 19./20.11.1976' – cit. in *Frankfurter Rundschau*, 9 December 1976, 14.

124 Marx, 'Die deutsche Ideologie', 382.

125 Rokeach, *The Open and Closed Mind*, 68. Cf. also Edelman, *The Symbolic Uses of Politics*, 39 ff. If loyalty is turned into a dogma, qualitative differentiation should no longer be applied when it comes to the demands on the loyalty of civil servants or citizens; cf. for a graphic example the quoted decision of the Federal Constitutional Court about the loyalty of civil servants.

emergency law, and to define internal enemies, the executive state presented itself to its citizens as a security-conscious enterprise and peacemaker. That its operative actions breached the confines of the *method Locke* and developed the features of an illiberal governmentality, here referred to as *method Hobbes* and *method Foucault*, was neither adequately noticed nor was it perceived as a scandal.

In turn, the civil rights and liberties of individuals and groups faded into the background. For their general security, they were integrated into the extended constitutional circle and politically taken into quasi-custody. Society finally appeared as the 'formed society'[126] that had been invoked in the mid-1960s. The 'forming' showed itself in its political behaviour and significantly quietist consciousness as well as in a sovereign super-ego state, to which individuals, groups and organizations had to answer for what they said and did. In this scenario, the defence of the liberal paradigm of law-rule and legal techniques of government gained urgency, despite all their ambiguities. Even Herbert Marcuse, one of the protagonists of critical theory, supported them: 'The rule of law, no matter how restricted, is still infinitely safer than rule above or without law'.[127] It remains to be seen whether this statement needs to be qualified.

[126] The concept of a 'formed society' can be traced back to the then Federal Chancellor Ludwig Erhard's speech at the 13th CDU Party Conference and characterizes a society freed from the categories of class struggle, purely geared towards free market prosperity and informed by psychological economic management.

[127] Marcuse, *One-dimensional Man*, 51.

6. Normalizing the state of exception: Counter-terrorism and 'whatever it takes'

6.1 TERROR AS MANIPULATIVE COMMUNICATION[1]

Those who commit acts of terror intend to occupy the mind.[2] They focus on the shock effect. That aside, emerging damage and victims usually are of no particular interest to them. From their perspective, terror differs from a common crime by reducing violence to its symbolic value. Every attack conveys a message presented with barbaric arrogance, often reinforced by a declaration of war in a letter or video claiming responsibility.[3] At the symbolic level, terror is communication, yet it is a one-way message interested in the 'profit of attention'[4] but not in mutual understanding. Those who pull the wire behind terror and those executing it stress their supposedly altruist motivation as well as the political or religious underpinning of their action to distance themselves from egoist crime and to force public attention: those not directly affected ought not to behave like a more or less interested audience, and the security services ought not to make use of the full scope of their discretion – i.e. to prevent terror and identify the perpetrators or to refrain from such action. On the one hand, terrorist acts are meant to force the political

---

[1] Preliminary considerations were published in an essay on combat law: 'Kritik des Bekämpfungsrechts', Kritische Justiz (2005), 370–86. The original version has been changed considerably as regards the concept of political technology, the relationship between rule of law and the state of exception, and terrorism and counter-terrorism as global phenomena.

[2] Wördemann, *Terrorismus*. This applies to terror attacks as well as to the certainly not naïvely so-called 'war on terror'.

[3] A different aspect is accentuated and pursued by Hoffmann, *Inside Terrorism*, ch. 1; Waldmann, *Terrorismus und Bürgerkrieg*, however, talks about 'low intensity wars'. Cf. also Altheide, *Terrorism and the Politics of Fear*; Münkler, *The New Wars* and Scheerer, *Die Zukunft des Terrorismus*.

[4] For this and the following, see Bung, 'Terror als Gegenstand einer Phänomenologie der Angst'.

class, the media, even whole societies and ultimately the global public, as far as it is created in moments of terror, to permanently engage with the presumed aims of its protagonists and, hence, also with the anxieties evoked by acts of terror.

On the other hand, with the bloody instrumental attack and the similarly cynical and excessive sacrifice of passers-by, the terrorist is determined to provoke the preventive-repressive apparatus of the state governed by law-rule into revealing itself to be an authoritarian regime in its counter-measures and criminal prosecution or to unmask the corruption and weakness of (Western) civilization. A fatal binarism[5] between the protagonists of terror and anti-terror develops that does not allow a third – critical or completely neutral – position. For the entirety of global anti-terror measures[6] – from legislative interventions,[7] detentions and cruel and inhuman interrogations, concrete police measures to attempts at neutrality, such as the French Sanctuary programme, as well as the accompanying academic discourse about freedom and security and media coverage – inevitably serves this manipulated communication, set off or maintained by a terrorist attack.

What has therefore to be discussed are the characteristics, risks and side effects of what was and is fashionably called 'new security architecture' in Western states constructed in the wake of the 'war on terrorism and organized crime'.[8] However, as regards the second crisis of law-rule since the end of the 1980s my main attention turns again to Germany, since here the ambivalence of the liberal paradigm may be regarded as

---

[5] Butler, *Precarious Life*.

[6] For the global dimension, see Ramraj et al., *Global Anti-Terrorism Law and Policy*; Roach, *The 9/11 Effect*; Daniel et al., *The Security of Freedom*; Engene, *Terrorism in Western Europe*; Tan, *A Handbook of Terrorism and Insurgency in Southeast Asia*; Darnstädt, *Der globale Polizeistaat*. For the situation in Germany, see Gustav-Heinemann-Initiative and Humanistische Union, *Graubuch Innere Sicherheit*. Cf. Graulich and Simon, *Terrorismus und Rechtsstaatlichkeit*.

[7] See Cole and Dempsey, *Terrorism and the Constitution*, part III (United States); the Terrorism Prevention and Investigation Measures Act 2011 and other measures – https://www.gov.uk/government/policies/protecting-the-uk-against-terrorism – (United Kingdom); Observer Research Foundation, *Counter-Terrorism in South-Asia*. See also: Roach, *September 11*; Jenkins 'In Support of Canada's Anti-Terrorism Act' (comparing Canadian, British and American counter-terrorism).

[8] For the contested term 'organized crime', see Lunde, *Organized Crime*; Lyman and Potter, *Organized Crime*; Mallory, *Understanding Organized Crime*; Albrecht, 'Feindbild Organisierte Kriminalität'.

typical of most Western countries with the exception of France. Moreover, it became clearly apparent in a technology of government that still reflects the characteristics of the *method Foucault* and emerges out of a combination of the *methods Hobbes* and *Locke*.

6.2 TERRORISM AND THE 'NEW SECURITY ARCHITECTURE'

The pillars of the 'new security architecture'[9] in Germany (and, *mutatis mutandis*, elsewhere) are: first, manifold measures bundled in three 'anti-terror packages'. Second, the data exchange between the security (police) and the intelligence services as well as a broad range of powers to intervene in data privacy, such as, in particular, the interception of telecommunications and access to online data, the recording of vehicle registration numbers, the use of security technology in identification documents and during border controls, dragnet investigations (*Rasterfahndung*), data retention and video surveillance. Third, counter-terrorism also comprised the tightening of the right of residence and assembly and also included criminal law. Fourth, institutionally the 'new architecture' is based on cooperation between the police, intelligence agencies and the military, and the Federal Criminal Police Office (*Bundeskriminalamt*). Finally and fifth, the emphasis on terrorism and 'organized crime' distinguishes the new agenda from previous security agendas. On closer inspection, its ad hoc character,[10] the rash speed of construction and the semantic and instrumental plasticity of these measures testify to a lack of

---

[9] For the restructuring of the security architecture in the US within and without the liberal paradigm, see Ackerman, *Before the Next Attack* and Cole and Dempsey, *Terrorism and the Constitution*. For corresponding developments in the EU, see Berndt, *Die 'Neue Europäische Sicherheitsarchitektur'*. Thiel recently provided a comprehensive study of the situation in Germany: *Die 'Entgrenzung' der Gefahrenabwehr*. See also Shapiro and Suzan, 'The French Experience of Counter-Terrorism'.

[10] The ad hoc character becomes particularly apparent in the bill complementing the bill combating terrorism (*Terrorismusbekämpfungsergänzungsgesetz*) and the bill for the criminal prosecution of the preparation of serious crimes of violence (*Gesetz zur Verfolgung der Vorbereitung von schweren Gewalttaten*), which provoked critics to assume that the *Rechtsstaat* was about to lose its nerve – Walter, 'Der Rechtsstaat verliert die Nerven'.

planning, coherence and stability, which denies the guiding principles of architecture and deconstructs the architectural metaphor.[11]

Spreading both nationally and globally, this 'security architecture' is in the following placed within the framework of 'combat law' (*Bekämpfungsrecht*), a concept derived from legislative activity not only aimed at transnational terrorism. Here, at the operational level a further stage becomes manifest in the normalization of the state of exception. The legislative rhetoric of 'combat' extends into the practice of executive security agencies. In the judicial discourse, it is translated into doctrinal justifications of state militancy vis-à-vis its 'enemies' and other extraordinary measures.

This militancy in word and deed marks, I believe, the second crisis of law-rule in a number of European countries. It began with a series of reactions to terrorist activities in the early 1990s, which coincided with NATO's review of its strategy and attempts at restructuring its institutions.[12] In contrast to the terrorist groups of the 1970s, which presented themselves as national and mostly operated nationally despite their internationalist rhetoric, the 'new' terrorism shifted its operations onto the transnational plane and relied on cross-border networks. These changes were addressed by NATO strategists[13] but also by the re-designers of law-rule and technologies of governing. The 'new security architecture' became the mantra for the new strategy against terrorism and 'organized crime' and required a linking-up of anti-terror conceptions and a framework of 'interlocking and mutually reinforcing institutions'. It continued to morph law-rule into a preventive or security state; a process that had already begun during the first crisis, triggered by nationalist terrorist groups (see Chapter 5).

While during the first crisis the combination of the *methods Locke* and *Hobbes* became manifest in the intrusions of what Max Weber might have called 'material' rationality into the formal structure of security law as well as in the overall reduced predictability of law-rule, the second crisis led to (a) tectonic shifts in the intervening powers of state agencies and agents responsible for the prevention of danger and criminal prosecution and intelligence; (b) a new institutional framework for the security and intelligence services and the armed forces. (c) These symptoms of crisis become apparent in the vocabulary and grammar of freedom and

[11] For such guiding principles as the pillars of a security architecture, see Ackerman, *Before the Next Attack*, especially 119.

[12] Cornish, 'European Security'.

[13] Berndt, *Die 'Neue Europäische Sicherheitsarchitektur'*, 133–45 with further references.

security. (d) In combination, these aspects imply a 'normalization' of the state of exception in political technology.

6.3 THE 'NORMALIZATION' OF THE STATE OF EMERGENCY

'Equal freedom for all' is the mantra of secular democratic societies. What turns out to be a promise for the rights-holder becomes an obligation for state representatives and officials. Geared towards this mantra, the practice of fundamental rights – their use which respects the rights of others, proportional respect for basic rights in state practice and, relatedly, scientifically founded legal reasoning as to their substance and scope – is expected to permanently inform and shape both a normalcy of freedom as well as its corresponding mentality. At the level of civic action, both prove their worth as readiness for conflict; at the level of the state's 'monopoly of the legitimate use of physical force',[14] they are to generate a climate of legality. Both aspects become particularly apparent in a culture of lively debate on the part of citizens and in statutes geared towards the averting of danger (police law) and a criminal law restrained by the *Rechtsstaat*.

The normative distinction of the legally constrained state of freedom receives its idealized contours through the contrasting gloomy image of the state of exception. The occasions of war, siege, and emergencies caused by catastrophe and domestic threat caused by revolt and turmoil are regarded as exceptions from normative normalcy. State authorities address them with an ensemble of power techniques, which is meant to protect from peril. In accordance with state- or constitution-centric, unwritten or legislated conceptions and corresponding state technologies, the state of exception reveals its exceptional character more or less clearly in its formal declaration, legal regulation and reference to a supra-positive legal source. Depending on the applied theoretical perspective and the practical-legal standardization beyond normalcy, it can be situated at the boundary of law or in a dark sphere between law and chaos.[15] As *political* dispositive, the state of exception transcends the

---

14 Weber, *Economy and Society*.

15 Exemplary for the different approaches to locating the state of emergency is Schmitt, *Political Theology*, 12: 'Unlike the normal situation, when the autonomous moment of the decision recedes to a minimum, the norm is *destroyed* in the exception. The exception remains, nevertheless, accessible to jurisprudence because both elements, the norm as well as the decision, *remain*

legal form by suspending the rules that apply to both the civic use of freedom and the state's exercise of power. As *legal* dispositive, it endangers the formal rationality of law-rule to the extent that it replaces general laws by specific – extraordinary – measures[16] and deactivates the normativity of what is regarded as the norm – its rules, limitations and checks on the exercise of power – in the name of 'materializations' dictated by the exceptional situation.

The Normalization of the State of Exception and the Crisis of the Law-rule

The second crisis of law-rule was unleashed by transnational terrorist networks and Mafia-like 'organized crime' from the end of the 1980s and the 1990s onwards. As has been argued above,[17] there is reason to enrich the historical phenomenology of concepts and regulatory patterns under emergency law[18] with the continuous and gradual 'normalization' of the state of exception: the *semantic* and *rhetorical trivialization* and playing down of exceptional measures; the drastic change of the *topography* of law-rule to the detriment of the protection of fundamental rights and liberties; and the corresponding introduction under emergency law of *powers to intervene* in the regular legal order, accompanied by doctrinal concepts of the exceptional, masked as regular law. On a case-by-case basis – usually if required, sometimes in advance – the 'unthinkable' is regulated or thought, the non-subsumable subsumed, and what transcends normalcy is standardized and smuggled into doctrinal considerations. In contrast to the formalism of the state of exception – its explicit declaration and conditions – normalized phenomena do not reveal their exceptional character but creep into the normativity of the legal everyday through the back door, so to speak.

This process of normalization did not simply overcome society and its regime of democratic legality like a metaphysical power in the 1990s;

---

within the framework of the juristic' (emphasis in the original). Agamben, *State of Exception*, qualifies the state of exception of the legal form of what cannot assume legal form. In contrast, Böckenförde develops in 'Ausnahmerecht und demokratischer Rechtsstaat', 264 ff., the model structure of an exceptional rule that requires positivization.

[16] Bung ('Terror als Gegenstand einer Phänomenologie der Angst') argues that when a state governed by the rule of law 'looks for unusual answers [...] it might potentially already have given up on itself' (65).

[17] See, in particular, Chapters 1 and 4.

[18] See also Ferejohn and Pasquino, 'The Law of the Exception'.

rather, first indications were already visible during the first crisis of the *Rechtsstaat*. Here, normalizations became manifest in certain boundary infringements, like illegal wiretapping and the practice of state agencies to bring citizens into disrepute as 'enemies of the constitution' in the construction of a metalegality and meta-fundamental rights to the detriment of the constitutional exercise of freedom. In the second crisis the move towards a surveillance state caused structural shifts, particularly in police law. The normalization of the state of exception dramatically intensified, with surveillance becoming systematic and with the inclusion of measures affecting life and health. It is not only that law-rule and the *method Locke* came under pressure and regressed here and there; rather, they were reshaped entirely by the concepts and instruments of the hyper-preventive security regime.

Threats to the Mentality of Freedom

The normalcy of freedom and its corresponding civic mentality are put at risk if the citizenry withdraws from the public or if public authorities violate the boundaries of law-rule as a 'regime of distance' from everyday passions and prejudices.[19] Civil desertion usually occurs in authoritarian and especially totalitarian regimes, which systematically encourage the withdrawal of the active citizen from the public sphere and the retreat into the private sphere so as to turn the public into a matter of state administration.[20]

In somewhat consolidated democratic regimes, the erosion of law-safeguarding guarantees and procedures jeopardizes citizens' willingness to act and may trigger those very fears law-rule is meant to constrain.[21] Catastrophic events, like the mass murder of 11 September 2001 or a series of brutal bomb attacks and their respective aftermaths, may generate feelings of fear and anxiety and hence the tendency to civil desertion.

Another source of fears concerns official threat scenarios, condensed, for instance, into the image of the 'ticking bomb' or the 'war against terror', and thereby legitimizing and triggering the panic-stricken reactions of the state. These rushed and unfocused actions can at the very

---

19 Both elements can also be linked more closely: the citizenry defects from the public *because* the public authorities violate the boundaries of the *Rechtsstaat* as a 'state system of distance' not only in individual cases.

20 Rödel et al., *Die demokratische Frage*.

21 See also the introductory considerations on fear in the preceding chapter; and Robin, *Fear*.

least intensify, perpetuate or even trigger fears regarding the threatening event. To the extent that these scenarios and reactions lead to the erosion of the rule of law and release the illiberal aspect of the *method Locke*, they produce the image of an unpredictable Leviathan and generate the very climate of diffuse fears regarding the state intervening in the sphere of freedom. The erosion of the *Rechtsstaat* as well as overreactions to catastrophic events undermine cognitive safety. Rightly or wrongly, citizens are worried that the exercise of their constitutional rights, especially in times of a prolonged 'war' against terror and organized crime, may come with some nasty surprises and cause hardly calculable risks.

Threats to normative normalcy lead, however, by no means necessarily to its liquidation or straight into the state of exception. But assassinations and attacks, if they assume the character of unpredictable catastrophes due to their frequency, scope and indeterminacy, encourage reactions that undermine any casual practice of freedom. Political decision-makers, especially those responsible for domestic security, tend to react to such threats in their political rhetoric as well as in their operations, with a rebalancing of their guiding principles, freedom and security, as well as the distinction between a normal and an exceptional state.[22] In an act of symbolic actionism, their techniques of governing reveal at the same time the illiberal aspect of the *method Locke* already analysed by Foucault.

6.4 THE LOGIC OF MILITANT LAW

The Rhetoric of Legislative Militancy

The executive desire for action becomes manifest in legislation that has the purpose of depicting a calming public image of a caring, proactive and decisive legislator. In this way, the legislator provides those agencies responsible for domestic security with ever new and extended powers to intervene, so as to give the frightened public the impression that everything necessary is being done to manage the threat.

This symbolic actionism is usually accompanied by a party-political discourse which revolves around the question of who (which party) is able to close the supposed security gaps most rigorously and, hence, to promise more security. This escalating security discourse is characterized

---

[22] Cf. Chapter 4, Section 2. Bung ('Terror als Gegenstand einer Phänomenologie der Angst', 66) rightly points to the fact that anxiousness determines this shift.

by a legislative rhetoric of militancy fuelled by itself. With regard to the self-description of the legislator's products, this means that legislation – initially laws aimed at preventing danger, then all kinds of laws – not only regulates via bans and commands but shows its military colours and *combats* rather than merely regulates. Legislation is meant to take up the fight against everything that could become a threat: 'organized crime',[23] money laundering and drug trafficking, tax evasion, the abuse of asylum, moonlighting, football hooliganism and graffiti, as well as, let's not forget, international terrorism.[24]

The Hyper-preventive Police Law

Combat law – or militant legislation – follows the logic of a perpetual normalized state of exception. With the semantic shift from regulation to 'combat' and the functional turn to instruments under quasi-emergency law, political technology is based in the long run on the conception of a militant, comprehensive and hyper-preventive regime for averting dangers and prosecuting crimes. The state authority gains additional intervention powers, which cover the lead-up to dangers, their monitoring and control, not only to avert concrete dangers but to be able to deal with still distant security risks, very much in accordance with the *method Foucault*. Additionally, combat law also becomes manifest in new, stricter criminal provisions that now cover the lead-up to offences, effectively shifting criminal liability forward; in this way, it assumes the character of an 'enemy criminal law' in combination, while the guarantees for criminal proceedings are also reduced.

On the way to new dynamic prevention officially geared towards 'organized crime' and terrorism, militant laws that totalize and toughen the regime for averting dangers also change the topography of law-rule. As will be outlined below, central categories and distinctions are razed that are meant to safeguard rights and liberties and to constrain state interventions; of special importance in this context are the concept of

---

23 For the official definition, see *Gemeinsame Arbeitsgruppe Justiz/Polizei*, RiStBV Anlage E. For criticism of the concept of 'organized crime' from different perspectives, see Pütter, *Der OK-Komplex*; Kinzig, *Die rechtliche Bewältigung von Erscheinungsformen organisierter Kriminalität*; P-A Albrecht, *Kriminologie* (München: Beck, 2005); id., 'Feindbild Organisierte Kriminalität – Brechstange gegen Freiheitsrechte' in T Müller-Heidelberg et al. (eds), *Grundrechte-Report 1998* (Reinbek bei Hamburg: Rowohlt, 1998), 23 ff.

24 For references, see E. Denninger, 'Freiheit durch Sicherheit?', *Strafverteidiger* (2002), 96 ff. and Frankenberg, 'Kritik des Bekämpfungsrechts'.

danger and the distinction between peacebreaker and non-peacebreaker. At the same time, the boundaries between police, secret services[25] and the military, between domestic security (averting of dangers) and external security (defence), between criminal law and the law of war are reduced and the threshold for intervention lowered.

Under the central notion of security, combat legislation generates a new rhetoric, conception and topography of prevention. In the name of 'new prevention', the efficacy of averting danger gains absolute priority over fundamental rights. According to the criticism provided by the *method Locke*, their exercise is made subject 'to the almost unconditional reservation of the executive' to the extent that 'the answer to the political question of security does not depend anymore on a verifiable concrete danger for an object of legal protection' or, respectively, on the probable cause of criminal prosecutions.[26] As a matter of fact, public answers are rarely given because the security agencies prefer to act in secrecy.[27] In short: discretion mutates into a prerogative.

The 'Right to Security' as the Basis of Combat Laws

Often referred to as the justification for measures taken, the 'right to security'[28] increasingly proves to be the legitimizing foundation for combat law. At first glance, it is derived from obligations to protect, embedded in guarantees under the constitutional rights to life and health, and seems therefore to give the state's responsibility to protect only a rights-frame. On closer scrutiny, however, the 'basic right to security' proves to be a meta-right (= power) of the state.[29] After all, citizens' rights and liberties are eclipsed by the comprehensive authority claim of the state – reminiscent of Hobbes. In this way, the state performs its duty to protect and by the same token deactivates its other duty to protect rights and liberties against state interventions, characteristic of the *method Locke*, in the name of this very 'fundamental right'. But even worse: the 'right to security' allows the exception – as a subcategory of the rule – to make itself at home in the law of normalcy. The borderline

---

[25] See B. Droste, *Handbuch des Verfassungsschutzrechts* (Boorberg: Stuttgart 2007).

[26] Lisken and Denninger, in id., *Handbuch des Polizeirechts*, C Rn. 91.

[27] See Cole et al., *Secrecy, National Security and the Vindication of Constitutional Law*.

[28] The most influential argument was developed by Isensee, *Das Grundrecht auf Sicherheit*.

[29] Cf. Chapter 5, Section 7.

cases of self-defence/assistance in an emergency (*Nothilfe*) and public emergency (*polizeilicher Notstand*) become detached from their legal conditions and perpetuate themselves.

6.5 THE ASYMMETRY BETWEEN FREEDOM AND SECURITY

The rhetorical shift from freedom to security,[30] from cognitive to existential safety – or from secured insecurity to insecure security – is reflected not only semantically but also structurally in the combat nature of police law. Somewhat less metaphorically, one can say that this shift changes the normative status of security and, hence, the structural asymmetry in the relationship between freedom and security.[31]

The Normalization of Security

This change is glossed over by a first methodical step in the normalization of security. This is based on the assumption that freedom and security as guiding principles stand side by side. For this purpose, we can, for instance, refer to the 'right to security' developed by Isensee or to Article 5 European Convention on Human Rights (ECHR), guaranteeing the 'right to liberty and security'. In this respect, it is often argued that the right to security 'cannot be understood in isolation but only in connection with the concept of freedom [and …] addresses "arbitrary" state interventions into civil rights and liberties of the individual'.[32]

From the assumption that freedom and security are normatively equivalent, we can derive that both can be balanced against each other without any problem. Balancing[33] suggests that freedom and security are equivalent principles of normal law-rule and compatible without any problems and, furthermore, follow a comparable logic of optimization.

---

30 See Hassemer, 'Zum Spannungsverhältnis von Freiheit und Sicherheit'; Hoffmann-Riem, 'Freiheit und Sicherheit im Angesicht terroristischer Anschläge'; Bielefeldt, *Freiheit und Sicherheit im demokratischen Rechtsstaat.*

31 Paradigmatic for the freedom/security controversy and the trade-offs of counter-terrorism: Waldron, *Torture, Terror, and Trade-Offs*, especially ch. 2 versus Posner and Vermeule, *Terror in the Balance*, 36–8.

32 Peukert, in Frowein and Peukert, *EMRK-Kommentar*, Art. 5 Rn. 4.

33 See Alexy, *A Theory of Constitutional Rights*. For a critical view: Ladeur, *Kritik der Abwägung in der Grundrechtsdogmatik*; Aleinikoff, 'Constitutional Law in the Age of Balancing'; Waldron, 'Security and Liberty'; Bronitt, 'Constitutional Rhetoric versus Criminal Justice Realities'.

An overriding preference for security, it is argued, is therefore out of the question. However, this is in fact the case. In a regime relying on political technology, the doctrines of constitutional rights and the doctrines of police law, cognitive safety morphs inexorably into a kind of existential safety, despite all rhetorical attempts to play this down.

The rise of existential safety is masked twice: first, by the claim that safety is still meant in a cognitive way; but this is obviously false, since the reference points of the new security are not even the precepts of determinacy, normative clarity and the effective and proportionate protection of rights that address arbitrary state interventions. These are severed from their normative basis, then undermined and given a new direction: now, they are meant to secure the existence of the state, of society or, more generally and illusorily, of life. After becoming comprehensive and existential, security quits the service of freedom.

Second, the decline of freedom is covered by the claim that freedom and security have always been principles or values of equal rank; so that freedom has actually in no way lost any significance. Against such an argument, we need to recall the fundamentally different initial positions of freedom and security, their specific relationship and their status in the *method Locke*. Freedoms empower citizens to act or to refrain from acting; they authorize them. On the part of the state, liberties are meant to function as negative competences.

Aside from this, equal rights and liberties are demanding in a normative sense. In a democratic context, they are geared towards participation in the common affairs of a society. Hence, they are meant to encourage initiatives out of the midst of society. In its normative link with equality, freedom finds its – admittedly neither clear nor uncontested – limitations when clashing with the rights of others; it carries its own inherent restraint.

The Excessiveness of Security

In the case of security, both aspects have a different twist. It is the task of the state to 'produce' security – a responsibility with a clear affinity to the *method Hobbes*. Moreover, security is qualified as a public good allocated by the legal order to the responsibility of state institutions and officials. The latter are granted by the legal order powers to intervene in societal areas, in social relations and the private decisions of citizens. Hence, a 'fundamental right' to security turns out to be a positive authorization that actuates the state's diffuse obligation to safeguard security. In contrast to the system of liberties, security carries no inherent constraint. On the contrary, as it has to satisfy needs and safeguard conditions, the scope of its tasks is inherently excessive.[34] When would one confidently be able to say that things are secure? It can hardly be disputed that insecurity always looms large and calls for more and further security measures.

Normatively speaking, an even more significant difference emerges, however, if one directly relates freedom and security. Freedom requires, as outlined above, a minimum of cognitive safety as a factual condition for its possibility. Cognitive safety is guaranteed, under a fairly consolidated law-rule, by the security agencies of the state and the courts. This safety gains its meaning through freedom and relates thereby asymmetrically to the latter. Without it, freedom would be scarcely more than an empty promise, and the call to exercise liberties would be a hollow one.

In the case of security, the situation is different again. It does not need freedom; at any rate, it does not depend on spheres of freedom as necessary conditions for its legitimation. Besides, it may be noted that civil liberties and rights are actually *guaranteed* by constitutional law, whereas security seeks its basis in the real and does not necessarily require a basis in constitutional norms, although the proponents of a concept of security (that emancipates itself from being restricted to the cognitive) do not grow tired of lending it a constitutional foundation, such as, for instance, the already mentioned 'right to security'.[35]

Therefore freedom and security only enter the same normative level and become commensurable when both are *assessed*, i.e. translated into values and *calculated*.[36] For such an operation, different methods are available. On the one hand, civil liberties and rights can be chosen as the starting point; they can then be translated into obligations to protect and are objectified in this way. The right to life and health, for instance, then corresponds to the state's duty to protect them, derived from the very same fundamental right. On the other hand, the point of departure might be security as a public collective good and state function. In this case, security – though not in a cognitive sense – or a supposed 'fundamental

---

34 It is instructive in this case that the official justification for the German *Terrorismusbekämpfungsgesetz* mentions security 37 times but freedom not even once; see Denninger, 'Freiheit durch Sicherheit?'. Consequently, following the logic of security, the EU pursues the aim set out in Art. 29 EU Treaty 'to provide citizens with a high level of safety within an area of freedom, security and justice'.

35 Isensee, *Das Grundrecht auf Sicherheit.*

36 For the issue of calculating the incalculable, see Jacques Derrida's second aporia, id., 'Force of Law'.

right to security' need only be reconstructed into a broad duty to protect. In contrast to individual civil liberties and rights, a comprehensive obligation to protect and a corresponding 'fundamental right' of state authorities do not have to shirk balancing as they will always prevail: as long as a state of security has not been achieved, it leaves every weighing up victorious and demands respective sacrifices from the freedom that loses out.

Freedom and security can therefore not easily be compared and then weighed up against each other. Their balancing rather requires a threefold change of perspective: the citizen turns into a potential offender, the state becomes the bearer of 'meta-rights'[37] and minority protection is transformed into the protection of the state. Thus, the system of liberties is eclipsed by security as the pervasive task of the state and, in turn, all individuals are ascribed, and have to carry, a general security burden.

Both the shift in perspective as well as the remodelling of the system of rights informs a security dispositive that brings the Hobbesian view to bear and links it up to the *method Foucault*: as Hobbes would have argued, freedom always carries the connotation of danger.[38] Hence, a democratic perspective can no longer be assumed or taken for granted; and, to use Hannah Arendt's words, the 'happiness of public liberty'[39] finds no support. In consequence, notions of security entertained by minorities stand no chance against those of the ruling majorities.

6.6 MILITANT LAW AS SPECIAL POLICE LAW

The turn to the *method Foucault* becomes particularly manifest, as will be shown next, in a combative police law. The new adjustment of the relationship between freedom and security in combative police law and criminal law leads to a split or paradigm shift. The rationality and techniques of 'classical' police law change from the reasonable creation of order with the help of specific, legally formed and constrained police interventions to avert dangers through direct behavioural control to a system of effective interventions geared towards indirect behavioural control by systematic, pre-emptive screening, monitoring and surveillance, aligned with concomitant deterrence. This shift starts at the level of (police) tasks and responsibilities, continues with powers to intervene

---

[37] See also the last two sections of Chapter 5.

[38] For an articulate statement of this position, see Lübbe, 'Freiheit und Terror'; Isensee, 'Der Verfassungsstaat als Friedensgarant'.

[39] Arendt, *On Revolution*.

and turns out to be of particular significance at the level of procedural guarantees and judicial review. At its core this system of interventions operates in the mode of an emergency law under quite relaxed factual and normative prerequisites.

Once more terrorism turns out to be the gate-opener to militant law-rule, which hides additional intervention powers and a lack of public and judicial control behind a mask of regular police law. Under the banner, initially, of preventing terrorist attacks, then of curbing 'organized crime' and 'crimes committed by foreigners',[40] and later other actual or imagined phenomena of criminal activity, the legislators (not only in Germany) departed from the provisions, structures and rationality of law-rule-oriented authorizations of the police. The latter would basically deploy what may be called a variety of legal techniques of governing: first, they narrowed down the task of police interventions to the preservation of 'public security and order'. Second, they standardized police measures, though with significant porosity and deviations, as conditional programmes. Third, they established clear and probable dangers as the threshold for interventions. Fourth, liability under standard police law focused on peacebreakers/offenders, and persons not responsible for a dangerous situation could only be required to support police action in emergency situations. Fifth, the conception of liberal police law as well as the *method Locke* could, at the very least, lay reasonable claim to provide for effective judicial review of police measures ex post facto, the crucial criteria being basic rights and the principle of proportionality.

In stark contrast, the new *hyper-preventive* police law that has been developing since the first post-war crisis of law-rule transcends by far the standard framework outlined above. Quite visibly, it transforms legal into political techniques of governing, combining the logic of the *method Hobbes* and the *method Foucault* in such a way that they accentuate the illiberal valences of the *method Locke*. The new 'special' police law and its corresponding criminal codes have come to characterize the legal regimes in many Western capitalist societies.[41] More dynamically than

---

[40] For a critical assessment, see Albrecht, *Kriminologie*, § 43.

[41] The hypertrophy of the security dispositive which inspired a regime of informational interventions is documented by US Department of Justice, 'Legal Authorities Supporting the Activities of the National Security Agency Described by the President' (Washington, DC, 19 January 2006); see also Cole and Dempsey, *Terrorism and the Constitution* (for the United States); the new regulations allowing the National Counterterrorism Center, among others, to monitor records of citizens have to be added; see *The New American*, 15 December 2012; also the recently published methods of the National Security

the legislative and operative measures of the first crisis of law-rule during the 1970s and 1980s, the second wave of counter-terrorism severed the ties of statutory authorizations of the police and security agencies from (1) the rationality, (2) the standardization, and (3) the judicial controls implied by the Lockean paradigm and concept of rule of law/*Rechtsstaat*, and thus normalized the state of exception on a wider front.

The Rationality of Hyper-prevention: From Adverting Dangers to Preventing Risks

Hyper-prevention begins with a definition of the tasks and purposes of police and security institutions. Key to the 'opening up' of police and security law in Germany was the actually rather inconspicuous purpose of 'preventing' – rather than prosecuting – crime, introduced as an additional authorization of the police at the end of the 1980s.[42] Preventing crime implied a temporal reorientation from past (or immediately imminent) events to the indefinite future and meant, in the words of the former President of the Federal Office of Criminal Investigation (BKA), that 'the police had to be at the site of the crime before the offender'.[43] Including computer technology in police operations was meant to both virtualize the knowledge basis for police measures and redirect the investigative focus from the individual suspect or peacebreaker to society in general.

Hyper-preventive or pre-emptive[44] reorientation of police work in general could only be implemented by adding a variety of informational

---

Agency geared towards screening and registering our digital life; see Schirrmacher, 'Der verwettete Mensch'. For a comparative analysis of counter-terrorism legislation in the UK, see Ken Macdonald of River Glaven, 'Review of Counter-Terrorism and Security Powers – Report Presented to Parliament' (Home Office, January 2011) and Smith, 'Balancing Liberty and Security?'

[42] For this issue, see Rachor, in Lisken and Denninger, *Handbuch des Polizeirechts*, F Rn. 160 ff., providing extensive and differentiated critical comment. Corresponding to this task, the norm in the Lower Saxon police law that authorized the gathering of data by wiretapping was recently held to be unconstitutional by the Federal Constitutional Court (*BVerfGE* 113, 348/364 ff.). The ruling is based mainly on the lack of legislative powers of the state and the violation of the principle of certainty under the rule of law. Cf. *BVerfGE* 110, 33/54.

[43] Quoted by Hartung, 'Kommissar Computer: Horst Herold und die Virtualisierung des polizeilichen Wissens'.

[44] For an instructive distinction between prevention and preemption, see Freedman, 'Prevention, Not Preemption'.

interventions to the arsenal of standard police measures. They reveal a somewhat desperate mindset on the part of the security engineer 'at the crossroads of radicalism and technology'[45] and on the day before and after another 11 September.[46] This mindset informs a security agenda which turns from prevention to pre-emption, from (concrete) dangers to (abstract) risks, from openly perceptible to secret measures covering wide target areas and directed against randomly targeted groups, such as convicted felons, 'dangerous elements', peacebreakers, schoolchildren, travellers[47] and other ordinary people.

The Structure of Hyper-prevention: Standard Powers versus Pre-emptive Informational Interventions

At the level of *authorization*, 'classical' police law is complemented on the one hand by extraordinary and warrantless measures directed against the body and freedom of movement of persons, like (pre-emptive) detentions and deportations, coercive interrogations and torture.[48] On the other hand, all-purpose informational interventions, not narrowly focused on particular cases, events and persons, characterize more generally and transnationally the new police law. All kinds of intelligence techniques are used. They comprise undercover agents and video surveillance of public spaces, warrantless wiretapping of private homes, banking DNA data, dragnet investigations, random police checks and systematic internet screenings, and, finally, surveillance with drones[49] to collect, store, process and transfer personal data so as to prepare and facilitate future criminal investigations, police or military action. The ensemble of informational interventions creates a hermeneutics of suspicion and

---

[45] As former President George W. Bush defined the problem of dealing with terrorist threats; quoted by Freedman, 'Prevention, Not Preemption', 105.

[46] Wolfgang Bosbach, Member of the Christian-Democratic Faction in the Federal Diet, and one of the leading party experts on security policy, once asked why every day is a September 12 for the security policy, see id., 'Warum für die Sicherheitspolitik jeder Tag der 12. September ist', 137 and 138.

[47] Their random identity checks, when encountered in facilities of international transport, at the road or a Federal waterway, are justified in the various police states of German states as 'the preventive combating of cross-border crime', if 'a person is encountered that are due to findings or police experience significant for cross-border crime'.

[48] These measures are primarily embraced by countries that are also fighting terrorism with military forces, such as the United States and the United Kingdom.

[49] See Manuel, 'State DNA Data Base and Data Bank Expansion Laws'.

coagulates into a normalized emergency law by combining a vague factual basis[50] with only very loosely, if at all, regulated decision-making procedures and extensive definitional powers of the police. Moreover, this regime of interventions relies not only on the discreet exchange of data between the police, security and intelligence agencies and the military[51] but also on the contributions of private organizations, which make data available, work as consultants, for example, for dragnet investigations, and cooperate in the outsourcing of torture and other coercive practices.[52]

Pre-emption calls for a softening, if not complete abandoning, of all categories that might constrain police authority. They are remodelled with far-reaching consequences: in the context of special authorizations, the concept of danger, once intended or at least aspiring to specify the threshold conditions for police interventions, dissolves. The dissolving or erosion begins with the phrase that possible 'indications' can 'justify the assumption' that a person could commit a criminal offence in the future; it is even accelerated once 'there are no specific requirements concerning the temporal proximity of the expected offence'.[53] Danger is replaced by its merely abstract assumption or by any uncertain and potentially dangerous behaviour the acting authorities might deem to become dangerous at some point. In the pre-emptive 'lead-up', powers under police law lose their conditional structure, which facilitates interventions on the part of the security agencies.[54] In particular, they are given power to define and decide when and which 'evidence' indicates a future criminal offence or danger. Accordingly, the term peacebreaker is replaced with 'endangerer' (*Gefährder*). Without there being any solid

---

[50] The authorizing norms do not refer to dangers but to 'actual indications' or 'facts' that justify the assumptions of the police.

[51] Undermining the functional separation of these institutions; for a random sample of opinions, see Müller-Wille, 'The Effect of International Terrorism on EU Intelligence Co-operation', who proposes a 'platform for the exchange of information'. Walsh, 'Intelligence-sharing in the EU', argues for more cooperation to 'tackle the problem of mistrust'. For a critical perspective, see Lisken and Denninger, in id., *Handbuch des Polizeirechts*, C Rn. 114 ff., and Gusy, 'Mehr als der Polizei erlaubt ist?'

[52] See Chapter 7, Section 5, regarding the 'outsourcing' of torture.

[53] Rachor, in Lisken and Denninger, *Handbuch des Polizeirechts*, F Rn. 177.

[54] For criticism of this development, see the decision of the Federal Constitutional Court of 27 July 2005 concerning data gathering for the purpose of prosecuting or preventing a criminal offence (*BVerfGE* 113, 348). For the lowering of the thresholds for intervention, see Poscher, 'Eingriffsschwellen im Recht der inneren Sicherheit'.

knowledge basis, 'endangerers' are taken to be 'persons of whom certain facts justify the assumption of the police that they will commit serious, politically motivated criminal offences'.[55]

With the extreme porosity of the central categories and the lowering of intervention thresholds, the statutes authorizing police measures open up a wide scope for 'operative police work'. The latter is characterized by blurring the boundary between repressive and preventive action and introducing the double authorization of the police.[56] Consequently, this double-functional, repressive-preventive purpose, knowing neither danger nor probable cause, also suspends the legal criteria of ascribing personal responsibility.

The Erosion of Legal Checks

At the level of legal checks, it takes its toll that the legislator hides behind the overall pre-emptive orientation and the corresponding ensemble of surveillance and control tools. Instead of regulating police operations, the legislator confines itself to defining the general goals of information gathering and risk management, and allows for the virtualization and 'subjectification' of operative knowledge. As the motivations of the security agencies to intervene dominate, police action is subject to a rather reduced standard of public control and judicial review. As the police authorities are authorized to act based on their experience, assessment of situations and assumptions, they are therefore entitled to produce their own knowledge-base undisturbed by legal criteria and are in the comfortable situation of being able to legitimize their operations by presenting their annual reports.[57] And, finally, if already 'indications'

---

[55] Deutscher Bundestag – Wissenschaftliche Dienste, 'Gefährder' – § 100a of the German Code of Criminal Procedure (StPO) allows the interception and recording of telecommunication without the knowledge of those affected for almost 100 serious offences: from high treason and endangering the democratic state based on the rule of law to genocide, manslaughter, child pornography, money laundering, fraud, falsification of documents and crimes against competition up to criminal offences against the Asylum Procedure Act and the Residence Act.

[56] The Federal Criminal Police Office Act of 7 July 1997 (BKAG) gave up the term 'crime prevention' (*vorbeugende Verbrechensbekämpfung*), still to be found in the police laws of States; instead it refers consistently to the prevention and prosecution of criminal offences (§ 1 sec. 3 BKAG).

[57] For the concept of the annual report (*Lagebericht*), see Bundeskriminalamt, *Kurzfassung des Lagebildes Organisierte Kriminalität Bundesrepublik Deutschland*.

'justify the assumption' that distant events may be considered dangerous or if police experience and assessment of situations can set off pre-emptive informational interventions, then police authorities are entitled to provide their own operational legitimacy in a quasi-self-referential move. A 'relatively strict legal obligation'[58] is thus replaced by trust in the truthfulness of the authorities' intentions and in the empirical soundness of their experience. In short, the police assume in individual cases the role of the legislator and operate on the basis of an intra-legal prerogative.

Blanket clauses tempt police authorities to focus primarily on generating circumstantial evidence to prevent danger and crime. In the absence of effective external control by the courts, police measures tend to follow a 'second code',[59] determined less by tactical-legal requirements than rather by prejudice, stereotypes and unquestioned everyday knowledge. Empirical cases illustrate that this subjectifiation of the knowledge-base entails institutionalized racial profiling.[60] Individuals or groups that are considered to be suspicious due to their origin, colour or appearance are statistically more often the focus of investigators than the rest of the population. In comparison with the 'normal citizen', they live in a legal sphere of reduced freedom, as the scope and intensity of state surveillance are measured according to the social status of the objects of social control.[61]

From Proportionality to the Uncontrollable Logic of Necessity

At the operational level, this special police law significantly softens the in any case elastic principle of proportionality for the constraining of operations and even annuls it in cases in which the life of persons or the security of the state are at stake. Regarding the appropriateness and necessity of measures, the principle of effective danger prevention has

---

[58] Note the contradictory wording.

[59] See Macnaughton-Smith, 'The Second Code Toward (or Away From) a Theory of Crime and Delinquency'.

[60] Herrnkind, 'Personenkontrollen und Schleierfahndung' and id., '"Schleierfahndung"'. For the problem of racial profiling, see Heumann and Cassak, *Good Cop, Bad Cop* and Benjamin Todd Jealous, 'Gastkommentar: Die üblichen Verdächtigen', *Amnesty Journal* (September 2004), http://www.amnesty.de/umleitung/2004/deu05/135?lang=de%26mimetype%3dtext%2fhtml.

[61] Albrecht Funk talks about 'different legal spheres' in 'Ausgeschlossene und Bürger', 255. With regard to informational interventions, the situation of foreigners can be characterized as 'second-class data protection'; see Frankenberg, 'Datenschutz und Staatsangehörigkeit'.

always offered a significant prerogative for assessment. Now, in the legitimizing context of counter-terrorism, it is considerably extended: pre-emptive measures 'without criminogenic valence' rest on self-produced police assessments, vague and unsupported/uncontrollable findings and everyday theories. Methodically controllable considerations about reasonableness fail because in the sphere leading up to a danger or crime or when the police operate on a large scale no individual 'case' exists. Moreover, the significance of the initial intervention (for example, taking a DNA sample or collecting personal data) tends to be underrated, when the consequences of the measure (data processing, distribution, its faults and side effects, etc.) remain excluded. Any ex post judicial review of this political technology is thinned out, bypassed or at least rendered considerably more difficult.

The difficulties of judicial review can be illustrated by the career of the principle of proportionality, once a law-rule pillar of police statutes and considered to be the most efficient legal check on police interventions. Today this principle is not only weakened; it is simply absent in some very crucial constellations: once confronted by claims for the protection of human life or the security of the state, reasoning in terms of proportionality is virtually neutralized. In potentially life-threatening situations when the ultimate harm is entirely unclear, the *potential* harm carries so much weight that it may justify even the most serious intervention, like coercive interrogations or torture. This logic also applies to allegedly state-threatening situations, i.e. 'attacks at the heart of the state'. In both constellations of threat, measuring proportionality becomes virtually impossible because every rational means-ends assessment under the principle of proportionality is bound to fail.

The special police law of normalized emergency, with its inherent peculiar political technology, hence, follows the logic of necessity. Whatever is claimed to be necessary to cope with a presumed or real threat normalizes public emergencies and balks at any significantly strict and potentially obstructive legal control of its proportionality.

And the erosion of judicial review is not even compensated by other forms of control. One would assume a check on the effectiveness of invasive police measures to replace the full fledged proportionality check. However, systematic evaluations of the effectiveness or efficiency of informational measures have not been undertaken yet: 'It is remarkable […] that there are hardly any reliable assessments of the success of the diverse, new means of surveillance.'[62] Sporadic obligations to report, selectively published material, common places and the praise of accidental findings do not even come close to an efficiency evaluation.[63] The actual police practice immunizes itself against empirical inquiries, while significant doubts remain about its effectiveness. In conclusion, some are outlined here.

First, regarding *dragnet investigations,* one cannot fail to note that the police necessarily operate in a reactive manner. The search pattern for a dragnet investigation can only be established once an event has already taken place that can be ascribed to a particular type (or group) of offender. Since it is unavoidable that the search pattern becomes public after the dragnet has been used, offenders can adapt their behaviour and make themselves inconspicuous. That aside, the sheer amount of data gathered can hardly be analysed accurately due to the large scope of a dragnet investigation. There is certainly cause to reflect on the effectiveness of such measures given that, for instance in Germany, in a large-scale dragnet investigation, data on about 250,000 individuals were stored and analysed to no avail.[64]

Second, with *random checks and surveillance* the police steer informational interventions in a conventional manner to whatever attracts their attention. The prototype of the 'sleeper' should, however, highlight that terrorists and organized criminals operating in networks are determined to move in society as inconspicuously as possible. Effectively, anticipatory investigation, aka averting danger, can therefore hardly focus alone or even primarily on the search for the conspicuous, if it intends to provide a minimum of existential or only cognitive safety.

Third, as long as there is no sufficiently strong empirical evidence, it should be assumed that *video surveillance* of public places and locations as well as similar measures lead rather to a shift of locale than a decline of crime.

In sum, the new security dispositive transforms law enforcement into the enforcement of politics, aka political technology, via manifold primarily informational interventions, which restructure the traditional

---

[62] This objection was raised by the former judge of the Federal Constitutional Court, Wolfgang Hoffmann-Riem, in his farewell address ('Das Bundesverfassungsgericht als Garant von Rechtsstaatlichkeit', 560).

[63] Denninger, 'Lauschangriff – Anmerkungen eines Verfassungsrechtlers' in *Strafverteidiger* 1998, 401 ff.; Petri, in Lisken and Denninger, *Handbuch des Polizeirechts*, H Rn. 199, and Rachor, ibid., F Rn. 435.

[64] Reference in the decision of the Federal Constitutional Court (*BVerfGE* 115, 320/324).

preventive legal techniques of the police and security institutions. Since the mid-1990s, within the framework of a 'new security architecture' geared officially towards terrorism and 'organized crime', society has become a prime target; and public spaces as well as the home and workplace have been under intense surveillance and monitoring – in a subcutaneous and inconspicuous but persistent manner which normalizes the state of exception to deal with the asymmetric war declared by terrorist networks and adversaries operating in criminal organizations.

That 'the war on …' has become such a pervasive metaphor should not be dismissed as 'only words' because it gives away the mindset of the latter-day political engineers. In a world of crises, which they experience as 'emergencies requiring extraordinary speed or secrecy', they seem to fear lest 'they come not in time to defend themselves from sudden blow'.[65]

6.7 'ENEMY CRIMINAL LAW' AND OTHER PHENOMENA OF MILITANT LAW

Counter-terrorism and related security projects, as well as the turn from prevention to pre-emption, supported by the rhetoric of war and combat, and the management of risks normalizing the exception have also infiltrated other areas of law.[66] I will briefly refer to some symptomatic phenomena. Despite their differences, they all point towards imagined emergency situations: 'enemy criminal law' (*Feindstrafrecht*), 'rescue torture' (*Rettungsfolter*), 'final and fatal shot' (*finaler Rettungsschuss*) and the 'rescue downing of aircraft' (*Rettungsabschuss*) hijacked by supposed terrorists. Having discussed these concepts as being structurally related to the Schmittian conception of norm and exception, I wish to analyse them now as features of the second crisis of law-rule and phenomena of normalization.

---

[65] Harrington, *The Commonwealth of Oceana*; for the complete quotation and commentary, see Ferejohn and Pasquino, 'The Law of the Exception', 213.

[66] So far the focus has been and will remain on domestic law. In international law, which cannot be discussed here, a similar issue can be highlighted in the crisis of multilateralism and the concomitant weakening of the *peace-keeping* function of international organizations as well as the softening of the ban on violence. All these developments show indications of a new global 'security architecture'. For an affirmative assessment, see Slaughter and Burke-White, 'An International Constitutional Moment'. For a critical analysis of the privileging of violence, see Berman, 'Privileging Combat?' and Kennedy, *Of War and Law*.

'Enemy Criminal Law' as the Normalization of the Exception

The chain of criminal combat laws[67] and their targets, notably terrorists and 'organized crime', inspired Günther Jakobs 'to describe [in civic criminal law and enemy criminal law] two poles of *one* world or two opposing tendencies in *one* context of criminal law'.[68] Initially, he was merely concerned with identifying 'enemy criminal law' in order to defend the standards of normal, civil criminal law. For this purpose, Jakobs initially analysed 'sprinkles' of enemy criminal law in the (German) Criminal Code and the Code of Criminal Procedure. He discovered the 'lex RAF', making punishable among other things the formation and membership of and support for terrorist organizations, and imposing incommunicado detention[69] on RAF prisoners, as well as the law of preventive measures (*Maßregelrecht*), providing for particularly dangerous or habitual offenders the possibility of detention for the purpose of incapacitation.[70] He established three characteristics for identifying enemy law and, we might add, combat law: its preventive orientations, the tightening of criminal sanctions and the reduction of guarantees in criminal proceedings. While these characteristics indicate that the 'enemy criminal law' normalizes the exception, Jakobs might

---

[67] Legislation for combating economic crime, terrorism, illegal drug trafficking and other forms of organized crime, sexual offences and other dangerous criminal offences as well as, finally, the *Verbrechensbekämpfungsgesetz* of 1994. For references, see Jakobs, 'Bürgerstrafrecht und Feindstrafrecht' and id., 'Das Selbstverständnis der Strafrechtswissenschaft', 51 ff.

[68] Jakobs, 'Bürgerstrafrecht und Feindstrafrecht', 88 (emphasis in the original).

[69] § 129a of the Criminal Code and the Contact Ban Act (*Kontaktsperregesetz*) were products of the German Autumn (*Deutscher Herbst*) 1977. The latter stated among other things: 'If imminent danger exists for life and limb or the freedom of a person, if certain facts justify the suspicion that this danger emanates from a terrorist organisation and if it is necessary in order to avert this threat to interrupt the communication of the prisoners among each other and to the outside world, including the written and verbal contact with their defence counsel, such a determination can be made' (§ 31(1) EGGVG).

[70] In particular, the highly contested, retroactive preventive detention (§ 66b of the Criminal Code) introduced in 2002 should correspond to Jakobs' concept of an enemy criminal law. Cf. Braums, 'Nachträgliche Sicherungsverwahrung: In dubio pro securitate' and the half-hearted decision by the Federal Constitutional Court: *BVerfGE* 109, 133/190; recently, Federal Constitutional Court (BVerfG), *Europäische Grundrechte-Zeitschrift* 2008, 636.

argue that in 1985 his 'cold'[71] assessments were meant to preserve the integrity of civic or standard criminal law by distinguishing it from 'enemy criminal law' and, more importantly, by insisting on the discreet positivization and differentiated legitimation of 'enemy criminal law', thus preventing the latter's normalization. His critical stance during the first crisis of the *Rechtsstaat*, he softened, however, in the second crisis when he gradually showed scholarly sympathy for – or at least justified the necessity of – an 'enemy criminal law'. In one of his many articles he asks

> whether the strict fixation on the category of the crime does impose an obligation on the state – the necessity to respect the offender as person – which is inappropriate vis-à-vis a terrorist who does not meet the general expectation towards personal behaviour.[72]

As regards the second crisis, Jakobs' reflections are instructive in a number of respects: his controversial conceptualization of an 'enemy criminal law' seamlessly follows the logic of militant combat law and its language of the battlefield. His considerations also rely on an extended security dispositive, when he refers *en passant* to a 'right to security' in order to legitimize philosophically his enemy criminal law. Furthermore, Jakobs embraces the preventive orientation with regard to 'enemies', respectively 'offenders for principle', as they were defined by the Italian Constitutional Court:[73]

> Certainly situations might arise, perhaps they are even given already, in which those norms indispensable for a liberal state lose their validity, when one waits with repression until the offender leaves his private sphere. But even under such circumstances, enemy criminal law can only be legitimized as exceptionally valid emergency criminal law.[74]

---

[71] Eser admitted that the 'coldness' of the Jakobsian concept made him 'shiver' in his 'Schlussbetrachtungen' (final conclusions), in Eser et al., *Die deutsche Strafrechtswissenschaft vor der Jahrtausendwende: Rückbesinnung und Ausblick*, 445.

[72] Jakobs, 'Das Selbstverständnis der Strafrechtswissenschaft', 51 ff.

[73] Quoted by Galli, 'The War on Terror and Crusading Judges'.

[74] Jakobs, 'Kriminalisierung im Vorfeld einer Rechtsgutsverletzung', 783 ff. Targeted at the fight against the RAF, these considerations can be transferred effortlessly to the transnational terrorism of the 1990s.

Finally, presenting the 'enemy criminal law' as 'what *must* be done against terrorists',[75] Jakobs not only subscribes again to the rationale of preventive combat law but, prompted by necessity, opens up the pathway to emergency measures. A number of scholars of criminal law and legislators have followed Jakobs' idea of pre-emptive criminalization (which is not to say he prompted the differential treatment of 'offenders for principle' in other countries). It was not only the usual suspects, the United States, Great Britain and Germany, that experienced a shift to preventive criminal laws, but also countries like Italy where the mandatory expulsion of foreigners convicted of terrorist offences and the listing of 'dangerous elements' testify to an intensified politicization of the law.[76] Whether offenders are explicitly named as 'enemies' as by Jakobs or whether they are treated as such, invariably the categories of criminal law and the law of war are blurred and the judges and prosecutors become crusaders pursuing a moral-legal battle against the enemy.[77]

'The Final and Fatal Shot'

The second crisis also coincides in several countries with controversies over the power of the police or security officials to shoot to kill.[78] The pertinent legislation and commentaries were not, however, related to counter-terrorism. In Germany the debate about the so-called 'final and fatal shot' (*finaler Rettungsschuss*) was set off by the first post-war bank robbery with hostage taking in 1971. In the course of the police action a hostage and one of the two perpetrators were killed. In the aftermath, advocates of shoot-to-kill criticized the (then generally and today in some federal states still valid) provisions under police law according to which firearms may only be used against persons to prevent them from attacking or fleeing.[79] To relieve the police and to clarify their powers – especially but not only in the case of hostage taking – scholars and a section of the police called for the legitimization of the shot with likely

---

[75] Jakobs, 'Bürgerstrafrecht und Feindstrafrecht', 92; emphasis in the original.

[76] Galli, 'The War on Terror and Crusading Judges', 164 ff.

[77] See Galli, 'The War on Terror and Crusading Judges', 169; Manacorda and Nieto Martin, *Criminal Law between War and Peace*; Gomez-Jara Diez, 'Enemy Combatants Versus Enemy Criminal Law'.

[78] On the use of lethal force, Bronitt et al., *Shooting to Kill*; Squires and Kennison, *Shooting to Kill*, especially ch. 7 (for Great Britain); Kahan et al., 'Whose Eyes are you Going to Believe?' and Harper, 'Shoot to Kill'.

[79] Examples can be found in legislation concerning direct coercion.

fatal effect if it is 'the only means to prevent an imminent mortal danger or an imminent danger of serious violation of bodily integrity'.[80] Despite significant police-tactical and legal reservations, this demand was included in the Model Draft for a Unitary Police Law and then adopted in their police law by ten states.

Advocates of the shoot-to-kill provision often argue that it is out of the question to adopt the legal justifications for self-defence and for public emergencies under criminal and civil law or even to assume an unwritten emergency law of the state. They call for the normalization of shooting to kill to legitimize it beforehand and to prevent circumstances where a police operation 'degenerates in extreme situations into a seminar about police law'. A second line of reasoning questions the effectiveness of shoot-to-wound because of traditional police responses that it just 'may not cut it'.[81] More recently, the shoot-to-kill advocates argue, now in the context of counter-terrorism, that the police like all security institutions should change their overall strategic orientation from 'reactive' to 'pro-active' measures.

Critics rejected the legal regulation of the final and fatal shot, because, apart from difficult practical issues, such an authority would transgress the boundaries of law-rule, contribute in everyday police practice to the lowering of inhibition levels and come 'dangerously close to the death penalty'.[82] However, the logic of combat law, if not the idea that normalizing the lethal use of force would make it more acceptable, has prevailed in most states and in the scholarly discourse.

The 'Rescue Downing' of Renegade Aircraft

For some time now, a similar controversy has surrounded the 'rescue downing' (*Rettungsabschuss*) of passenger aircraft that are under the control of supposed terrorists. This was triggered by the attack on the World Trade Center on 11 September 2001 and, in Germany, re-energized when a mentally ill 'stray pilot' threatened to plunge his motor glider into one of the skyscrapers in Frankfurt. Two years later the Federal Diet (*Bundestag*) enacted the Aviation Security Act,[83] which

80 See § 42(2) of the Model Draft for a Unitary Police Law (MEPolG).

81 References in Schenke, *Polizei- und Ordnungsrecht*, Rn. 560 ff.; Merten, 'Zum Streit um den Todesschuß. Vom Tätermitleid zur Opferpreisgabe?', 604; Harper, 'Shoot to Kill'.

82 References in Rachor, in Lisken and Denninger, *Handbuch des Polizeirechts*, F Rn. 990 ff.

83 Act of 11 January 2005, *BGBl.* I, 78.

authorized air security authorities, airlines and airport operators to implement stricter security measures, especially tightened identity and reliability checks on employees at airports and airlines in order to prevent attacks like that of 9/11.[84] The controversy focused in particular on a provision authorizing the 'direct use of armed force' against a passenger aircraft 'when, according to the specific circumstances, the conclusion can be reached that the aircraft is meant to be used against the lives of individuals and that the downing is the only means of defence against this imminent danger' (§ 14(3)).

This authorization by simple statute was meant to integrate the armed forces into the executive concept of combating dangers and risks and potentially to use them domestically for the very first time. Due to a constitutional reservation, any domestic deployment of the armed forces that does not serve defensive purposes requires the explicit approval of the Basic Law. Apart from the exceptional situations of revolt, disasters or grave accidents and catastrophes,[85] the domestic deployment of the armed forces with the use of armed force – not for the purpose of defending Federal territory[86] but to safeguard air traffic against hijacking, sabotage and especially terrorist attacks by so-called renegade aircraft – lacked constitutional backing. Therefore the governments of some Federal states and the Christian-Democratic parliamentary group tabled draft legislation that intended to change the deployment opportunities provided by the Basic Law.[87]

---

[84] Interestingly, pilots who (like the 'stray pilot' mentioned) only possess a licence for microlights and gliders were exempt.

[85] 'The authorisation of the armed forces under § 14.3 of the Aviation Security Act to use direct armed force against an aircraft is not in harmony with these regulations. Article 35.2 sentence 2 of the Basic Law rules out the use of direct armed force in the case of a regional emergency situation.' Federal Constitutional Court of Germany (*BVerfGE* 115, 118/142, 146 ff.).

[86] Under Art. 115a Basic Law, the vague term of defence is defined as actual or imminent armed attack on Federal territory. The state of defence needs by the way to be determined by the *Bundestag* with the consent of the *Bundesrat* on application of the Federal Government.

[87] See Art. 87a.2–4 Basic Law and Art. 35.2 and 3 Basic Law. The suggested amendments were however rejected by the majority of the *Bundestag*, *BT-Plenarprotokoll* 15/115, 10545. For this reason alone, it was foreseeable that the Federal Constitutional Court would rule that § 14.3 Aviation Security Act was unconstitutional.

The public debate in Germany – and concerning a comparable case in Poland[88] – focused almost exclusively on the compatibility of the authorization of the downing with the constitutional protection of human dignity and life. As already in the case of the 'final and fatal shot', the advocates of 'rescue downing' argued in its favour with reference to the ethics of rescue in order to open the way for relativizing both human dignity, arguably conceptualized as not only balancing-proof (*abwägungsfest*), and the right to life, considered to be hostile to balancing (*abwägungsfeindlich*).[89] Earlier, the Federal Minister of the Interior had argued with regard to the necessity of killings in exceptional situations:

> Is there not even a right to self-defence vis-à-vis terrorists who plan mass murder? This leads to the question of whether the killing of one person is also justified as self-defence in extreme cases.[90]

To legitimize 'self-defence', reference was again made to the 'right to security' 'not directly but indirectly' contained in the Basic Law.[91] One of the more bizarre justifications was based on the 'theory' that passengers agree to the presumed downing of their aircraft once they enter it as well as the theory that free citizens have an obligation to possibly sacrifice their lives for the community in extreme situations.[92] Patently absurd seems to be the idea that passengers were functional components of the threatened aircraft.

On the other hand, critics of the 'downing licence' argued that the imminently threatened lives of uninvolved airplane passengers were of equal value with the potentially threatened lives of persons on the ground, and that airplane passengers would be killed on the basis of a hypothetical scenario and not of a certain course of events. And, finally, they rejected the quantification of life and concluded that the state's

---

88 Federal Supreme Court, Judgment of 30 September 2008 – K44/07, concerning Art. 122 of the Act of 3 July 2002 – The Aviation Act.

89 For the debate regarding the Aviation Security Act, see Hartleb, 'Der neue § 14 III LuftSiG und das Grundrecht auf Leben'; Bernhard Schlink, *Der Spiegel* No. 3 of 17 January 2005, 34 ff.; Merkel, 'Wenn der Staat Unschuldige opfert'; id., '§ 14 Abs. 3 Luftsicherheitsgesetz: Wann und warum darf der Staat töten?'; Sattler, 'Terrorabwehr durch die Streitkräfte nicht ohne Grundgesetzänderung'; Wieland, 'Verfassungsrechtliche Grundlagen polizeiähnlicher Einsätze der Bundeswehr'.

90 Otto Schily, *Der Spiegel* No. 18 of 26 April 2004, 47.

91 Schily, 'Interview', *Süddeutsche Zeitung* of 29 October 2001.

92 Cf. Depenheuer, *Selbstbehauptung des Rechtsstaates*, who criticized the decision of the Federal Constitutional Court as 'constitutional autism'.

obligation to not kill its citizens outweighs its obligation to protect them against threats by other citizens or even terrorists.

The Federal Constitutional Court ended this debate temporarily by rejecting an ethics of rescue and, hence, also the theory of the citizen-sacrifice in favour of a questionable civic security. The Court decided:

> In such an extreme situation, which is, moreover, characterized by the cramped conditions of an aircraft in flight, the passengers and the crew are typically in a desperate situation. They can no longer influence the circumstances of their lives independently from others in a self-determined manner.
>
> This makes them objects not only of the perpetrators of the crime. Also the state which in such a situation resorts to the measure provided by § 14.3 of the Aviation Security Act treats them as mere objects of its rescue operation for the protection of others. The desperateness and inescapability which characterize the situation of the people on board the aircraft who are affected as victims also exist vis-à-vis those who order and execute the shooting down of the aircraft. Due to the circumstances, which cannot be controlled by them in any way, the crew and the passengers of the plane cannot escape this state action but are helpless and defenceless in the face of it with the consequence that they are shot down in a targeted manner together with the aircraft and as a result of this will be killed with near certainty. Such a treatment ignores the status of the persons affected as subjects endowed with dignity and inalienable rights. By their killing being used as a means to save others, they are treated as objects and at the same time deprived of their rights; with their lives being disposed of unilaterally by the state, the persons on board the aircraft, who, as victims, are themselves in need of protection, are denied the value which is due to a human being for his or her own sake.[93]

In contrast to the demands of state practice and of a significant number of scholarly voices in the discourse on security and freedom, both courts – the Federal Constitutional Court of Germany as well as the Federal Supreme Court in Poland – resisted the temptation to sacrifice primarily the right to life on the altar of aviation security: after all, it did not sanction the citizen sacrifice as a 'solidarity obligation' in order to 'preserve the legally constituted order'.

Whether this concludes the matter of 'rescue downings' is highly questionable, however. Every once in a while the logic of pre-emption prompts governments to return to the issue and seek to gain authorization for the downing of renegade aircraft. And the 'renegade concept' of

---

93 Federal Constitutional Court (*BVerfGE* 115, 118/154).

NATO, which inspired the downing of 'aircraft with a terrorist background', could further encourage such efforts.[94] More promising (for the protagonists) seem to be efforts to pave the way for the domestic use of the military and to turn what was meant to be an exception, reserved for situations of emergency beyond the power of the police, into the norm.

'Rescue Torture'

In close conceptual and political proximity to the 'final and fatal shot' and the 'rescue downing of aircraft', the matter of 'rescue torture' has proved to be a talking point since the mid-1990s. In most countries the legal discourse was sparked by counter-terrorism or 9/11; in Germany by a theoretical thought experiment.[95] The controversy continued in many national 'epistemic communities' in the following decade, with significant intensity and apologetic bias as will be shown in the following chapter. Here, it may suffice to identify rescue torture as a doctrinal phenomenon of normalization within the overall scheme of militant combat law.

Under the spell of the archetypical figure of militant police law – the terrorist, later complemented by the hostage taker – the advocates develop their doctrine justifying 'rescue torture' or 'new torture' from the perspective of danger prevention. The resolution of a 'tragic' or dilemma decision, they argue, may require that the bodily and mental integrity of an offender or even suspect be subordinated to the protection of the dignity and life of those threatened by him, a reasoning that equates with a pattern of thought that fits seamlessly into the context of fighting the enemy under emergency law. With torture's *ultima ratio* of averting danger, another element – Günther Jakobs would talk of a 'sprinkle' – of the legally masked 'enemy criminal law' joins the already discussed shoot-to-kill as well as the downing of aircraft. However, whereas the term 'enemy criminal law' reveals its exceptional character and therefore lends itself to contestation, the advocates of state brutality in interrogations veil their doctrinal constructs in normalizing semantic obscurity and

---

[94] See Dreist, 'Einsatz der Bundeswehr im Innern', 86; Niklaus, *Zum Abschuss freigegeben?* Cf. also BT-Stenographischer Bericht, 96. Sitzung, *Plenarprotokoll* 15/96, 10 March 2004, 8585.

[95] Brugger, 'Darf der Staat ausnahmsweise foltern?'. Furthermore, id., 'Vom unbedingten Verbot der Folter zum bedingten Recht auf Folter?'; id., 'Würde gegen Würde'; id., 'Das andere Auge – Folter als zweitschlechteste Lösung'. For a critical perspective, see Denninger, '"Rechtsstaat" oder "Rule of law"?' and Chapter 7 with further references.

talk euphemistically of 'rescue torture' or 'self-defence torture',[96] 'forcible lifesaving cooperation enforcement' or 'self-inflicted rescue interrogation'.[97]

The phenomena of combat law exceed the boundaries of law-rule by far and put illiberal governmentality into the limelight. In the excessiveness of security decoupled from freedom, in addition to the *method Hobbes* and the *method Foucault* even elements of the *method Machiavelli* come into play, when and to the extent that security services defend their 'principality', their position of power, in the absence of legislative barriers and judicial controls and smuggle concepts and legitimatory patterns of a state of emergency into the normative routine of normal law-rule – where it dresses itself in the very law whose logic it contradicts.

6.8 SOME EFFECTS OF COMBAT LAW AND SECURITY MENTALITY

From Cognitive to Existential Safety

In a constantly monitored and screened society, the shift from old to new prevention comes with a loss of freedom and cognitive safety. However, the accompanying political discourse on security/freedom also entails the message that this loss is compensated for: from the barely understood symbolism of militant legislation, from scholarly doctrines of combat law or from the umbrella term 'homeland security' (comprising the reorganized security institutions of the United States) the passive civic audience can unsuspectingly derive the claim to be protected against all common life risks. In the shadow of catastrophic events, exaggerated threat scenarios and the hectic production of measures, the normalized state of exception intangibly produces a corresponding mentality on the part of the audience: a diffuse sense of threat and fear of crime coagulate into a vague need for what may be termed 'existential certainty'. Together with the security promises of the state, these ubiquitous fears force onto the defensive the anyway not very popular because of strenuous testing and enduring of freedom's everyday risks. Where fears are transformed into

---

96 For references, see Bowden, 'The Dark Art of Interrogation', 70, 76, and Chapter 7.

97 Concerning the euphemistic terms '*gewaltsame lebensrettende Kooperationserzwingung*' and '*selbstverschuldete Rettungsbefragung*' see Trapp, *Folter oder selbstverschuldete Rettungsbefragung?*

anxiety and the sense of being threatened spreads, cognitive uncertainty occurs, as does 'the loss of rationality and autonomy which play into the hands of the compensatory power increase of state agencies'.[98]

Situations and scenarios of threat and anxiety also intensify the Hobbesian uncertainty that accompanies every regime of freedom; it addresses the issue of whether and how the released flurry of civic initiative can be controlled effectively, the multitude of actions and their consequences can be coordinated and unavoidable societal conflicts can be constrained. Where Hobbes' question of security dominates, the publicly declared willingness to live with certain risks, to tolerate differences – poignantly formulated, to tolerate foreigners and others who deviate from 'normal image' and 'normal behaviour' – has to defend itself against the accusation that it trivializes the dangers threatening society.[99] Whoever criticizes the concept of the enemy is charged by the dramatizers and supporters of the combat rhetoric with 'problem disposal via concept rejection'.[100] Substantively, the accusation addressed to the court majority by a constitutional judge on the occasion of the decision about dragnet investigations, which she disapproved of, is similarly clear. In her view the majority's decision failed to appreciate that the legislator cannot be denied the power to 'readjust the threshold for intervention in the face of a changed security situation and threat quality within the framework of its obligation to risk prevention [...] for the purpose of risk management'.[101]

The Costs of Risk Prevention under Emergency Law

In political technology geared towards combating, the turn towards a mentality of security becomes manifest in the prima facie not unreasonable attitude to restrict liberties to create space for effective measures of danger prevention. During the second crisis of law-rule, this happened in fact as shown by the significant and excessive extension of state intervention powers. At second glance, given the dramatic risks and side effects, one could at least expect proof of the success and effectiveness of

---

[98] Bung, 'Terror als Gegenstand einer Phänomenologie der Angst', 66; see also Chapter 5.

[99] See also Butler, *Precarious Life*, ch. 3 ('Indefinite Detention').

[100] Depenheuer, *Selbstbehauptung des Rechtsstaates*, 57.

[101] Dissenting opinion of Judge Haas, Federal Constitutional Court of Germany (*BVerfGE* 115, 320/380). For a more differentiated argument, see Roellecke, 'Der Rechtsstaat im Kampf gegen den Terror', when he refers to the issue of (legal) waiver.

police interventions in social processes. However, this fails to materialize despite the repeated use of the instruments and historical experience. Security experts are loath to admit that the results of random police checks, apart from accidental findings, are rather meagre; and that dragnet investigations rarely produce conclusive evidence. It has not become known that the broad informational interventions under special police law are subject to strict monitoring of their effectiveness, which has the character of an evaluation. It is the constitutive characteristic of the discourse on torture that the uncertainty of the rescue and, hence, its proportionality as well as the conditions of the procedurally correct and proportional use of torture methods, including the professional training of torturers, are not reflected seriously. Also ignored are the almost certainly devastating effects of a legally sanctioned practice of torture on the normative tissue of law-rule and on society. Jakobs' account is blind to the fact that an 'enemy criminal law' is likely to produce more enemies, to provide them with arguments for recruiting sympathizers and, hence, could increase the supposed danger it intends to combat. At the same time, his analysis of contact bans and solitary confinement imposed on RAF terrorists provides ample illustration of the counterproductive effects of measures under enemy criminal law.

Regarding the downing of aircraft one misses any consideration that, depending on the situation, a significant aviation incident is characterized by large uncertainties and that the motives and aims of the hijackers as well as the fate of the passengers remain speculative up until the very last moment, i.e. that the command for the downing could come too early or too late. Interestingly enough, the security technicians were only reproached with failing to consider these problems by the Federal Constitutional Court and military experts.[102] In short, under the flag of combat law, practice and scholarship cultivate a security operation partly established and exercised in the sphere of the exceptional without even taking much notice of reality.

Risks and Side Effects of the Shift in Mentality

The shift in mentality to security also becomes obvious in the recently pronounced, pithy as well as diffuse, rhetoric of sacrifice in jurisprudence.[103] From the perspective of mentality, the rediscovery of the

---

[102] *BVerfGE* 115, 118/155 ff.

[103] For a detailed account, see Chapter 4. Typical of the rhetoric of sacrifice: Depenheuer, *Selbstbehauptung des Rechtsstaates*, 75 ff.; Haltern, 'Internationales Verfassungsrecht?', 555: 'The area of political imagination in the nation state

citizen-sacrifice can be read as both a heroic and an impotent contribution by intellectuals to the war against transnational terrorism. This rhetoric of sacrifice differs significantly from the reactions of the 'community of rights companions', who by and large do not have an appetite for heroics. What comes to the fore here is a political quietism in everyday life rather unaffected by demands for freedom. It readily accepts the illusory promise of existential safety and in turn even spurs on the discourse of outbidding in security policy as well as the semantics and logic of combative police law 'from below' by the thoughtless waiver of liberties. Depending on temperament, the burden of security is accepted emphatically or lethargically. With its anticipatory waiver of both basic rights and proof of the effectiveness of anti-terror measures, the civic audience accommodates the technicians of the state who claim to fight terrorism, 'organized crime', radical Islamism and whatever it considers to be dangerous. The maxims that, first, in matters of security the state can do no wrong and, second, that citizens have nothing to hide meet the mentality of engineers half way.

As side effects of this, prejudice against 'foreigners' and 'dangerous elements' is given house room, and a punitive climate fosters the articulation of a hardly tamed desire for sanctions against suspects and even more so against convicted criminals. In demands for deportation of foreigners, summary proceedings and lifelong imprisonment, the downside of the expectations of security becomes manifest.[104]

Under the unacknowledged regime of anxiousness, such a mentality of security could become a problem for the security services, which operate relieved of civic criticism and freed from the constraints of law-rule. Indeed, if the sacrifice of freedom and the submissive tolerance towards interventions of the security state intensify the desire for 'existential

---

starts with the sacrifice that assimilates "us" to the law. From the perspective of liberalism, this is an unpopular statement since here the state does not demand to die but to provide protection. However, political theory has to be able to explain the phenomenon of self-sacrifice and killing.' For a more differentiated account of the sacrifice from the perspective of the social contract, see Enders, 'Der Staat in Not', 1043 ff., who develops in the context of terror prevention a general obligation to solidarity, if necessary at the risk of one's own life in order to preserve the legally constituted order. For the theory of the sacrifice in general, see Münkler and Fischer, '"Nothing to Kill or Die for ..."'.

[104] Günther, 'Kritik der Strafe I'.

certainty', then this civic 'self-disempowerment'[105] corresponds ultimately with the overtaxing of the preventive state, which is not given the obligation to provide comprehensive personal care and comprehensive protection of society without reason. It is not accidental that the security technicians usually promise more security that they can actually provide. And it may only be a matter of time until those disappointed in their expectations realize that they have relinquished the secured insecurity that comes with a legal regime of freedom – not for the fantasy world of a comprehensively protected existence, but for highly insecure freedom in a normalized emergency regime promising illusory security.

---

[105] Bung, 'Terror als Gegenstand einer Phänomenologie der Angst' – following Fromm, *Die Furcht vor der Freiheit* and Neumann, 'Anxiety and Politics' – refers to 'losses of rationality and autonomy due to fear or anxiety' (66).

7. Normalizing torture as a technique of governing: What 'the exigencies of war' demand?[1]

7.1 THE DOMESTICATION OF A TABOO[2]

In awe of the sacred or for fear of demons, 'savages' avoid the taboo.[3] It is also fear which dictates that neurotics obey the forbidden. Those who deem themselves civilized may prefer the guidance of convention or wisdom to respect what is taboo or to approach the unfamiliar with caution.[4]

Torture might qualify as both the unfamiliar and a taboo. Until recently torture, in Freudian terms, was not 'generally accessible', being removed from public scrutiny as well as surrounded by the aura of the dangerous and strictly prohibited. Even legal norms declaring this practice unlawful dared not spell out the law of torture[5] in detail, as if the taboo even prohibited semantic approaches or defended its religious dimension.

In this last chapter I look at the torture debate and the practice of torture in the United States and at the discourse on torture in German

[1] 'The principle has been more and more acknowledged that the unarmed citizen is to be spared in person, property, and honor as much as the exigencies of war will admit.' (Art. 22 of the 'Lieber Code'; Francis Lieber, 'Instructions for the Government of Armies of the United States in the Field', promulgated as General Order No. 100 by President Abraham Lincoln, 24 April 1863.

[2] The following text is based on an earlier publication which has been considerably revised and updated for this publication to accentuate the global perspective and includes additional comparative material; cf. Frankenberg, 'Torture and Taboo: An Essay Comparing Paradigms of Organized Cruelty', 56 *American Journal of Comparative Law* 403 (2008).

[3] Freud, *Totem and Taboo*.

[4] Reimann, 'Tabu', 420.

[5] 'No one shall be subjected to torture or to cruel, inhuman or degrading treatment or punishment.' (Art. 5 Universal Declaration of Human Rights 1948); and 'No one shall be subjected to torture or to inhuman or degrading treatment or punishment.' (Art. 3 European Convention on Human Rights 1952).

legal academia. I discuss three common misunderstandings of the phenomenon that also shape the recent controversies. Then I wish to introduce the structural elements of the different paradigms of torture and focus on those features of the 'new torture' that have been claimed to distinguish it from its evil ancestry: the rescue motive and the close relationship to law. The imaginary novelty of 'rescue torture' is also unmasked in the context of legal doctrines that are meant to guide in the proportionate application of 'rescue torture'. The final discussion will focus on strategic and semantic practices of camouflaging violations of the taboo.

What used to be taboo mutated, after a moment of initial reticence,[6] first in the media and then, which is of particular interest here, in the legal discourse, to a domestic animal. In German legal academia domestication began with juridical speech-acts that were almost innocently rooted in the everyday. Long before 11 September, in 1996 a legal scholar and philosopher of law inquired: 'May Government Ever Use Torture?'[7] This also happened quite some time before the 'war on terror' had entered its intense phase, and some years after the provocation by the grand master of systems theory, Niklas Luhmann, in a lecture given at the University of Heidelberg. To introduce his topic as to whether 'there (are) non-renounceable norms in our societies' he presented the following case:

> Imagine that you are a police officer. In your country – and this might also be Germany in a not too distant future – there are many leftist and rightist terrorists, and every day there are murders, killings, arson attacks, and damages affecting numerous innocent parties. Imagine that you captured the leader of such a group. You could, if you tortured him, presumably save the life of many people – ten, hundred, or thousand, – we may vary the case. Would you do it?[8]

Whether you would in fact *do* 'it', Luhmann did not really care to know. As a theoretician he was merely interested in the functional differentiation between the systems of law and morality and wondered if it could be sustained in extreme and borderline situations.[9] Likewise the scholar

---

[6] See Poscher, 'Die Würde des Menschen ist unantastbar'.

[7] Brugger, 'May Government Ever Use Torture?'; the original German version appeared in 1996.

[8] Luhmann, 'Are There Still Indispensable Norms in Our Society?'.

[9] Strangely enough, he recommended at the end of the article, regardless of all legalistic concerns, 'a licence for torture issued by internationally supervised courts, monitored by television in Geneva or Luxemburg, so as not to sacrifice

of public law and legal philosopher Winfried Brugger, who had in fact listened to Luhmann's lecture, did not want to know whether you would *do* 'it', but if and under what circumstances the law might justify the use of coercion. He argued, in a lawyer's practical spirit, for a legal solution. And moved from 'the strict prohibition of torture to its conditional licence', somewhat uneasily admitting that this might be 'the second-best solution'.[10]

What could be misunderstood, in the beginning, as a naïve 'why not ask?' soon developed into a full-fledged exercise in legal doctrine concerning human dignity and the proportionality of police measures, and even including, as a sombre highlight, a torture case for students in public law, meant to prepare them for the graduate exam.[11] Starting from the romantic setting of Heidelberg, calculated state violence gradually turned into a legal commodity for everyday use – like any other standard, if certainly more drastic, police measure. Any observer of the German legal-scientific community might be surprised by the stream of publications that have addressed the topic of torture since the middle of the 1990s, unwarranted by the actual state practice. And she would most likely be astonished that a theoretical provocation should set off a doctrinal debate. This debate was soon intensified by a kidnapping and murder case in Frankfurt, when the vice president of the police threatened the suspected kidnapper with 'extremely painful coercion'.[12] The torture discourse became more dynamic after a series of terrorist attacks, first in New York and then in other European cities. Legal scholars got accustomed to thinking 'the unthinkable', arguing that the banned practice should be permissible or morally justifiable under certain circumstances, or that it might be 'an option'.

Next to the 'new' torture nurtured in legal/philosophical academia, another one soon emerged that had been presumed dead and that nobody had missed except sadists and cynics. In Guantánamo and Abu Ghraib, but not only there, the latter had apparently been included in the arsenal

innocent people to the fanaticism of terrorists'. Luhmann, 'Are There Still Indispensable Norms in Our Society?', 27.

[10] See Brugger, 'Vom unbedingten Verbot der Folter zum bedingten Recht auf Folter?'. See also id., 'Das andere Auge', 8.

[11] See Brugger, 'Würde gegen Würde'.

[12] This 'case' is likely to go down in the German history of penal law as a *cause célèbre*. The literature covering the 'Fall Daschner' (the said Vice President of the police) can hardly be grasped; see only Zagolla, *Im Namen der Wahrheit*, notably 196 ff.; Erb, 'Notwehr als Menschenrecht'; Lochte, *Der Fall Jakob von Metzler*; Ziegler, 'Das Folterverbot in der polizeilichen Praxis'.

of governmental technology.[13] Both the 'new' torture being discussed and the 'old' torture being practised encroach upon what many prohibitions have intended to remove, with almost religious strictness, from governmental intervention.

Comparatively speaking, the US-American legal discourse, motivated and accelerated by the anti-terror politics of the Bush/Cheney government, covers a wider spectrum of argument. The advocates of coercion are united, though, by the rhetoric of necessity.[14] The 'war on terror', 9/11, an imperial president who authorized interrogation measures that may arguably be qualified as torture[15] or 'rescue torture', practised notably in Guantánamo and Abu Ghraib, shook up the legal profession and became the focal points of critical and apologetic juridical interventions in the wake of the Military Commissions Act of October 2006 and the earlier Patriot Act – a euphemistic and Orwellian shorthand for its full name: 'Uniting and Strengthening America by Providing Appropriate Tools Required to Intercept and Obstruct Terrorism Act of 2001'.[16]

In general, quite a few participants in the discourse moved from strict prohibition to a conditional licence, if only for exceptional cases.[17] While

---

[13] Hersh, 'Torture at Abu Ghraib'; Human Rights Watch, 'The Road to Abu Ghraib'; Sands, *Torture Team*.

[14] See Greenberg, *The Torture Debate in America*. For a critical perspective see Sands, *Torture Team*; Kutz, 'Torture, Necessity and Existential Politics', who argues that the invocation of 'emergency powers' by the Bush/Cheney government follows the Schmittian script. See also Scheuerman, 'Emergency Powers and the Rule of Law After 9/11' and the controversy documented by the contributions in Levinson, *Torture*.

[15] International Committee of the Red Cross, 'ICRC Report on the Treatment of Fourteen High Value Detainees in CIA Custody', http://www.nybooks.com/icrc-report.pdf (13 November 2009) and Danner, 'US Torture'.

[16] See Abraham, 'The Bush Regime from Elections to Detentions', who compared these two acts to the Nazi *Ermächtigungsgesetz* [Empowerment Act] of 1933; Levinson, *Torture*; McCoy, *Foltern und Foltern lassen* and Sands, *Torture Team*. A critical distance from torture guides Bruce Ackerman's draft of a 'framework' for the state of exception: Ackerman, *Before the Next Attack*. See also the 'Report to Congress on Implementation of sec. 1001 of the USA-PATRIOT Act', US Department of Justice, Office of the Inspector General, 17 July 2003. For a critique of the anti-terrorism measures, see Goodin, *What's Wrong with Terrorism*; Tushnet, *The Constitution in Wartime*; for a defence of the Bush/Cheney strategy, see Yoo, *The Powers of War and Peace*. See also Poole, 'Courts and Conditions of Uncertainty in "Times of Crisis"'. For a comprehensive review of anti-terrorism measures – such as internet monitoring, detentions, renditions, etc. – see Cole and Dempsey, *Terrorism and the Constitution*.

[17] For references see Strauss, 'Torture' and Levinson, *Torture*.

some invoked the survival rule to limit extremely coercive interrogations to situations when they are – in Abraham Lincoln's words – an 'indispensable necessity for the preservation of the nation', other authors operated with more lenient necessity standards: such as 'a grave risk or danger for the nation', a 'tendency toward self-destruction' or simply a 'rule of priority' – referring to 'seasons of public danger' as George Mason might have remarked. Yet others argued that torture should be banned but quietly practised, as a certain two-facedness is called for in the fight against terrorists. The unqualified apologists of torture[18] as a blatantly political technology were strictly opposed by scholars sustaining its prohibition on moral and legal grounds.[19] Moderate opposition came from others who desperately tried to give torture a legal dressing, i.e. defining it as a legal technique of governing; they advocated the ex ante legal regulation of coercion to make public and transparent an already ongoing 'promiscuous' practice or they favoured torture warrants because torture 'should damn well have court approval'.[20]

The discourse in both interpretive communities (and in many others) calls into question what multiple norms – laid down in national, supranational and international documents absolutely prohibit. Many seem to be prepared to violate what has been introduced here as a taboo. Considering the many layers of prohibitive norms that persuasively if not always with sufficient determinacy outlaw torture I do not want to discuss in detail the merits of the arguments for and against calculated brutality practised or condoned by government agencies under exceptional circumstances, regardless of whether dictated by catastrophes or academic thought experiments.[21]

---

[18] As to the debate concerning emergency powers in the US, see Ferejohn and Pasquino, 'The Law of the Exception'; Ackerman, 'The Emergency Constitution'; id., *Before the Next Attack* and Dyzenhaus, 'Schmitt v. Dicey'.

[19] For a survey of the stand-off between critics and apologists and the topography of normative and empirical arguments, see Waldron, *Torture, Terror, and Trade-Offs* versus Posner and Vermeule, *Terror in the Balance.*

[20] Dershowitz, *Why Terrorism Works*; id., *Preemption*, 3; id., 'The Torture Warrant'. Similarly, Mirko Bagaric and Julie Clarke advocate the adoption of a legal framework to regulate torture which under certain circumstances may be morally justifiable: Bagaric and Clarke, 'Not Enough Official Torture in the World?'. For a critique of any ex ante or ex post justification of torture see Strauss, 'Torture' and Scarry, 'Five Errors in the Reasoning of Alan Dershowitz'.

[21] Concerning the debate about the law of the exception in the US discourse see Ferejohn and Pasquino, 'The Law of the Exception'; Ackerman, 'The Emergency Constitution' and Dyzenhaus, 'Schmitt v. Dicey'.

Rather than adding a further opinion to the maze of justifications and refutations, I briefly address some of the problems the advocates of torture (and, albeit to a lesser degree, of coercive interrogation) have to cope with. However, I start with a review of the discourse as to how the arguments of justification are structured, how they can be situated in their historical context and located in relation to normal legal competencies and emergency powers. By comparing the structures of justificatory paradigms, I neither suggest nor imply that the different historical and political contexts can be disregarded or equated. The structural approach might help, though, to elucidate the role of law and ultimately to answer the intriguing question of how a strict legal prohibition can be relativized, normalized and then come in again by the back door.

7.2 A 'RETURN' TO THE 'MIDDLE AGES'?

Seismographs of human rights violations register all over the world the manifold incidents of organized cruelty executed or tolerated by states. Human Rights Watch, anti-torture committees and, with remarkable persistence, Amnesty International, keep us informed about the ubiquitous violations of the taboo.[22] Unwillingly they help sustain the common image – and misconception – of a random, medieval practice which has returned. A *return* may be noted only in regions – actually: under regimes – where cruelty, as practised or tolerated by governments, for whatever official purposes, had been disapproved of or regarded as taboo to this very day. 'Return' would therefore mean that torture has become acceptable contrary to an established practice based on categorical legal prohibitions.[23] Not in exotic countries where crazy tyrants rage or where, as some like to assume, a cruel 'asianism'[24] stops at nothing, but even under the hands and eyes of 'governments of laws and not of men'.[25]

Torture is widely associated with the dark Middle Ages and characterized as the senseless and indiscriminate application of extreme physical pain and mental agony, directed against whoever was suspected of a

---

[22] Amnesty International reports of torture in 153 countries, http://www.uni-kassel.de/fb5/frieden/themen/Menschenrechte/folter.html.

[23] See the Universal Declaration of Human Rights (1948) and the European Convention on Human Rights (1952).

[24] In his otherwise very informative and to be recommended study, *La torture*, Alec Mellor held 'asianism' responsible for the proliferation of torture in the 20th century.

[25] Massachusetts Constitution of 2 March 1780, Part I, Art. XXX.

crime or not even that. To begin with the Middle Ages: it is correct that torture, also referred to as the 'painful question', is always located in the shadow of history and can be traced back to the medieval administration of justice. Its origins, however, reach back to the Greco-Roman world whence violence in criminal legal procedures accompanied the reception of Roman law and proliferated since the 13th century all over Europe, including the Holy Roman Empire of the German Nation.[26] During the first half of the 18th century the extortion of confessions in criminal trials within and without the Inquisition was discontinued.[27] In Prussia, King Frederick I permitted torture subject to royal review in 1720. By the time of Frederick the Great, 'the new law of proof had already displaced judicial torture from its former regularity'.[28] Hence it comes as no surprise that, within a month of his accession to the throne, the monarch widely considered enlightened should have abolished torture in 1740, but felt obliged to allow it for 'especially serious cases'. Provoked by various requests for permission to put suspects to torture, Frederick ordered the complete cessation of judicial torture in 1754.[29] Historians have noted similar developments elsewhere in continental Europe, the abolition legislation substituting the new law of proof for the old law of torture.

At first glance, the image of the medieval nature of torture is underscored by the standard historical accounts, before John Langbein's study revealed the relationship between torture and the proof system, and by the prevailing opinion in philosophy that positioned the end of torture in the account of the Enlightenment. Reliance on Thomasius, Voltaire, Montaigne, Bentham, Beccaria and other critics as principal witnesses seems to be problematic, though. Contrary to views relating the sceptical discourse on torture[30] to the philosophy of the Enlightenment, this discourse can be traced back to antiquity, enlisting Aristotle and Cicero among many other prominent opponents.[31] And contrary to the once dominant interpretation, the enlightened midwives of modernity were neither always nor even primarily led by their worry about the individual bestowed with reason and dignity. Like many of his contemporaries,

---

[26] Lea, *A History of the Inquisition of the Middle Ages*; Langbein, *Torture and the Law of Proof*, ch. 1, and Peters, *Torture*.

[27] Langbein, *Torture and the Law of Proof*, ch. 4.

[28] Ibid., at 61.

[29] Ibid., at 62.

[30] De La Bruyère, *Les Caractères*: 'La question est une invention merveilleuse et tout à fait sûre pour perdre un innocent qui a la complexion faible, et sauver un coupable qui est né robuste.'

[31] Ibid., at 8–12.

Cesare Beccaria, while denouncing torture as 'barbarism', was mainly concerned about the lack of effectiveness and the faultiness of a procedure which uses pain as the 'measuring pole for truth'[32] – very much like Frederick the Great finding it both 'gruesome' and 'an uncertain means to discover the truth'.[33] In retrospect, one may therefore not implausibly assume that after the murderous witch-trials there were no significant incidents and cases in which to apply torture and that it was abolished jointly with the 'collapsing of the [old] proof system'[34] and because there was ample evidence of its dysfunctional results.

The medieval image of torture is further at odds with its more recent history. For state violence – despite its formal abolition in the 18th century throughout Europe – accompanied like an ugly shadow a modernity which by definition was deemed civilized and respectful of the individual's right to physical integrity. Interestingly enough, the past decennium was labelled somewhat paradoxically as 'the century of human rights and torture' by Hannah Arendt.[35] And the 21st century – at least up until this point – does not seem to be steering a different course.

To turn to a second misunderstanding: apart from barbaric witch-hunts[36] and tyrannical orgies, history reveals that torture was almost never applied *indiscriminately*. On the contrary, one may detect changing patterns of selectivity.[37] The Greeks reserved torture for slaves and traitors. The law of the Roman Republic added free citizens. Medieval and later canon law, following the letters and logic of the papal Bull *Ad extirpanda*, primarily brought heretics to the torture rack. During the 13th and 14th centuries the circle of victims was considerably extended on the basis of secular criminal law to 'unwholesome people' (*landschädliche Leute*) and whoever was suspected of witchcraft. While there never existed a uniform practice of judicial torture in the different European countries, one may still conclude that, as a rule, the 'painful question' was directed against certain types of perpetrators – or rather: suspects. Children and juveniles, honourable persons and aristocrats usually, though not always, enjoyed the privilege of being exempt from the painful question. Its application was further reserved for certain categories of penal acts, preferably heresy and high treason.

---

32 Kiesow, 'Das Experiment mit der Wahrheit'.

33 Ibid., with further references.

34 This is Kiesow's interpretation ('Das Experiment mit der Wahrheit'), 101.

35 See Mellor, *La torture* and Arendt, *The Origins of Totalitarianism*.

36 Cf. Behringer, *Hexen und Hexenprozesse in Deutschland*, and from a contemporary perspective: Spee von Langenfeld, *Cautio Criminalis*.

37 See Peters, *Torture*, with further references.

Finally, the idea of a *disorderly practice* misses crucial aspects of the history of torture, at least of the regularized torture in continental criminal and canon procedures.[38] To be sure, within the framework of the Inquisition and other criminal trials, cruel treatment did not follow strict provisions of procedural law according to any current understanding of due process. Step by step, however, regulatory insights and norms were – at least at certain historical moments – implemented. The extortion of confessions was only to be applied upon a sufficient suspicion that an exceptional crime had been committed. The Roman canon law required 'half proof' for torture. And in general it had to be applied '*messiglich auß Vernunft*', which is to say: within reason.[39]

Such indeterminate standards left sufficient room for arbitrariness and violence, above all in the execution of witch-hunts. Nevertheless, torture was integrated into a para-legal setting based on canon law, imperial privileges or resolutions of the Imperial Diet [*Reichstag*]. That is why contemporaries could consider torture as basically 'legal'. According to contemporary sources, its normal application was 'embedded in a genuine algebra of real, direct, indirect, legitimate, presumptive, artificial, manifest, remarkable, incomplete, light, partial, urgent, necessary, near or distant proofs and evidence'.[40] As a matter of fact, apart from excesses, judicial torture appears to have been 'a court procedure with strict rules', devised by a 'jurisprudence of torture', following a 'juridical code of suffering'.[41]

In the context of criminal trials, judicial torture functioned as a method or procedure of proof, as a tool for the ascertainment of truth.[42] The extorted confession was understood as *proving* the guilt of the accused and *justifying* the judge's verdict. Thus, repressive torture, as a 'creature of the so-called statutory system of proofs' – the Roman canon law of evidence – replaced archaic practices like the oath, the ordeal or duel,[43] accompanied the new understanding of combating crime as a public task,

---

[38] See Langbein, *Torture and the Law of Proof*, 12–16; van Caenegem, 'La preuve dans le droit du moyen age occidental'; Fiorelli, *La tortura giudiziaria nel diritto commune*.

[39] See Langbein, *Torture and the Law of Proof*, 13–16.

[40] Kiesow, 'Das Experiment mit der Wahrheit', 101, concerning the characterization of evidence in contemporary sources.

[41] Langbein, *Torture and the Law of Proof*, 3–5 and 12–15, and Foucault, *Discipline and Punish*, 46.

[42] The application of torture within the execution of criminal sentences is not considered here.

[43] Langbein, *Torture and the Law of Proof*, 3.

and the rise and fall of the Inquisition. Calculated violence, one may somewhat daringly conclude, modernized criminal procedure.

The limitation of violent interrogations to certain crimes and criminals – or rather: suspects – and to certain methods suggests a correspondence between the Inquisition and other criminal trials on the one hand and the modest beginnings of what may be called juridification on the other. These tender shoots should not be taken to play down the brutality of the 'painful question'.[44] The inquisitorial 'queen of agony' knew quite well how to produce extremely gruesome pains when she bent over the body to extract from it the 'material truth'. She was partial to applying her tools to those joints of the body that are particularly sensitive to pain. She ordered the victim to be bound in the most gruesome way, broken upon the wheel or subjected to thumb- or leg-screws. If necessary, she repeated the cruel procedure until the suspect began to speak. More often than not, she rated silence as a confession because it was taken to indicate the support of the devil.

During the 19th century the repressive-procedural practice appeared to retreat from Europe to islands beyond the pale of the 'community of civilized states'. Torture was said to rage where relicts of the Inquisition – in particular its evidence system focusing on the confession – survived in peace and quiet outside the luminous beam of the Enlightenment. Meanwhile, in Europe contemporary critics celebrated the end of torture. Victor Hugo wrote in 1851, prematurely as it would turn out:

> Torture has already disappeared in the abyss of dregs where the Inquisition lies and whither the death penalty will follow soon.[45]

7.3 THE NEW PARADIGM?

At the beginning of the 20th century, the contours of a different paradigm, both ancient and new, become manifest, including torture in the arsenal of tyrannical and authoritarian techniques of governing respectively. Under dictatorial regimes orgies of torture reduce the inquisitorial 'queen of agony' to a cameo on the stage of violence enacted by or in the name of governments. Despite those islands of quasi-inquisitorial trials and judicial torture in countries where circumstantial evidence is either not admitted or not considered a sufficient basis for

---

44 See the common torture devices reproduced in Langbein, *Torture and the Law of Proof*, 19–26, and Dirnbeck, *Die Inquisition*.

45 Quoted from Szeemann et al., *Aubes – Rêveries au bord de Victor Hugo*.

conviction (as for instance in Turkey), it is the political paradigm that coins the 20th century's mark of Cain.

As distinct from its judicial sibling while sharing its regularity, political torture – also referred to in the language of normalization as 'modern torture'[46] (for the purpose of de-barbarization) – generally eschews the light of the public sphere and is practised in the dark. It stays hidden in the sense that it remains outside or at the margins of prevailing political discourse.[47]

To a much lesser degree this applies to the blood feasts of tyrants which at times celebrate the excesses of cruelty conspicuously and are therefore seen as perpetuating the tradition of witch-hunts. However, the political paradigm is marked less by the random, orgiastic brutality of dictators than by the gruesome, calculated technology of agony as developed and applied by regimes of terror. That is why it qualifies as the 'legitimate' successor of ritualized procedural torture with random excesses, as practised in inquisitorial and other criminal trials.

Modern political torture seems to have very little in common with its judicial predecessor as it needs neither specific incidents nor serious crimes to be unleashed. It may be triggered by the slightest suspicion, a presumptive 'insult of the ideal personality of the state'[48] or any behaviour identified as oppositional. It shares, however, a certain selectivity with the judicial torture practice: its political agenda is reflected in the selection of its victims. As an example one may refer to a decree issued by Heinrich Himmler in 1942:

> [For the purpose of extorting confessions or prying information] the 'third degree' may only be applied to communists, Marxists, Jehovah's Witnesses, saboteurs, members of resistance movements, antisocial elements, oppositional elements or political or ethnic vagabonds.[49]

As distinct from their inquisitorial forerunners, the torturers of dictators and their commanders are not pursuing a truth, however illusionary it

---

[46] See Parry, 'The Shape of Modern Torture'; Parry, 'Torture in the Modern World'; Rejali, *Torture and Modernity* and the rather naïve and empirically ignorant review written by Chirot, 'Torture and Modernity'.

[47] Parry, 'The Shape of Modern Torture', 521.

[48] Art. 8 of the Turkish Antiterror Law No. 3713. The discrepancy between the constitutional and legal prohibition of torture and its still rather widespread practice in Turkey has been repeatedly noted by the European Commission for the Prevention of Torture, e.g. 10th Report on the CPT's Activities (1999) – accessed on 25 December 1999.

[49] Quoted in Peters, *Torture*, 125.

may be. Inspired by their various political ideologies, the executors of violence are bent on seeking revenge, on humiliating and destroying. In the cellars of the Gestapo, in Soviet Gulags, in the dungeons of colonial rulers and military Juntas, in the interrogation cells of numerous secret police forces and military installations 'political torture' is executed with beastly cruelty and an archaic lust in the victims' suffering.[50] Obedient henchmen and technicians of authoritarian regimes inflict pain and fear for the sake of domination by breaking resistance and demoralizing oppositional minds,[51] and by terrorizing the unsuspecting public into submission, which marks modern torture as a mechanism to produce 'disciplinary knowledge'.[52]

The torturers of dictators and terror regimes do not seek to extort a 'material truth', however illusionary, from their victims. Yet, with regard to the thirst for information one may draw a line from the extortion of information about 'oppositional elements' and traitors to the judicial extraction of truth in inquisitorial and other criminal trials.

As regards its relationship to law, political torture appears to have no affinity to the legalized or rather juridified procedures of judicial torture as a legal technique of governing. While the political torturer may deem his trade to be his duty (or inevitable to save his own skin), he may not, however, seriously consider his methods and practice to be legal in any substantial and understandable sense. William Blackstone's casual and all-too-fine distinction regarding the torture rack as 'an instrument of the state, not of the law',[53] which was validated in the 19th and, more terribly and on a mass scale, throughout the 20th century,[54] captures quite succinctly the distance of political torture practices from the legal claims of judicial torture and between the enforcement of politics and law enforcement.

---

[50] This lust refers to the tyrannical blood feasts mentioned before and defeats even an analytical distinction.

[51] Parry ('The Shape of Modern Torture') characterizes modern torture as 'total domination' (525).

[52] See Foucault *'Society Must be Defended'*; id., *Power/Knowledge*, 92–106.

[53] Blackstone, *Commentaries on the Laws of England*; see also Peters, *Torture*, 103–40 with further references.

[54] See Mellor, *La torture*; Alleg, *La question*; Levine, *The Third Degree*. As a document on the brutality of political torture as a system of hatred, see *The Report of the Argentine National Commission on the Disappeared: Nunca Más* (1986). Dershowitz (see id., *Preemption*) claims that torture is used 'promiscuously' today.

Political cruelty always had a military companion[55] from which it was at best only analytically distinguishable, mainly with regard to the strategic ends pursued in the different historical-political contexts. Not merely at first glance, affinities and correspondences abound. Both authoritarian regimes and military commanders share the concept of the victim as enemy as well as having a preventive orientation. Within political and military contexts, coercive interrogation methods were systematically developed, at times even with scientific support.[56] The application of violence by degrees is meant to render difficult the proof that the cruelty applied in interrogations qualifies as torture. Today, the infamous 'third degree' comprises practices which focus less on the joints of the body but rather on the sensory system and the psyche so as to leave no traces behind, examples being sensory deprivation, isolation cells, electro-shocks, the 'water method', jailing victims with rats or insects, and other forms of extreme emotional destabilization.[57]

All potential informants qualify as victims: prisoners of war, spies, insurgents, legal or illegal combatants, saboteurs, and members of the civil population. In military prisons and camps, calculated cruelty becomes an element of modern warfare – and during the two world wars the warfare was total. Without abandoning the politics of terror, military torture is primarily targeted at ferreting out useful information. Like calculated political torture, it pursues a preventive goal: the prevention of danger caused by an enemy. And thus, both political and military brutally coercive interrogation relates to the most recent pattern of practice and interpretation: the so-called 'rescue torture' or 'necessity torture'.[58]

A comparison between faded inquisitorial and the ongoing political-military cruelty in interrogation situations on the one hand and the new paradigm on the other, though not unproblematic, reveals striking affinities and contrasts. Despite claims to novelty and legal decency, 'rescue

---

55 The calamity and barbarism of war has always inspired attempts to ban 'unnecesary cruelty'; see e.g. Art. 16 of the 'Lieber Code': '[M]ilitary necessity does not admit of cruelty … nor of torture to extort confessions.'

56 Concerning the supportive advisory role of physicians and behavioural scientists at Guantánamo Bay see Mayer, 'The Experiment', 60 and Parry, 'The Shape of Modern Torture', 522.

57 Regarding the torture methods in the 20th century see Peters, *Torture*, 169–76; Amnesty International, '*Wer der Folter erlag* …' and the reports in *Nunca Más*.

58 In his introduction to Alleg's, *La question*, Jean-Paul Sartre denounces torture as a 'plague' and rescue torture as 'hypocrisy'.

torture'[59] (used here as a shorthand for both variations) is less exceptional than its justifiers are inclined to suggest.

In fact, 'rescue torture' resembles its inquisitorial and judicial predecessor in that it does not shun the light of the public, but knocks on the door of the legal citadel and calls for a doctrinal invitation or 'court approval'.[60] While it certainly stands aloof from witch-hunts and tyrannical orgies of pain, the new paradigm still resides in the ugly neighbourhood of political and military coercion whose rhetoric of necessity it echoes and, if only implicitly, the concept of a war with its inherent friend/enemy distinction. And it reiterates the shift in the political-military approach to controlling harmful conduct by moving away from the traditional reliance on the deterrent and reactive approaches of criminal and police law against wrongdoers towards more preventive and proactive approaches against evildoers.

Today 'rescue torture' has become part and parcel of counter-terrorism[61] and also, if on a lower scale, of combating crime. Both the terrorist and the perpetrator who threatens the life of his victims – notably the kidnapper – are treated de facto and de jure as enemies.

Differences between macro crimes and micro crimes, between al-Qaeda and the law student from Frankfurt who kidnapped and murdered a young boy, as well as between the protection of society and the protection of victims are blurred in the universal founding moment of the new paradigm: the *ticking-bomb* scenario,[62] which is sometimes referred to as a case for Dirty Harry.[63] Only the captured terrorist-suspect

---

[59] From the vast body of literature, see only: Walter et al., *Terrorism as a Challenge for National and International Law*; Beestermöller and Brunkhorst, *Rückkehr der Folter* and Nitschke, *Rettungsfolter im modernen Rechtsstaat.* For further references see also Chapters 4, 5 and 6.

[60] 'I'm not in favor of torture, but if you're going to have it, it should damn well have court approval' (Dershowitz, *Why Terrorism Works*).

[61] See Walter et al., *Terrorism as a Challenge for National and International Law*; Neumann, 'Comment, Counter-Terrorist Operations and the Rule of Law'; Gearty, 'Terrorism and Human Rights' and Dyzenhaus, *The Constitution of Law.* The political-legal discourse has for quite some time been accompanied by media productions supporting or opposing the 'Whatever it Takes' logic of counter-terrorism; see Mayer, 'Whatever it Takes'.

[62] Cf. Brecher, *Torture and the Ticking Bomb*; Dyzenhaus, 'The Permanence of the Temporary'; Luban, 'Liberalism, Torture and the Ticking Bomb'; Althoff, *Terrorism, Ticking Time-Bombs and Torture*; and Zedner, 'Terrorism, the Ticking Bomb and Criminal Justice Values', arguing that the ticking-bomb scenario may have a restraining effect.

[63] Steinhoff, 'Torture'.

knows where the bomb is hidden and how it can be defused. Only the arrested kidnapper-suspect knows where to find the victim and how she can be rescued. Are the police not obliged to do anything, indeed anything possible, to save the lives of hundreds of people or of one boy?

Along the lines of an answer to this not completely rhetorical question, violence may equally be applied in situations of police and military danger. Its preventive – or rather: pre-emptive – orientation is only one small step away from the *rescue motive*:

> You know what is sometimes said for the justification of executioners: that one has to come to the decision to torture persons, when their confession saves the lives of hundreds.[64]

On closer scrutiny, this motive is not at all peculiar to the 'new torture' but operates as a more or less visible accomplice in all paradigms inspiring the recurrent attempts to justify violence in interrogation procedures. The Inquisition introduced the rescue motive under the guise of a paternalistic form of ethical perfectionism: coercion was meant to save the sinner's soul, if need be against her will, from the grasp of the devil. The Christian duty to liberate the 'true self' from the evil allowed the Inquisitor to ignore the actual pain and agony of the existing self and to regard torture as a blessing.[65] Together with the *mise en scène* of power and the search for truth, the inquisitorial torture's construction of meaning relied on *saving souls* as a central motive.

In military scenarios the rescue motive reappears without a Christian blessing or ideology. Coercion is not utilized to save the prisoner's better self but, with a more secular twist, to save the company, the army or ultimately society and the state from perfidious enemy attacks. The same applies to the political paradigm. It is true that within this paradigm the rescue motive has often thinned out to a mere pretext; it is still invoked, however, to justify violence against all individuals and groups, habitually referred to as 'foreign elements', threatening the stability of the system, the international reputation of the regime, the Turkishness of Turkey and so forth.

Aside from the rescue motive, the advocates of the 'new' torture derive its exceptionalism explicitly or implicitly from its *legality*: it is to be

64 Jean-Paul Sartre, 'Introduction' to Alleg, *La question*. Sartre goes on to characterize torture as a 'plague' and decribes the use of torture to save others as 'hypocrisy' (11).

65 Augustine, *De civitate dei*, XIII; Forst, *Toleranz im Konflikt*, 78 ff.; Berlin, 'Two Concepts of Liberty'.

regulated by law, institutionalized as a legal practice or legitimized by a court decision (warrant), and therefore also executed in the name of the *law* – according to the liberal paradigm: in the name of the popular sovereign. Thus the torture victim becomes a member of 'We the people', who 'are all torturers'[66] because, according to the common understanding of democracy, they ultimately authorize it. Consequently, those who are out to justify torture should not talk about a 'self-inflicted' but a 'self-authorized' rescue interrogation and deny the victim of torture, following Hobbes' logic of *volenti non fit iniuria*,[67] recourse to rights and courts. Not even the rules and regulations of the Inquisition would imply that those subject to torture also authorized it. Besides, advocates of the new and thoroughly secular paradigm of torture, however diligently they base it on a reasoned elaboration, balancing human dignity and the right to life and health, still have to accept the Inquisition as an unpleasant, if historically distant, neighbour-in-law.

The legal correspondence between 'rescue torture' and both the 'defence torture', respectively the torture to defend the system, and the political-military paradigm is less tangible. The former finds no support in international law.[68] The latter two tend to borrow their thin coat of legality – or actually: legitimacy – from an imagined or real *état de siège*. Within the context of counter-terrorism, an updated version of the *état de siège* seems to have migrated into the legal realm.[69] There it operates as a background assumption and facilitates the normalization of torture as a political technology for extreme situations.

Compared with its political and military siblings, 'rescue torture' usually seeks a warmer legal outfit. While the German academic discourse focuses on the ticking bomb and extreme situations and proportionality, US discourse participants prefer arguments of necessity and utility or address the question of whether torture should be legally regulated, institutionalized and court sanctioned or remain in the dark and secret sphere of the extra-legal – 'how this practice fits into legal norms and traditions, and how it ought to be regulated'.[70]

With questions like these, polite as they may seem, the advocates of coercive governmental technologies contemplate a legal licence to enter

---

66 Danner, 'We Are All Torturers Now'.

67 See above (Chapter 1, Section 2) for discussion of Hobbes, *Leviathan*.

68 Bruha, 'Folter und Völkerrecht' and Bruha and Steiger, *Das Folterverbot im Völkerrecht*, 12 ff.

69 See Parry, 'The Shape of Modern Torture', 522–5, 526–8.

70 Posner and Vermeule, 'Should Coercive Interrogations Be Legal?', 1.

the taboo zone by loosening whatever ties of due process and human rights restrictions there may be.

In Germany, where the doctrine of 'rescue torture' did not crystallize around a massive and unprecedented terrorist attack or a comparable human catastrophe, one might have expected vehement criticism[71] or at least moderately critical reactions,[72] reminding the justifiers of historical precedents and of the disastrous effects once one unleashes the demons to be banned by the taboo or, in a more pragmatic attitude, of the 'slippery slope'[73] we had better keep away from. Therefore it comes as a surprise how many scholars joined the justifiers even before 9/11.[74]

The spirit of the *ticking bomb*, which does not want to be late, fabricated new laws and arguments. In the United States, it was said, since 9/11 the Bush administration, supported by academic voices, changed the rules on how to deal with terrorism and created conditions where the ends justify the means.[75] Likewise, German scholars soon brought up other extreme police measures for discussion. Initially, they

---

[71] See only Kiesow, 'Das Experiment mit der Wahrheit'; Hecker, 'Relativierung des Folterverbots in der BRD?'; Marx, 'Folter', at 278; Jahn, 'Gute Folter – schlechte Folter?'; Denninger, 'Recht, Gewalt und Moral'.

[72] Compare Reemtsma, *Folter im Rechtsstaat?*, advocating a ban on torturous practices, with Ignatieff, *The Lesser Evil*, allowing a balancing of evils in extreme situations.

[73] For a more general account see Schauer, 'Slippery Slopes'; with regard to counter-terrorism, see Ginbar, *Why Not Torture Terrorists?*, who rather unusually opens his analysis with considerations from the perspective of the torturer.

[74] The chairman of the German Judges' Association [*Deutscher Richterbund*] Geert Mackenrodt, *Frankfurter Rundschau* (22 February 2003); Bund deutscher Kriminalbeamter, *Darmstädter Echo* (22 February 2003); M. von Schmude, 'Müssen wir foltern?', *Frankfurter Rundschau* (28 December 2001); Report in *Der Spiegel* 51/2001, 15; Kirchhof, 'Die Zulässigkeit des Einsatzes staatlicher Gewalt in Ausnahmesituationen' and Christian Starck, in von Mangoldt and Klein, *Grundgesetz-Kommentar I*, Art. 1 I No. 71. M. Herdegen, in Maunz and Dürig, *Grundgesetz*, Art. 1 Rn. 44 ff. and 90, focuses on the purpose of a violent measure and thus allows for 'the threat or application of physical harm which, because of the purpose to save lives, does not violate the guarantee of human dignity'. Rather more cautiously H. Dreier (in Dreier, *Grundgesetz I*, Art. 1 Rn. 133) considers similar rights to dignity which 'do not exclude a priori the legal idea of a justifying collision of duties'; in general he considers torture illegal (Art. 1 Rn. 72 and Art. 104 Rn. 54 ff.). A similar argument had been suggested by Wittreck, 'Menschenwürde und Folterverbot'. Regarding the justification of torture see also Trapp, 'Wirklich "Folter"?'

[75] See Greenberg and Dratel, *The Torture Papers*; Steyn, 'Guantanomo Bay'; Scheppele, 'North American Emergencies'.

reintroduced the 'final rescue shot', which is to say: the right of the police not only to disable dangerous persons but to shoot to kill. And the former civil-rights lawyer and German Minister of the Interior suggested pre-emptive measures: 'Don't we have an emergency law against terrorists who plan mass murders? Which leads to the question, whether the killing of a person may be justified in extreme cases as self-defence.'[76] He implied a positive answer. Following this logic of normalizing the state of exception, the German law-maker recently authorized the armed forces to shoot down airplanes presumed to be in the hands of terrorists, a provision that was struck down by the Federal Constitutional Court.[77]

7.4 PRACTICAL CONSEQUENCES OF 'RESCUE TORTURE'

If we look more closely at the legal arguments designed to justify torture in extreme or exceptional situations,[78] we generally discover a logic which operates in a Manichean world, where the military, the security institutions and the police, and the executive power in general tend to appear as representatives of the good which needs to be defended against the evil and evildoers threatening society and against all those who seem not to realize how dramatic the dangers that have to be prevented are. So, as a rule, those who justify torture defer to the executive,[79] opt for a combination of the *method Hobbes* and the *method Foucault* and abstain from looking at the actual application of the brutality they condone.

(1) Beginning with deference and the *method Hobbes*, various pathways that lead to the normative justification of torture, all of them on offer in legal academia, need to be differentiated.

First, one may bypass principled prohibition and taboo by invoking a *state of exception* and neither maintaining a veneer of

---

[76] The former German Minister of the Interior, Otto Schily, 'Interview', *Der Spiegel* 18/2004, 47. A similar statement was issued by the security expert for the Christian Social Union (CSU), Norbert Geis, in *Der Tagesspiegel* (21 February 2003).

[77] The decision of the First Senate of 15 February 2006 – 1 BvR 357/05 – held that § 14(3) of the Luftsicherheitsgesetz (Air Security Act) violated the right to life (Art. 2(2) German Basic Law) and the protection of human dignity (Art. 1(1) German Basic Law). See above Chapter 6, Section 7.

[78] As regards the function of *ticking-bomb* scenarios for the construction of a dualist legal structure, see Chapter 4, Section 6.

[79] Explicitly so: Posner and Vermeule, *Terror in the Balance*, Introduction.

legality nor supporting the justifiers of torture with substantial legal arguments. This would be a basically Schmittian position, discussed above in Chapter 4, giving *priority* to the exigencies of the 'war on terror'.

Second, one may follow a fairly large group of authors who leave the realm of law (or who already work in the field of philosophy) and turn to ethics for support.[80] Calling the decisional situation provoked by terrorists a 'tragic choice' helps invoke an 'ethics of prudence rather than first principle' and opens the way to a reshaping of constitutional-legal arrangements in times of crisis. At first glance, this proposition appears to be attractive as it contrasts the absolute protection of dignity and the strict prohibition of torture[81] with the potential suffering of whoever is threatened by the 'ticking bomb' and introduces an ethic of responsibility for extreme situations. However, this ethic not only justifies torturing a terrorist or kidnapper who can defuse the ticking bomb but turns into an ethic of sacrifice when the downing of a renegade aircraft implies the killing of innocent passengers. A utilitarian or consequentialist ethic has to disregard a certain type of consequence, though, namely those damages resulting from the application of torture and afflicting not only the torture victim but also the torturer, the texture of the rule of law and the society that tolerates torture as a governmental technique.

Third, authors preferring a legal blanket[82] to cover torture have several options: unless they opt and wait for new legal/ constitutional institutions,[83] they may justify torture in terms of *necessity* and, thus, come close to the Schmittian position. Or they may consider torture to be, on balance, the *lesser evil.* This approach calls for empirical evidence regarding the necessity or the different evils, and the findings have to be supported by a modestly

---

80 E.g. Althoff, 'A Defense of Torture'. For a – not very persuasive – distinction between 'intended main consequences' and unintended side effects, see Lamprecht, *Darf der Staat foltern, um Leben zu retten?*; and also the very similar arguments of Posner and Vermeule, 'Should Coercive Interrogations Be Legal?'; and id., *Terror in the Balance*, ch. 6.

81 For a defence of the absolute prohibition on torture, see Fiss, 'The War Against Terrorism and the Rule of Law' and Strauss, 'Torture'.

82 For references see Gross, 'Chaos and Rules'; see also Alan Dershowitz's torture-warrant proposal to regulate the application of torture rather than legally banning it. For a critique of this proposal, see Ackerman, *Before the Next Attack* and Scarry, 'Five Errors in the Reasoning of Alan Dershowitz'.

83 Tushnet, 'Controlling Executive Power in the War on Terrorism'.

persuasive normative evaluation – in the light of first- and second- and arguably third-order consequences – to pass as a plausible weighing of 'the exigencies of war'.[84] Concern for potential consequences or a utilitarian calculus is meant to force onto the defensive the supposedly naïve adherents of dignity/right to life/integrity of law-rule defenders of the prohibition of torture.

Fourth, another (rather popular, particularly but not exclusively, in the German context) option is to focus the *legal* balancing on both a *proportionality* reasoning[85] and the *comparative value* and weight of the *dignities* and *rights* to life of the terrorist/perpetrator and their victim(s) – with a predictable outcome. This approach, which purports to defend the principle of legality in times of crisis, shifts the focus away from the state and the practice of torture to the structure of the legal justification. Its preoccupation with doctrine prevents its protagonists from 'taking a good look' at what they justify or normalize.[86] Whoever follows this path has to cope with the argument that the rule of law ceases to exist if torture is permitted:

> Torture cannot be reconciled with the *Rechtsstaat* because it attacks and, in the extreme case, breaks and destroys the individual and its capability to be a legal subject.[87]

Justifiers of torture try to neutralize this objection, which would defeat their project by shifting the focus away from the modified law-rule, which goes along with the application of torture, and away from a society that tolerates torture as a technique of governing.[88] Instead they redirect attention to the victim and the

---

84 Ignatieff, *The Lesser Evil*, argues on principle against torture but in favour of torture, if necessary, in *ticking-bomb* situations.

85 The concise article by May, 'Torturing Detainees During Interrogation', provides an excellent and also historically informed argument on proportionality.

86 Posner and Vermeule ('Should Coercive Interrogation Be Legal?') provide a fitting example as they refer fairly indiscriminately and intermittently to coercive interrogation and torture without really specifying the practices these terms imply. Also Brugger in his many publications never took the time to describe the phenomenon at any length.

87 Reemtsma, *Folter im Rechtsstaat?*, 125. See also von Bernstorff, 'Pflichtenkollision und Menschenwürdegarantie'. As regards the intention to break and destroy an individual, see Sands, *Torture Team*, and Danner 'US Torture'.

88 The aspect is highlighted by e.g. Reemstma, *Folter im Rechtsstaat?*, and May, 'Torturing Detainees During Interrogation'.

justificatory structure of their argument. Brugger, who tenaciously pursued a justificatory course, discovered a *Wertungslücke* (value gap) in ticking-bomb situations. To remove human dignity from any balancing, he holds, denies a normatively adequate answer to the collision of the victim's dignity and the kidnapper's or bomb planter's dignity. In a second step, Brugger and others construct a conflict of duties: in a ticking-bomb situation, i.e. a multipolar constitutional relationship, *respect* for the dignity and integrity of a perpetrator requires the state to abstain from torture. At the same time, the duty to *protect* the dignity and life of the victim obliges the state to act accordingly. With regard to human dignity, the duty to protect collides with the duty to respect: 'To respect and protect it shall be the duty of all state authority' (Article 1(1) BL). If, on the other hand, one defended the strict prohibition of torture, one would claim a priority for the duty to *respect*,[89] which could be defended from the perspective of the inviolability of human dignity.[90] In addition one might say that the state, in the execution of the duty to protect, is limited to the application of legal measures. This reasoning the protagonists of 'rescue torture' are loath to accept. According to their argumentative strategy, the kidnapper-terrorist's evil deed and the victim's innocent suffering both constitute a normative asymmetry, based on a hierarchy of human dignity claims which then (pre)determines the outcome of the balancing operation. Strictly speaking, there is no balancing but a rule of collision that turns out to be a rule of preference in favour of the victim. First, the kidnapper's or terrorist's claims to dignity and physical integrity are ranked as inferior. Second, the police or the military are introduced as the altruistic executors of the state's duty to protect individuals, groups or the whole society. Third, they are granted extraordinary powers in extreme situations where differences between danger and risk, a suspected danger and an imaginary danger are levelled to make possible interventions even if the chances of rescue are unclear. Errors as to who controls the source of danger and how the danger can be most effectively averted are taken for granted. Whoever assumes that there are situations in

[89] See the decisions of the Federal Constitutional Court concerning renegade aircraft (*BVerfGE* 115, 118) and preventive custody (*BVerfGE* 109, 133). For a differentiated treatment of the duty to respect and to protect: von Bernstorff, 'Pflichtenkollision und Menschenwürdegarantie' with further references.

[90] 'Human dignity shall be inviolable' (Art. 1(1) Basic Law).

which there is no alternative to torture[91] has to apply torture even on a mere suspicion. Fourth, in the end it is actually not the state that is acting but human beings. And 'because of the life-saving purpose'[92] they – the torturer and whoever ordered torture – should be freed from the risk of possible criminal sanctions 'in the line of duty'. That is why the justifiers come up with two types of violence and distinguish 'good' rescue torture from those cruel and degrading interrogation practices which gave torture its bad name. As a matter of consequence, the police or military officer cannot be blamed for violating human dignity,[93] because the actually, or potentially, prevented innocent suffering outbalances the perpetrator's pain and justifies emergency measures. Ultimately, the advocates of justified coercion hold the kidnapper or terrorist liable for what happens to him in the interrogation room. According to this logic, the individual was destroyed under torture and has ceased to exist as a person. And the non-person as object of brutality is held responsible for an action which can be attributed only to persons.[94] Thus, the torturer is purged from violating the taboo. And her critic may be charged with hardheartedly neglecting the plight and suffering of innocent victims and not understanding the – undoubtedly – difficult situation of the police.

(2) The empirical aspects of torture and some of its factual and normative problems can only be briefly discussed here. Still, it seems to be in order to list some of the basic problems connected with the legal *justification* and *application* of torture: the legal regulation of torture presupposes a plausible definition, which, as will be shown immediately, is an almost impossible task because of the polysemy of torture. At the least, one would have to differentiate torture from coercive interrogation, a task in which prolific legal authors have failed. Then there is the problem of how to regulate torture. Should it be based on a conditional programme? Or should the acting agencies and officials be granted a wide or narrow margin of discretion? Should torture be limited to certain categories

---

[91] Thus argues Merkel, 'Folter und Notwehr', 391.

[92] Herdegen, in Maunz and Dürig, *Grundgesetz*, Art. 1 No. 45.

[93] Referring to the extreme situation of kidnapping: Di Fabio, 'Grundrechte als Werteordnung'. For a justification of an enemy criminal law directed against terrorists and organized crime, see Jakobs, 'Kriminalisierung im Vorfeld einer Rechtsgutsverletzung'.

[94] See the detailed argument provided by Günther, 'Folter kennt keine Grenze'.

of offenders – terrorists, kidnappers? Regarding the application: what degree of probable cause could justify which degree of torture? What kind of evidence is required? Which torture methods could be legally applied? Who would qualify as a lawful torturer and supervisor of the torture process, etc.?

(3) The advocates of torture, regardless which pathway to justification they choose, tend to underestimate (to put it mildly) the problem of *uncertainty*. Some of the recent doctrines covering calculated state brutality betray a certain historical naïvety as well as a rather peculiar and narrow construction of the rescue scenario. At times not without concern, but still quite uninhibited, they negate not only the available evidence concerning the devastating effects of torture methods but also even crucial insights that once de-legitimated torture as 'counter-productive' and therefore puzzle even seasoned experts today.[95] To begin with, the rescue motive, necessity and lesser-evil argument imply the *timeliness* and *usefulness* of the knowledge extracted under coercion. Yet, the justificatory discourse, though claiming to be geared towards practice, does not even address, let alone answer, a number of crucial practical questions. It overlooks that whoever is tortured may not have the coveted knowledge and therefore may not be the right person. That she may say anything just to end the suffering, if only for the time being.[96] Also that the person under torture may have other reasons for not disclosing the information remains a rather remote possibility in the rescue scenario. And, finally, that the information might be obtainable more easily in a different venue or that the intended rescue might come too late even with the extorted information is hardly taken into consideration.

In short: numerous problems of uncertainty and error concerning the execution of 'rescue torture' are almost methodically left out of the account.[97] Such ignorance or neglect is no accident or oversight: dealing with the risks of uncertainty would invariably bring about the collapse of the doctrinal bridge across assumed value gaps or

---

[95] For a discussion of the counter-productive aspects (and the problem of uncertainty), see Bowden, 'The Dark Art of Interrogation' and McCoy, *Foltern und Foltern lassen*.

[96] Instructive information is provided by Bowden, 'The Dark Art of Interrogation', and Danner, 'US Torture'.

[97] For similar arguments see Poole, 'Courts and Conditions of Uncertainty'; Scarry, 'Five Errors in the Reasoning of Alan Dershowitz'.

undermine the privileging of the state's duty to protect or call into question the lesser evil strategy.

(4) What if the person to be tortured in fact does have the knowledge required for rescue? Then the forcibly extracted confession could prove useful. Nevertheless, some nasty questions would have to be addressed: how may the 'new torture' be applied *lege artis* (in terms of procedure, due process and substance)? How may it go as easily as possible (proportionality!) on basic rights? To indicate – as happened in the Frankfurt case – that violence would be executed by experienced police officers who 'hold a licence by the German Sports Association … to prevent the occurrence of injuries' and would, of course, be supervised by a medical doctor[98] has a very bureaucratic and unwittingly ironic touch, but hardly meets even the most modest standards of due process. From the rules regulating violence as an element of political technology we may infer that a professional, experienced in the trade of inflicting pain, and medical supervision may have the blessing of tradition, but scarcely suffice to gain court approval (vehemently called for by Alan Dershowitz).[99]

(5) More importantly, the justificatory discourse necessary to ascertain its legal credentials would have to deal, to some extent at least, with the practical side of proportionality governing all police and military measures under domestic and international law. On the part of the practitioners and their legal advisers, however, differentiated considerations correlating the infliction of pain with the dimension of the danger, the person under interrogation and the threatening evil are still outstanding.

Should we hope and wait for a manual of legally admissible violence – or not? If at all conceivable (a critic has already ironically invoked a necessary 'federal torture ordinance'), such a torturer's manual might indeed correspond to the practical purpose and logic of 'rescue torture', but would inevitably transgress the boundaries of law-rule and undermine the imagination of due process. Ultimately, an explicit and operative legal concept of 'rescue torture' would deconstruct the legal form and its claim to legality as well as the vision, however ideological, of a society ruled

---

[98] Report in the *Frankfurter Rundschau* (22 February 2003) and *Der Spiegel* 9/2003 (24 February 2003); Heiner Busch, 'Rechtsstaatlich geregelte Folter?', in *Bürgerrechte & Polizei/CILIP 74* (2003).

[99] Dershowitz, 'The Torture Warrant'; see also Bagaric and Clarke's argument in id., 'Not Enough Official Torture in the World?'.

by law. In the end, assuming torture 'works', this method of political technology would have found its way into the legal order and helped to defuse the ticking bomb. By the same token, the normativity of the norm would have been undermined at its most sensitive spot – the relationship to violence. And the imaginary barrier that keeps us away from violent ages and brutal regimes elsewhere would have been rescinded.

7.5 THE POLYSEMY OF TORTURE AND ITS ABUSES

The impossibility of answering most of the crucial practical questions raised by the legalization/legal justification for torture may be one of the reasons why authors favour an *extra-legal* emergency regime or *virtualize* torture as a thought experiment,[100] or simply stick with the less dramatic term *coercive interrogation*[101] instead. A further question is raised by political-military practitioners who prefer to deny or camouflage illegal violence rather than admitting that a taboo is being violated. Whereas the extra-legal state of exception has been dealt with above,[102] the virtualization of torture deserves some comments.

(1) *Virtualization* guided by theory and logic leads the advocates of 'rescue' or 'necessity torture' away from the realm of real agony and brutality into the world of academic imaginations. Offices, conferences and faculty clubs are sites where theoretical-doctrinal proposals are produced, where legal scholars construct extreme situations – state of exception, emergency, catastrophes, etc. – as a testing ground for normative principles and taboos. These extreme situations, they suggest, will never occur but must be thought through because any legal order (they claim to defend) has to reckon with extreme cases and handle them appropriately. For that purpose they imagine an empirically highly implausible 'case': the terrorist, the ticking bomb and the police officer in the airplane. And of course they exclude from their imagination the problems of

[100] Like many participants in the German academic discourse (see Chapter 4). See, for instance, Merkel, 'Folter und Notwehr'; Brugger, 'Vom unbedingten Verbot der Folter zum bedingten Recht auf Folter' and Trapp, 'Wirklich "Folter"?'

[101] Which is not really an easy way out, as, for example, Posner and Vermeule may have learned ('Should Coercive Interrogation Be Legal?') and id., *Terror in the Balance*.

[102] Certainly not sufficiently (see Chapters 1 and 4).

uncertainty mentioned before. And of course the application of torture seems inevitable, even reasonable, because otherwise the normative order would be compromised.

Another academic exercise runs like this (and amounts to the same abstract reasoning): one enumerates a long list of conditions before torture may be applied. First, 'a clear, immediate and significant danger to the life and physical integrity of an innocent person'. Second, 'the danger must be caused by an identifiable perpetrator'. Third, 'the perpetrator is the only person who can remove the danger by returning within the borders of the law'. Fourth, 'the perpetrator must be obliged to do so'. And finally: 'the application of physical pain is the only promising means to obtain the information'.[103] In the end, it seems clear that all of these conditions will never be met in real life and therefore reasoning about torture is not that problematic and might be helpful, after all, in critical situations. So, whatever modality the legal scholar may choose, we are invariably led to believe that we are only participating in an academic thought experiment. Virtual torture then, and no need to worry.

The UN Convention Against Torture, however, may have reckoned with the unbridled imagination in academia and already anticipated such (theoretical as well as, even more so, practical) attempts to bypass the torture ban and therefore intended it to be implemented 'with religious austerity':[104]

> No exceptional circumstances whatsoever, whether a state of war or a threat of war, internal political instability or any other public emergency, may be invoked as a justification of torture. (Art. 2(2))

A different strategy is preferred, first and foremost, by practitioners (but also embraced by legal scholars). Rather than virtualizing torture they semantically *normalize* it as a standard military, respectively doctrinally justifiable practice. In both state practice and legal discourse this strategy exploits the polysemy of torture to support a posture of denial.

To begin with the legal discourse: 'rescue torture' comes across as a fairly unsophisticated concept as it still reveals the violence

---

[103] Brugger, 'Würde gegen Würde' and id., 'May Government Ever Use Torture?'

[104] Freud, *Totem and Taboo*, 303.

implied at the moment of rescue. Other formulas, such as 'self-inflicted rescue interrogation',[105] deny the act of state brutality and play down the torture situation, reducing it to the level of a normal questioning by the police. The following brief report about CIS methods of interrogation illustrates the brutality that has to be justified 'away'.[106] Instructive in this respect is also the 53-page report submitted by US General Antonio M. Taguba in February 2004 in which he listed some of the wrongdoing:

> Breaking chemical lights and pouring the phosphoric liquid on detainees; pouring cold water on naked detainees; beating detainees with a broom handle and a chair; threatening male detainees with rape; allowing a military police guard to stitch the wound of a detainee who was injured after being slammed against a wall in his cell; sodomizing a detainee with a chemical light and perhaps a broom stick; and using military dogs to frighten and intimidate detainees with threats of attack, and in one instance actually biting a detainee.[107]

Those who trivialize torture provide legal arguments for regimes, such as, for instance, the Bush/Cheney Adminstration which authorized an 'alternative set of procedures' for interrogations in Guantánamo that has been identified as torture.[108] Their parasitic exploitation of the polysemy of torture amounts to nothing less than a denial of the violation of the taboo. In this vein, states spare no trouble to argue that they neither practise nor tolerate torture – 'even if that involves admitting the conduct was cruel, inhuman or degrading'.[109] This strategy is met halfway by the authors of legal documents who camouflage torturous coercion with a 'generalized vocabulary', criticized by historians as the 'language of Eden'.[110]

The strict wording of the prohibition of torture demonstrates that its indeterminacy shifts the juridical (and also the practitioners') discourse from inventing exceptions to manipulating the definition

---

[105] Trapp, 'Wirklich "Folter"?' and id., *Folter oder selbstverschuldete Rettungsbefragung?* See also Lenzen, 'Einleitung', who, in a distancing move, puts torture in quotation marks.

[106] Danner, 'US Torture', based on a report of the International Red Cross.

[107] Quoted by Hersh, 'Torture at Abu Ghraib' and May, 'Torturing Detainees During Interrogation', 194.

[108] By the retired Judge and former Counsel for the Administration, Susan J. Crawford, quoted by Danner, 'US Torture'. For a detailed account see Sands, *The Torture Team.*

[109] Parry, 'The Shape of Modern Torture', 520.

[110] Peters, *Torture*, 152.

and, thus, opens up semantic spaces for escape attempts from the taboo zone. Traces of such attempts can also be found in the euphemizing and cynical language of 'extreme prison conditions', 'disadvantageous' or 'full coercive treatment', 'torture lite' or 'extra encouragement' in interrogation situations.[111]

(2) A third move is brought into play where euphemisms fail because cruelty, like electro-shocks or the method of water-boarding, evidently reaches the level of torture or has been publicly portrayed as such. When torture threatens to leave the realm of remote possibilities and to undermine the palliative rhetoric of interrogation techniques, its commanders and practitioners resort to deceptive manoeuvres so as to camouflage the chains of command and to defer legal responsibility as well as to prevent or curb public protest.

Torture by proxy and offshore torture[112] illustrate that, in keeping with the logic of outsourcing,[113] political office-holders, military commanders and secret services have taken to delegating the application of violence to proxy-holders well-known for brutal interrogation techniques, like Jordan, Pakistan, Singapore, Somalia, Uzbekistan or Egypt. In a flanking movement military interrogations have also been *privatized.* Not only interrogations involving torture but also the transfer of torture victims, i.e. illegal renditions, have been subcontracted to private security services, non-governmental organizations so to say.

---

[111] As to the empirical dimension of military and secret service torture methods, see Bowden, 'The Dark Art of Interrogation'; Hersh, *Chain of Command*, 19–20; id., 'Torture at Abu Ghraib'; Human Rights Watch, 'The Road to Abu Ghraib'; Sands, *Torture Team* and Parry, 'Escalation and Necessity'.

[112] See Committee on International Human Rights of the Association of the Bar of the City of New York and Center for Human Rights and Global Justice, New York University School of Law, 'Torture by Proxy: International and Domestic Law Applicable to "Extraordinary Renditions"'; Interview with Jane Mayer, *The New Yorker* (14 February 2005); 'Torture by Proxy', *The New York Times* (8 March 2005).

[113] Mayer, 'Outsourcing Torture'. Dana Priest, 'CIA Holds Terror Suspects in Secret Prisons', *The Washington Post* (2 November 2005); American Civil Liberties Union, 'Extraordinary Renditions – In Depth'; Amnesty International, '"Rendition" and Secret Detention: A Global System of Human Rights Violations'; Human Rights Watch, 'The Road to Abu Ghraib'; Sands, *Torture Team*; International Committee of the Red Cross, *Report on the Treatment of Fourteen 'High Value Detainees' in CIA Custody*; Danner, 'US Torture'.

While torture by proxy refers to its agent, offshore torture designates the territorial aspect: suspects are transferred to military bases outside the country, such as Guantánamo, and secret detention camps or prisons where they are either subjected to torturous treatment or passed on to the proxy-holders. As a prerequisite to torture by proxy, the US Army has installed special removal units since the beginning of the 1990s and increasingly after 11 September to deliver persons suspected of terrorism outside regular extradition procedures, by illegal renditions, to 'reliable regimes' known for their 'brass-knuckled quest for information'. Because of the secret and irregular nature of these renditions, the mandator of torture may deny any responsibility, very much like an innocent bystander, with only the risk of being charged with a violation of international law for the rendition.[114] Thus torture by proxy or offshore permits the actual instigator to cultivate a rule-of-law image at home[115] and invites other clients and collaborators to freely utilize the intelligence obtained by brutal violence.

Any promptings of the conscience – a rare phenomenon in the engineering mindset of political technicians – are likely to be silenced by the 'responsibility for our security' or similar imperatives of the 'war on terror' as illustrated by the statement of the former German Minister of the Interior:

> If we had to vouch for the information of other secret services that they were obtained by observance of the proprieties of constitutional principles we might as well shut down business.[116]

---

[114] See Parry, 'The Shape of Modern Torture', 528–33; Bartelt, 'Das Rendition-Programm der USA und die Rolle Europas'; Marty, 'Alleged Secret Detentions and Unlawful Interstate Transfers'; Amnesty International, 'Partners in Crime'.

[115] Unless political office-holders, like the Vice President of the USA, suggest almost publicly that their own secret service – the CIA – be exempt from the prohibition on torture, and unless a presidential executive order condones those interrogation techniques. See the report in *Human Rights News*, New York (21 December 2004), http://www.hrw.org/en/news/2004/12/20/us-did-president-bush-order-torture.

[116] The Minister of the Interior, Wolfgang Schäuble, as quoted by *Der Spiegel online* (1 January 2006), http://www.spiegel.de/politik/deutschland/0,1518,393047,00.html.

From the beginning to the end, security,[117] the keyword in the discourse on torture, operates as a multi-purpose concept: it redirects attention from the sites of brutality to the citadel of law, where extreme situations and doctrines are invented and arguments are exchanged. Security inspires the turn to ethics or cost-benefit analyses to lower the – anyway not insurmountable – legal barriers against governmental coercion. Security comes across as a good end that defines necessity and justifies even bad means. Security also prompts a utilitarian calculus: it is not the individual's but the greater number's happiness that counts. And, finally, both the rationality of security and its utilitarian calculus open up the porous texture of law even further and integrate torture into the law-rule of law as one of the normalized emergency powers.

AFTERWORD

In all probability we have to reckon with dangers; according to the logic of terror we have to reckon with further terrorist attacks. No one would be so foolish as to deny that and to be unprepared to avert dangers accordingly. Nevertheless, it would not only be foolish but also dangerous to gauge the techniques of governing in such a way that they operated as if 'every day [were] 12 September' and therefore required security policy 'never to be a day too late to counter a danger'.[118] For such a mindset and policy would send society into a constant state of alarm and stir up the desire for security, procuring further emergency powers for the security-state, lowering the threshold for state interventions and weakening judicial control still further.

Security has become the password of political technology. The message it has been sending out for quite some time is that less freedom and more surveillance and control are the price citizens and also Angela Merkel as Chancellor have to pay as their contribution to the prevention of the return of 9/11. This message implies that there will be no defence of the liberal valence of the *method Locke*, but that citizens must get accustomed to measures introduced here as the political technology

---

[117] For a sample of the critiques of the security imperative dominating the academic and political discourses on anti-terrorism, see Waldron, 'Security and Liberty'; Frankenberg, 'Kritik des Bekämpfungsrechts'; Loader and Walker, *Civilizing Security*.

[118] Bosbach, 'Warum für die Sicherheitspolitik jeder Tag der 12. September ist', 137 and 138.

implied by *the method Hobbes* and *the method Foucault*. It further implies that citizens cannot be trusted with facing and, according to their capabilities, opposing dangers and insecurity or enduring what cannot be avoided. On the other hand, the very same citizens are required to acquiesce in a civilizational rapture or even, as office-holders, to execute cruel and degrading interrogation and detention measures. This is precisely the subtext of academic doctrines and theories of justification. To be sure, academic 'rescue' doctrines, by the same token supporting military and secret service agendas and deferring to the executive power, entertain a different relationship with governmental brutality and coercion than their practitioners. However, they basically agree that, to win the 'war on …', the mandate of the security state comprises whatever it takes, including violence and pre-emptive strikes.

This book, predictably, can neither offer a solution to the problem of torture nor promise that things will change for the better. At the least, Niklas Luhmann's theoretical question as to whether there are non-renounceable norms can be answered, if only tentatively. From counter-terrorism in real life and in academia one may infer that necessity or, to be precise, necessity's agents know no law. To be precise: necessity knows no non-renounceable norms. There is no good reason, however, to join the ranks of the justifiers and practitioners of cruelty organized and practised by governments. On the contrary, the visual instruction on torture, the endless apologetic discourse on emergency measures and calls for civic sacrifice and deference to the executive power strongly suggest that one had better resist the *ultima ratio* logic aligned with the imperative of security. While the *method Locke* and legal techniques of governing, after what we have learned about the contribution of law and legal scholars to counter-terrorism, cannot be invoked without misgivings, democratic legality can still be defended, in the spirit of Herbert Marcuse.[119] Here the defence has focused on the critique of the ambivalences of law-rule.

On a more practical note, touching upon the religious dimension of a taboo, one might want to add: whoever advocates 'rescue torture' may claim to be more sensitive to the dilemma of police and military officers who have to decide in situations of extreme danger. One should be aware, though, that these advocates invite us to sign a pact with the devil.

119 'The rule of law, no matter how restricted, is still infinitely safer than rule above or without law.' Marcuse, *One-dimensional Man*, 51.

Bibliography

Abendroth, Wolfgang, 'Zum Begriff des demokratischen und sozialen Rechtsstaates im Grundgesetz der Bundesrepublik Deutschland', in Ernst Forsthoff (ed.), *Rechtsstaatlichkeit und Sozialstaatlichkeit* (Darmstadt: Wissenschaftliche Buchgesellschaft, 1968), 114 ff.

Abraham, David, 'The Bush Regime from Elections to Detentions: A Moral Economy of Carl Schmitt and Human Rights', 62 *University of Miami Law Review* 249–73 (2007–08).

Ackerman, Bruce, 'The Emergency Constitution', 113 *Yale Law Journal* 1029 (2004).

Ackerman, Bruce, *Before the Next Attack: Preserving Civil Liberties in an Age of Terrorism* (New Haven: Yale University Press, 2006).

Adorno, Theodor W., *The Authoritarian Personality* (New York: Harper, 1950).

Adorno, Theodor W., *Aesthetic Theory* [1970], R. Hullot-Kentor transl. (Minneapolis: University of Minnesota Press, 1997).

Agamben, Giorgio, *Homo Sacer: Sovereign Power and Bare Life*, Daniel Heller-Roazen transl., Werner Hambacher and David E. Wellbery (eds.) (Stanford: Stanford University Press, 1998).

Agamben, Giorgio, *State of Exception* (Chicago: University of Chicago Press, 2005).

Albrecht, Peter-Alexis, 'Feindbild Organisierte Kriminalität', in Till Müller-Heidelberg et al. (eds.), *Grundrechte-Report 1998* (Reinbek/Hamburg: Rowohlt, 1998), 23 ff.

Albrecht, Peter-Alexis, *Die vergessene Freiheit: Strafrechtsprinzipien in der europäischen Sicherheitsdebatte* (Berlin: Berliner Wissenschafts-Verlag, 2003).

Albrecht, Peter-Alexis, *Kriminologie*, 3rd ed. (München: C.H. Beck, 2005).

Albrow, Martin, *Abschied vom Nationalstaat* (Frankfurt: Suhrkamp, 1998).

Aleinikoff, T. Alexander, 'Constitutional Law in the Age of Balancing', 96 *Yale Law Journal* 943 (1983).

Alexy, Robert, *A Theory of Constitutional Rights* (New York: Oxford University Press, 2010).

Allan, Trevor, *Law, Liberty and Justice: The Legal Foundations of British Constitutionalism* (Oxford: Clarendon Press, 1993).

Alleg, Henri, *La question* (Paris: Minuit, 1958).
Altheide, David L., *Terrorism and the Politics of Fear* (Oxford: AltaMira Press, 2006).
Althoff, Fritz, 'Terrorism and Torture', 17 *International Journal of Applied Philosophy* 105 (2003).
Althoff, Fritz, 'A Defense of Torture: Separation of Cases, Ticking Time-Bombs and Moral Justification', *International Journal of Applied Philosophy* (2005).
Althoff, Fritz, *Terrorism, Ticking Time-Bombs and Torture: A Philosophical Analysis* (Chicago: Chicago University Press, 2012).
American Civil Liberties Union, 'Extraordinary Renditions – In Depth' (11 May 2006), http://www.aclu.org/safefree/torture/25546res20060511.html.
Amnesty International (ed.), *'Wer der Folter erlag … ' – Ein Bericht über die Anwendung der Folter in den 80er Jahren* (Frankfurt: Fischer, 1984).
Amnesty International, 'Partners in Crime. Europe's Role in US Renditions', EUR 01/008/2006 (2006).
Amnesty International, '"Rendition" and Secret Detention: A Global System of Human Rights Violations', POL 30/003/2006 (1 January 2006).
Anderson, Benedict, *Imagined Communities. On the Origin and Spread of Nationalism* (London: Verso, 1991).
Anschütz, Gerhard, *Die Verfassung des Deutschen Reiches vom 11. August 1919*, 14th ed. (Berlin: Stilke, 1933).
Arendt, Hannah, *The Origins of Totalitarianism* (New York: Meridian Books, 1951).
Arendt, Hannah, *On Revolution* (London: Penguin, 1990).
Aretin, Johann Christian von, *Staatsrecht der konstitutionellen Monarchie I* (Altenburg: Literatur-Comptoir, 1824).
Argentine National Commission on the Disappeared (ed.), *Nunca Más* (New York: Farar, Strauss & Giroux, 1986).
Arndt, Adolf, 'Der Rechtsstaat und sein polizeilicher Verfassungsschutz', *Neue Juristische Wochenschrift* 897 (1961).
Arndt, Adolf, 'Demokratie – Wertsystem des Rechts', in Adolf Arndt and Michael Freund, *Notstandsgesetz – aber wie?* (Köln: Verlag Wissenschaft und Politik, 1962), 7 ff.
Augsberg, Steffen, '"Denken vom Ausnahmezustand her". Über die Unzulässigkeit der anormalen Konstruktion und Destruktion des Normativen', in Felix Arndt et al. (eds.), *Freiheit – Sicherheit – Öffentlichkeit* (Baden-Baden: Nomos, 2009), 17 ff.
Aust, Stefan, *The Baader-Meinhof Group: The Inside Story of a Phenomenon* (London: Bodley Head, 1987).

Bacon, Francis, 'Of Regiment', in *Complete Essays* (New York: Dover Publications, 2008).
Baeyer, Walter von and Baeyer-Katte, Wanda von, *Angst* (Frankfurt: Suhrkamp, 1971).
Bagaric, Mirko and Clarke, Julie, 'Not Enough Official Torture in the World? The Circumstances in Which Torture is Morally Justifiable', 39 *University of San Francisco Law Review* 581 (2005).
Bagaric, Mirko and Clarke, Julie, *Torture: When the Unthinkable is Permissible* (Albany: State of New York Press, 2007).
Bähr, Otto, *Der Rechtsstaat* (Kassel: Wigand, 1864).
Balkin, Jack M., 'The Constitution in the National Surveillance State', 93 *Minnesota Law Review* 1 (2009).
Ball, Kirstie and Webster, Frank (eds.), *The Intensification of Surveillance: Crime, Terrorism and Warfare in the Information Age* (London: Pluto Press, 2003).
Baratta, Alessandro, 'Zur Entwicklung des modernen Rechtsstaatsbegriffs', in Friedrich-Wilhelm Baer-Kaupert (ed.), *Liber amicorum B.C.H. Aubin* (Kehl: Engel, 1979), 1 ff.
Bartelt, Dawid D., 'Das Rendition-Programm der USA und die Rolle Europas', 36 *Aus Politik und Zeitgeschichte* 31–8 (2006).
Bäumlin, Richard and Ridder, Helmut, 'Art. 20 Abs. 1–3 III Rn. 30 ff.', in *Alternativkommentar zum GG*² (Neuwied/Darmstadt: Luchterhand, 1984).
Baumann, Zygmunt, *Modernity and Ambivalence* (Oxford: Blackwell Publishers, 1993).
Beck, Ulrich, *Risk Society – Towards a New Modernity* (New Delhi: Sage, 1992).
Beestermöller, Gerhard and Brunkhorst, Hauke, *Rückkehr der Folter. Der Rechtsstaat im Zwielicht?* (München: C.H. Beck, 2006).
Behrendt, Ethel Leonore, *Rechtsverzicht als Rechtsgewinn?* (München: Meta A. Verlag, 1981).
Behringer, Wolfgang (ed.), *Hexen und Hexenprozesse in Deutschland*, 4th ed. (München: Deutscher Taschenbuch Verlag, 2000).
Benjamin, Walter, 'Critique of Violence', in *Reflections, Essays, Aphorisms and Autobiographical Writings*, Peter Demetz (ed.) (New York: Schocken Books, 2003), 277–300.
Benjamin, Walter, 'Über den Begriff der Geschichte, These VIII', in: Walter Benjamin, *Gesammelte Schriften, 1. Abhandlungen, 2. Teil*, Rolf Tiedemann and Hermann Schweppenhäuser (eds.) (Frankfurt: Suhrkamp, 1991), 697 ff.
Benz, Arthur, 'Nationalstaat', in Arthur Benz et al. (eds.), *Handbuch Governance: Theoretische Grundlagen und empirische Anwendungsfelder* (Wiesbaden: Verlag für Sozialwissenschaften, 2007), 339 ff.

Berg, Wilfried, 'Der Rechtsstaat und die Aufarbeitung der vorrechtsstaatlichen Vergangenheit', 51 *Veröffentlichungen der Vereinigung der Deutschen Staatsrechtslehrer* 46 (1992).

Berlin, Isaiah, 'Two Concepts of Liberty', in Isaiah Berlin, *Four Essays on Liberty* (Oxford: Oxford University Press, 1969), 118 ff.

Berman, Nathaniel, 'Privileging Combat? Contemporary Conflict and the Legal Construction of War', 42 *Columbia Journal of Transnational Law* 1 (2004).

Berndt, Michael, *Die 'Neue Europäische Sicherheitsarchitektur'* (Wiesbaden: Verlag für Sozialwissenschaften, 2007).

Bernstorff, Jochen von, 'Pflichtenkollision und Menschenwürdegarantie: Zum Vorrang staatlicher Achtungspflichten im Normbereich von Art. 1 GG', 47 *Der Staat* 21 (2008).

Bethge, Horst and Roßmann, Erich (eds.), *Der Kampf gegen das Berufsverbot* (Köln: Pahl/Rugenstein, 1973).

Bettermann, Karl August, *Der totale Rechtsstaat* (Göttingen: Vandenhoeck und Ruprecht, 1986).

Bielefeldt, Heiner, *Freiheit und Sicherheit im demokratischen Rechtsstaat*, Deutsches Institut für Menschenrechte (ed.) (Berlin: Deutsches Institut für Menschenrechte, 2004).

Binder, Julius, 'Autoritärer Staat und Rechtsstaat' [1934], in Eckart Jakob, *Grundzüge der Rechtsphilosophie Julius Binders* (Baden-Baden: Nomos, 1996), 233 ff.

Blackstone, William, *Commentaries on the Laws of England* (Oxford: Oxford University Clarendon Press, 1765–9).

Blanke, Bernard, 'Der Deutsche Faschismus als Doppelstaat', *Kritische Justiz* 221 (1975).

Blanke, Thomas and Frankenberg, Günter, 'Zur Kritik und Praxis des Radikalenerlasses', *Kritische Justiz* 45 (1979).

Bloch, Ernst, *Natural Law and Human Dignity*, Dennis J. Schmidt transl. (Cambridge, MA: MIT Press, 1987).

Blumenberg, Hans, *The Legitimacy of the Modern Age* (Cambridge, MA: MIT Press, 1999).

Bobbitt, Philip, *Terror and Consent: The Wars for the Twenty-First Century* (Harmondsworth: Penguin, 2013).

Böckenförde, Ernst-Wolfgang, *Der Staat als sittlicher Staat* (Berlin: Duncker & Humblot, 1978).

Böckenförde, Ernst-Wolfgang, 'Der verdrängte Ausnahmezustand: Zum Handeln der Staatsgewalt in außergewöhnlichen Lagen', *Neue Juristische Wochenschrift* 1881 (1978).

Böckenförde, Ernst-Wolfgang, 'Rechtsstaat und Ausnahmerecht', *Zeitschrift für Parlamentsfragen* 591 (1980).

Böckenförde, Ernst-Wolfgang, 'Ausnahmerecht und demokratischer Rechtsstaat', in Hans Jochen Vogel (ed.), *Die Freiheit des Anderen. Festschrift für Martin Hirsch* (Baden-Baden: Nomos, 1981), 259 ff.

Böckenförde, Ernst-Wolfgang, 'Grundrechte als Grundsatznormen. Zur gegenwärtigen Lage der Grundrechtsdogmatik', 29 *Der Staat* 1 (1990).

Böckenförde, Ernst-Wolfgang, 'Entstehung und Wandel des Rechtsstaatsbegriffs', in Ernst-Wolfgang Böckenförde, *Recht, Staat, Freiheit*, 2nd ed. (Frankfurt: Suhrkamp, 1992), 143 ff.

Bodin, Jean, *Six Books of the Commonwealth*, M.J. Tooley (ed.) (Oxford: Basil Blackwell, 2009).

Bohlender, Matthias, 'Metamorphosen des Gemeinwohls: Von der Herrschaft guter polizey zur Regierung durch Freiheit und Sicherheit', in Herfried Münkler and Harald Bluhm (eds.), *Gemeinwohl und Gemeinsinn. 1. Historische Semantiken politischer Leitbegriffe* (Berlin: Akademie Verlag, 2001), 247 ff.

Boldt, Hans, *Rechtsstaat und Ausnahmezustand* (Berlin: Duncker & Humblot, 1967).

Boldt, H. and Stolleis, M., 'Geschichte der Polizei in Deutschland', in H. Lisken and E. Denninger (eds.), *Handbuch des Polizeirechts*, 4th ed. (München: C.H. Beck, 2007).

Bonß, Wolfgang, *Vom Risiko. Unsicherheit und Ungewißheit in der Moderne* (Hamburg: Hamburger Edition, 1995).

Borgs-Maciejewski, Hermann, 'Parlament und Nachrichtendienste', *Aus Politik und Zeitgeschichte. Beilage zur Zeitschrift Das Parlament*, B 6, 12 (1977).

Borgs-Maciejewski, Hermann and Ebert, Frank, *Das Recht der Geheimdienste. Kommentar zum Bundesverfassungsschutzgesetz sowie zum G 10* (Stuttgart: Boorberg, 1986).

Bosbach, Wolfgang, 'Der Rechtsstaat in Zeiten des Terrors – Warum für die Sicherheitspolitik jeder Tag der 12. September ist', in Stefan Huster and Karsten Rudolph (eds.), *Vom Rechtsstaat zum Präventionsstaat* (Frankfurt: Suhrkamp, 2008), 137 ff.

Boucher, David and Kelly, Paul, *The Social Contract from Hobbes to Rawls* (London: Routledge, 1994).

Bowden, Mark, 'The Dark Art of Interrogation', *The Atlantic* 51 (October 2003).

Braum, Stefan, 'Nachträgliche Sicherungsverwahrung: In dubio pro securitate?', *Zeitschrift für Rechtspolitik* 105 (2004).

Braunthal, Gerard, *Political Loyalty and Public Service: The 1972 Decree against Radicals and its Consequences* (Boston: University of Massachusetts Press, 1992).

Brecher, Bob, *Torture and the Ticking Bomb* (Oxford: Blackwell, 2007).

Bredekamp, Horst, *Thomas Hobbes Visuelle Strategien. Der Leviathan – Das Urbild des modernen Staates – Werkillustrationen und Portraits* (Berlin: Akademie Verlag, 1999).

Bredekamp, Horst, 'Ikonographie des Staates – der Leviathan und die Folgen', *Kritische Justiz* 395 (2000).

Brink, Josef and Keller, Rainer, 'Politische Freiheit und strafrechtlicher Gewaltbegriff', *Kritische Justiz* 107 (1983).

Bronitt, Simon, 'Constitutional Rhetoric versus Criminal Justice Realities: Unbalanced Responses to Terrorism' 14 *Public Law Review* 76 (2003).

Bronitt, Simon, Gani, Miriam and Hufnagel, Saskia (eds.), *Shooting to Kill: Socio-Legal Perspectives on the Use of Lethal Force* (Oxford: Oxford University Press: 2012).

Brugger, Winfried, 'Würde gegen Würde – Examensklausur im öffentlichen Recht', *Verwaltungsblätter für Baden-Württemberg* 414 (1995).

Brugger, Winfried, 'Darf der Staat ausnahmsweise foltern?', 35 *Der Staat* 67 (1996).

Brugger, Winfried, 'May Government Ever Use Torture? Two Responses from German Law', 48 *American Journal of Comparative Law* 661 (2000).

Brugger, Winfried, 'Vom unbedingten Verbot der Folter zum bedingten Recht auf Folter?', *Juristenzeitung* 165 (2000).

Brugger, Winfried, *Freiheit und Sicherheit. Eine staatstheoretische Skizze mit praktischen Beispielen* (Baden-Baden: Nomos, 2004).

Brugger, Winfried, 'Das andere Auge – Folter als zweitschlechteste Lösung', in Peter Nitschke (ed.), *Rettungsfolter im modernen Rechtsstaat?* (Bochum: Kamp, 2005).

Bruha, Thomas, 'Folter und Völkerrecht', *Aus Politik und Zeitgeschichte. Beilage zur Zeitschrift Das Parlament* 36 (2006).

Bruha, Thomas and Steiger, Dominik, *Das Folterverbot im Völkerrecht*, Beiträge zur Friedensethik, 39 (Stuttgart: Kohlhammer, 2006).

Bruyère, Jean de La, *Les Caractères* [1688] (Paris: Classiques Garnier, 1962).

Bundeskriminalamt (ed.), *Kurzfassung des Lagebildes Organisierte Kriminalität 2007 Bundesrepublik Deutschland* (Wiesbaden: Bundeskriminalamt, 2007).

Bung, Jochen, 'Terror als Gegenstand einer Phänomenologie der Angst', 3 *WestEnd. Neue Zeitschrift für Sozialforschung* 64 (2006).

Bung, Jochen, 'Sichtbare und unsichtbare Handlungen', 120 *Zeitschrift für die gesamte Strafrechtswissenschaft* 526 (2008).

Burwell, Frances G. et al., *Transatlantic Transformation: Building a NATO-EU Security Architecture* (Washington: The Atlantic Council, 2006).

Busch, Heiner, 'Rechtsstaatlich geregelte Folter? Der Fall Daschner und die politische Falle', *Bürgerrechte & Polizei/CILIP* 74/62 (2003).

Butler, Judith, *Precarious Life: The Power of Mourning and Violence* (Brooklyn: Verso, 2006).

Caenegem, Raoul C. Van, 'La preuve dans le droit du moyen âge occidental', 17 *Recueils de la Société Jean Bodin pour l'histoire comparative des institutions* 691 (1965).

Canaris, Claus-Wilhelm, 'Grundrechte und Privatrecht', 184 *Archiv für die civilistische Praxis* 201 (1984).

Casson, Douglas, 'Emergency Judgment: Carl Schmitt, John Locke, and the Paradox of Prerogative', 36 *Politics & Policy* 944–71 (2008).

Cerella, Antonio, *Il ritorno della violenza: Le BR dal ventennio rosso al XXI secolo* (Rome: Il Filo, 2007).

Charvat, J.P. 'A Study of UK Anti-Terror Law', in J.P. Charvat (ed.), *Legal Aspects of Combating Terrorism* (IOS Press, 2008).

Chirot, D., 'Torture and Modernity: Self, Society, and State in Modern Iran, by Darius M Rejali', 23 *Contemporary Sociology* 678 (1994).

Cobler, Sebastian, *Law, Order, and Politics in West Germany* (Middlesex: Penguin, 1978).

Cole, David and Dempsey, James X., *Terrorism and the Constitution – Sacrificing Civil Liberties in the Name of National Security* (New York: New Press, 2002).

Cole, David, Fabbrini, Federico and Vedaschi, Arianna (eds.), *Secrecy, National Security and the Vindication of Constitutional Law* (Cheltenham, UK and Northampton, MA, USA: Edward Elgar Publishing, 2013).

Committee on International Human Rights of the Association of the Bar of the City of New York and Center for Human Rights and Global Justice, New York University School of Law, 'Torture by Proxy: International and Domestic Law Applicable to "Extraordinary Renditions"' (29 October 2004).

Cornish, Paul, 'European Security: The End of Architecture and the New NATO', 72 *International Affairs* 751 (1996).

Cortés, Juan Donoso, *Obras I and IV* (Madrid: Imprenta de Tejado, 1854–5).

Creveld, Martin van, *The Rise and Decline of the State* (Cambridge: Cambridge University Press, 1999).

Daniel, Ronald J., Macklem, Patrick and Roach, Kent (eds.), *The Security of Freedom: Essays on Canada's Anti-Terrorism Bill* (Toronto: University of Toronto Press, 2001).

Danner, M., 'We Are All Torturers Now', *New York Times* (6 January 2005).

Danner, Mark, 'US Torture: Voices from the Black Sites', 56 (6) *The New York Review of Books* (2009).
Darnstädt, Thomas, *Der globale Polizeistaat* (München: Goldmann, 2010).
Dartnell, Michael Y., *Action Directe: Ultra Left Terrorism in France 1979–1987* (London: Frank Cass Publishers, 1995).
Degenhart, Christoph, 'Rechtsstaat – Sozialstaat, Anmerkungen zum aktuellen Problemstand', in Norbert Achterberg (ed.), *Recht und Staat im sozialen Wandel. Festschrift für Hans Ulrich Scupin* (Berlin: Duncker & Humblot, 1983), 537 ff.
Deleuze, Gilles, 'Was ist ein Dispositiv?', in François Ewald and Bernhard Waldenfels (eds.), *Spiele der Wahrheit. Michel Foucaults Denken* (Frankfurt: Suhrkamp, 1991), 153 ff.
Denninger, Erhard (ed.), *Freiheitliche demokratische Grundordnung. Materialien zum Staatsverständnis und zur Verfassungswirklichkeit in der Bundesrepublik*, 2 vols. (Frankfurt: Suhrkamp, 1977).
Denninger, Erhard, 'Verfassungstreue und Schutz der Verfassung', *Veröffentlichungen der Vereinigung der Deutschen Staatsrechtslehrer* 37 (Berlin: de Gruyter, 1979), 7 ff.
Denninger, Erhard, 'Der Präventionsstaat', *Kritische Justiz* 1 (1988).
Denninger, Erhard, *Der gebändigte Leviathan* (Baden-Baden: Nomos, 1990).
Denninger, Erhard, 'Verfassungsrechtliche Schlüsselbegriffe', in Erhard Denninger, *Der gebändigte Leviathan* (Baden-Baden: Nomos, 1990), 158 ff.
Denninger, Erhard, 'Vom Elend des Gesetzgebers zwischen Übermaßverbot und Untermaßverbot', in Herta Däubler-Gmelin et al. (eds.), *Gegenrede. Aufklärung – Kritik – Öffentlichkeit – Festschrift für Ernst Gottfried Mahrenholz* (Baden-Baden: Nomos, 1994), 561 ff.
Denninger, Erhard, 'Die Wirksamkeit der Menschenrechte in der deutschen Verfassungsrechtsprechung', *Juristenzeitung* 1129 (1998).
Denninger, Erhard, 'Lauschangriff – Anmerkungen eines Verfassungsrechtlers', *Strafverteidiger* 401 (1998).
Denninger, Erhard, 'Staatliche Hilfe zur Grundrechtsausübung durch Verfahren, Organisation und Finanzierung', in Josef Isensee and Paul Kirchhof (eds.), *Handbuch des Staatsrechts der Bundesrepublik Deutschland*, vol. 5, 2nd ed. (Heidelberg: C.F. Müller, 2000), § 113.
Denninger, Erhard, 'Freiheit durch Sicherheit?', *Strafverteidiger* 96 ff. (2002).
Denninger, Erhard, '"Rechtsstaat" oder "Rule of law" – was ist das heute?', in Cornelius Prittwitz et al. (eds.), *Festschrift für Klaus Lüderssen* (Baden-Baden: Nomos, 2002), 41 ff.

Denninger, Erhard, 'Normalfall oder Grenzfall als Ausgangspunkt rechtsphilosophischer Konstruktion?', in Winfried Brugger and Görg Haverkate (eds.), *Grenzen als Thema der Rechts- und Sozialphilosophie* (Stuttgart: Franz Steiner Verlag, 2002), 37 ff.

Denninger, Erhard, 'Recht, Gewalt und Moral – ihr Verhältnis in nachwestfälischer Zeit', *Kritische Justiz* 359 ff (2005).

Depenheuer, Otto, *Selbstbehauptung des Rechtstaates*, 2nd ed. (Paderborn: Schöningh, 2008).

Derrida, Jacques, *Of Grammatology* (Baltimore: Johns Hopkins University Press, 1998).

Derrida, Jacques, 'Force of Law: The "Mystical" Foundation of Justice', 11 *Cardozo Law Review* 921–1045 (1990).

Dershowitz, Alan M., *Why Terrorism Works* (New Haven, CT: Yale University Press, 2002).

Dershowitz, Alan M., 'The Torture Warrant: A Response to Professor Strauss', 48 *New York Law School Law Review* 275 (2003–04).

Dershowitz, Alan M., *Preemption. A Knife that Cuts Both Ways* (New York: W.W. Norton Company, 2006).

Dicey, Albert V., *Introduction to the Study of the Law of the Constitution*, 10th ed. (London: Macmillan, 1959).

Dieckmann, Hubertus-Emmanuel, *Überpositives Recht als Prüfungsmaßstab im Geltungsbereich des Grundgesetzes?* (Berlin: Duncker & Humblot, 2006).

Di Fabio, Udo, 'Grundrechte im präzeptoralen Staat am Beispiel hoheitlicher Informationstätigkeit', *Juristenzeitung* 689 (1993).

Di Fabio, Udo, *Risikoentscheidungen im Rechtsstaat* (Tübingen: Mohr Siebeck, 1994).

Di Fabio, Udo, 'Grundrechte als Werteordnung', *Juristenzeitung* 1 (2004).

Di Fabio, Udo, 'Sicherheit in Freiheit', *Neue Juristische Wochenschrift* 421 (2008).

Dirnbeck, Josef, *Die Inquisition. Eine Chronik des Schreckens* (Augsburg: Pattloch, 2002).

Dobbelstein, Rainer and Gellert, Claudius, 'Shades of a New McCarthyism in West Germany? A Political and Legal Analysis of the Campaign against Radicals in the West German Civil Service', *Revue de Droit International des Sciences Diplomatiques et Politiques* 64 (1977).

Dreier, Horst (ed.), *Grundgesetz. Kommentar I*, 2nd ed. (Tübingen: Mohr Siebeck, 2004); *Kommentar III*, 2nd ed. (Tübingen: Mohr Siebeck, 2008).

Dreier, Ralf, *Rechtsbegriff und Rechtsidee* (Frankfurt: Metzner, 1986).

Dreist, Peter, 'Einsatz der Bundeswehr im Innern – Das Luftsicherheitsgesetz als Anlass zum verfassungsrechtlichen Nachdenken', in

Ulrich Blaschke et al. (eds.), *Sicherheit statt Freiheit? Staatliche Handlungsspielräume in extremen Gefährdungslagen* (Berlin: Duncker & Humblot, 2005), 77 ff.
Droste, Bernadette, *Handbuch des Verfassungsschutzrechts* (Stuttgart: Boorberg, 2007).
Duhm, Dieter, *Angst im Kapitalismus*, 11th ed. (Lampertheim: Kübler, 1975).
Dunn, John, *The Political Thought of John Locke: An Historical Account of the Argument of the Two Treatises of Government* (Cambridge: Cambridge University Press, 1969).
Duso, Giuseppe, 'Repräsentative Demokratie. Entstehung, Logik und Aporien ihrer Grundbegriffe', in Karl Schmitt (ed.), *Herausforderungen der repräsentativen Demokratie* (Baden-Baden: Nomos, 2003), 11 ff.
Dworkin, Ronald, *Taking Rights Seriously* (Cambridge, MA: Harvard University Press, 1978).
Dyson, Kenneth, 'Anticommunism in the Federal Republic of Germany: The Case of Berufsverbot', 28 *Parliamentary Affairs* 51 (1974–5).
Dyzenhaus, David, *Legality and Legitimacy. Carl Schmitt, Hans Kelsen and Hermann Heller in Weimar* (Oxford: Oxford University Press, 1997).
Dyzenhaus, David, *The Constitution of Law: Legality in a Time of Emergency* (Cambridge: Cambridge University Press, 2006).
Dyzenhaus, David (ed.), *Law as Politics – Carl Schmitt's Critique of Liberalism* (Durham, NC: Duke University Press, 1998).
Dyzenhaus, David, '*Schmitt v. Dicey*: Are States of Emergency Inside or Outside the Legal Order?', 27 *Cardozo Law Review* 2005 (2005–06).
Dyzenhaus, David, 'The Permanence of the Temporary: Can Emergency Powers be Normalized?', in Ronald Daniels, Patrick Macklem and Kent Roach (eds.), *The Security of Freedom: Essays on Canada's Anti-Terrorism Bill* (Toronto: Toronto University Press).
Edelman, Murray, *The Symbolic Uses of Politics* (Chicago: University of Illinois Press, 1985).
Enders, Christoph, 'Der Staat in Not', *Die Öffentliche Verwaltung* 1039 (2007).
Engelmann, Bernt, *Trotz alledem. Deutsche Radikale 1777–1977* (München: Bertelsmann, 1977).
Engels, Friedrich, *Herr Eugen Dühring's Revolution in Science – Anti-Dühring* (Chicago: C.H. Kerr & Co, 1935).
Engels, Friedrich, 'Herrn Eugen Dührings Umwälzung der Wissenschaft (Anti-Dühring)', in Karl Marx and Friedrich Engels, *Werke XX* (Berlin: Dietz Verlag, 1962), 16 ff.

Engene, Jan Oskar, *Terrorism in Western Europe* (Cheltenham, UK and Northampton, MA, USA: Edward Elgar Publishing, 2004).
Erb, Volker, 'Notwehr als Menschenrecht Zugleich eine Kritik der Entscheidung des LG Frankfurt am Main im "Fall Daschner"', *Neue Zeitschrift für Strafrecht* 593 (2005).
Erhard, Ludwig, 'Rede auf dem XIII. Parteitag der CDU', 35 *Archiv der Gegenwart* 11775 (1965).
Ericson, Richard V. and Haggerty, Kevin, *Policing the Risk Society* (Toronto: University of Toronto Press, 1997).
Ericson, Richard V. and Haggerty, Kevin D., *The New Politics of Surveillance and Visibility* (Toronto: University of Toronto Press, 2006).
Eser, Albin, 'Schlussbetrachtungen', in Albin Eser et al. (ed.), *Die deutsche Strafrechtswissenschaft vor der Jahrtausendwende. Rückbesinnung und Ausblick* (München: C.H. Beck, 2000), 437 ff.
Euchner, Walter, 'Demokratietheoretische Aspekte der politischen Ideengeschichte', in Gisela Kress and Dieter Senghaas (eds.), *Politikwissenschaft. Eine Einführung in ihre Probleme*, 3rd ed. (Frankfurt: Europäische Verlagsanstalt, 1971), 38 ff.
Ewald, François, *L'État providence* (Paris: Bernard Grasset, 1986).
Ferejohn, John and Pasquino, Pasquale, 'The Law of the Exception: A Typology of Emergency Powers', 2 *International Journal of Constitutional Law* 210 (2004).
Fetscher, Iring, 'Einleitung', in Thomas Hobbes, *Leviathan* (1651), Iring Fetscher (ed.) (Frankfurt: Suhrkamp, 1984), IX ff.
Fiorelli, Piero, *La tortura giudiziaria nel diritto commune*, 2 vols. (Rome: Giuffré, 1953–4).
Fiss, Owen, 'The War Against Terrorism and the Rule of Law', 26 *Oxford Journal of Legal Studies* 235 (2006).
Fitzpatrick, Peter and Golder, Ben, *Foucault's Law* (New York: Routledge, 2009).
Forst, Rainer, *Kontexte der Gerechtigkeit* (Frankfurt: Suhrkamp, 1994).
Forst, Rainer, *Toleranz im Konflikt* (Frankfurt: Suhrkamp, 2003).
Forsthoff, Ernst, 'Der Ausnahmezustand der Länder', *Annalen des Deutschen Reichs für Gesetzgebung, Verwaltung und Volkswirtschaft, Jg. 1923–1925* (München: Schweitzer Verlag, 1926), 138 ff.
Forsthoff, Ernst, *Der totale Staat* (Hamburg: Hanseatische Verlagsanstalt, 1933).
Forsthoff, Ernst, 'Die Bindung an Gesetz und Recht (Art. 20 Abs. 3 GG)', *Die Öffentliche Verwaltung* 41 (1959).
Forsthoff, Ernst, 'Der introvertierte Rechtsstaat und seine Verortung', 2 *Der Staat* 385 (1963).

Forsthoff, Ernst (ed.), *Rechtsstaatlichkeit und Sozialstaatlichkeit* (Darmstadt: Wissenschaftliche Buchgesellschaft, 1968).

Forsthoff, Ernst, 'Begriff und Wesen des sozialen Rechtsstaates', in Ernst Forsthoff (ed.), *Rechtsstaatlichkeit und Sozialstaatlichkeit* (Darmstadt: Wissenschaftliche Buchgesellschaft, 1968), 165 ff.

Forsthoff, Ernst, *Der Staat der Industriegesellschaft* (München: C.H. Beck, 1971).

Forsthoff, Ernst, 'Die Umbildung des Verfassungsgesetzes', in Mehdi Tohidipur (ed.), *Der bürgerliche Rechtsstaat I* (Frankfurt: Suhrkamp, 1978), 177 ff.

Foschepoth, Josef, *Überwachtes Deutschland. Post- und Telefonüberwachung in der Bundesrepublik* (Göttingen: Vandenhoeck Ruprecht, 2013).

Foucault, Michel, *Der Wille zum Wissen. Sexualität und Wahrheit I* (Frankfurt: Suhrkamp, 1977).

Foucault, Michel, *Discipline and Punish. The Birth of the Prison* (New York: Pantheon, 1978).

Foucault, Michel, *Dispositive der Macht. Über Sexualität, Wissen und Wahrheit* (Berlin: Merve Verlag, 1978).

Foucault, Michel, *Power/Knowledge: Selected Interviews and Other Writings 1972–77* (New York: Pantheon, 1980), 92 ff.

Foucault, Michel, 'The Confessions of the Flesh', in *Power/Knowledge. Selected Interviews and Other Writings*, Colin Gordon (ed.) (New York: 1980), 194–228.

Foucault, Michel, *The Birth of the Clinic: An Archeology of Medical Perception* (London: Routledge, 1989).

Foucault, Michel, *Madness and Civilization: A History of Insanity* (New York: Routledge, 1989).

Foucault, Michel, 'Governmentality' (Lecture at the Collège de France), in Graham Burchell, Colin Gordon and Peter Miller (eds.), *The Foucault Effect: Studies in Governmentality* (Hemel Hempstead: Harvester Wheatsheaf, 1991), 87–104.

Foucault, Michel, 'Security, Territory, Population', in Michel Foucault, *Ethics: Subjectivity and Truth*, Paul Rabinow (ed.) (New York: The New Press, 1997), 73–9.

Foucault, Michel, *Schriften in vier Bänden [Dits et Écrits] 1976–1979*, Daniel Defert and François Ewald (eds.) (Frankfurt: Suhrkamp, 2003).

Foucault, Michel, *Society Must be Defended: Lectures at the Collège de France, 1975–76*, David Macey transl. (London: Penguin, 2003).

Foucault, Michel, 'Die Sicherheit und der Staat', in Daniel Defert and François Ewald (eds.), *Die Analytik der Macht* (Frankfurt: Suhrkamp, 2005), 137 ff.

Foucault, Michel, *Sicherheit, Territorium, Bevölkerung: Geschichte der Gouvernementalität I*, 4th ed. (Frankfurt: Suhrkamp, 2006).
Foucault, Michel, *Security, Territory, Population: Lectures at the College de France, 1977–78* (Hampshire: Palgrave, 2009).
Foucault, Michel, *The Birth of Biopolitics: Lectures at the Collège de France 1978–1979* (New York: Palgrave, 2010).
Fraenkel, Ernst, *The Dual State* (New York: Octagon Books, 1969).
Frahm, Friedrich, 'Entstehungs- und Entwicklungsgeschichte der Preußischen Verfassung', *Forschungen zur Brandenburgischen und Preußischen Geschichte* 41 (1928), 248 ff.
Frankenberg, Günter, 'Angst im Rechtsstaat', *Kritische Justiz* 353 (1977).
Frankenberg, Günter, 'Staatstreue. Die aktuelle Spruchpraxis zu den Berufsverboten', *Kritische Justiz* 276 (1980).
Frankenberg, Günter, 'Passive Resistenz ist keine Nötigung', *Kritische Justiz* 301 (1985).
Frankenberg, Günter (ed.), *Auf der Suche nach der gerechten Gesellschaft* (Frankfurt: Fischer, 1994).
Frankenberg, Günter, *Die Verfassung der Republik* (Frankfurt: Suhrkamp, 1997).
Frankenberg, Günter, 'Datenschutz und Staatsangehörigkeit', in Dieter Simon and Manfred Weiss (eds.), *Zur Autonomie des Individuums* (Baden-Baden: Nomos, 2000), 99 ff.
Frankenberg, Günter, 'The Learning Sovereign', in András Sajó (ed.), *Militant Democracy* (Utrecht: Eleven International Publishing, 2004), 113–32.
Frankenberg, Günter, 'Kritik des Bekämpfungsrechts', *Kritische Justiz* 370 (2005).
Frankenberg, Günter, 'Torture and Taboo: An Essay Comparing Paradigms of Organized Cruelty', 56 *American Journal of Comparative Law* 403 (2008).
Frankenberg, Günter, 'Die europäische Union der Staatstechniker und Experten', in Michael Bäuerle et al. (eds.), *Demokratie-Perspektiven. Festschrift für Brun-Otto Bryde zum 70. Geburtstag* (Tübingen: Mohr Siebeck, 2013), 141–55.
Freedman, Lawrence, 'Prevention, Not Preemption', 26 *The Washington Quarterly* 105–14 (2003).
Ferejohn, John and Pasquino, Pasquale, 'The Law of Exception: A Typology of Emergency Powers', 2 *International Journal of Constitutional Law* 210–39 (2004).
Freud, Sigmund, 'Introductory Lectures on Psycho-analysis' [1916/1917], in Sigmund Freud, *The Standard Edition of the Complete Psychological Works*, Vol. XVI, James Strachey (ed.) (London: Vintage, 2001).

Freud, Sigmund, *Civilization and its Discontents* (London: Penguin, 2002).

Freud, Sigmund, 'Inhibitions, Symptoms and Anxiety', in Sigmund Freud, *The Standard Edition of the Complete Psychological Works*, Vol. XX (London: Vintage, 2007).

Freud, Sigmund, *Totem and Taboo: Resemblances between the Psychic Lives of Savages and Neurotics* (New York: Moffat, Yard & Co., 1918).

Friedrich, Carl J., *Constitutional Government and Democracy* (Boston: Ginn, 1941).

Frisch, Max, 'We Hope', 60 (4) *World Literature Today* 536–40 (1986).

Fromm, Erich, *Die Furcht vor der Freiheit* (Frankfurt: Ullstein, 1988).

Fromm, Erich, Horkheimer, Max and Marcuse, Herbert, *Studien über Autorität und Familie* (Paris: Libraire Félix Alcan, 1936).

Frowein, Jochen Abraham and Peukert, Wolfgang, *Europäische Menschenrechtskonvention. EMRK-Kommentar*, 2nd ed. (Kehl: Engel, 1996).

Funk, Albrecht, 'Ausgeschlossene und Bürger. Das ambivalente Verhältnis von Rechtsgleichheit und sozialem Ausschluß', *Kriminologisches Journal* 243 (1995).

Funk, Albrecht and Werkentin, Falco, 'Der Todesschuß der Polizei', *Kritische Justiz* 121 (1976).

Funk, Albrecht and Werkentin, Falco, 'Der Musterentwurf für ein einheitliches Polizeigesetz – ein Muster exekutiven Rechtsstaatsverständnisses', *Kritische Justiz* 407 (1976).

Furedi, Frank, *Politics of Fear. Beyond Left and Right* (London: Continuum, 2005).

Fürmetz, Gerhard (ed.), *Schwabinger Krawalle. Protest, Polizei und Öffentlichkeit zu Beginn der 60er Jahre* (Essen: Karltext Verlag, 2006).

Galli, Francesca, 'The War on Terror and Crusading Judges', in Aniceto Masferrer (ed.), *Post 9/11 and the State of Permanent Legal Emergency* (Dordrecht: Springer 2012) 153.

Gallie, Walter Bryce, 'Essentially Contested Concepts', 56 *Proceedings of the Aristotelian Society* 167 (1955–6).

Galtung, Johan, 'Violence, Peace and Peace Research', *Journal of Peace Research* 6 (1969), 167–91.

Garland, David, *The Culture of Control* (Oxford: Oxford University Press, 2001).

Gauchet, Marcel, 'Des deux corps du roi au pouvoir sans corps. Christianisme et politique', (14, 15) *Le Débat* 133, 147 (1981).

Gauchet, Marcel, 'Pacification, démocratique, desertion civique', 60 *Le Débat* 87–98 (1990).

Gearty, Connor, 'Terrorism and Human Rights', 19 *Legal Studies* 367 (1999).

Geertz, Clifford, 'Centers, Kings, and Charisma: Reflections on the Symbolics of Power', in Sean Wilentz (ed.), *Rites of Power* (Philadelphia: University of Pennsylvania Press, 1985), 13 ff.

Gerber, Carl Friedrich von, *Grundzüge eines Systems des deutschen Staatsrechts*, 3rd ed. (Leipzig: Tauchnitz, 1880).

Gerstenberger, Heide, 'Zur Theorie der historischen Konstitution des bürgerlichen Staates', 8/9 *Prokla* 207 (1973).

Gerstenberger, Heide, 'Klassenantagonismus, Konkurrenz und Staatsfunktionen', *Gesellschaft – Beiträge zur Marxschen Theorie 3* (Frankfurt: Suhrkamp, 1975), 7 ff.

Giddens, Anthony, 'Risk and Responsibility', 62 *Modern Law Review* 1–10 (1999).

Ginbar, Yuval, *Why Not Torture Terrorists? Moral, Practical and Legal Aspects of the 'Ticking Bomb' Justification of Torture* (Oxford: Oxford University Press, 2010).

Ginzburg, Carlo, 'Welt der Leviathane: Furcht, Verehrung, Schrecken – Thomas Hobbes' politische Theologie', 83 *Lettre International* 23 (2008).

Gladstone, W.E. and Brinkmann, G., 'Militant Democracy and Radicals in the West German Civil Service', 46 *The Modern Law Review* 584–600 (1983).

Goldsworthy, Jeffrey, 'Legislative Sovereignty and the Rule of Law', in Tom Campbell, K.D. Ewing and Adam Tomkins (eds.), *Sceptical Essays on Human Rights* (Oxford: Oxford University Press, 2001).

Gomez-Jara Diez, C., 'Enemy Combatants Versus Enemy Criminal Law', 11 *New Criminal Law Review* 529 (2008).

Goodin, Robert E., *What's Wrong with Terrorism?* (Cambridge: Polity, 2006).

Gough, John W., *Fundamental Law in English Constitutional History* (Oxford: Clarendon Press, 1955).

Gramm, Christof, 'Der wehrlose Verfassungsstaat?', *Deutsches Verwaltungsblatt* 653–61 (2006).

Grasskamp, Walter, *Die unästhetische Demokratie. Kunst in der Marktgesellschaft* (München: C.H. Beck, 1992).

Graulich, Kurt and Simon, Dieter (eds.), *Terrorismus und Rechtsstaatlichkeit. Analysen, Handlungsoptionen, Perspektiven* (Berlin: Oldenbourg Akademieverlag, 2007).

Greenberg, Karen J. (ed.), *The Torture Debate in America* (New York: Cambridge University Press, 2006).

Greenberg, Karen J. and Dratel, Joshua L. (eds.), *The Torture Papers. The Road to Abu Ghraib* (New York: Cambridge University Press, 2005).

Grimm, Dieter, 'Reformalisierung des Rechtstaats als Demokratiepostulat?', *Juristische Schulung* 704 (1980).

Groh, Ruth, *Arbeit an der Heillosigkeit der Welt. Zur politisch-theologischen Mythologie und Anthropologie Carl Schmitts* (Frankfurt: Suhrkamp, 1998).

Gross, Oren, 'Chaos and Rules: Should Responses to Violent Crisis Always Be Constitutional?', 112 *Yale Law Journal* 1011 (2002–03).

Gross, Oren and Ní Aoláin, Fionnula, *Law in Times of Crisis* (Cambridge: Cambridge University Press, 2006).

Grosser, Alfred, 'Die Bundesrepublik, der internationale und der innere Friede. Ansprache anlässlich der Verleihung des Friedenspreises des deutschen Buchhandels 1975', in Erhard Denninger (ed.), *Freiheitliche demokratische Grundordnung. Materialien zum Staatsverständnis und zur Verfassungswirklichkeit in der Bundesrepublik I* (Frankfurt: Suhrkamp, 1977), 54 ff.

Groth, Klaus, 'Die Transformation der Verfassung durch die Berufsverbote', *Kritische Justiz* 295 (1975).

Günther, Klaus, *Der Sinn für Angemessenheit* (Frankfurt: Suhrkamp, 1988).

Günther, Klaus, 'Welchen Personenbegriff braucht die Diskurstheorie des Rechts? Überlegungen zum internen Zusammenhang zwischen deliberativer Person, Staatsbürger und Rechtsperson', in Hauke Brunkhorst and Peter Niesen (eds.), *Das Recht der Republik. Festschrift für Ingeborg Maus* (Frankfurt: Suhrkamp, 1999), 83 ff.

Günther, Klaus, 'Kritik der Strafe I', 1 *WestEnd. Neue Zeitschrift für Sozialforschung* 117 (2004).

Günther, Klaus, 'Folter kennt keine Grenze', *ZEIT online* (14 March 2008).

Gustav Heinemann-Initiative and Humanistische Union (ed.), *Graubuch Innere Sicherheit. Die schleichende Demontage des Rechtsstaates nach dem 11. September 2001* (Norderstedt: Books on Demand, 2009).

Gusy, Christoph, *Weimar – Die wehrlose Republik?* (Tübingen: Mohr Siebeck, 1991).

Gusy, Christoph, 'Vom Deutschen Reich zur Weimarer Republik', *Juristenzeitung* 758 (1999).

Gusy, Christoph, 'Mehr als der Polizei erlaubt ist? Die Nachrichtendienste im Anti-Terrorkampf', in Stefan Huster and Karsten Rudolph (eds.), *Vom Rechtsstaat zum Präventionsstaat* (Frankfurt: Suhrkamp, 2008), 120 ff.

Habermas, Jürgen, *Theory and Practice* (London: Heinemann, 1974).

Habermas, Jürgen, *The Philosophical Discourse of Modernity: Twelve Lectures*, Frederick Lawrence transl. (Cambridge, MA: MIT Press, 1987).

Habermas, Jürgen, 'Die Schrecken der Autonomie', in Jürgen Habermas, *Eine Art Schadensabwicklung* (Frankfurt: Suhrkamp, 1987), 101 ff.

Habermas, Jürgen, *Between Facts and Norms: Contributions to a Discourse Theory of Law and Democracy*, William Regh transl. (Cambridge, MA: MIT Press, 1996).
Haltern, Ulrich, 'Internationales Verfassungsrecht? Anmerkungen zu einer kopernikanischen Wende', 128 *Archiv des öffentlichen Rechts* 511 (2003).
Hampton, Jean, *Hobbes and the Social Contract Tradition* (Cambridge: Cambridge University Press, 1986).
Hanebeck, Alexander, *Der demokratische Bundesstaat des Grundgesetzes* (Berlin: Duncker & Humblot, 2004).
Harper, Timothy, 'Shoot to Kill', *The Atlantic* (1 October 2000).
Harrington, James, *The Commonwealth of Oceana* [1656], J.G.A. Pocock (ed.) (Cambridge: Cambridge University Press, 1992).
Harscher von Almendingen, Ludwig, 'Grundzüge zu einer neuen Theorie über Verletzungen des guten Namens und der Ehre. Ein philosophisch-juridischer Versuch', in Karl Grolman (ed.), *Magazin für die Philosophie und Geschichte des Rechts und der Gesetzgebung*, vol. 1 (Gießen: Heyer, 1800), 1 ff. and 133 ff., vol. 2 (Gießen: Heyer, 1807), 1 ff.
Hartleb, Torsten, 'Der neue § 14 III LuftSiG und das Grundrecht auf Leben', *Neue Juristische Wochenschrift* 1397 (2005).
Hartung, Lea, 'Kommissar Computer. Horst Herold und die Virtualisierung des polizeilichen Wissens', in Georgia Schulze et al. (eds.), *Neue Analysen zu Staat, Recht und Polizei* (Freie Universität Berlin, 2010).
Hase, Friedhelm, Ladeur, Karl-Heinz and Ridder, Helmut, 'Nochmals: Reformalisierung des Rechtsstaats als Demokratiepostulat?', *Juristische Schulung* 794 (1981).
Hassemer, Winfried, 'Zum Spannungsverhältnis von Freiheit und Sicherheit. Drei Thesen', *Vorgänge* 10 (2002).
Hatemi, Peter K., McDermott, Rose et al., 'Fear as a Disposition and an Emotional State', 57 *American Journal of Political Science* 279–293 (2013).
Hawel, Marcus, 'Dämmerung des demokratischen Rechtsstaates? Zur Renaissance des Dezisionismus', *Kritische Justiz* 64 (2009).
Hecker, Wolfgang, 'Relativierung des Folterverbots in der BRD?', *Kritische Justiz* 210 (2003).
Heinemann, Gustav, 'Freimütige Kritik und demokratischer Rechtsstaat', in Martin Lotz, *Bibliographie, Archiv der sozialen Demokratie*, Friedrich-Ebert-Stiftung (ed.) (Bonn: Peter Millard, 1976).
Heller, Hermann, 'Der Begriff des Gesetzes in der Reichsverfassung' [1928], in Hermann Heller, *Gesammelte Schriften*, vol. 2 (Leiden: A.W. Sijthoff, 1971), 203 ff.

Heller, Hermann, *Rechtsstaat oder Diktatur*? (Tübingen: Mohr Siebeck, 1930).

Heller, Hermann, *Staatslehre*, 3rd ed. (Tübingen: Mohr Siebeck, 1983).

Herrnkind, Martin, 'Personenkontrollen und Schleierfahndung', *Kritische Justiz* 188 (2000).

Herrnkind, Martin, '"Schleierfahndung". Institutionalisierter Rassismus und weitere Implikationen sogenannter verdachtsunabhängiger Polizeikontrollen', in Komitee für Grundrechte und Demokratie (ed.), *Verpolizeilichung der Bundesrepublik Deutschland* (Köln: Komitee für Grundrechte und Demokratie, 2002), 99 ff.

Hersh, Seymour M., *Chain of Command. The Road from 9/11 to Abu Ghraib* (New York: Harper Collins, 2004).

Hersh, Seymour M., 'Torture at Abu Ghraib', *The New Yorker* (10 May 2004).

Hess, Henner, 'Terrorismus und Terrorismus-Diskurs', in Henner Hess et al. (eds.), *Angriff auf das Herz des Staates: Soziale Entwicklung und Terrorismus*, vol. 1 (Frankfurt: Suhrkamp, 1988), 55 ff.

Hess, Henner et al. (eds.), *Angriff auf das Herz des Staates. Soziale Entwicklung und Terrorismus*, 2 vols. (Frankfurt: Suhrkamp, 1988).

Hesse, Konrad, 'Grundfragen einer verfassungsmäßigen Normierung des Ausnahmezustandes', *Juristenzeitung* 105 (1960).

Hesse, Konrad, *Grundzüge des Verfassungsrechts der Bundesrepublik Deutschland*, 20th ed. (Heidelberg: C.F. Müller, 1995).

Hetzer, Wolfgang, *Rechtsstaat oder Ausnahmezustand? Souveränität und Terror* (Berlin: Duncker & Humblot, 2008).

Heuer, Jens-Uwe, *Die Rechtsordnung der DDR. Anspruch und Wirklichkeit* (Baden-Baden: Nomos, 1995).

Heumann, Milton and Cassak, Lance, *Good Cop, Bad Cop: Racial Profiling and Competing Views of Justice* (New York: Peter Lang, 2003).

Heuschling, Luc, *État de droit, Rechtsstaat, Rule of Law* (Paris: Dalloz, 2002).

Hilger, Christian, *Rechtsstaatsbegriffe im Dritten Reich* (Tübingen: Mohr Siebeck, 2003).

Hillgruber, Christian, 'Der Staat des Grundgesetzes – nur "bedingt abwehrbereit"?', *Juristenzeitung* 209 (2007).

Hobbes, Thomas, *Elements of Law, Natural and Politic* [1640], John C.A. Gaskin (ed.) (Oxford: Oxford University Press, 1999).

Hobbes, Thomas, *De Cive* [1642], Howard Warrender (ed.) (Oxford: Clarendon Press, 1983).

Hobbes, Thomas, *Leviathan* [1651], Richard Tuck (ed.) (Cambridge: Cambridge University Press, 1996.

Hobbes, Thomas, *Thomae Hobbesii Malmesburiensis Vita* (London, 1679).
Hoffmann, Bruce, *Inside Terrorism*, 2nd ed. (New York: Columbia University Press, 2006).
Hoffmann, Bruce, *Right-wing Terrorism in Europe Since 1980* (Santa Monica: RAND, 1984).
Hofmann, Hasso, 'Von den Ursprüngen deutschen Rechtsstaatsdenkens in der nachchristlichen Sozialphilosophie', *Juristische Schulung* 9 (1984).
Hofmann, Hasso, *Legitimität gegen Legalität. Der Weg der politischen Philosophie Carl Schmitts*, 3rd ed. (Berlin: Duncker & Humblot, 1995).
Hofmann, Hasso, 'Souverän ist, wer über den Ausnahmezustand entscheidet', 44 *Der Staat* 171 (2005).
Hoffmann-Riem, Wolfgang, *Modernisierung von Recht und Justiz* (Frankfurt: Suhrkamp, 2000).
Hoffmann-Riem, Wolfgang, 'Freiheit und Sicherheit im Angesicht terroristischer Anschläge', *Zeitschrift für Rechtspolitik* 497 (2002).
Hoffmann-Riem, Wolfgang, 'Das Bundesverfassungsgericht als Garant von Rechtsstaatlichkeit', *Europäische Grundrechte-Zeitschrift* 557 (2008).
Holdsworth, William Searle, *A History of English Law II*, 2nd ed. (London: Methuen, 1914).
Honneth, Axel, *The Critique of Power: Reflective Stages in a Critical Social Theory* (Cambridge, MA: MIT Press, 1991).
Honneth, Axel, *Das Andere der Gerechtigkeit* (Frankfurt: Suhrkamp, 2000).
Horn, Klaus, 'Über den Zusammenhang zwischen Angst und politischer Apathie', in Herbert Marcuse et al. (eds.), *Aggression und Anpassung in der Industriegesellschaft* (Frankfurt: Suhrkamp, 1968), 59 ff.
Horn, Klaus, *Psychoanalyse – Kritische Theorie des Subjekts. Aufsätze 1969–1972* (Amsterdam: de Munter, 1972).
Huber, Hans, 'Niedergang des Rechts und Krise des Rechtsstaates', in Max Imboden (ed.), *Demokratie und Rechtsstaat. Festgabe zum 60. Geburtstag von Zaccaria Giacometti* (Zürich: Polygraphischer Verlag, 1953), 59 ff.
Human Rights Watch, 'The Road to Abu Ghraib', http://www.hrw.org/reports/2004/usa0604/usa0604.pdf (2004).
Humboldt, Wilhelm von, *Ideen zu einem Versuch, die Grenzen der Wirksamkeit des Staates zu bestimmen* (Breslau: Trewendt Verlag, 1851).
Humboldt, Wilhelm von, *The Sphere and Duties of Government: The Limits of State Action* [German orig.: 1792] (London: John Chapman, 1854).

Huntington, Samuel P., *The Clash of Civilizations and the Remaking of World Order* (New York: Touchstone Books, 1996).

Hurrelmann, Achim et al. (eds.), *Zerfasert der Nationalstaat? Die Internationalisierung politischer Verantwortung* (Frankfurt: Campus Verlag, 2008).

Huster, Stefan and Rudolph, Karsten (eds.), *Vom Rechtsstaat zum Präventionsstaat* (Frankfurt am Main: Suhrkamp, 2008).

Hutchinson, Allan C. and Monahan, Patrick (eds.), *The Rule of Law: Ideal or Ideology* (Toronto: Carswell, 1987).

Ignatieff, Michael, *The Lesser Evil. Political Ethics in an Age of Terror* (Princeton: Princeton University Press, 2004).

Ihering, Rudolf von, *The Struggle for Law* [1879] (Chicago: Callaghan & Co, 1915).

Imbusch, Peter, 'The Concept of Violence', in Wilhelm Heitmeyer and John Hagan (eds.), *International Handbook of Violence Research I* (Norwell: Kluwer, 2003), 13–40.

International Commission of Jurists, *States of Emergency and their Impact on Human Rights* (Geneva: The Commission, 1983).

International Commission of the Red Cross, *Report on the Treatment of Fourteen 'High Value Detainees' in CIA Custody* (Washington: ICRC, 14 February 2007).

International Monetary Fund (IMF), *Good Governance: The IMF's Role* (Washington, DC: IMF, 1997).

Isensee, Josef, 'Wehrhafte Demokratie', (3) *Das Parlament* 1 (17 January 1976).

Isensee, Josef, *Das Grundrecht auf Sicherheit. Zu den Schutzpflichten des freiheitlichen Verfassungsstaates* (Berlin: De Gruyter, 1983).

Isensee, Josef (ed.), *Vergangenheitsbewältigung durch Recht. Drei Abhandlungen zu einem deutschen Problem* (Berlin: Duncker & Humblot, 1992).

Isensee, Josef, 'Das Grundrecht als Abwehrrecht und staatliche Schutzpflicht', in Josef Isensee and Paul Kirchhof (eds.), *Handbuch des Staatsrechts der Bundesrepublik Deutschland*, vol. V, 2nd ed. (Heidelberg: C.F. Müller, 2000), § 111.

Isensee, Josef, 'Normalfall oder Grenzfall als Ausgangspunkt rechtsphilosophischer Konstruktion?', in Winfried Brugger and Görg Haverkate (eds.), *Grenzen als Thema der Rechts- und Sozialphilosophie* (Stuttgart: Franz Steiner Verlag, 2002), 51 ff.

Isensee, Josef, 'Der Verfassungsstaat als Friedensgarant (II)', 414 *Die politische Meinung* 66 (2004).

Isensee, Josef, 'Menschenwürde – die säkulare Gesellschaft auf der Suche nach dem Absoluten', 131 *Archiv des öffentlichen Rechts* 173 (2006).

Jacobson, Arthur J. and Schlink, Bernhard (eds.), *Weimar: A Jurisprudence of Crisis* (Berkeley: University of California Press, 2000).

Jahn, Matthias, 'Gute Folter – schlechte Folter?', *Kritische Vierteljahresschrift für Gesetzgebung und Rechtswissenschaft* 24 (2004).

Jakab, András, 'Das Grunddilemma und die Natur des Staatsnotstandes', *Kritische Justiz* 323 (2005).

Jakobs, Günther, 'Kriminalisierung im Vorfeld einer Rechtsgutsverletzung', 97 *Zeitschrift für die gesamte Strafrechtswissenschaft* 751 (1985).

Jakobs, Günther, 'Das Selbstverständnis der Strafrechtswissenschaft vor den Herausforderungen der Gegenwart (Kommentar)', in Albin Eser et al. (eds.), *Die deutsche Strafrechtswissenschaft vor der Jahrtausendwende. Rückbesinnung und Ausblick* (München: C.H. Beck, 2000) 47 ff.

Jakobs, Günther, *Staatliche Strafe: Bedeutung und Zweck* (Paderborn: Schöningh, 2004).

Jakobs, Günther, 'Bürgerstrafrecht und Feindstrafrecht', *Online-Zeitschrift für Höchstrichterliche Rechtsprechung im Strafrecht* 88 (2004).

Jakobs, Günther, 'Terroristen als Personen im Recht', 117 *Zeitschrift für die gesamte Strafrechtswissenschaft* 839 (2005).

Jakobs, Günther, 'Zur Theorie des Feindstrafrechts', in Henning Rosenau and Sangyun Kim (eds.), *Straftheorie und Strafgerechtigkeit* (Frankfurt: Peter Lang, 2010), 167–82.

Janus, Eric S., 'The Preventive State, Terrorists and Sexual Predators', William Mitchell College of Law Research Paper No. 11 (2005).

Jellinek, Georg, *Allgemeine Staatslehre*, 2nd ed. [1905] (Tübingen: Mohr & Siebeck, 1928).

Jenkins, David, 'In Support of Canada's Anti-Terrorism Bill. A Comparison of Canadian, British and American Anti-Terrorism Law', 66 *Saskatchewan Law Review* 419 (2003).

Jennings, Andrew, *Foul! The Secret World of FIFA* (London: HarperCollins, 2012).

Jerouschek, Günter and Kölbel, Ralf, 'Folter von Staats wegen?', *Juristenzeitung* 613–20 (2003).

Jowell, Jeffrey, 'The Rule of Law Today', in Jeffrey Jowell and Dawn Oliver (eds.), *The Changing Constitution*, 3rd ed. (Oxford: Oxford University Press, 1994).

Jünger, Ernst, 'Technology as the Mobilization of the World through the Gestalt of the Worker', in Carl Mitcham and Robert Mackey (eds.),

Philosophy and Technology – Readings in the Philosophical Problems of Technology (New York: Macmillan Publishing, 1983), 269–90.

Jünger, Ernst, *Der Arbeiter. Herrschaft und Gestalt* (Stuttgart: Klett-Cotta, 2007).

Justi, Johann H.G. von, *Die Natur und das Wesen der Staaten als Grundwissenschat der Staatskunst, der Policey und aller Regierungswissenschaften, desgleichen als die Quelle aller Gesetze*, 2nd ed. (Mitau: Steidel, 1771).

Kägi, Werner, *Die Verfassung als rechtliche Grundordnung des Staates* (Zürich: Polygraphischer Verlag, 1945).

Kägi, Werner, 'Rechtsstaat und Demokratie. Antinomie und Synthese', in Mehdi Tohidipur (ed.), *Der bürgerliche Rechtsstaat I* (Frankfurt: Suhrkamp, 1978), 127 ff.

Kahan, Dan M., Hoffman, David A. and Braman, Donald, 'Whose Eyes are you Going to Believe? *Scott v. Harris* and the Perils of Cognitive Illiberalism', 122 *Harvard Law Review* 837 (2009).

Kant, Immanuel, 'On the Old Saw: That May be Right in Theory, but Won't Work in Practice', E.B. Ashton transl. (Philadelphia: University of Princeton Press, 1974).

Kant, Immanuel, *'Perpetual Peace': A Philosophical Essay* (London: G. Allen and Unwin, 1917).

Kant, Immanuel, 'Zum Ewigen Frieden. Ein philosophischer Entwurf' [1795], *Werkausgabe XI* (Frankfurt: Suhrkamp, 1977), 191 ff.

Kant, Immanuel, *The Metaphysics of Morals* [1797], in Immanuel Kant, *Practical Philosophy*, Mary J. Gregor and Allen W. Wood (eds.), *The Cambridge Edition of the Works of Immanuel Kant* (Cambridge: Cambridge University Press, 1996), 353–603.

Kantorowicz, Ernst H., *The King's Two Bodies* (Princeton: Princeton University Press, 1957).

Kantorowicz, Ernst H., 'Mysteries of State. An Absolutist Concept and its Late Mediaeval Origins', in Ernst H. Kantorowicz, *Selected Studies* (Locust Valley/New York: J.J. Augustin, 1965), 381 ff.

Kaufmann, Erich, 'Die Gleichheit vor dem Gesetz im Sinne des Art. 109 der Reichsverfassung', 3 *Veröffentlichungen der Vereinigung der Deutschen Staatsrechtslehrer* 1 (1927).

Kegley, Charles W. and Raymond, Gregory A., 'Global Terrorism and Military Prevention: Policy Problems and Normative Perils', 41 *International Politics* 37–49 (2004).

Kelsen, Hans, *General Theory of Law and State* [1925] (Cambridge, MA: Harvard University Press, 1945).

Kelsen, Hans, *Reine Rechtslehre*, 2nd ed. (Wien: Deuticke, 1960), repr.: (Wien: Österreichischer Staatsdruck, 1992).

Kennedy, David, 'Challenging Expert Rule: The Politics of Global Governance', 27 *Sydney Journal of International Law* 5 (2005).
Kennedy, David, 'The Mystery of Global Governance', 34 *Ohio Northern University Law Review* 827 (2008).
Kennedy, David, *Global Governance? New Thinking about Law and Politics* (Princeton: Princeton University Press, 2011).
Kennedy, David, *Of War and Law* (Princeton: Princeton University Press, 2006).
Kersting, Wolfgang, *Die politische Philosophie des Gesellschaftsvertrags* (Darmstadt: Wissenschaftliche Buchgesellschaft, 1994).
Kersting, Wolfgang, *Niccolò Machiavelli*, 3rd ed. (München: C.H. Beck, 2006).
Kierkegaard, Søren, 'Repetition', in *Kierkegaard's Writings VI: Fear and Trembling/Repetition* (Princeton: Princeton University Press, 1983).
Kierkegaard, Søren, *Fear and Trembling* [1843] (London: Penguin, 2005).
Kierkegaard, Søren, *The Concept of Anxiety* [1844] (Princeton: Princeton University Press, 1981).
Kiesow, Rainer Maria, 'Das Experiment mit der Wahrheit. Folter im Vorzimmer des Rechts', 3 *Rechtsgeschichte* 98 (2003).
Kinzig, Jörg, *Die rechtliche Bewältigung von Erscheinungsformen organisierter Kriminalität* (Berlin: Duncker & Humblot, 2004).
Kirchheimer, Otto, 'Legalität und Legitimität', in Otto Kirchheimer, *Politische Herrschaft. Fünf Beiträge zur Lehre vom Staat* (Frankfurt: Suhrkamp, 1967), 7 ff.
Kirchhof, Paul, 'Die Zulässigkeit des Einsatzes staatlicher Gewalt in Ausnahmesituationen', in Deutsche Sektion der Internationalen Juristen-Kommission (ed.), *Rechtsstaat in der Bewährung, vol. 2. Die Zulässigkeit des Einsatzes staatlicher Gewalt in Ausnahmesituationen* (Karlsruhe: C.F. Müller, 1976), 83 ff.
Kirshner, Jonathan (ed.), *Globalization and National Security* (London: Routledge, 2005).
Kistner, Thomas, *FIFA-Mafia. Die schmutzigen Geschäfte mit dem Weltfußball* (München: Droemer, 2012).
Klein, Hans Hugo, 'Vom sozialistischen Machtstaat zum demokratischen Rechtsstaat', *Juristenzeitung* 53 (1990).
Klinsman, Gary W., Buse, Dieter K. and Steedman, Mercedes (eds.), *Whose National Security? Canadian Surveillance and the Creation of Enemies* (Toronto: Between the Lines, 2000).
Koellreutter, Otto, *Der nationale Rechtsstaat* (Tübingen: Mohr Siebeck, 1932).
Koellreutter, Otto, 'Leviathan und totaler Staat', 59 *Reichsverwaltungsblatt* 803 (1938).

Koja, Friedrich, *Der Staatsnotstand als Rechtsbegriff* (Salzburg: Pustet, 1979).

Komitee für Grundrechte und Demokratie (ed.), *Ohne Zweifel für den Staat* (Reinbek/Hamburg: Rowohlt, 1982).

Körtner, Ulrich H.J., *The End of the World: A Theological Interpretation* (Kentucky: Westminster J. Know Press, 1995).

Koschorke, Albrecht, Frank, Thomas, Lüdemann, Susanne and Matala de Mazza, Ethel, *Der fiktive Staat. Konstruktionen des politischen Körpers in der Geschichte Europas* (Frankfurt: Fischer, 2007).

Krane, Christian, *'Schleierfahndung'. Rechtliche Anforderungen an die Gefahrenabwehr durch ereignisunabhängige Personenkontrollen* (Stuttgart: Boorberg, 2003).

Kretschmer, Bernhard, 'Folter in Deutschland – Rückkehr einer Ungeheuerlichkeit?', *Recht und Politik* 102 (2003).

Kühnl, Reinhard, *Formen bürgerlicher Herrschaft. Liberalismus – Faschismus* (Reinbek/Hamburg: Rowohlt, 1971).

Kunig, Philip, *Das Rechtsstaatsprinzip* (Tübingen: Mohr Siebeck, 1986).

Kutz, Christopher, 'Torture, Necessity and Existential Politics', 95 *California Law Review* 235 (2007).

Laak, Dirk van, *Gespräche in der Sicherheit des Schweigens. Carl Schmitt in der Geistesgeschichte der frühen Bundesrepublik* (Berlin: Akademie Verlag, 1993).

Laband, Paul, *Das Staatsrecht des Deutschen Reiches II*, 5th ed. (Tübingen: Mohr Siebeck, 1911).

Ladeur, Karl-Heinz, *Kritik der Abwägung in der Grundrechtsdogmatik* (Tübingen: Mohr Siebeck, 2004).

Lamprecht, Florian, *Darf der Staat foltern, um Leben zu retten?* (Paderborn: Mentis Verlag, 2009).

Langbein, John H., *Torture and the Law of Proof* (Chicago: University of Chicago Press, 1977).

Lange, Hans-Jürgen (ed.), *Wörterbuch zur Inneren Sicherheit* (Wiesbaden: Verlag für Sozialwissenschaften, 2006).

Lea, Henry Charles, *A History of the Inquisition of the Middle Ages* (New York: Harper & brothers, 1887).

Lefort, Claude, *Fortdauer des Theologisch-Politischen?* (Wien: Passagen Verlag, 1999).

Leibholz, Gerhard, *Strukturprobleme der modernen Demokratie* (Karlsruhe: C.F. Müller, 1958).

Leisner, Walter, 'Rechtsstaat – ein Widerspruch in sich?', *Juristenzeitung* 537 (1977).

Lemke, Thomas, 'The Birth of Bio-Politics: Michel Foucault's Lectures at the Collège de France on Neo-liberal Governmentality', 20 *Economy and Society* 190–207 (2001).

Lenin, Vladimir I., *Staat und Revolution* (Berlin: Dietz, 1948).
Lenzen, Wolfgang, 'Einleitung', in Wolfgang Lenzen (ed.), *Ist Folter erlaubt? Juristische und philosophische Aspekte* (Paderborn: Mentis Verlag, 2006), 7 ff.
Lepsius, Oliver, 'Das Luftsicherheitsgesetz und das Grundgesetz', in Fredrik Roggan (ed.), *Mit Recht für Menschenwürde und Verfassungsstaat. Festgabe für Dr. Burkhard Hirsch* (Berlin: Berliner Wissenschafts-Verlag, 2006), 47 ff.
Lerche, Peter, 'Grundrechte der Soldaten', in Karl August Bettermann, Hans Carl Nipperdey and Ulrich Scheuner (eds.), *Die Grundrechte*, vol. 4, 1st half binding (Berlin: Duncker & Humblot, 1960), 447 ff.
Levine, Emanuel H., *The Third Degree: American Police Methods* (New York: Vanguard Press, 1930).
Levinson, Sanford (ed.), *Torture: A Collection* (New York: Oxford University Press, 2004).
Lewis, James A., *Globalization and National Security* (Washington: CSIS, 2004).
Lieber, Francis, 'Instructions for Government Armies of the United States in the Field' (1862), in US War Department (ed.), *The War of Rebellion: A Compilation of the Official Records of the Union and the Confederate States* (Washington, DC: Government Printing Office, 1899).
Lietzmann, Hans J., 'Von der konstitutionellen zur totalitären Diktatur. Carl J. Friedrichs Totalitarismustheorie', in Alfons Söllner et al. (eds.), *Totalitarismus – Eine Ideengeschichte des 20. Jahrhunderts* (Berlin: Akademie Verlag, 1997), 161 ff.
Lietzmann, Hans J., *Die Entwicklung der Totalitarismustheorie Carl J. Friedrichs* (Opladen: Leske u. Budrich, 1999).
Lindner, Josef Franz, 'Die Würde des Menschen und sein Leben', *Die Öffentliche Verwaltung* 577 (2006).
Lisken, Hans and Denninger, Erhard (eds.), *Handbuch des Polizeirechts*, 4th ed. (München: C.H. Beck, 2007).
Loader, Ian and Walker, Neil, *Civilizing Security* (Cambridge: Cambridge University Press, 2007).
Lochte, Adrienne, *Sie werden dich nicht finden. Der Fall Jakob von Metzler* (München: Droemer, 2004).
Locke, John, *Two Treatises of Government* [1689], Peter Laslett (ed.) (Cambridge: Cambridge University Press, 1967).
Loewenstein, Karl, 'Militant Democracy and Fundamental Rights', 31 *American Political Science Review* 417 (1937).
Losano, Mario G., 'Der nationale Staat zwischen Regionalisierung und Globalisierung', in: Jörg Huber (ed.), Darstellung: Korrespondenz – Interventionen (Zürich: Springer, 2000), 187 ff.

Loughlin, Martin, *Public Law and Political Theory* (Oxford/New York: Oxford University Press, 1992).

Loughlin, Martin, *The Foundations of Public Law* (Oxford: Oxford University Press, 2010).

Luban, David, 'Liberalism, Torture and the Ticking Bomb', 91 *Virginia Law Review* 1425 (2005).

Lübbe, Hermann, 'Freiheit und Terror', 31 *Merkur* 819 (1977).

Lübbe-Wolff, Gertrude, 'Rechtsstaat und Ausnahmerecht', *Zeitschrift für Parlamentsfragen* 110 (1980).

Luhmann, Niklas, 'Metamorphosen des Staates', in Niklas Luhmann, *Gesellschaftsstruktur und Semantik. Studien zur Wissenssoziologie der modernen Gesellschaft IV* (Frankfurt: Suhrkamp, 1999), 101 ff.

Luhmann, Niklas, 'Are There Still Indispensable Norms in Our Society?', in Todd Cesaratto (ed.), *Soziale Systeme* (Stuttgart: Lucius & Lucius, 2008), 14 ff.

Lunde, Paul, *Organized Crime* (New York: Dk Publishers, 2006).

Lyman, Michael O. and Potter, Gary W., *Organized Crime*, 4th ed. (Upper Saddle River: Prentice Hall, 2007).

Lyon, David, *Surveillance after September 11* (London: Polity, 2003).

Lyon, David, *Surveillance Society* (Buckingham: Open University Press, 2001).

MacCormick, Neil, 'Der Rechtsstaat und die rule of law', *Juristenzeitung* (1984), 65 ff.

MacCormick, Neil, *Rhetoric and the Rule of Law. A Theory of Legal Reasoning* (Oxford: Oxford University Press, 2005).

MacCrudden, Christopher and Chambers, Gerald (eds.), *Individual Rights and the Law in Britain* (Oxford: Clarendon Press, 1994).

Machiavelli, Niccolò, *The Prince* [1532], Quentin Skinner and Russell Price (eds.) (Cambridge: Cambridge University Press, 1988).

Machiavelli, Niccolò, *The Discourses*, Bernard Crick (ed.) (London: Penguin, 1984).

MacNaughton-Smith, Peter, 'The Second Code Toward (or Away From) a Theory of Crime and Delinquency', 7 *Criminology* 15 (1969).

Macpherson, Crawford B., *The Political Theory of Possessive Individualism: From Hobbes to Locke* (Oxford: Clarendon, 1962).

Mallory, Stephen, *Understanding Organized Crime* (Burlington: Jones & Bartlett, 2007).

Manacorda, Stefano and Nieto Martin, Adrán (eds.), *Criminal Law between War and Peace* (Cuenca: Ediciones de la Universidad de Castilla-La Mancha, 2009).

Mangoldt, Hermann von, Klein, Friedrich and Starck, Christian (eds.), *Grundgesetz, vol. 1: Präambel, Artikel 1 bis 19*, 5th ed. (München: C.H. Beck, 2005).

Manow, Philip, 'Der demokratische Leviathan – eine kurze Geschichte parlamentarischer Sitzanordnungen seit der französischen Revolution', *Leviathan* 32 (2004), 319 ff.

Manow, Philip, *In the King's Shadow: The Political Anatomy of Democratic Representation* (London: Polity, 2010).

Manuel, Virna A., 'State DNA Data Base and Data Bank Expansion Laws: Is it Time for California to Expand its DNA Data Base Law to Include all Convicted Felons?' 31 *Washington State University Law Review* 339 (2004).

Marcuse, Herbert, *One-dimensional Man: Studies in the Ideology of Advanced Industrial Society* (Boston: Beacon Press Books, 1967).

Marshall, Thomas H., *Citizenship and Social Class* (Cambridge: Cambridge University Press, 1950).

Marty, D., 'Alleged Secret Detentions and Unlawful Interstate Transfers', *Information Memorandum II, AS/Jur.* (7 June 2006).

Marx, Karl, 'Die deutsche Ideologie', in Karl Marx, *Frühschriften*, Siegfried Landshut (ed.) (Stuttgart: Kröner, 1953).

Marx, Reinhard, 'Folter – eine zulässige polizeiliche Präventionsmaßnahme?', *Kritische Justiz* 278 (2004).

Mau, Steffen, *Transnationale Vergesellschaftung* (Frankfurt: Campus Verlag, 2007).

Maunz, Theodor and Dürig, Günter (eds.), *Grundgesetz. Loseblatt-Kommentar* (München: C.H. Beck, 1958).

Maus, Ingeborg, *Bürgerliche Rechtstheorie und Faschismus. Zur sozialen Funktion und aktuellen Wirkung der Theorie Carl Schmitts*, 2nd ed. (München: C.H. Beck, 1980).

Maus, Ingeborg, *Rechtstheorie und Politische Theorie im Industriekapitalismus* (München: Fink, 1986).

Maus, Ingeborg, 'Entwicklung und Funktionswandel der Theorie des bürgerlichen Rechtsstaats', in Ingeborg Maus, *Rechtstheorie und Politische Theorie im Industriekapitalismus* (München: Fink, 1986), 11 ff.

Maus, Ingeborg, 'Verrechtlichung, Entrechtlichung und der Funktionswandel von Institutionen', in Ingeborg Maus, *Rechtstheorie und Politische Theorie im Industriekapitalismus* (München: Fink, 1986), 277 ff.

Maus, Ingeborg, 'Perspektiven "reflexiven Rechts" im Kontext gegenwärtiger Deregulierungstendenzen', *Kritische Justiz* 390 (1986).

Maus, Ingeborg, *Zur Aufklärung der Demokratietheorie* (Frankfurt: Suhrkamp, 1992).

May, Larry, 'Torturing Detainees During Interrogation', 19 *International Journal of Applied Philosophy* 193 (2005).

Mayer, Jane, 'Outsourcing Torture. The Secret History of America's "Extraordinary Rendition" Program', *The New Yorker* (14 February 2005).

Mayer, Jane, 'The Experiment. The Military Trains People to Withstand Interrogation – Are those Methods being Misused at Guantánamo?', *The New Yorker* (11 July 2005).

Mayer, J. 'Whatever it Takes: The Politics of the Man behind "24"', *The New Yorker* (27 February 2007).

Mayer, Otto, *Deutsches Verwaltungsrecht*, 3rd ed. (München: Duncker & Humblot, 1924).

Mayntz, Renate, 'Verwaltungsreform und gesellschaftlicher Wandel', in Edgar Grande and Rainer Prätorius (eds.), *Modernisierung des Staates? Staatslehre und politische Verwaltung* (Baden-Baden: Nomos, 1997), 65 ff.

Mayntz, Renate, 'Governance Theory als fortentwickelte Steuerungstheorie?', in Gunnar Folke Schuppert (ed.), *Governance-Forschung. Vergewisserung über Stand und Entwicklungslinien* (Baden-Baden: Nomos, 2005), 11 ff.

McCormick, John, 'Addressing the Political Exception: Machiavelli's "Accidents" and the Mixed Regime', 87 *American Political Science Review* 4 (1993).

McCormick, John, *Carl Schmitt's Critique of Liberalism: Against Politics as Technology* (Cambridge: Cambridge University Press, 1997).

McCormick, John, 'Irrational Choice and Mortal Combat as Political Destiny: The Essential Carl Schmitt', 10 *Annual Review of Political Science* 315 (2007).

McCoy, Alfred, *Foltern und foltern lassen. 50 Jahre Folterforschung und -praxis von CIA und US-Militär* (Frankfurt: Zweitausendeins Verlag, 2005).

McMahan, Jeff, 'Torture in Principle and in Practice', 22 *Public Affairs Quarterly* 111 (2008).

Mehring, Reinhard, *Carl Schmitt. Aufstieg und Fall* (München: C.H. Beck, 2009).

Meinert, Günter, 'Städtische Regierungskunst: Aspekte einer Good Urban Governance', *Bundeszentrale für politische Bildung* 1 (21 November 2006).

Mellor, Alec, *La torture. Son histoire, son abolition, sa réapparition au XXe siècle* (Paris: Horizons littéraires, 1949).

Merk, Hans Günther and Werthebach, Eckart, *Innere Sicherheit*, 2nd ed. (Karlsfeld: Südwestdeutsche Verlagsanstalt, 1986).

Merkel, Reinhard, 'Wenn der Staat Unschuldige opfert', 29 *Die Zeit* 33 (8 July 2004), http://www.zeit.de/2004/29/Abschussgesetz.

Merkel, Reinhard, '§ 14 Abs. 3 Luftsicherheitsgesetz: Wann und warum darf der Staat töten?', *Juristenzeitung* 373 (2007).
Merkel, Reinhard, 'Folter und Notwehr', in Michael Pawlik and Rainer Zaczyk (eds.), *Festschrift für Günther Jakobs zum 70. Geburtstag* (Köln: Heymanns, 2007), 375 ff.
Merkel, Reinhard, 'Folter als Notwehr', 11 *Die Zeit* 46 (6 March 2008).
Merten, Detlef, 'Rechtsstaatsdämmerung', in Manfred Schreiber (ed.), *Polizeilicher Eingriff und Grundrechte. Festschrift zum 70. Geburtstag von Rudolf Samper* (Stuttgart: Boorberg, 1982), 35 ff.
Merten, Detlef, 'Zum Streit um den Todesschuß. Vom Tätermitleid zur Opferpreisgabe?', in Kay Hailbronner (ed.), *Staat und Völkerrechtsordnung. Festschrift für Karl Doehring* (Berlin: Springer, 1989), 579 ff.
Meyer, Georg and Anschütz, Gerhard, *Lehrbuch des deutschen Staatsrechts*, repr. of the 7th ed., München: Duncker & Humblot, 1919 (Berlin: Duncker & Humblot, 2005).
Michelman, Frank, 'Law's Republic', 97 *Yale Law Journal* 1493 (1988).
Mill, John Stuart, *On Liberty* (London: Parker and Son, 1859).
Miller, Seumas, *Terrorism and Counter-Terrorism* (Oxford: Blackwell, 2009).
Minow, Martha, 'The Constitution as Black Box During National Emergencies', 75 *Fordham Law Review* 593 (2006).
Mohl, Robert von, *Das Staatsrecht des Königreichs Württemberg*, 2 vols. (Tübingen: Laupp, 1829).
Mohl, Robert von, *Die Polizei-Wissenschaft nach den Grundsätzen des Rechtsstaates*, 2 vols. (Tübingen: Laupp, 1832 and 1833).
Mohnhaupt, Heinz and Grimm, Dieter, *Verfassung. Zur Geschichte des Begriffs von der Antike bis zur Gegenwart* (Berlin: Duncker & Humblot, 1995).
Monahan, Torin, *Surveillance and Security: Technological Politics in Everyday Life* (New York: Routledge, 2006).
Monson, Robert A., 'Political Toleration versus Militant Democracy: The Case of West Germany', 7 *German Studies Review* 301 (1984).
Montesquieu, Charles de, *The Spirit of the Laws* (New York: Prometheus Books, 2012).
Moore, Michael S., 'Torture and the Balance of Evils', 23 *Israel Law Review* 280 (1989).
Mopin, Michel et al., *L'Assemblée nationale* (Paris: Biro, 1992).
Mouffe, Chantal, *On the Political* (New York: Routledge, 2005).
Mulgan, Geoff, 'Vom Staat und Glück', *ZEIT-online* (11 March 2004), www.zeit.de/2004/12/Essay_Mulgan.
Müller, Adam Heinrich, *Elemente der Staatskunst* (Berlin: Sander, 1809).

Müller, Adam Heinrich, 'Erste Vorlesung über König Friedrich II. und die Natur, Würde und Bestimmung der preußischen Monarchie', *Pantheon* 179 (1810).
Müller, Ingo, 'Die DDR – ein "Unrechtsstaat"?', *Neue Justiz* 281 (1992).
Müller-Wille, Björn, 'The Effect of International Terrorism on EU Intelligence Co-operation', 46 *Journal of Common Market Studies* 49 (2008).
Münch, Ingo von, 'Rechtsstaat versus Gerechtigkeit?', 33 *Der Staat* 165 (1994).
Münch, Ingo von and Kunig, Philip (eds.), *Grundgesetz-Kommentar*, vol. 3, Art. 70–146, vols. 4–5 (München: C.H. Beck, 2003).
Münkler, Herfried, *The New Wars* (Cambridge: Polity, 2004).
Münkler, Herfried, *Machiavelli* (Frankfurt: Fischer, 2004).
Münkler, Herfried, 'Machiavelli, Niccolò', in Neil Smelser and Paul Baltes (eds.), *International Encyclopedia for the Social and Behavioral Sciences*, vol. XIII (Amsterdam: Elsevier, 2001), 9107–11.
Münkler, Herfried and Fischer, Karsten, '"Nothing to Kill or Die for …" – Überlegungen zu einer politischen Theorie des Opfers', *Leviathan* 343 (2000).
Neumann, Franz L., 'Anxiety and Politics', in *The Democratic and The Authoritarian State: Essays in Political and Legal Theory* (Glencoe: Free Press, 1957).
Neumann, Franz L., *The Democratic and The Authoritarian State: Essays in Political and Legal Theory* (Glencoe: Free Press, 1957).
Neumann, Franz L., *The Rule of Law: Political Theory and the Legal System* (Bloomsbury: Berg Publishers, 1986).
Neumann, Franz L., 'The Concept of Political Freedom', in W.E. Scheuerman (ed.), *The Rule of Law under Siege, Selected Essays of Franz L. Neumann and Otto Kirchheimer* (Berkeley: University of California Press, 1996), part III, 195.
Neuman, Gerald, 'Comment, Counter-Terrorist Operations and the Rule of Law', 15 *European Journal of International Law* 15 (2004), 1019–29.
Niklaus, René, *Zum Abschuss freigegeben? Eine interpretative Mikro-Policy-Analyse des Sicherheitskonzeptes zur Abwehr terroristischer Gefahren aus dem Luftraum* (Marburg: Tectum Verlag, 2006).
Nitschke, Peter (ed.), *Rettungsfolter im modernen Rechtsstaat? Eine Verortung* (Bochum: Kamp, 2005).
Noack, Paul, *Carl Schmitt. Eine Biographie* (Berlin: Propyläen Verlag, 1993).
Nollau, Günther, *Wie sicher ist die Bundesrepublik?* (München: Goldmann, 1976).

Noman, Akbar et al. (eds.), *Good Growth and Governance in Africa: Rethinking Development Strategies* (Oxford: Oxford University Press, 2011).

Nozick, Robert, *Anarchie. Staat – Utopia*, 2nd ed. (München: Olzog Verlag, 2006).

Obinger, Herbert and Zohlnhöfer, Reimut, 'Abschied vom Interventionsstaat? Der Wandel staatlicher Subventionsausgaben in den OECD-Ländern seit 1980', 13 *Swiss Political Science Review* 203 (2007).

Observer Research Foundation (ed.), *Counter-Terrorism in South-Asia* (New Delhi: KW Publishers, 2011).

O'Connor, James, *The Fiscal Crisis of the State* (New York: St. Martin's Press, 1973).

Oertzen, Peter von, *Die soziale Funktion des staatsrechtlichen Positivismus* (Frankfurt: Suhrkamp, 1974).

Oeter, Stefan, *Integration und Subsidiarität im deutschen Bundesstaatsrecht* (Tübingen: Mohr Siebeck, 1998).

Özbudun, Ergun and Turhan, Mehmet, *Emergency Powers – Report of the European Commission for Democracy Through Law* (Strasbourg: The European Council, 1995).

Offe, Claus, 'Editorial', in Murray Edelman, *Politik als Ritual* (Frankfurt: Campus Verlag, 1976), VII ff.

Opitz, Sven, 'Zwischen Sicherheitsdispositiven und Securitization: Zur Analytik illiberaler Gouvernementalität', in Patricia Purtschert, Katrin Meyer and Yves Winter (eds.), *Gouvernementalität und Sicherheit* (Bielefeld: Transcript Verlag, 2008), 201 ff.

Orford, Anne, *International Authority and the Responsibility to Protect* (Cambridge: Cambridge University Press, 2011).

Parry, John T., 'The Shape of Modern Torture: Extraordinary Rendition and Ghost Detainees', 6 *Melbourne Journal of International Law* 516 (2005).

Parry, John T., 'Torture in the Modern World', Lewis & Clark College – Law School (December 2005), http://ssrn.com/abstract=899113.

Parry, John T., 'Escalation and Necessity: Defining Torture at Home and Abroad', in Sanford Levinson (ed.), *Torture: A Collection* (Oxford/New York: Oxford University Press, 2009), 145 ff.

Pasquino, Pasquale, 'Locke on King's Prerogative', 26 *Political Theory* 198 (1998).

Pateman, Carole, *The Sexual Contract* (Stanford: Stanford University Press, 1988).

Pawlik, Michael, '§ 14 Abs. 3 des Luftsicherheitsgesetzes – ein Tabubruch?', *Juristenzeitung* 1045 (2004).

Perels, Joachim, 'Der soziale Rechtsstaat im Widerstreit', *Kritische Justiz* 295 (2006).

Peters, Edward, *Torture* (Philadelphia: University of Philadelphia Press, 1996).

Pieroth, Bodo, 'Der Rechtsstaat und die Aufarbeitung der vorrechtsstaatlichen Vergangenheit', 51 *Veröffentlichungen der Vereinigung der Deutschen Staatsrechtslehrer* 91 (1992).

Pieroth, Bodo, Schlink, Bernhard and Kniesel, Michael, *Polizei- und Ordnungsrecht*, 4th ed. (München: C.H. Beck, 2007).

Placidus, Johann Wilhelm, *Litteratur der Staatslehre. Ein Versuch* (Straßburg, 1798).

Polanyi, Karl, *The Great Transformation* (Boston: Beacon Press, 2001).

Poole, Thomas, 'Courts and Conditions of Uncertainty in "Times of Crisis"', *Public Law* 234 (2008).

Poscher, Ralf, 'Die Würde des Menschen ist unantastbar', *Juristenzeitung* 756 (2004).

Poscher, Ralf, 'Eingriffsschwellen im Recht der inneren Sicherheit', 41 *Die Verwaltung* 345 (2008).

Posner, Eric A., *The Perils of Global Legalism* (Chicago: University of Chicago Press, 2009).

Posner, Eric A. and Vermeule, Adrian, 'A "Torture" Memo and its Tortuous Critics', *Wall Street Journal* (6 July 2004).

Posner, Eric A. and Vermeule, Adrian, 'Should Coercive Interrogations Be Legal?', University of Chicago Law School, Working Paper (March 2005).

Posner, Eric A. and Vermeule, Adrian, *Terror in the Balance. Security, Liberty, and the Courts* (Oxford: Oxford University Press, 2007).

Prantl, Heribert, *Der Terrorist als Gesetzgeber. Wie man mit Angst Politik macht* (München: Droemer, 2008).

Prempeh, H. Kwasi, 'Presidential Power in Comparative Perspective: The Puzzling Persistence of Imperial Presidency of Post-Authoritarian Africa', 35 *Hastings Constitutional Law Quarterly* 4 (2008).

Preuß, Ulrich K., *Legalität und Pluralismus. Beiträge zum Verfassungsrecht der Bundesrepublik Deutschland* (Frankfurt: Suhrkamp, 1973).

Preuß, Ulrich K., 'Gesellschaftliche Bedingungen der Legalität', in Ulrich K. Preuß, *Legalität und Pluralismus. Beiträge zum Verfassungsrecht der Bundesrepublik Deutschland* (Frankfurt: Suhrkamp, 1973), 7 ff.

Preuß, Ulrich K., 'Juristen', in Hanspeter Knirsch, Bernhard Nagel and Wolfgang Voegeli (eds.), *"Radikale" im öffentlichen Dienst? Eine Dokumentation* (Frankfurt: Fischer, 1973), part IV, 118 ff.

Preuß, Ulrich K., *Bildung und Herrschaft. Beiträge zu einer politischen Theorie des Bildungswesens* (Frankfurt: Fischer, 1975).

Preuß, Ulrich K., 'Zum Begriff des Politischen bei Carl Schmitt', in *Politische Verantwortung und Bürgerloyalität* (Frankfurt: Fischer, 1984), 198 ff.

Preuß, Ulrich K., 'Souveränität – Zwischenbemerkungen zu einem Schlüsselbegriff des Politischen', in Tine Stein et al. (eds.), *Souveränität, Recht, Moral. Die Grundlagen politischer Gemeinschaft* (Frankfurt: Campus Verlag, 2007), 313 ff.

Pütter, Norbert, *Der OK-Komplex* (Münster: Westfälisches Dampfboot, 1998).

Püttner, Günter, 'Der informale Rechtsstaat', *Kritische Vierteljahresschrift für Gesetzgebung und Rechtswissenschaft* 63 (1991).

Quaritsch, Helmut, 'Kirchen und Staat. Verfassungs- und staatstheoretische Probleme der staatskirchenrechtlichen Lehre der Gegenwart', 1 *Der Staat* 175 (1962).

Radbruch, Gustav, 'Die Erneuerung des Rechts', in Werner Maihofer (ed.), *Naturrecht oder Rechtspositivismus?* (Darmstadt: Wissenschaftliche Buchgesellschaft, 1966), 1 ff.

Ramraj, Victor V., *Emergencies and the Limits of Legality* (Cambridge: Cambridge University Press, 2008).

Ramraj, Victor V., Hor, Michael and Roach, Kent (eds.) *Global Anti-Terrorism Law and Policy* (Cambridge: Cambridge University Press, 2011).

Rankin, Robert S. and Dallymayr, Winfried R., *Freedom and Emergency Powers in the Cold War* (New York: Appleton-Century-Crofts, 1964).

Rawls, John, *A Theory of Justice* (Cambridge, MA: Harvard University Press, 1971).

Reemtsma, Jan Philipp, *Folter im Rechtsstaat?* (Hamburg: Hamburger Edition, 2005).

Reemtsma, Jan Philipp, *Vertrauen und Gewalt. Versuch über eine besondere Konstellation der Moderne* (Hamburg: Hamburger Edition, 2008).

Reimann, Horst, 'Tabu', in Görres-Gesellschaft (ed.), *Staatslexikon. Recht – Wirtschaft – Gesellschaft*, vol. 5, 7th ed. (Freiburg: Herder, 1989), 421 ff.

Reinach, Théodore, *De l'état de siège et des institutions de salut public a Rome, en France et dans les Législations étrangères* (Paris: Cotillon, 1885).

Reinhard, Wolfgang, *Geschichte der Staatsgewalt. Eine vergleichende Verfassungsgeschichte Europas von den Anfängen bis zur Gegenwart* (München: C.H. Beck, 1999).

Rejali, Darius M., *Torture and Modernity: Self, Society, and State in Modern Iran* (Boulder: Westview Press, 1994).

Rejali, Darius M., *Torture and Democracy* (Princeton: Princeton University Press, 2007).

Richter, Horst-Eberhard, *Eltern, Kind und Neurose*, 2nd ed. (Reinbek/ Hamburg: Rowohlt, 1969).

Ridder, Helmut, 'Die soziale Ordnung des Grundgesetzes', in Josef Mück (ed.), *Verfassungsrecht. Bad Wildunger Beiträge zur Gemeinschaftskunde*, vol. 5 (Opladen: Westdeutscher Verlag, 1975), 85 ff.

Ridder, Helmut, 'Vom Wendekreis der Grundrechte', *Leviathan* 467 (1977).

Ritter, Gerhard A., *Der Sozialstaat – Entstehung und Entwicklung im internationalen Vergleich*, 2nd ed. (München: Oldenbourg, 1991).

Roach, Kent, *September 11: Consequences for Canada* (McGill-Queens Press, 2003).

Roach, Kent, *The 9/11 Effect: Comparative Counter-Terrorism* (New York: Cambridge University Press, 2011).

Robert, Philippe, *Le citoyen, le crime et L'État* (Genf: Droz, 1999).

Robin, Corey, *Fear: The History of a Political Idea* (Oxford: Oxford University Press, 2004).

Rödel, Ulrich, Frankenberg, Günter and Dubiel, Helmut, *Die demokratische Frage* (Frankfurt: Suhrkamp, 1989).

Roellecke, Gerd, 'Der Rechtsstaat im Kampf gegen den Terror', *Juristenzeitung* 265 (2006).

Rokeach, Milton, *The Open and Closed Mind* (New York: Basic Books, 1960).

Rosenau, James N. and Czempiel, Ernst-Otto (eds.), *Governance Without Government. Order and Change in World Politics* (Cambridge: Cambridge University Press, 1992).

Rossiter, Clinton Lawrence, *Constitutional Dictatorship. Crisis Government in the Modern Democracies* (Princeton: Princeton University Press, 1948; new ed.: New Brunswick: Transaction Publishers, 2007).

Roßnagel, Alexander, *Digitalisierung der Grundrechte* (Opladen: Westdeutscher Verlag, 1990).

Rotteck, Carl von and Welcker, Carl (eds.), *Das Staats-Lexikon: Encyclopädie der sämmtlichen Staatswissenschaften für alle Stände*, 15 vols. (Altona: J.F. Hammerich, 1846).

Rousseau, Jean-Jacques, 'The Social Contract' [1762], in Jean-Jacques Rousseau, *'The Social Contract' and Other Political Writings*, Victor Gourevitch (ed.) (Cambridge: Cambridge University Press, 1997).

Rüthers, Bernd, *Die unbegrenzte Auslegung*, 6th ed. (Tübingen: Mohr Siebeck, 2005).

Ryffel, Hans, *Grundprobleme der Rechts- und Staatsphilosophie* (Neuwied: Luchterhand, 1969).

Sajó, András (ed.), *Militant Democracy* (Den Haag: Eleven International Publishers, 2004).

Saliger, Frank, 'Feindstrafrecht: Kritisches oder totalitäres Strafrechtskonzept?', *Juristenzeitung* 756 (2006).

Sands, Philippe, *Torture Team. Deception, Cruelty and the Compromise of Law* (London: Penguin, 2008).

Sartori, Giovanni, *Il Sultanato* (Rome: Laterza, 2009).

Sattler, Henriette, 'Terrorabwehr durch die Streitkräfte nicht ohne Grundgesetzänderung', *Neue Zeitschrift für Verwaltungsrecht* 1286 (2004).

Scarry, Elaine, 'Five Errors in the Reasoning of Alan Dershowitz', in Sanford Levinson (ed.), *Torture: A Collection* (New York: Oxford University Press, 2004), 281 ff.

Scharpf, Fritz W., *Die politischen Kosten des Rechtsstaats* (Tübingen: Mohr Siebeck, 1970).

Scharpf, Fritz W., *Games Real Actors Play. Actor-Centered Institutionalism in Policy Research* (Boulder: Westview Press, 1997).

Schäuble, Wolfgang, 'Aktuelle Sicherheitspolitik im Lichte des Verfassungsrechts', *Zeitschrift für Rechtspolitik* 210 (2007).

Schauer, Frederick, 'Slippery Slopes', 99 *Harvard Law Review* 361 (1985).

Scheerer, Sebastian, 'Ein theoretisches Modell zur Erklärung sozialrevolutionärer Gewalt', in Henner Hess et al., *Angriff auf das Herz des Staates: Soziale Entwicklung und Terrorismus*, vol. 1 (Frankfurt: Suhrkamp, 1988), 75 ff.

Scheerer, Sebastian, 'Deutschland: Die ausgebürgerte Linke', in Henner Hess et al., *Angriff auf das Herz des Staates: Soziale Entwicklung und Terrorismus*, vol. 1 (Frankfurt: Suhrkamp, 1988), 191 ff.

Scheerer, Sebastian, *Die Zukunft des Terrorismus. Drei Szenarien* (Lüneburg: zu Klampen, 2002).

Scheidemantel, Heinrich Gottfried, *Das Staatsrecht nach der Vernunft und den Sitten der vornehmsten Völker betrachtet*, 3 vols. (Jena: Croecker, 1770–73).

Schenke, Wolf-Rüdiger, *Polizei- und Ordnungsrecht*, 5th ed. (Heidelberg: C.F. Müller, 2007).

Scheppele, Kim Lane, 'North American Emergencies: The Use of Emergency Powers in Canada and the United States', 4 *International Journal of Constitutional Law* 213 (2006).

Scheuerman, William, 'Legal Indeterminacy and the Origins of Nazi Legal Thought: The Case of Carl Schmitt', 17 *History of Political Thought* 571 (1996).

Scheuerman, William E., *The Rule of Law under Siege, Selected Essays, Part III: The Concept of Political Freedom*, Franz L. Neumann (ed.) (Berkeley: University of California Press, 1996).

Scheuerman, William, 'Emergency Powers and the Rule of Law After 9/11', 14 *Journal of Political Philosophy* 61 (2006).

Schirrmacher, Frank, 'Der verwettete Mensch', *Frankfurter Allgemeine Zeitung* (17 June 2013).

Schlink, Bernhard, 'Rechtsstaat und revolutionäre Gerechtigkeit', *Neue Justiz* 433 (1994).

Schlink, Bernhard, 'Das Opfer des Lebens', *Merkur* 1021 (2005).

Schmitt, Carl, *Gesetz und Urteil* (Berlin: Otto Liebmann, 1912).

Schmitt, Carl, *Unabhängigkeit der Richter, Gleichheit vor dem Gesetz und Gewährleistung des Privateigentums nach der Weimarer Verfassung* (Berlin: de Gruyter, 1926).

Schmitt, Carl, *Verfassungslehre* (München: Duncker & Humblot, 1928).

Schmitt, Carl, 'Die Wendung zum totalen Staat', 7 *Europäische Revue* 241 (1931).

Schmitt, Carl, *Staat, Bewegung, Volk* (Hamburg: Hanseatische Verlagsanstalt, 1933).

Schmitt, Carl, 'Der Führer schützt das Recht', *Deutsche Juristen-Zeitung* 945 (1934).

Schmitt, Carl, 'Was bedeutet der Streit um den Rechtsstaat?', *Zeitschrift für die gesamte Staatswissenschaft* 189 (1935).

Schmitt, Carl, 'Der Rechtsstaat', in Hans Frank (ed.), *Nationalsozialistisches Handbuch für Recht und Gesetzgebung* (München: Zentralverlag, 1935), 3 ff.

Schmitt, Carl, 'Völkerrechtliche Probleme im Rheingebiet (1928)', in Carl Schmitt, *Positionen und Begriffe im Kampf mit Weimar – Genf – Versailles, 1923–1939* (Hamburg: Hanseatische Verlagsanstalt, 1940), 97 ff.

Schmitt, Carl, 'Staatsethik und pluralistischer Staat (1930)', in Carl Schmitt, *Positionen und Begriffe im Kampf mit Weimar – Genf – Versailles, 1923–1939* (Hamburg: Hanseatische Verlagsanstalt, 1940), 133 ff.

Schmitt, Carl, 'Die staatsrechtliche Bedeutung der Notverordnung, insbesondere ihre Rechtsgültigkeit (1931)', in Carl Schmitt, *Verfassungsrechtliche Aufsätze aus den Jahren 1924–1954*, repr. of 1st ed. (Berlin: Duncker & Humblot, 1958), 3rd ed. (Berlin: Duncker & Humblot, 1985), 235 ff.

Schmitt, Carl, *Political Theology: Four Chapters on the Concept of Sovereignty*, George D. Schwab transl. (Boston: MIT Press, 1985).

Schmitt, Carl, *Die Diktatur*, 5th ed. (Berlin: Duncker & Humblot, 1989).

Schmitt, Carl, *The Concept of the Political*, George Schwab (ed.) (Chicago: The University of Chicago Press, 1996).

Schmitt, Carl, *Der Hüter der Verfassung*, 4th ed. (Berlin: Duncker & Humblot, 1996).

Schmitt, Carl, *Legality and Legitimacy*, Jeffrey Seitzer transl. (Durham, NC: Duke University Press, 2004).

Schmitt, Carl, *Constitutional Theory*, Ellen Kennedy transl. (Durham: Duke University Press, 2008).

Schmitt, Carl, *Political Theology II: The Myth of the Closure of Any Political Theology*, Michael Hoelzl and Graham Ward transl. (Cambridge: Polity Press, 2008).

Schneider, Peter, *Ausnahmezustand und Norm: Eine Studie zur Rechtslehre von Carl Schmitt* (Stuttgart: Deutsche Verlagsanstalt, 1957).

Schröder, Meinhard, 'Staatsrecht an den Grenzen des Rechtsstaates', *Archiv des öffentlichen Rechts* 103 (1978), 121 ff.

Schumacher, Joachim, *Die Angst vor dem Chaos. Über die falsche Apokalypse des Bürgertums* (Bodenheim: Athenaeum Verlag, 1987).

Schuster, Rudolf, 'Relegalisierung der KPD oder Illegalisierung der NPD? Zur politischen und rechtlichen Problematik von Parteiverboten', 4 *Zeitschrift für Politik* 413 (1968).

Schwagerl, Hans Joachim, *Verfassungsschutz in der Bundesrepublik Deutschland* (Heidelberg: C.F. Müller, 1985).

Schweitzer, C.C., 'Emergency Powers in the Federal Republic of Germany', 22 *The Western Political Quarterly* 112 (1969).

Seifert, Jürgen, *Der Notstandsausschuß* (Frankfurt: Europäische Verlagsanstalt, 1968).

Seifert, Jürgen, *Kampf um Verfassungspositionen* (Köln: Europäische Verlagsanstalt, 1974).

Sen, Amartya, *Identity and Violence: The Illusion of Destiny* (New York: W.W. Norton, 2007).

Senghaas, Dieter, 'Zur Pathologie organisierter Friedlosigkeit', in Ekkehart Krippendorff (ed.), *Friedensforschung* (Köln: Kiepenheuer & Witsch, 1968), 217 ff.

Shapiro, Jeremy and Suzan, Bénédicte, 'The French Experience of Counter-Terrorism', 45 *Survival* 67–98 (2003).

Shklar, Judith, 'Political Theory and the Rule of Law', in Allan C. Hutchinson and Patrick Monahan (eds.), *The Rule of Law: Ideal or Ideology* (Carswell: Transnational Pub, 1987), 1.

Shklar, Judith, 'Liberalism of Fear', in Nancy Rosenblum (ed.), *Liberalism and the Moral Life* (Cambridge, MA: Harvard University Press, 1989), 21–38.

Shue, Henry, 'Torture', 7 *Philosophy and Public Affairs* (1978).

Shue, Henry and Rodin, David (eds.), *Preemption: Military Action and Moral Justification* (Oxford: Oxford University Press, 2009).

Sieyès, Emmanuel Joseph, *Qu'est-ce que le Tiers-État?* (Genf: Droz, 1970).

Singelnstein, Tobias and Stolle, Peer, *Die Sicherheitsgesellschaft. Soziale Kontrolle im 21. Jahrhundert* (Wiesbaden: Verlag für Sozialwissenschaft, 2006).

Skinner, Quentin, *Freiheit und Pflicht. Thomas Hobbes' politische Theorie* (Frankfurt: Suhrkamp, 2008).

Skinner, Quentin, *Hobbes and Republican Liberty* (Cambridge: Cambridge University Press, 2008).

Skinner, Quentin, *Machiavelli* (Oxford: Oxford University Press, 1981).

Slaughter, Anne-Marie and Burke-White, William, 'An International Constitutional Moment', 43 *Harvard International Law Journal* 1 (2002).

Smith, Brian C., *Good Governance and Development* (Hampshire: Palgrave Macmillan, 2007).

Smith, Tony, 'Balancing Liberty and Security? A Legal Analysis of UK Anti-Terrorist Legislation', 13 *European Journal of Criminal Policy and Research* 73 (2007).

Sobota, Katharina, *Das Prinzip Rechtsstaat* (Tübingen: Mohr Siebeck, 1997).

Spee von Langenfeld, Friedrich, *Cautio Criminalis* (Rinteln: Lucius, 1631).

Squires, Peter and Kennison, Peter, *Shooting to Kill: Policing, Firearms and Armed Response* (Oxford: Wiley, 2010).

Stahl, Friedrich Julius, *Die Philosophie des Rechts*, vol. 2, repr. of the 5th ed. (Tübingen, 1878), 6th ed. (Hildesheim: Georg Olms Verlag, 1963).

Starck, Christian, 'Übermaß an Rechtsstaat?', *Zeitschrift für Rechtspolitik* 209 (1979).

Starck, Christian, 'Der Rechtsstaat und die Aufarbeitung der vorrechtsstaatlichen Vergangenheit', 51 *Veröffentlichungen der Vereinigung der Deutschen Staatsrechtslehrer* 9 (1992).

Steinhoff, Uwe, 'Torture – The Case for Dirty Harry and Against Alan Dershowitz', 23 *Journal of Applied Philosophy* 337 (2006).

Sternberger, Dolf, 'Das Menschenrecht nach Glück zu streben', in Dolf Sternberger, *Staatsfreundschaft* (Frankfurt: Insel Verlag, 1980), 95 ff.

Sterzel, Dieter (ed.), *Kritik der Notstandsgesetze. Kommentierungen*, 2nd ed. (Frankfurt: Suhrkamp, 1969).

Steyn, Johan, 'Guantanamo Bay: The Legal Black Hole', *International and Comparative Law Quarterly* 53 (2004), 1 ff.

Stollberg-Rilinger, Barbara, *Des Kaisers alte Kleider. Verfassungsgeschichte und Symbolsprache des Alten Reiches* (München: C.H. Beck, 2008).

Stolleis, Michael, 'Löwe und Fuchs. Eine politische Metapher zur Zeit der Entstehung des modernen Staates', in Ingo von Münch (ed.),

Staatsrecht, Völkerrecht, Europarecht. Festschrift für Hans-Jürgen Schlochauer (Berlin: de Gruyter, 1981), 151 ff.

Stolleis, Michael, *Geschichte des öffentlichen Rechts in Deutschland*, vol. 1, *1600–1800: Reichspublizistik und Policeywissenschaft* (München: C.H. Beck, 1988); vol. 2, *1800–1914: Staatsrechtslehre und Verwaltungswissenschaft* (München: C.H. Beck, 1992); vol. 3, *1914–1945: Staats- und Verwaltungswissenschaft in Republik und Diktatur* (München: C.H. Beck, 1999).

Stolleis, Michael, 'Die Entstehung des Interventionsstaates und das öffentliche Recht', *Zeitschrift für Neuere Rechtsgeschichte* 129 (1989).

Stolleis, Michael, 'Rechtsstaat', in Adalbert Erler et al. (eds.), *Handwörterbuch zur deutschen Rechtsgeschichte IV* (Berlin: E. Schmidt Verlag, 1990), 367 ff.

Stolleis, Michael, *Staat und Staatsräson in der frühen Neuzeit* (Frankfurt: Suhrkamp, 1990).

Stolleis, Michael, '"Staatsethik", oder: Vom sittlichen Staat zu den Bürgertugenden', *Kritische Vierteljahresschrift für Gesetzgebung und Rechtswissenschaft* (1995), 58 ff.

Stolleis, Michael, 'Besatzungsherrschaft und Wiederaufbau deutscher Staatlichkeit 1945–1949', in Josef Isensee and Paul Kirchhof (eds.), *Handbuch des Staatsrechts der Bundesrepublik Deutschland*, vol. I, 3rd ed. (Heidelberg: C.F. Müller, 2003), § 7.

Stolleis, Michael, *The Eye of the Law: Two Essays on Legal History* (Oxford/New York: Routledge, 2008) (orig. *Das Auge des Gesetzes. Geschichte einer Metapher* (C.H. Beck, 2004).

Stolleis, Michael, 'Rechtskolumne. Angst essen Seele auf', *Merkur* 1145 (2007).

Stratenwerth, Günter and Kuhlen, Lothar, *Strafrecht. Allgemeiner Teil I*, 5th ed. (Köln: Heymanns, 2004).

Strauss, Marcy, 'Torture', 48 *New York Law School Law Review* 201 (2003–04).

Sunstein, Cass, *Gesetze der Angst* (Frankfurt: Suhrkamp, 2007).

Sunstein, Cass, 'Probability Neglect: Emotions, Worst Case Scenarios, and Law', 110 *Yale Law Journal* 1 (2000).

Szeemann, Harald et al. (eds.), *Aubes – Rêveries au bord de Victor Hugo* (Paris: Paris Musées, 2002).

Tamanaha, Brian Z., *On the Rule of Law: History, Politics and Theory* (Cambridge: Cambridge University Press, 2004).

Tan, Andrew T.H. (ed.), *The Politics of Terrorism: A Survey* (London: Routledge, 2011).

Tan, Andrew T.H. (ed.), *A Handbook of Terrorism and Insurgency in Southeast Asia* (Cheltenham, UK and Northampton, MA, USA: Edward Elgar Publishing, 2006).

Thatcher, Margaret, *Statecraft: Strategies for a Changing World* (Scranton: Harper, 2002).

Theobald, Christian, *Zur Ökonomik des Staates. Good Governance und die Perzeption der Weltbank* (Baden-Baden: Nomos, 2000).

The Report of the Argentine National Commission on the Disappeared: Nunca Más (New York: Farrar, Straus & Giroux, 1986).

Thiel, Markus, *Die 'Entgrenzung' der Gefahrenabwehr* (Tübingen: Mohr Siebeck, 2011).

Thoma, Richard, 'Rechtsstaatsidee und Verwaltungsrechtswissenschaft', 4 *Jahrbuch des öffentlichen Rechts der Gegenwart* 196 (1910).

Thoma, Richard, 'Der Vorbehalt der Legislative und das Prinzip der Gesetzmäßigkeit von Verwaltung und Rechtsprechung', in Gerhard Anschütz and Richard Thoma (eds.), *Handbuch des Deutschen Staatsrechts II* (Tübingen: Mohr Siebeck, 1932), § 76, 221 ff.

Tingsten, Herbert, *Les pleins pouvoirs. L'expansion des pouvoirs gouvernementaux pendant et après la Grande Guerre* (Paris: Librairie Stock, 1934).

Trapp, Rainer, *Folter oder selbstverschuldete Rettungsbefragung?* (Paderborn: Grin Verlag, 2006).

Trapp, Rainer, 'Wirklich "Folter" oder nicht vielmehr selbstverschuldete Rettungsbefragung?', in Wolfgang Lenzen (ed.), *Ist Folter erlaubt? Juristische und philosophische Aspekte* (Paderborn: Mentis Verlag, 2006), 95 ff.

Tully, James, *A Discourse on Property. John Locke and his Adversaries* (Cambridge: Cambridge University Press, 1980).

Tushnet, Mark, 'Controlling Executive Power in the War on Terrorism', 118 *Harvard Law Review* 2673 (2004–05).

Tushnet, Mark (ed.), *The Constitution in Wartime. Beyond Alarmism and Complacency* (Durham: University of North Carolina Press, 2005).

UNESCAP, 'What is Good Governance?', http://www.unescap.org/pdd/prs/ProjectActivities/Ongoing/gg/governance.asp (2011).

Varon, Jeremy, *Bringing the War Home: The Weather Underground, the Red Army Faction, and Revolutionary Violence in the Sixties and Seventies* (Berkeley: University of California Press, 2004).

Vesting, Thomas, 'Die Staatsrechtslehre und die Veränderung ihres Gegenstandes: Konsequenzen von Europäisierung und Internationalisierung', 63 *Veröffentlichungen der Vereinigung der Deutschen Staatsrechtslehrer* 41 (2004).

Vico, Giambattista, *De antiquissima Italorum Sapientia ex linguae Latinae originibus eruenda* (Naples: Mosca, 1710).

Vico, Giambattista, *On the Most Ancient Wisdom of the Italians* (New Haven: Yale University Press, 2011).

Vogel, Jochen, 'Zur Diskussion um die Normenflut', *Juristenzeitung* 321 (1979).
Voigt, Rüdiger (ed.), *Verrechtlichung* (Königstein: Athenaeum Verlag, 1980).
Vondung, Klaus, *Die Apokalypse in Deutschland* (München: Deutsher Taschenbuch Verlag, 1988).
Vorländer, Hans, 'Gründung und Geltung. Die Konstitution der Ordnung und die Legitimität der Konstitution', in Gert Melville and Hans Vorländer (ed.), *Geltungsgeschichten. Über die Stabilisierung und Legitimierung institutioneller Ordnungen* (Köln: Böhlau, 2002), 243 ff.
Waldmann, Peter, *Terrorismus. Provokation der Macht*, 2nd ed. (Hamburg: Murmann Verlag, 2005).
Waldmann, Peter, *Terrorismus und Bürgerkrieg. Der Staat in Bedrängnis* (München: Gerling Akademie Verlag, 2003).
Waldron, Jeremy, 'Security and Liberty: The Image of Balance', 11 *Journal of Politics & Philosophy* 191 (2003).
Waldron, Jeremy, 'Torture and Positive Law: Jurisprudence for the White House', 50 *Columbia Law Review* 1681 (2005).
Waldron, Jeremy, *Torture, Terror, and Trade-Offs. Philosophy for the White House* (Oxford: Oxford University, 2010).
Walsh, James I., 'Intelligence-sharing in the EU: Institutions Are Not Enough', 44 *Journal of Common Market Studies* 626 (2006).
Walter, Bernd, 'Schleierfahndung', *Kriminalistik* 668 (2004).
Walter, Christian et al. (eds.), *Terrorism as a Challenge for National and International Law: Security versus Liberty?* (Berlin: Springer, 2004).
Walter, Tonio, 'Der Rechtsstaat verliert die Nerven', *Kritische Justiz* 443 (2008).
Weber, Max, *Economy and Society*, 3 vols. (Berkeley: University of California Press, 1978).
Weinacht, Paul-Ludwig, '"Staatsbürger" – Zur Geschichte und Kritik eines politischen Begriffs', 8 *Der Staat* 41 (1969).
Welcker, Karl Theodor, *Die letzten Gründe von Recht, Staat und Strafe* (Gießen: Heyer, 1813).
Wieland, Joachim, 'Verfassungsrechtliche Grundlagen polizeiähnlicher Einsätze der Bundeswehr', in Dieter Fleck (ed.), *Rechtsfragen der Terrorismusbekämpfung durch Streitkräfte* (Baden-Baden: Nomos, 2004), 14 ff.
Wiesbrock, Heinz (ed.), *Die politische und gesellschaftliche Rolle der Angst* (Frankfurt: Europäische Verlagsanstalt, 1967).
Wiethölter, Rudolf, 'Materialisierungen und Prozeduralisierungen von Recht', in Gert Brüggemeier and Christian Joerges (eds.), *Workshop zu Konzepten des postinterventionistischen Rechts, ZERP-Materialien 4* (Bremen: Zentrum für Europäische Rechtspolitik, 1984), 25 ff.

Wiggershaus, Renate and Wiggershaus, Rolf, 'Was schützt das "Gesetz zum Schutz des Gemeinschaftsfriedens"?', *Kritische Justiz* 175 (1976).
Wisner, David A., *The Cult of the Legislator in France 1750–1830* (Oxford: Voltaire Foundation, 1997).
Wittreck, Fabian, 'Menschenwürde und Folterverbot. Zum Dogma von der ausnahmslosen Unabwägbarkeit des Art. 1 Abs. 1 GG', *Die Öffentliche Verwaltung* 873 (2003).
Wördemann, Franz, *Terrorismus. Motive, Täter, Strategien* (München: Piper, 1977).
Yoo, John, *The Powers of War and Peace. The Constitution and Foreign Affairs After 9/11* (Chicago: University of Chicago Press, 2005).
Young, Iris, *Justice and the Politics of Difference* (Princeton: Princeton University Press, 1990).
Zacher, Hans F. et al. (eds.), *Verrechtlichung von Wirtschaft, Arbeit und sozialer Solidarität* (Baden-Baden: Nomos, 1984).
Zacher, Hans F., 'Das soziale Staatsziel', in Josef Isensee and Paul Kirchhof (eds.), *Handbuch des Staatsrechts der Bundesrepublik Deutschland*, vol. II, 3rd ed. (Heidelberg: C.F. Müller, 2004), § 28.
Zagolla, Robert, *Im Namen der Wahrheit. Folter in Deutschland vom Mittelalter bis heute* (Berlin: be.bra Verlag, 2006).
Zangl, Bernhard, *Die Internationalisierung der Rechtsstaatlichkeit* (Frankfurt: Campus Verlag, 2006).
Zedner, Lucia, 'Terrorism, the Ticking Bomb and Criminal Justice Values', 73 *Criminal Justice Matters* 18 (2008).
Ziegler, Ole, 'Das Folterverbot in der polizeilichen Praxis. Der "Fall Daschner" als Beleg für die rechtsstaatliche Absolutheit des Folterverbotes', *Kritische Vierteljahresschrift für Gesetzgebung und Rechtswissenschaft* 50 (2004).

Index